MW01257231

Verse by Verse Commentary on the Book of

ACTS

Enduring Word Commentary Series
By David Guzik

The grass withers, the flower fades,
but the word of our God stands forever.
Isaiah 40:8

Commentary on Acts

Copyright ©2019 by David Guzik

Printed in the United States of America
or in the United Kingdom

Print Edition ISBN: 1-56599-047-1

Enduring Word

5662 Calle Real #184

Goleta, CA 93117

Originally published in 2000, updated in 2019

Electronic Mail: ewm@enduringword.com

Internet Home Page: www.enduringword.com

Contents

Acts 1 - Jesus Ascends to Heaven, A New Apostle Chosen

A. Prologue.

1. (1) Reference to former writings.

The former account I made, O Theophilus, of all that Jesus began both to do and teach.

a. **The former account I made**: The **former account** is the Gospel of Luke. At one time the Gospel of Luke and the Book of Acts were joined together as one book with two volumes.

i. Imagine what it would be like if the Book of Acts wasn't in the Bible. You pick up your Bible and see the ministry of Jesus ending in the Gospel of John; next you read about a man named Paul writing to the followers of Jesus in Rome. Who was Paul? How did the gospel get from Jerusalem to Rome? The Book of Acts answers these questions. "A great New Testament scholar has said that the title of *Acts* might be, 'How they brought the Good News from Jerusalem to Rome.'" (Barclay)

ii. That expansion from Jerusalem to Rome is a remarkable story. "Humanly speaking, [Christianity] had nothing going for it. It had no money, no proven leaders, no technological tools for propagating the gospel. And it faced enormous obstacles. It was utterly new. It taught truths that were incredible to the unregenerate world. It was the subject to the most intense hatreds and persecutions." (Boice)

iii. Acts is written in the literary style of the Greek translation of the Old Testament, known as the Septuagint. "Since Luke can write in a different style (Lk. 1:1-4), this is something deliberate. Probably he regarded himself as recording *sacred history*." (Marshall)

iv. We really don't know all that much about Luke from the New Testament.

- We know that he was a physician (Colossians 4:14).

- We know that he was a Gentile (from his name).

- We know that he was a devoted companion of Paul (from the text of Acts, and Colossians 4:14, Philemon 24, and 2 Timothy 4:11).

v. There was a time when many scholars and critics thought that Acts was sort of a romance novel of the early church, written more than 100 years after the events supposedly happened. But William Ramsay, a noted archaeologist and Bible scholar, proved that the historical record of Acts is remarkably accurate regarding the specific practices, laws and customs of the period it claims to record. It is definitely the work of contemporary eyewitnesses.

vi. In the mid-1960's, A.N. Sherwin-White, an expert in Graeco-Roman history from Oxford, wrote about Acts: "The historical framework is exact. In terms of time and place the details are precise and correct... As documents these narratives belong to the same historical series as the record of provincial and imperial trials in epigraphical and literary sources of the first and early second centuries AD...For Acts the confirmation of historicity is overwhelming...Any attempt to reject its basic historicity even in matters of detail must now appear absurd. Roman historians have long taken it for granted."

vii. John Calvin wrote that the Book of Acts was "a kind of vast treasure." D. Martyn Lloyd-Jones called Acts "that most lyrical of books...Live in that book, I exhort you: It is a tonic, the greatest tonic I know of in the realm of the Spirit." (Cited in Stott)

b. **Theophilus**: This man might have been a Christian wanting instruction. He might have been a Roman official being briefed by Luke about the history of the Christian movement. Or, the name could be symbolic, because the name **Theophilus** means "God-lover."

i. In the introduction to the first volume (Luke 1:3), Luke addresses Theophilus with title *most excellent*, which was a way to address people who held high office.

ii. Since Acts ends with Paul awaiting trial before Caesar, some have wondered if Luke-Acts are not "defense briefs" on Paul's behalf to give a Roman official background on Paul's case. Luke arrived in Jerusalem with Paul in Acts 21:17; he left with him again on the journey to

Rome in Acts 27:1. In those two years, Luke had plenty of time to research and write his Gospel and the Book of Acts.

iii. "Ancient books were generally written on papyrus scrolls. It was practical to have a scroll about thirty-five feet in length. When it got any longer it got too bulky to carry around. This physical limitation has determined the length of many books of the Bible." (Boice) Luke used two scrolls to tell his story, and one we call "The Gospel of Luke" and the other we call "The Book of Acts."

iv. Luke wanted to show Theophilus and the Romans:

- That Christianity is *harmless* (some Romans officials had embraced it themselves).

- That Christianity is *innocent* (Roman judges could find no basis for prosecution).

- That Christianity is *lawful* (as the true fulfillment of Judaism, which was an approved religion in the Roman Empire).

c. **Of all that Jesus began both to do and teach**: Notice that **the former account** concerned **all that Jesus *began* both to do and teach**. Luke's Gospel describes only the *beginning* of Jesus' work; Acts describes its *continuation*; and the work of Jesus *continues* to our present day.

i. We must remember that Acts does not give us a full history of the church during this period. For example, the churches in Galilee and Samaria are barely mentioned (Acts 9:31), and the establishing of a strong church in Egypt during this time isn't mentioned at all.

ii. Acts spans a period of about 30 years, and takes us up to about A.D. 60 or 61, with Paul in Rome waiting to appear before Caesar Nero. This same Nero began his infamous persecutions of Christians in A.D. 64.

iii. Wonderfully, what Jesus began still continues. There is a real sense in which the Book of Acts continues to be written today. Not in an authoritative Scriptural sense; but in the sense of God's continued work in the world by His Spirit, through His church.

iv. "The Acts of the Apostles should therefore be studied mainly for this double purpose: first, to trace our Lord's unseen but actual *continuance of his divine teaching and working*; and, secondly, to trace the *active ministry of the Holy Spirit* as the abiding presence in the church." (Pierson)

2. (2-3) The last work of Jesus before His ascension to heaven.

Until the day in which He was taken up, after He through the Holy Spirit had given commandments to the apostles whom He had chosen, to whom He also presented Himself alive after His suffering by many infallible proofs, being seen by them during forty days and speaking of the things pertaining to the kingdom of God.

a. **Until the day in which He was taken up**: Jesus, **through the Holy Spirit**, instructed the apostles regarding what to do in His absence. He **had given commandments to the apostles**.

i. Significantly, Jesus did this **through the Holy Spirit**. This was the resurrected, glorified Lord Jesus Christ, risen with all authority and sovereignty. Yet He still chose to not rely on His own resources (as it were), but relied on the power and the presence of the indwelling **Holy Spirit**.

ii. The **Holy Spirit** – the Third Member of the Holy Trinity – is the aspect of God that lives and empowers and inspires man. The Holy Spirit has a work among those who are not yet believers, but also a great and significant work in those who believe.

iii. If the glorified, resurrected Jesus needed and relied on the Holy Spirit, so should we. This is a pattern for the rest of the Book of Acts, which shows us what the Holy Spirit does operating through the church. "The disciple is not above his Master, nor the servant above his Lord. If even he was indebted to the Holy Spirit for the power of his ministry, surely we cannot afford to attempt the work appointed us without the same anointing." (Pierson)

b. **To whom He also presented Himself alive after His suffering by many infallible proofs**: Jesus also established the fact of His resurrection with **many infallible proofs** during the **forty days** after his resurrection but before His ascension. He left *no possible doubt* that He was resurrected, exactly as He had promised.

i. In 1 Corinthians 15:6 Paul described one of these **many infallible proofs**: *He was seen by over five hundred brethren at once, of whom the greater part remain to the present.* More than 500 people saw the resurrected Jesus, and most of them were still alive some 25 years later in the days of Paul's ministry.

c. **Speaking of the things pertaining to the kingdom of God**: The teaching Jesus gave during that period after His resurrection and before His ascension is not recorded, but we are told that He used that time to speak **of the things pertaining to the kingdom of God**.

i. Some Gnostic and New Age teachers would like to think that Jesus used those 40 days to teach His followers strange and obscure doctrines that must be rediscovered with new revelations today. But Luke told us that Jesus simply taught them much the same things and themes that He had taught them in His earthly ministry: **The things pertaining to the kingdom of God.**

B. The ascension of Jesus.

1. (4-5) Jesus' final instructions to the disciples.

And being assembled together with *them*, He commanded them not to depart from Jerusalem, but to wait for the Promise of the Father, "which," *He said*, "you have heard from Me; for John truly baptized with water, but you shall be baptized with the Holy Spirit not many days from now."

a. **He commanded them not to depart from Jerusalem**: Jesus had nothing else for the disciples to do other than to **wait** for the coming of the Holy Spirit (**the Promise of the Father**). Jesus knew that they really could do nothing effective for the Kingdom of God until the Spirit came.

- **To wait** means that it was worth waiting for.
- **To wait** means that they had a promise it would come.
- **To wait** means they must *receive* it; they couldn't create it themselves.
- **To wait** means that they would be tested by waiting, at least a little.

b. **He commanded... the Promise of Father... baptized with the Holy Spirit**: This is another example of how the fact of the Trinity – that there is One God in Three Persons – is woven into the fabric of the New Testament. Here we see that **He** (Jesus) told of the **Promise of the Father**, which is the coming of the **Holy Spirit**.

i. It is significant that this coming, filling, and empowering of the Holy Spirit is called "**the Promise of the Father**."

- It shows that we should wait for it with eager anticipation; a "**Promise of the Father**" could only be good.
- It shows that it is reliable; the Father would never **Promise** something He could not fulfill.
- It shows that the **Promise** belongs to all His children, since it comes from God as our **Father**.
- It shows that it must be received by faith, as is the pattern with the promises of God throughout the Bible.

ii. "The 'promise of the Father' now became also the promise of the Son." (Pierson)

c. **You shall be baptized with the Holy Spirit**: The idea of being **baptized** is to be immersed or covered over in something; even as John baptized people in water, so these disciples would be "immersed" in the Holy Spirit.

i. It may be more useful to describe the baptism of the Holy Spirit as a *condition* than as an *experience*. We should perhaps ask, "*Are you* baptized in the Holy Spirit?" instead of asking, "*Have you been* baptized in the Holy Spirit?"

d. **Not many days from now**: They knew that this **Promise of the Father** would come, but not immediately. It would be **days from now**, but not **many days**. Jesus had a purpose in not telling them exactly when it would come.

2. (6) The disciples ask Jesus a final question before His ascension.

Therefore, when they had come together, they asked Him, saying, "Lord, will You at this time restore the kingdom to Israel?"

a. **Therefore, when they had come together**: This would be the last time they would see Jesus in His physical body, until they went to heaven to be with Him forever. There is nothing specific in the text to show us that they *knew* this would be their last time seeing Him on earth, other than the weight of the question they were about to ask.

b. **Lord, will You at this time restore the kingdom to Israel?** This was a question asked many times before, but it had a special relevance now. They knew that Jesus had instituted the New Covenant (Luke 22:20). They also knew that the restoration of **the kingdom to Israel** was part of the New Covenant (as seen in Jeremiah 23:1-8, Ezekiel 36:16-30, Ezekiel 37:21-28).

i. It was actually reasonable for them to wonder when the *rest* of the New Covenant would be fulfilled. The response of Jesus in the following verses also indicates that He did not rebuke them or even correct them for the question. He simply told them that the answer wasn't for them to know.

ii. "The verb *restore* shows that they were expecting a political and territorial kingdom; the noun *Israel* that they were expecting a national kingdom; and the adverbial clause *at this time* that they were expecting its immediate establishment." (Stott)

iii. The disciples certainly knew the many Old Testament prophecies describing the spiritual *and* national rebirth of Israel. The disciples probably thought that the spiritual rebirth seemed certain, so the national would also come.

3. (7-8) Jesus' final teaching and final promise before His ascension.

And He said to them, "It is not for you to know times or seasons which the Father has put in His own authority. But you shall receive power when the Holy Spirit has come upon you; and you shall be witnesses to Me in Jerusalem, and in all Judea and Samaria, and to the end of the earth."

a. **It is not for you to know**: Jesus warned the disciples against inquiring into aspects of the timing of God's kingdom, because those things belong to God the Father alone (**which the Father has put in His own authority**).

i. It was wise for Jesus not to outline His plan over the next 2,000 years. It was good for the disciples to not know that the full restoration of the kingdom to Israel that they hoped would happen soon would not come for some 2,000 years. It might overly discourage them in the work they had to do right then, and might make them think less of the aspect of the kingdom of God that *was* present with them.

ii. At the same time, Jesus did not say that there was to be *no* restoration of the kingdom to Israel; He simply said that speculation into the time and date of this restoration was not proper for the disciples.

iii. **In His own authority**: The resurrected, ascended Jesus again showed His submission to the Father. His submission to the Father was not temporary, but eternal.

b. **But you shall receive power**: If the national kingdom they wanted would be delayed, the **power** they needed would not. They would soon receive power with the coming of the **Holy Spirit**.

i. With their question about the restoration of the kingdom to Israel, it is possible that the disciples still saw **power** too much in terms of Caesar's kind of power, and not enough in terms of God's kind of power.

c. **And you shall be witnesses to Me**: The natural result of receiving this promised power would be that they would become **witnesses** of Jesus, all over the earth.

i. Notice that this really wasn't a command; it was a simple statement of fact: *When* **the Holy Spirit has come upon you... you** *shall* be **witnesses of Me**. The words **shall be** are in the indicative, not the imperative. Jesus didn't recommend that they become **witnesses**; He said they would **be witnesses**.

ii. If we want to **be witnesses**, we need to be filled with the Holy Spirit. The best training program for evangelism is of little effectiveness without the filling of the Holy Spirit.

iii. Isaiah 43:10 has the Lord proclaiming to His people *You are My witnesses*. A cultic group today claims that this is their mandate for being "Jehovah's Witnesses." Unfortunately, they fail to see Isaiah 43:10 in the context of Acts 1:8; we are truly *Yahweh's Witnesses* when we are *Jesus' Witnesses*.

d. **In Jerusalem, and in all Judea and Samaria, and to the end of the earth**: The progress of the spread of the gospel message from **Jerusalem**, to **Judea and Samaria**, and then **to the end of the earth** becomes the outline of Acts.

- Acts 1-7 describes the gospel in **Jerusalem**.
- Acts 8-12 speak of the gospel in **Judea and Samaria**.
- Acts 13-28 tells of the gospel going **to the end of the earth**.

i. We may imagine the objections the disciples might think of to the places of ministry Jesus described.

- **Jerusalem** was where Jesus was executed at the word of an angry mob.
- **Judea** rejected His ministry.
- **Samaria** was regarded as a wasteland of impure half-breeds.
- In the **uttermost parts of the earth**, the Gentiles were seen by some Jews of that day as nothing better than fuel for the fires of Hell.

ii. Yet God wanted a witness sent to all of these places, and the Holy Spirit would empower them to do this work.

4. (9-11) Jesus ascends into heaven.

Now when He had spoken these things, while they watched, He was taken up, and a cloud received Him out of their sight. And while they looked steadfastly toward heaven as He went up, behold, two men stood by them in white apparel, who also said, "Men of Galilee, why do you stand gazing up into heaven? This *same* Jesus, who was taken up from you into heaven, will so come in like manner as you saw Him go into heaven."

a. **He was taken up, and a cloud received Him out of their sight**: Jesus was taken up from them as He blessed them (Luke 24:50). As He slowly disappeared into the sky, surrounded by a **cloud** they continued to gaze upward.

> i. The **cloud** that **received Him** is suggestive of the cloud of glory (called the *Shekinah*) that is associated with the presence of God in the Old and New Testaments.

b. **While they watched, He was taken up**: It was important for Jesus to leave His disciples in this manner. In theory, He certainly could have simply vanished to heaven and the Father's presence in a secret sort of way. But by ascending in this manner, Jesus wanted His followers to know that He was gone for good, as opposed to the way He appeared and reappeared during the 40 days after His resurrection.

> i. Remember Jesus' words to His disciples in John 16:7: *It is to your advantage that I go away; for if I do not go away, the Helper will not come to you; but if I depart, I will send Him to you.* Now the disciples could know that that promise would be fulfilled. The Holy Spirit was coming because Jesus promised to send the Spirit when He left.

c. **Why do you stand gazing up into heaven?** The **two men** (apparently angels) told the disciples to put their attention in the right place (obedience to Jesus' command to return to Jerusalem), not in wondering where and how Jesus went. Jesus told them to go to the ends of the *earth*, and they stood **gazing up into heaven**.

> i. Morgan speculated that the **two men** were possibly Moses and Elijah. It seems best to say they were angels.

d. **This same Jesus**: This is a glorious phrase. It reminds us that the Jesus ascended to heaven and seated at the right hand of God the Father is the **same Jesus** of the Gospels. He is the **same Jesus** of love, grace, goodness, wisdom, and care.

e. **Will so come in like manner as you saw Him go into heaven**: Jesus will return just as He left.

- He left *physically* and **will so come in like manner**.
- He left *visibly* and **will so come in like manner**.
- He left from the *Mount of Olives* and **will so come in like manner**.
- He left in the *presence of His disciples* and **will so come in like manner**.
- He left *blessing His church* and **will so come in like manner**.

C. Matthias is appointed to replace Judas.

1. (12-14) The followers of Jesus return to Jerusalem.

Then they returned to Jerusalem from the mount called Olivet, which is near Jerusalem, a Sabbath day's journey. And when they had entered, they went up into the upper room where they were staying: Peter, James, John, and Andrew; Philip and Thomas; Bartholomew and Matthew; James *the son* of Alphaeus and Simon the Zealot; and Judas *the son* of James. These all continued with one accord in prayer and supplication, with the women and Mary the mother of Jesus, and with His brothers.

a. **They returned to Jerusalem**: This was notable *obedience*. Jesus told them to return to Jerusalem and wait for the coming of the Holy Spirit (Acts 1:4), and that is exactly what they did. They didn't forget the sermon right after they heard it, and they actually did what Jesus told them to do, even though He was no longer physically present with them.

b. **A Sabbath's day journey**: The Mount of Olives was just outside of ancient Jerusalem. This describes a short distance, the only kind allowed on the Sabbath.

c. **When they had entered, they went up into the upper room**: Acts 1:15 tells us that there were about 120 present. This included the eleven disciples (the twelve minus Judas) are present; along with Mary, the mother of Jesus, the brothers of Jesus (such as James and Jude), the women who followed Jesus, and others.

   i. The brothers of Jesus never seemed to be supportive of His ministry before His death and resurrection (John 7:5, Mark 3:21). After encountering the resurrected Jesus, they were changed into true followers of Jesus.

   ii. Calvin translates **with the women** as *with their wives*, a reference to the wives of the apostles.

d. **These all continued with one accord**: This is notable *unity*. When we saw the disciples in the Gospels, it seemed that they always fought and bickered. What had changed? Peter still had the history of denying the Lord; Matthew was still a tax collector; Simon was still a zealot. Their differences were still there, but the resurrected Jesus in their hearts was greater than any difference.

e. **These all continued with one accord in prayer and supplication**: This was notable *prayer*. They **all** prayed, and they **continued** in **prayer and supplication**. The idea of **supplication** is a sense of desperation and earnestness in prayer.

   i. Already, we see three important steps in making godly decisions: The disciples were in obedience, they were in fellowship, and they were in prayer.

2. (15-20) Peter suggests selecting a replacement for Judas.

And in those days Peter stood up in the midst of the disciples (altogether the number of names was about a hundred and twenty), and said, "Men *and* brethren, this Scripture had to be fulfilled, which the Holy Spirit spoke before by the mouth of David concerning Judas, who became a guide to those who arrested Jesus; for he was numbered with us and obtained a part in this ministry." (Now this man purchased a field with the wages of iniquity; and falling headlong, he burst open in the middle and all his entrails gushed out. And it became known to all those dwelling in Jerusalem; so that field is called in their own language, Akel Dama, that is, Field of Blood.) "For it is written in the book of Psalms:

'Let his dwelling place be desolate,
And let no one live in it';

and,

'Let another take his office.'

a. **Peter stood up in the midst of the disciples**: Here, Peter took a natural leadership role among the disciples. There is nothing wrong with seeing Peter as the leader of the first group of the apostles, even as he often was the spokesman among the disciples during the earthly ministry of Jesus.

i. However, the idea that the authority of Peter was *supreme* and that *he handed it down in unbroken succession*, is unbiblical and wrong.

b. **Men and brethren, this Scripture had to be fulfilled**: Peter's words show wisdom we did not often see in him before. He began by noting that Judas didn't spoil God's plan, he fulfilled it (**this Scripture had to be fulfilled**). This is something that only wise and mature disciples can see in the aftermath of evil.

c. **Falling headlong, he burst open in the middle and all his entrails gushed out**: Luke's historical note calls attention to how Judas died. Matthew 27:5 says that Judas hanged himself, but apparently he failed in the attempt, fell, and was killed by the impact of falling from the tree in the **Field of Blood**.

i. It was a **Field of Blood** not only because Judas spilled his blood there, but also because the field was purchased with the "blood money" given to the betrayer of Jesus.

d. **For it is written**: Peter, quoting from two separate Psalms, showed why God wanted them to choose another disciple to officially replace Judas.

i. This was notable *reliance on God's Word*. This wasn't the wisdom of man at work, but a principle revealed in Scripture. Also, this is the first time in the New Testament we read that Peter quoted Scripture.

ii. **Let his habitation be desolate**: David, the writer of these quoted Psalms, knew what it was like to be betrayed by another. When David was a fugitive from Saul, a man named Doeg betrayed him (1 Samuel 21-22), and many innocent people died as a result. David may have penned these very words in reference to this betrayer.

iii. **Let another take his office**: When David was betrayed, he desired that the betrayer would be desolate and that another fill the betrayer's office. It wasn't hard to understand that the Son of David - Jesus, whom David often prefigured - would desire the same thing.

iv. This was notable *desire for God's will*. Because of the principle of the quoted Scripture, they decided to replace Judas because they believe it is what Jesus wanted, not because it is what they wanted.

3. (21-23) Qualifications are stated and two men are nominated.

"Therefore, of these men who have accompanied us all the time that the Lord Jesus went in and out among us, beginning from the baptism of John to that day when He was taken up from us, one of these must become a witness with us of His resurrection." And they proposed two: Joseph called Barsabas, who was surnamed Justus, and Matthias.

a. **One of these must become a witness with us**: The disciples were bold enough to make a decision because they knew from God's Word that this is what He wanted. The apostles did not sense an outpouring of the Holy Spirit upon them; that was yet to come. But God did not leave them without guidance. They knew what to do from the Word.

i. Of course, even if we do sense a special guidance from the Holy Spirit, we *still* have God's voice permanently established in His Word. Any perceived guidance from the Holy Spirit will never disobey God's written word to us.

b. **Who have accompanied us all the time**: Whoever replaced Judas must be one who had been with them since John baptized them, who stayed with them during the days of Jesus' earthly ministry, and who saw the resurrected Jesus.

i. We find no evidence that these qualifications were discovered either in the Scriptures or by special leading of the Holy Spirit. We might say that they simply used their *sanctified common sense*. These seemed to be logical, common sense requirements for the successor to Judas' office as disciple.

ii. Their common sense was sanctified because it came as they were in obedience, in fellowship, in prayer, in the Scriptures, and desiring God's will.

iii. This was notable *sanctified common sense*. It didn't answer everything, but it did narrow it down to two men.

c. **One of these must become a witness with us of His resurrection**: This was the main job of the disciple that would replace Judas. Now that Jesus had ascended to heaven, it was more important than ever to have **a witness…of His resurrection**.

i. We also can be witnesses of His resurrection, both by trusting and proclaiming the apostolic testimony, and our own testimony that the risen Jesus lives in and through us.

4. (24-26) The disciples pray and cast lots to select a replacement for Judas.

And they prayed and said, "You, O Lord, who know the hearts of all, show which of these two You have chosen to take part in this ministry and apostleship from which Judas by transgression fell, that he might go to his own place." And they cast their lots, and the lot fell on Matthias. And he was numbered with the eleven apostles.

a. **And they prayed**: They prayed first, and it was easy to pray because they had already been praying (Acts 1:14).

i. This was a notable way of *doing what Jesus would do*. We remember that when Jesus chose His disciples, He prayed (Luke 6:12-13). The disciples, following Jesus, prayed for wisdom to know who the Lord would add to their number.

b. **And they cast their lots**: This was essentially rolling dice or drawing straws for the answer. Many people have questioned the method for choosing one of the two men; it seems that despite all these wonderful spiritual steps, they ended up rolling dice to pick the winner. It is fair to ask, "Is this any way to choose an apostle?"

i. Nevertheless, this was notable *reliance on God*. Though they were not yet filled with the Holy Spirit as they soon would be, they still wanted to choose a method that would make them rely on God. Perhaps they remembered Proverbs 16:33: *The lot is cast into the lap, but its every decision is from the LORD*.

ii. The casting of lots may be an imperfect way to discern God's will, but it is much better than the methods many Christians use today – that is, to rely on emotions, to rely on circumstances, or feelings, or carnal desires, and so forth.

c. **And the lot fell on Matthias**: Some insist that Matthias was the wrong choice and the use of lots in making the decision was not right. The idea is that God would have eventually chosen Paul if the office had been left vacant. But we must respect the testimony of the Scriptures; God did not want to leave the office vacant. If it were left unfilled, it might be seen as a victory for Satan; as if Jesus chose 12, but one came up short and therefore Satan defeated Jesus' desire to have 12 apostles.

i. Even though we read nothing more of Matthias, we should not assume he was a failure as an apostle. Except for Peter and John, none of the original twelve are mentioned again after Acts 1. Matthias was no more of a failure than Matthew or Andrew or Thomas or any of the others.

ii. As for Paul, he clearly considered himself an apostle, but *one born out of due time* (1 Corinthians 15:8). It doesn't seem that he objected to the selection of Matthias.

iii. Revelation 21:14 brings up an interesting question. It tells us that each of the twelve foundations of the New Jerusalem has the name of one of the *twelve apostles of the Lamb*. When we get to heaven, it will be interesting to see if the twelfth apostle of the Lamb is Paul or Matthias.

d. **And he was numbered with the eleven apostles**: No one can fault all the things they did *before* they cast lots. We must believe that all these things put them into the place where God would truly guide their decision.

i. We would not make many wrong decisions if we did all the things the disciples did before making big decisions.

- The disciples obeyed.
- The disciples were in unity and fellowship.
- The disciples were in prayer.
- The disciples were in the Scriptures.
- The disciples wanted to do God's will.
- The disciples used sanctified common sense.
- The disciples did what Jesus did.
- The disciples did what they could do to rely on God.

Acts 2 - The Holy Spirit is Poured Out on the Church

A. The initial experience of the filling of the Holy Spirit.

1. (1-4a) The disciples are filled with the Holy Spirit.

When the Day of Pentecost had fully come, they were all with one accord in one place. And suddenly there came a sound from heaven, as of a rushing mighty wind, and it filled the whole house where they were sitting. Then there appeared to them divided tongues, as of fire, and *one* sat upon each of them. And they were all filled with the Holy Spirit.

a. **The Day of Pentecost**: This was a Jewish feast held 50 days after Passover. It celebrated the firstfruits of the wheat harvest.

i. In the Jewish rituals of that time, the first sheaf reaped from the barley harvest was presented to God at Passover. But at Pentecost, the firstfruits of the wheat harvest were presented to God; therefore, Pentecost is called *the day of the firstfruits* (Numbers 28:26).

ii. Jewish tradition also taught that **Pentecost** marked the day when the Law was given to Israel. The Jews sometimes called **Pentecost** *shimchath torah*, or "Joy of the Law."

iii. On the Old Testament **Day of Pentecost** Israel received the Law; on the New Testament **Day of Pentecost** the Church received the Spirit of Grace in fullness.

iv. "It was the best-attended of the great feasts because traveling conditions were at their best. There was never a more cosmopolitan gathering in Jerusalem than this one." (Hughes)

v. Leviticus 23:15-22 gives the original instructions for the celebration of Pentecost. It says that two loaves of *leavened* bread were to be waved before the Lord by the priest as part of the celebration. "Were there not two loaves? Not only shall Israel be saved, but the multitude of the Gentiles shall be turned unto the Lord Jesus Christ." (Spurgeon)

b. **When the Day of Pentecost had fully come**: It was now 10 days after the time Jesus ascended to heaven (Acts 1:3), and since Jesus commanded them to wait for the coming of the Holy Spirit.

> i. The disciples were not strangers to the person and work of the Holy Spirit.
>
> - The disciples saw the Holy Spirit continually at work in the ministry of Jesus.
> - The disciples experienced something of the power of the Spirit as they stepped out and served God (Luke 10:1-20).
> - The disciples heard Jesus promise a new, coming work of the Holy Spirit (John 14:15-18).
> - The disciples received the Holy Spirit in a new way after Jesus finishes His work on the cross and instituted the New Covenant in His blood (John 20:19-23).
> - The disciples heard Jesus command them to wait for a promised baptism of the Holy Spirit that would empower them to be witnesses (Acts 1:4-5).
>
> ii. They waited until **the Day of Pentecost had fully come**, but they didn't know ahead of time how long they would have to wait. It would be easy for them to think it would come the same afternoon Jesus ascended to heaven; or after 3 days, or 7 days. But they had to wait a full 10 days, until **the Day of Pentecost had fully come**.
>
> iii. The only possible Scriptural precedent for this might be Jeremiah 42:7: *Ten days later the word of the LORD came to Jeremiah*. But who would have suspected that? God used this time to break them down and then to build them up. We can imagine how their patience and kindness and compassion was tested during this time, yet they all stayed together.
>
> iv. What this passage tells us about the gift of the Holy Spirit.
>
> - The gift of the Holy Spirit is promised to us.
> - The gift of the Holy Spirit is worth waiting for.
> - The gift of the Holy Spirit comes as He wills, often not according to our expectation.
> - The gift of the Holy Spirit can come upon not only individuals, but also upon groups (see also Acts 2:4, 4:31, 10:44).

- The gift of the Holy Spirit is often given as God deals with the flesh and there is a dying to self.

v. What this passage does *not* tell us about the gift of the Holy Spirit.

- The gift of the Holy Spirit is given according to formula.
- We earn the gift of the Holy Spirit by our seeking.

c. **They were all with one accord in one place**: They were gathered together sharing the same heart, the same love for God, the same trust in His promise, and the same geography.

i. Before we can be filled, we must recognize our emptiness; by gathering together for prayer, in obedience, these disciples did just that. They recognized they did not have the resources in themselves to do what they could do or should do; they had to instead rely on the work of God.

d. **Suddenly there came a sound from heaven**: The association of the sound of a **rushing mighty wind**, filling the **whole house**, with the outpouring of the Holy Spirit is unusual. But it probably has connection with the fact that in both the Hebrew and Greek languages, the word for *spirit* (as in *Holy Spirit*) is the same word for *breath* or **wind** (this also happens to be true in Latin). Here, the **sound from heaven** was the sound of the Holy Spirit being poured out on the disciples.

i. The **sound** of this fast, **mighty wind** would make any of these men and women who knew the Hebrew Scriptures think of the presence of the Holy Spirit.

- In Genesis 1:1-2, it is the Spirit of God as the breath/wind of God, blowing over the waters of the newly created earth.
- In Genesis 2:7, it is the Spirit of God as the breath/wind of God, blowing life into newly created man.
- In Ezekiel 37:9-10, it is the Spirit of God as the breath/wind of God, moving over the dry bones of Israel bringing them life and strength.

ii. This single line tells us much about how the Holy Spirit moves.

- **Suddenly**: Sometimes God moves suddenly.
- **Sound**: It was real, though it could not be touched; it came by the ears.
- **From heaven**: It wasn't of earth; not created or manipulated or made here.
- **Mighty**: Full of force, coming with great power.

e. **There appeared to them divided tongues as of fire, and one sat upon each of them**: These **divided tongues, as of fire**, appearing over each one, were also unusual. It probably should be connected with John the Baptist's prophecy that Jesus would *baptize you with the Holy Spirit and with fire* (Matthew 3:11).

i. The idea behind the picture of **fire** is usually purification, as a refiner uses fire to make pure gold; or fire can burn away what is temporary, leaving only what will last. This is an excellent illustration of the principle that the filling of the Holy Spirit is not just for abstract power, but for *purity*.

ii. In certain places in the Old Testament, God showed His special pleasure with a sacrifice by lighting the fire for it Himself – that is, fire from heaven came down and consumed the sacrifice. The experience of the followers of Jesus on Pentecost is another example of God sending fire from heaven to show His pleasure and power, but this time, it descended upon *living sacrifices* (Romans 12:1).

iii. The Holy Spirit *sat* **upon each of them**. "The word 'sat' has a marked force in the New Testament. It carries the idea of a *completed preparation*, and a certain *permanence of position and condition*." (Pierson)

iv. Under the Old Covenant, the Holy Spirit rested on God's people more as a *nation*, that is, Israel. But under the New Covenant, the Holy Spirit rests upon God's people as *individuals* - the tongues of fire **sat upon *each* of them**. This strange phenomenon had never happened before and would never happen again in the pages of the Bible, but was given to emphasis this point, that the Spirit of God was present with and in and upon *each individual*.

f. **And they were all filled with the Holy Spirit**: Essentially, the **rushing mighty wind** and the **tongues, as of fire**, were only unusual, temporary phenomenon, which accompanied the true gift – being **filled with the Holy Spirit**.

i. While it would be wrong to expect a **rushing mighty wind** or **tongues, as of fire**, to be present today when the Holy Spirit is poured out, we can experience the true gift. We, just as they, can be **all filled with the Holy Spirit**.

ii. But we should do what the disciples did before and during their filling with the Holy Spirit.

- The disciples were filled *in fulfillment of a promise*.
- They were filled as they *received in faith*.

- They were filled *in God's timing*.
- They were filled *as they were together in unity*.
- They were filled *in unusual ways*.

iii. This coming and filling of the Holy Spirit was so good, so essential for the work of the community of early Christians, that Jesus actually said that it was *better* for Him to leave the earth bodily so He could send the Holy Spirit (John 16:7).

2. (4b-13) The phenomenon of speaking in tongues.

And began to speak with other tongues, as the Spirit gave them utterance. And there were dwelling in Jerusalem Jews, devout men, from every nation under heaven. And when this sound occurred, the multitude came together, and were confused, because everyone heard them speak in his own language. Then they were all amazed and marveled, saying to one another, "Look, are not all these who speak Galileans? And how *is it that* we hear, each in our own language in which we were born? Parthians and Medes and Elamites, those dwelling in Mesopotamia, Judea and Cappadocia, Pontus and Asia, Phrygia and Pamphylia, Egypt and the parts of Libya adjoining Cyrene, visitors from Rome, both Jews and proselytes, Cretans and Arabs–we hear them speaking in our own tongues the wonderful works of God." So they were all amazed and perplexed, saying to one another, "Whatever could this mean?" Others mocking said, "They are full of new wine."

a. **And began to speak with other tongues**: In response to the filling of the Holy Spirit, those present (not only the twelve apostles) **began to speak with other tongues**. These were languages that they were never taught, and they spoke these languages, speaking **as the Spirit gave them utterance**.

b. **Devout men, from every nation under heaven**: The multitude from many nations gathered in Jerusalem because of the Feast of Pentecost. Many of these were the same people who gathered in Jerusalem at the last feast, Passover, when an angry mob demanded the execution of Jesus.

c. **And when this sound occurred**: A crowd quickly gathered, being attracted by **this sound**, which was either the sound of the *rushing mighty wind* or the sound of speaking in **other tongues**. When the crowd came, they heard the Christians speaking in their own foreign languages. Apparently, the Christians could be heard from the windows of the upper room, or they went out onto some kind of balcony or into the temple courts.

i. Not many homes of that day could hold 120 people. It is far more likely that this upper room was part of the temple courts, which was a huge structure, with porches and colonnades and rooms. The crowd came from people milling about the temple courts.

d. **We hear them speaking in our tongues the wonderful works of God**: This is what the crowd heard the Christians speak. From this remarkable event, **all** were **amazed and perplexed**, but **some** used it as a means of honest inquiry and asked, "**Whatever could this mean?**" **Others** used it as an excuse to dismiss the work of God and said, "**They are full of new wine.**"

i. **Look, are not all these who speak Galileans?** People from Galilee (**Galileans**) were known to be uncultured and poor speakers. This was all the more reason to be impressed with their ability to speak eloquently in other languages. "Galileans had difficulty pronouncing gutturals and had the habit of swallowing syllables when speaking; so they were looked down upon by the people of Jerusalem as being provincial." (Longenecker)

ii. They all spoke in different tongues, yet there was a unity among the believers. "Ever since the early church fathers, commentators have seen the blessing of Pentecost as a deliberate and dramatic reversal of the curse of Babel." (Stott)

e. **Whatever *could* this mean?** What are we to make of the phenomenon of speaking in tongues? Speaking in tongues has been the focal point for significant controversy in the church. People still ask the same question these bystanders asked on the day of Pentecost.

i. There is no controversy that God, at least at one time, gave the church the gift of tongues. But much of the controversy centers on the question, "what is God's *purpose* for the gift of tongues?"

ii. Some think that the gift of tongues was given primarily as a sign to unbelievers (1 Corinthians 14:21-22) and as a means to miraculously communicate the gospel in diverse languages. They believe there is no longer the need for this sign, so they regard tongues as a gift no longer present in the church today.

iii. Others argue that the gift of tongues, while a sign to unbelievers as stated by 1 Corinthians 14:21-22, are *primarily* a gift of communication between the believer and God (1 Corinthians 14:2, 13-15), and is a gift still given by God today.

iv. Many mistakenly interpret this incident in Acts 2, assuming that the disciples used tongues to preach to the gathered crowd. But a careful look shows this idea is wrong. Notice what the people heard the disciples say: **Speaking... the wonderful works of God**. The disciples declared the praises of God, thanking Him with all their might in unknown tongues. The gathered crowd merely *overheard* what the disciples exuberantly declared to God.

v. The idea that these disciples communicated to the diverse crowd in tongues is plainly wrong. The crowd *had* a common language (Greek), and Peter preached a sermon to them in that language! (Acts 2:14-40)

f. **We hear them speaking in our tongues the wonderful works of God**: The gift of tongues *is* a personal language of prayer given by God, whereby the believer communicates with God beyond the limits of knowledge and understanding (1 Corinthians 14:14-15).

i. The Gift of Tongues has an important place in the devotional life of the believer, but a small place in the corporate life of the church (1 Corinthians 14:18-19), especially in public meetings (1 Corinthians 14:23).

ii. When tongues *is* practiced in the corporate life of the church, it must be carefully controlled, and never without an interpretation given by the Holy Spirit (1 Corinthians 14:27-28).

iii. The ability to pray in an unknown tongue is not a gift given to every believer (1 Corinthians 12:30).

iv. The ability to pray in an unknown tongue is *not* the primary or singularly true evidence of the filling of the Holy Spirit. This emphasis leads many to seek the gift of tongues (and to counterfeit it) merely to prove to themselves and others that they really are filled with the Holy Spirit.

g. **Began to speak with other tongues as the Spirit gave them utterance**: Was this speaking in tongues in Acts 2 the same *gift of tongues* described in 1 Corinthians 12 and 14?

i. Some say we are dealing with two separate gifts. They argue that the 1 Corinthians gift must be regulated and restricted, while the Acts 2 gift can be used any time without regulation. Those who believe they are two separate gifts emphasize that the speech of Acts 2 was immediately recognized by foreign visitors to Jerusalem, while the speech of 1 Corinthians was unintelligible to those present except with a divinely granted gift of interpretation.

ii. However, this doesn't take into account that the differences have more to do with the *circumstances* in which the gifts were exercised than with the gifts *themselves*.

iii. In Jerusalem, the group spoken to was uniquely multi-national and multi-lingual; at feast time (Pentecost), Jews of the dispersion from all over the world were in the city. Therefore, the likelihood that foreign ears would hear a tongue spoken in their language was much greater. On the other hand, in Corinth (though a rather cosmopolitan city itself), the gift was exercised in a local church, with members all sharing a common language (Greek). If one had the same diversity of foreigners visiting the Corinthian church when all were speaking in tongues, it is likely that many would hear members of the Corinthian church **speaking in our own tongues the wonderful works of God**.

iv. As well, it should never be assumed that each person among the 120 who spoke in tongues on the Day of Pentecost spoke in a language immediately intelligible to human ears present that day. We read they *all…began to speak with other tongues*; therefore there were some 120 individuals speaking in tongues. Since the nations spoken of in Acts 2:9-11 number only fifteen (with perhaps others present but not mentioned), it is likely that many (if not most) of the 120 spoke praises to God in a language that was not understood by someone immediately present. The text simply does not indicate that someone present could understand *each person* speaking in tongues.

v. However, we should not assume those who were not immediately understood by human ears spoke "gibberish," as the modern gift of tongues is sometimes called with derision. They may have praised God in a language completely unknown, yet completely human. After all, what would the language of the Aztecs sound like to Roman ears? Or some may have spoke in a completely unique language given by God and understood by Him and Him alone. After all, communication with God, not man, is the purpose of the gift of tongues (1 Corinthians 14:2). The repetition of simple phrases, unintelligible and perhaps nonsensical to human bystanders, does not mean someone speaks "gibberish." Praise to God may be simple and repetitive, and part of the whole dynamic of tongues is that it bypasses the understanding of the speaker (1 Corinthians 14:14), being understood by God and God alone.

vi. All in all, we should regard the gift of Acts 2 and the gift of tongues in 1 Corinthians as the same, simply because the same term is used for both in the original language (*heterais glossais*). Also, the verb translated *gave them utterance* in Acts 2:4 is frequently used in Greek literature in connection with spiritually prompted (ecstatic) speech, not mere translation into other languages.

B. Peter's sermon on the day of Pentecost.

1. (14-15) Peter begins his sermon.

But Peter, standing up with the eleven, raised his voice and said to them, "Men of Judea and all who dwell in Jerusalem, let this be known to you, and heed my words. For these are not drunk, as you suppose, since it is *only* the third hour of the day.

a. **Peter, standing up with the eleven**: Peter stood and preached to the crowd as a representative of the whole group of apostles.

i. We should notice that the speaking in tongues stopped when Peter began to preach. The Holy Spirit now worked through Peter's preaching and would not work *against* Himself through tongues at the same time.

b. **Raised his voice**: There was a remarkable change in Peter. He had courage and boldness that was a complete contrast to his denials of Jesus before being filled with the Holy Spirit.

i. On the Day of Pentecost Peter didn't teach as the rabbis in his day usually did, who gathered disciples around them, sat down, and instructed them and any others who might listen. Instead, Peter proclaimed the truth like a herald.

ii. This remarkable sermon had no preparation behind it – it was spontaneously given. Peter didn't wake up that morning knowing he would preach to thousands, and that thousands would embrace Jesus in response. Yet we could say that this was a well-prepared sermon; it was prepared by Peter's prior life with God and relationship with Jesus. It flowed spontaneously out of that life, and out of a mind that thought and believed deeply.

iii. It is good to remember that what we have in Acts 2 is a small portion of what Peter actually said. Acts 2:40 tells us, *And with many other words he testified and exhorted them.* Like almost all the sermons recorded in the Bible, what we have is a Holy Spirit inspired abridgment of a longer message.

c. **For these are not drunk**: Peter deflected the mocking criticism that the disciples were drunk. In that day it was unthinkable that people would be so drunk so early in the day (about 9:00 in the morning).

i. Commentator Adam Clarke says that most Jews - pious or not - did not eat or drink until after the **third hour of the day**, because that was the time for prayer, and they would only eat after their business with God was accomplished.

d. **These are not drunk**: We shouldn't think that the Christians were acting as if they were drunk. The idea of "being drunk in the Spirit" has no foundation in Scripture; the comment from the mockers on the Day of Pentecost had no basis in reality.

> i. "Nor, must we add, did the believers' experience of the Spirit's fullness *seem* to them or *look* to others like intoxication, because they had lost control of their normal mental and physical functions. No, the fruit of the Spirit is 'self-control,' not the loss of it." (Stott)

2. (16-21) Quoting Joel 2, Peter explains the strange events at Pentecost.

But this is what was spoken by the prophet Joel:

'And it shall come to pass in the last days, says God,
That I will pour out of My Spirit on all flesh;
Your sons and your daughters shall prophesy,
Your young men shall see visions,
Your old men shall dream dreams.
And on My menservants and on My maidservants
I will pour out My Spirit in those days;
And they shall prophesy.
I will show wonders in heaven above
And signs in the earth beneath:
Blood and fire and vapor of smoke.
The sun shall be turned into darkness,
And the moon into blood,
Before the coming of the great and awesome day of the LORD.
And it shall come to pass
***That* whoever calls on the name of the LORD**
Shall be saved.'

> a. **But this is what was spoken by the prophet Joel**: In the midst of this great outpouring of the Holy Spirit, among signs and wonders and speaking in tongues, what did Peter do? Essentially, he said, "Let's have a Bible study. Let's look at what **the prophet Joel** wrote."

> > i. This introduces the first of three Old Testament passages Peter will quote: Joel 2:28-32, Psalm 16:8-11, and Psalm 110:1.

> > ii. This focus on God's Word did not quench the moving of the Holy Spirit; it fulfilled what the Holy Spirit wanted to do. All the signs and wonders and speaking in tongues were preparing for this work of God's Word.

> > iii. Unfortunately, some people set the Word against the Spirit. They almost think it's more spiritual if there is no Bible study. Sadly, this is

often due to the weak and unspiritual teaching of some who teach the Bible.

b. **The prophet Joel**: This quotation from Joel 2:28-32 focuses on God's promise to pour out His Spirit on all flesh. What happened on the day of Pentecost was a *near* fulfillment of that promise, with the *final* fulfillment coming in the last days (which Peter had good reason to believe he was in).

i. Joel mostly prophesied about judgment that was coming to ancient Israel. Yet in the midst of the many warnings of judgment, God also gave several words of promise – promises of future blessing, like this one that announces an outpouring of the Holy Spirit.

c. **It shall come to pass in the last days**: The idea of the **last days** is that they are the times of the Messiah, encompassing both His humble coming and His return in glory. Because Jesus had already come in humility, they were aware that His return in glory could be any time.

i. Though there would be some 2,000 years until Jesus returned, until this point, history had been running *towards* the point of the ultimate establishment of God's kingdom on earth. But from this time on, history runs *parallel* to that point, ready at any time for the consummation.

ii. It may also be helpful to see the **last days** as something like a season – a general period of time – more than a specific *period*, such as a week. In the whole span of God's plan for human history, we are in the season of the **last days**.

iii. "Peter did not say of that pentecostal enduement, 'Now *is fulfilled* that which was spoken by the prophet Joel,' but, more guardedly, '*This is that* which was spoken;' that is to say, Joel's words furnish the *explanation* of this first Pentecost, though this does not finish their *fulfillment*." (Pierson)

d. **I will pour out of My Spirit on all flesh**: In using the quotation from Joel, Peter explained what these curious onlookers saw - the Holy Spirit poured forth upon the people. Before the Holy Spirit was given in drops, now He is *poured* forth – and **on all flesh**.

i. This was a glorious emphasis on Pentecost. Under the Old Covenant, certain people were filled with the Spirit at certain times for specific purposes. Now, under the New Covenant, the outpouring of the Holy Spirit is for all who call upon the name of the LORD, even **menservants** and **maidservants**.

ii. "There had been no provision for, and no promise of, an abiding presence of the Holy Spirit in the life of any Old Testament saint." (Hughes). This changes under the New Covenant.

e. **Whoever calls on the name of the Lord shall be saved**: Peter also used this passage from Joel to an evangelistic purpose. This outpouring of the Holy Spirit meant that God now offered salvation in a way previously unknown – to **whoever calls on the name of the Lord**, whether they are Jew or Gentile.

i. It would be many years until the gospel was offered to Gentiles, yet Peter's sermon text announced the gospel invitation by saying, *whoever* **calls on the name of the Lord shall be saved**.

ii. The idea is expressed in Proverbs 18:10: *The name of the Lord is a strong tower; the righteous run to it and are safe.*

3. (22-24) Peter introduces the focus of the sermon: The resurrected Messiah, Jesus of Nazareth.

"Men of Israel, hear these words: Jesus of Nazareth, a Man attested by God to you by miracles, wonders, and signs which God did through Him in your midst, as you yourselves also know—Him, being delivered by the determined purpose and foreknowledge of God, you have taken by lawless hands, have crucified, and put to death; whom God raised up, having loosed the pains of death, because it was not possible that He should be held by it.

a. **Men of Israel, hear these words**: Many people would think it would be enough for Peter to stop after the quotation from Joel, considering all we have in it. Joel told us of:

- An outpouring of the Holy Spirit.
- Miraculous dreams, visions, and prophecy.
- Signs and wonders regarding the Day of the Lord.
- An invitation to call on the name of the Lord.

i. But it wasn't enough, because Peter had not yet spoken about the saving work of Jesus on our behalf. Everything until this point had been introduction, explaining the strange things they just saw. Now Peter would bring the essential message.

b. **Men of Israel, hear these words**: This was much as Peter had already said, *let this be known to you, and heed my words* (Acts 2:14). Peter wanted people to pay attention, and he spoke as if he had something important to say - something some teachers fail to do.

c. **As you yourselves also know**: Peter refered to what these people already knew about Jesus. They already knew of His life and miraculous works. Often in speaking to people about Jesus, we should start with what they *already* know about Him.

d. **Being delivered by the determined counsel and foreknowledge of God**: Peter knew that Jesus' death was in the plan of God. At the same time, those who rejected Him and called for His execution were responsible for the actions of their **lawless hands**.

> i. Peter did not flinch at saying, "You crucified this Man who God sent." His first concern was not to please his audience, but to tell them the truth. The Spirit-filled Peter was a different man that the Peter who a few months before, even knowing Jesus (Matthew 26:69-75).

e. **It was not possible**: Peter knew that Jesus could not remain bound by death, as explained by the following quotation from Psalm 16. It was not possible that Jesus should remain a victim of the sin and hatred of man; He would certainly triumph over it.

> i. **Having loosed the pains of death**: In the phrase **pains of death**, the word **pains** is actually the word for "birth pains." In this sense, the *tomb* was a *womb* for Jesus.

> ii. "It was not possible that the chosen one of God should remain in the grip of death; 'the abyss can no more hold the Redeemer than a pregnant woman can hold the child in her body.'" (Bruce, quoting Bertram)

4. (25-33) Quoting Psalm 16, Peter explains the resurrected Jesus.

"For David says concerning Him:

'I foresaw the LORD always before my face,
For He is at my right hand, that I may not be shaken.
Therefore my heart rejoiced, and my tongue was glad;
Moreover my flesh also will rest in hope.
For You will not leave my soul in Hades,
Nor will You allow Your Holy One to see corruption.
You have made known to me the ways of life;
You will make me full of joy in Your presence.'

"Men *and* brethren, let *me* speak freely to you of the patriarch David, that he is both dead and buried, and his tomb is with us to this day. Therefore, being a prophet, and knowing that God had sworn with an oath to him that of the fruit of his body, according to the flesh, He would raise up the Christ to sit on his throne, he, foreseeing this, spoke concerning the resurrection of the Christ, that His soul was not left in

Hades, nor did His flesh see corruption. This Jesus God has raised up, of which we are all witnesses. Therefore being exalted to the right hand of God, and having received from the Father the promise of the Holy Spirit, He poured out this which you now see and hear.

a. **For David says concerning Him**: Peter recognized that though this Psalm spoke of David, it spoke of someone greater than David – the Messiah, Jesus the Christ. Jesus may have taught Peter this when He instructed the disciples in the Scriptures (Luke 24:44-45).

b. **Your Holy One**: Jesus bore the full wrath of God on the cross, *as if* He were a guilty sinner, guilty of *all* our sin, even being made sin for us (2 Corinthians 5:21). Yet, that work was an act of holy, giving love for us, so that Jesus Himself did not become a sinner, even though He bore the full *guilt* of our sin.

i. This is the gospel message; that Jesus took our punishment for sin on the cross and remained a perfect Savior through the whole ordeal - *proved* by His resurrection. Apart from the resurrection, we would have no *proof* that Jesus successfully, perfectly, paid for our sins.

c. **Nor will You allow Your Holy One to see corruption**: Because Jesus bore our sin without becoming a sinner, He remained the **Holy One**, even in His death. Since it is incomprehensible that God's Holy One should be bound by death, the resurrection was absolutely inevitable.

i. Instead of being punished for His glorious work on the cross, Jesus was rewarded, as prophetically described in the Psalm: **You have made known to me the ways of life; You will make me full of joy in Your presence**.

d. **David… is both dead and buried**: Peter points out that this Psalm cannot be speaking of its human author, **David** - he is dead and remains buried. The Psalm must speak prophetically of the Messiah, Jesus.

e. **This Jesus God has raised up, of which we are all witnesses**: Jesus of Nazareth, the man they all knew (*as you yourselves also know*, Acts 2:22), was the one who fulfilled this prophetic Psalm. How did Peter know this? He saw the resurrected Jesus! The basic *evidence* of the resurrection was simply the report of reliable eyewitnesses: **Of which we are all witnesses**.

f. **He poured out this which you now see and hear**: Peter affirms that what the crowd saw was the work of the risen and ascended Jesus, who has sent His Holy Spirit upon His church.

5. (34-36) Quoting Psalm 110, Peter explains the Divine Messiah.

For David did not ascend into the heavens, but he says himself:

'The LORD said to my Lord,
"Sit at My right hand,
Till I make Your enemies Your footstool."'

"Therefore let all the house of Israel know assuredly that God has made this Jesus, whom you crucified, both Lord and Christ."

a. **The LORD said to my Lord**: This begins the third Old Testament passage Peter used in his sermon, Psalm 110:1. This verse of the Old Testament is quoted in the New Testament more than any other single verse; either quoted or referred to at least 25 times. In this Psalm, David understood and proclaimed the *deity* of the Messiah.

i. In this Psalm, King David – by the inspiration of the Holy Spirit – recorded that Yahweh, Israel's covenant God (**The LORD**), spoke to David's Lord (**my Lord**) as God. Peter used this to show that the Messiah, who is the focus of Psalm 110, is in fact Divine – He is God.

b. **Therefore let all the house of Israel know**: The sermon concludes with a summary. Simply, all Israel should know that even though they crucified Jesus, God has declared Him **both Lord and Christ**.

i. It is as if Peter said, "You were all wrong about Jesus. You crucified Him as if He were a criminal, but by the resurrection, God proved that He is Lord and Messiah."

ii. When Peter exhorted them *whoever calls on the name of the Lord shall be saved* (Acts 2:21), there is little doubt who the **Lord** is that he spoke of: **Jesus**.

iii. "That the early Christians meant to give Jesus the title *Lord* in this highest sense of all is indicated by their not hesitating on occasion to apply to him passages of Old Testament scripture referring to Yahweh." (Bruce)

C. The response to Peter's preaching.

1. (37) They respond with a question: **What shall we do?**

Now when they heard *this*, they were cut to the heart, and said to Peter and the rest of the apostles, "Men *and* brethren, what shall we do?"

a. **Now when they heard this…"What shall we do?"** This was obviously a significant work of the Holy Spirit. The great crowd listening to Peter was deeply moved by Peter's bold proclamation of the truth. *They* asked Peter how they should respond.

i. It is wrong to think that Peter offered no kind of invitation or challenge for his listeners to respond. Acts 2:40 says, *And with many other words he testified and exhorted them, saying, "Be saved from this perverse generation."* Peter clearly did exhort them to respond, and invited his listeners to *"Be saved."* Nevertheless, the multitude responded with remarkable initiative.

ii. The response of the crowd also helps us to put the events of that Day of Pentecost into perspective. The exercise of the gift of tongues produced nothing in the listeners except for astonishment and mocking. It wasn't until the gospel was preached that conviction from the Holy Spirit came. This was the work God really wanted to accomplish.

b. **Cut to the heart**: This is a good way of describing the conviction of the Holy Spirit. They now knew that they were responsible for the death of Jesus (as each of us are), and that they had to *do* something in response to this responsibility.

i. Peter had some previous experience with cutting. When Jesus was arrested, Peter cut off the right ear of one of the men who came to arrest Jesus (John 18:10). All this was an embarrassing mess that Jesus had to clean up. That showed Peter in the flesh, doing the best *he* could with a literal sword of human power.

ii. When the resurrected Jesus changed Peter's life and when the power of the Holy Spirit had come upon him, he did some much more effective cutting; cutting hearts, opening them to Jesus. This is what Peter could do in the power of the Spirit, doing God's *best* with the sword of the Spirit, God's Word. Which sword was more powerful?

c. **Men and brethren, what shall we do?** When God is working on someone's heart, they *want* to come to Him; they will act to come to God.

i. It has been said that in normal seasons of Christian work the evangelist seeks the sinner. Yet in times of revival or awakening, things change: the sinner seeks the evangelist. This Day of Pentecost in Acts 2 was one of those great seasons of God's work.

2. (38-40) Peter invites the multitude to come to Jesus.

Then Peter said to them, "Repent, and let every one of you be baptized in the name of Jesus Christ for the remission of sins; and you shall receive the gift of the Holy Spirit. For the promise is to you and to your children, and to all who are afar off, as many as the Lord our God will call." And with many other words he testified and exhorted them, saying, "Be saved from this perverse generation."

a. **Then Peter said to them**: This was in response to the question, *"What shall we do?"* Peter must have been pleasantly amazed to see what God had done in this situation. Instead of people wanting to crucify him because of Jesus, thousands of people wanted to trust in Jesus as Lord and Messiah.

b. **Repent, and let every one of you be baptized**: Responding to the question, "*What shall we do?*" Peter gave them something to *do*. This means that we must *do* something to be saved, we must *do* something to follow Jesus; it doesn't just "happen."

    i. Peter *did not* say, "There's nothing you can do. If God saves you, you're saved. If God doesn't save you, you'll never be saved." Though it was true that only God could do the saving, the people had to receive through repentance and faith, faith leading to action such as baptism.

c. **Repent**: The first thing Peter told them to *do* is **repent**. To repent does not mean to feel sorry, but it means to change one's mind or direction. They had thought a certain way about Jesus before, considering Him worthy of crucifixion. Now they must turn their thinking around, embracing Jesus as Lord and Messiah.

    i. **Repent** sounds like such a harsh word in the mouths of many preachers and in the ears of many listeners, but it is an essential aspect of the gospel. **Repent** has been rightly called "the first word of the gospel."

    ii. When John the Baptist preached he said, "*Repent, for the kingdom of heaven is at hand!*" (Matthew 3:2). When Jesus began to preach He said, "*Repent, for the kingdom of heaven is at hand*" (Matthew 4:17). Now when Peter began to preach, he started with **repent**.

    iii. Repentance must never be thought of as something we must do *before* we can come back to God. Repentance describes what coming to God is. You can't turn *towards* God without turning *from* the things He is against.

    iv. In this sense, **repent** is a word of great hope. It says, "You don't have to continue the way you've been going, you can turn to God."

    v. "The old-fashioned grace of repentance is not to be dispensed with; there must be sorrow for sin; there must be 'a broken and a contrite heart.' This, God will not despise; but a 'conversion' which does not produce this result, God will not accept as genuine." (Spurgeon)

d. **Be baptized in the name of Jesus Christ**: This was the second thing Peter said they must do. For them to **be baptized in the name of Jesus Christ** was an expression of their belief and complete trust in Him.

    i. Baptism made a clear statement. In that day, Jews were not commonly baptized, only Gentiles who wanted to become Jews. For these Jewish men and women to be baptized showed just how strongly they felt they needed Jesus.

ii. "While baptism with water was the expected symbol for conversion, it was not an indispensable criterion for salvation." (Longenecker)

e. **The promise is to you and to your children, and to all who are afar off**: As they repented and demonstrated faith and obedience by baptism, the gift of the Holy Spirit would be given to them as it was given to the original group of disciples. Peter also specifically promised that the **promise** of the Holy Spirit would be given to those who believe in all succeeding generations (**all who are afar off**).

i. They saw the glorious work of the Holy Spirit among the disciples, and Peter told them that it was something that these people could take part in; they didn't only have to be observers. And since the promise is for **all who are afar off**, it includes all people up to the present time.

ii. It is also important to note that Peter did not say that the unbelieving, unaware **children** of his listeners should be baptized. He simply said that the promise of **the remission of sins** and the **gift of the Holy Spirit** were for *all* who would repent and believe with active faith, even to coming generations and **all who are afar off, as many as the Lord God will call**.

iii. "That is to say, that great covenant promise, 'Whosoever shall call on the name of the Lord shall be saved,' is meant for you, is meant for your children, is meant for Hottentots, is meant for Hindoos, is meant for Greenlanders, is meant for everybody to whom the Lord's call is addressed." (Spurgeon)

f. **And with many other words he testified and exhorted them**: Peter's sermon didn't end there. He continued to urge the crowd to come to Jesus in repentant surrender.

g. **Be saved from this perverse generation**: Any generation that is responsible for putting Jesus to death is a **perverse generation**. But since *every* generation is responsible for Jesus' death, every generation needs salvation.

3. (41) The response to Peter's sermon.

Then those who gladly received his word were baptized; and that day about three thousand souls were added *to them*.

a. **About three thousand souls were added to them**: This day of Pentecost saw an amazing harvest of souls. The church went from about 120 people to 3,120 people in one day.

i. Think of how this touched lives beyond that one day. Many of the 3,000 were undoubtedly pilgrims who came to Jerusalem for the feast of Pentecost. They expected something special from God, but not anything like this. Many in this crowd went back home, traveling far from Jerusalem, taking the good news of Jesus Christ with them.

b. **Those who gladly received his word were baptized**: Those who believed on Jesus that day did so **gladly**, even making a dramatic statement in baptism. They would not have submitted to baptism unless they were fully convinced of who Jesus was and their great need for Him as a Savior.

i. How could you baptize 3,000 people? There were huge resources of water available on the temple mount, and pools and reservoirs nearby, so it was not difficult to find a place where the baptisms could take place.

ii. God continues to do such great things. After the 1990 Summer Harvest Crusade, there was a mass baptism at Corona del Mar. They couldn't count how many were baptized, but more than 5,000 people attended the event. It was reported as the largest baptism service in American history.

D. The life of these first believers.

1. (42) The foundation of their Christian life.

And they continued steadfastly in the apostles' doctrine and fellowship, in the breaking of bread, and in prayers.

a. **And they continued steadfastly**: On the day of Pentecost the sound of the rushing wind, the tongues of fire, and the conversion of 3,000 were all remarkable events. But the things described in Acts 2:42 were the abiding legacy of God's work.

b. **They continued steadfastly in the apostles' doctrine**: They relied on the apostles to communicate to them who Jesus was and what He had done. They just trusted in Jesus; now they wanted to know more.

i. **Continued steadfastly** uses a Greek verb communicating "a steadfast and single-minded fidelity to a certain course of action." (Longenecker) There was to be no departure from the **apostles' doctrine**, because it was the truth of God.

ii. Thankfully, God allows us to sit under the **apostles' doctrine** - the New Testament record. Every pastor should seek to be unoriginal in the sense that we don't have our own doctrine, but the **apostles' doctrine**.

c. **They continued in steadfastly in…fellowship**: The ancient Greek word *koinonia* (translated here as **fellowship**) has the idea of association, communion, fellowship, and participation; it means to *share* in something.

i. The Christian life is meant to be full of **fellowship**, of sharing one with another.

- We share the same Lord Jesus.
- We share the same guide for life.
- We share the same love for God
- We share the same desire to worship Him.
- We share the same struggles and the same victories.
- We share the same job of living for Him.
- We share the same joy of communicating the gospel.

d. **They continued in steadfastly… in the breaking of bread**: Even living so close to the time when Jesus was crucified, they still never wanted to forget what He did on the cross. How much more important is it for us to never forget?

e. **They continued in steadfastly… in prayers**. Whenever God's work is done, God's people gather for prayer and worship.

i. "In the Greek the definite article occurs before the word 'prayer.' The text actually says, 'to the prayers.' They devoted themselves 'to *the* breaking of bread and to *the* prayers.' Obviously, that is a reference to something formal – to worship in which the people got together and praised God." (Boice)

f. **The apostles' doctrine and fellowship, in the breaking of bread, and in prayers**: Everything else we read about the power and glory of the early church flows from this foundation of the word, fellowship, remembrance of Jesus' work on the cross, and prayer.

i. From Luke's description of the early Christian community, "The educated reader would have got the impression here that the Greek ideal of society had been realized." (Dictionary of New Testament Theology)

ii. "It is presented as a model church, but this does not mean that it was perfect. A few chapters further on, we are going to find that it was far from perfect." (Boice)

2. (43) The presence of the power of God.

Then fear came upon every soul, and many wonders and signs were done through the apostles.

a. **Then fear came upon every soul**: This was evidence of the power of God. One of the greatest, most powerful works God can do is to change the human heart towards a reverent honor of the Lord.

b. **Many signs and wonders were done**: This was evidence of the power of God. Where God is at work, lives will be touched in miraculous ways.

3. (44-45) Their close hearts and sharing in the common life of Jesus.

Now all who believed were together, and had all things in common, and sold their possessions and goods, and divided them among all, as anyone had need.

a. **Now all who believed were together, and had all things in common**: With the influx of more that 3,000 believers, most of whom stayed in Jerusalem and didn't have jobs, the family of Christians *had* to share if they were to survive.

i. We shouldn't regard this as an early experiment in communism because it was *voluntary, temporary*, and *flawed* to the extent that the church in Jerusalem was in continual need of financial support from other churches. Also, we don't have any evidence this continued very long.

b. **All who believed were together**: The Jews had a tremendous custom of hospitality during any major feast like Pentecost. Visitors were received into private homes, and no one could charge for giving a bed or a room to a visitor or for supplying their basic needs. The Christians took this tremendous feast-time hospitality and made it an everyday thing.

c. **Sold their possessions and their goods, and divided them among all, as anyone had need**: The power of God is evident here because Jesus became much more important to them than their possessions.

4. (46-47) The Christian family lived together and grew.

So continuing daily with one accord in the temple, and breaking bread from house to house, they ate their food with gladness and simplicity of heart, praising God and having favor with all the people. And the Lord added to the church daily those who were being saved.

a. **So continuing daily with one accord in the temple, and breaking bread from house to house**: The church is meant to worship God and learn His Word together. Yet it is meant to do more; God wants us to share our *lives* with one another.

b. **Praising God and having favor with all the people**: Their Christian experience was daily, joyful and simple - good examples for us to follow.

c. **And the Lord added to the church daily those who were being saved**: This is God's prescription for church growth. If we take care to follow the example of Acts 2:42-47a, God will take care of growing the church Himself.

Acts 3 - A Lame Man Healed

A. The healing of the paralytic at the Gate Beautiful.

1. (1-3) The request of the paralyzed beggar.

Now Peter and John went up together to the temple at the hour of prayer, the ninth *hour*. And a certain man lame from his mother's womb was carried, whom they laid daily at the gate of the temple which is called Beautiful, to ask alms from those who entered the temple; who, seeing Peter and John about to go into the temple, asked for alms.

a. **Now Peter and John went up together**: Peter and John were both commissioned by Jesus and recognized by the early Christians as *apostles* – special ambassadors of Jesus. Acts 2:43 told us, *many signs and wonders were done through the apostles*. Acts 3 tells us of a specific example, one of the *many*.

i. We can think of at least three reasons why Luke found it important to share the story of *this* miracle. First, to give an example of what he mentioned in Acts 2:43. Second, to give an excuse for telling us about another sermon of Peter. Third, to show why these earliest Christians were persecuted, because that is what this beautiful story leads to.

b. **At the hour of prayer**: Apparently Peter and John saw no problem in continuing their Jewish custom of prayer at certain hours of the day.

i. Morgan points out that Peter and John were *not* going to the temple at the hour of *sacrifice*, but **at the hour of prayer** that followed the afternoon sacrifice. They realized that the sacrificial system was fulfilled in the perfect sacrifice Jesus offered on the cross.

ii. Calvin saw a missionary intent in what Peter and John did: "Furthermore, if any man ask, whether the apostles went up into the temple that they might pray according to the rite of the law, I do not think that that is a thing so likely to be true, as they might have better opportunity to spread abroad the gospel."

iii. **The ninth hour**: "Perhaps this time of day, even then, held special significance for them because it was the hour when Jesus cried from the cross, 'It is finished' (John 19:30)." (Hughes)

c. **The gate of the temple which is called Beautiful**: The Jewish historian Josephus described this gate on the temple mount; made of fine Corinthian brass, seventy-five feet high with huge double doors, so beautiful that it "greatly excelled those that were only covered over with silver and gold." (Cited in Stott)

d. **A certain man lame from his mother's womb was carried... asked for alms**: The lame man simply wanted to be *supported* in the condition that he was in. God had something better in mind; Jesus wanted to completely change his condition.

i. Of course, the lame man felt he had no other option than to be supported in his condition; and it was certainly better for him to be supported than to starve to death.

ii. In addition, the man had good reason to believe that begging at the **Beautiful** gate could support him. There was (and is) a strong tradition of alms-giving (giving to the poor, especially beggars) in Judaism, and doing it as an act of righteousness.

2. (4-6) What Peter said to the lame man.

And fixing his eyes on him, with John, Peter said, "Look at us." So he gave them his attention, expecting to receive something from them. Then Peter said, "Silver and gold I do not have, but what I do have I give you: In the name of Jesus Christ of Nazareth, rise up and walk."

a. **Fixing his eyes on him**: The man must have been happy and encouraged when Peter and John looked at him intently. Most people who want to ignore beggars are careful to not make eye contact with them. When they looked at the lame man so intently, he probably thought he had a big gift coming.

b. **He gave them his attention, expecting to receive something from them**: The lame man returned the eye contact with Peter and John; perhaps he stretched out his hand or a cup to receive their generosity.

i. The lame man was correct in **expecting to receive something from them**, but he received much more than the monetary donation he would have been satisfied with!

ii. Many have yet to come to the place where they really expect something from God. This is *faith*, plain and simple – even if the man expected less than Jesus wanted to give.

iii. Better yet, we should expect the right things from God. We are often much too ready to settle for much less than God wants to give to us, and our low expectations often rob us.

c. **Silver and gold I do not have**: Peter didn't have any money, but he did have authority from Jesus to heal the sick (**what I do have I give to you**). Peter knew what it was like to have God use him to heal others, because Jesus had trained him in this (Luke 9:1-6).

i. For some people, to say "**silver and gold I do not have**" is about the worst thing that can be said. They feel the church is in ruins if it must say "**silver and gold I do not have**." But it is much worse if the church never has the spiritual power to say, "**In the name of Jesus Christ of Nazareth, rise up and walk**"?

ii. There is a story – perhaps true – about a humble monk walking with a Roman Catholic cardinal at a time in the Middle Ages when the Roman Catholic church was at its zenith of power, prestige and wealth. The cardinal pointed to the opulent surroundings and said to the monk, "We no longer have to say, **silver and gold I do not have**." The monk replied, "But neither can you say, **In the name of Jesus Christ of Nazareth, rise up and walk**."

iii. When Peter and John gave him no money, we might have heard the lame man complain: "You don't care about me. You won't support me. Look at the mess I'm in." But Peter and John wanted something greater than supporting the man in his condition. They wanted to transform his life by the power of the risen Jesus Christ.

iv. "It is not the Church's business in this world to simply make the present condition more bearable; the task of the Church is to release here on earth the redemptive work of God in Christ." (LaSor)

d. **What I do have I give you**: He gave the lame man power in the name of Jesus, but he could not give it unless *he had it in his own life*. Many people want to be able to say, "**rise up and walk**" without having received the power of Jesus to transform their own life.

i. **In the name of Jesus Christ of Nazareth**: "Jesus was from Nazareth – he was a Nazarene, and this had been used to insult Christ during his life on earth. But now Peter waved it like a banner." (Hughes)

3. (7-10) The healing of the lame man.

And he took him by the right hand and lifted *him* up, and immediately his feet and ankle bones received strength. So he, leaping up, stood and walked and entered the temple with them–walking, leaping, and praising God. And all the people saw him walking and praising God. Then they knew that it was he who sat begging alms at the Beautiful Gate of the temple; and they were filled with wonder and amazement at what had happened to him.

a. **And he took him by the right hand and lifted him up**: It was one thing to say, "**rise up and walk**," but it was a much greater thing to so boldly take the man's hand and lift him to his feet. At this moment, Peter received the *gift of faith* described in 1 Corinthians 12:9 – a supernatural ability to trust God in a particular situation.

i. This wasn't something Peter did on a whim or as a promotional event; he did it under the specific prompting of the Holy Spirit. God gave Peter the supernatural ability to trust Him for something completely out of the ordinary.

b. **Immediately his feet and bones received strength**: Strength did not come to the lame man until Peter said "**rise up and walk**," and not until Peter **took him by the right hand and lifted him up**.

i. "Perhaps only medical men can fully appreciate the meaning of these words; they are peculiar, technical words of a medical man. The word translated *feet* is only used by Luke, and occurs nowhere else. It indicates his discrimination between different parts of the human heel. The phrase *ankle-bones* is again a medical phrase to be found nowhere else. The word 'leaping up' describes the coming suddenly into socket of something that was out of place, the articulation of a joint. This then is a very careful medical description of what happened in connection with this man." (Morgan)

c. **Entered the temple... walking, leaping, and praising God**: As soon as he was healed, the formerly lame man did three good things. First, he attached himself to the apostles (**entered the temple with them**). Secondly, he immediately started to use what God had given him (**walking, leaping**). Finally, he began to praise and worship God (**praising God**).

d. **Then they knew that it was he who sat begging alms**: This man was more than 40 years old (Acts 4:22), and had been crippled since birth. He was a familiar sight at this temple gate (Acts 3:10). Therefore, Jesus must have passed him by many times without healing him.

i. We can say that one Jesus didn't heal his is because God's timing is just as important as His will, and it was for the greater glory of God that Jesus heal this man from heaven through His apostles.

B. Peter preaches to the gathered crowd.

1. (11-12) Introduction: Why do you think *we* have done something great?

Now as the lame man who was healed held on to Peter and John, all the people ran together to them in the porch which is called Solomon's, greatly amazed. So when Peter saw *it,* he responded to the people: "Men of Israel, why do you marvel at this? Or why look so intently at us, as though by our own power or godliness we had made this man walk?

a. **Held on to Peter and John**: Since he could walk, it wasn't for support. Perhaps he held on to them out of gratitude, perhaps out of a combined sense of fear and surprise – since a crowd quickly gathered as **the people ran together to them... greatly amazed**.

b. **When Peter saw it, he responded to the people**: Peter wisely took advantage of the gathering crowd. Yet he knew that the phenomenon of the miraculous in itself brought no one to Jesus, it merely aroused interest. Though they were **greatly amazed**, they weren't saved yet.

i. This might have been a good time for a testimony service, for the healed man certainly had a great experience. Yet Peter knew that what the crowd needed to hear – even more than the healed man's experience – was the gospel of Jesus Christ, and a call to repent and believe. The healed man didn't know enough yet to share that, so Peter did the talking.

ii. Peter knew that saving faith did not come by seeing or hearing about miracles, rather *faith comes by hearing, and hearing by the word of God* (Romans 10:17).

c. **Why look so intently at us, as though by our own power or godliness we had made this man walk?** Peter denied that the healing was due to either his **power or godliness**.

i. Many evangelists or preachers today who would never claim to heal in their own power still give the impression that healing happens because they are so spiritual, so close to God, or so godly. Peter knew that it was all of Jesus and nothing was of him.

d. **Why do you marvel at this?** Peter's point was simple: Jesus healed all sorts of people when He walked this earth, so why should it seem strange that He continues to heal from heaven?

2. (13-15) Peter preaches Jesus.

The God of Abraham, Isaac, and Jacob, the God of our fathers, glorified His Servant Jesus, whom you delivered up and denied in the presence of Pilate, when he was determined to let *Him* go. But you denied the Holy One and the Just, and asked for a murderer to be granted to you, and killed the Prince of life, whom God raised from the dead, of which we are witnesses.

a. **God of Abraham, Isaac, and Jacob**: By opening with this reference to God, Peter made it clear that he spoke to them about the God of Israel, the God represented in the Hebrew Scriptures.

b. **His Servant Jesus**: The greatness of Peter's sermon is that it was all about Jesus. The focus on the sermon was not on Peter nor on anything he did, but all about Jesus.

i. The first thing Peter said about Jesus in this sermon drew attention to the idea that Jesus was the perfect **Servant** of the Lord, and spoken of in the Hebrew Scriptures (as in Isaiah 42 and 52:13-53:12). "The concept of the 'servant of the Lord' was well-known in Israel because of Isaiah 53 and other texts." (Boice)

c. **Whom you delivered up and denied**: Peter boldly set the guilt of Jesus' death squarely where it belonged. **Pilate**, the Roman governor, was **determined to let Him go**, but the Jewish mob insisted on the crucifixion of Jesus (John 18:29-19:16).

i. This does *not* mean that the Jewish people of that day *alone* were responsible for the death of Jesus. They Romans – Gentiles – were also responsible. The Romans would not have crucified Jesus without pressure from the Jewish leaders, and the Jews could not have crucified Jesus without Roman acceptance of it. God made certain that both Jew and Gentile shared in the guilt of Jesus' death. In fact, it was not political intrigue or circumstances that put Jesus on the cross; it was our sin. If you want to know who put Jesus on the cross, look at me – or look in the mirror.

ii. Peter was not afraid to confront their sin, and he showed amazing boldness. "One commentator says that the miracle of the speech of Peter is a far more wonderful one than the miracle wrought in the healing of the man who lay at the Beautiful Gate." (Morgan)

iii. Yet notice the contrast. In God's estimation Jesus is the exalted **Servant**, promised centuries before in the Hebrew Scriptures. In man's estimation Jesus was only worthy to be tortured and crucified.

d. **Holy One**: Here Peter exalted Jesus as *God*. The term **Holy One** is used more than 40 times in the Old Testament as a high and glorious title for Yahweh, the covenant God of Israel.

e. **Asked for a murderer to be granted to you**: One of the ironies of the crucifixion of Jesus is that while the crowd rejected Jesus, they embraced a criminal and a murderer named Barabbas (Luke 23:13-25, John 18:39-40). Peter *boldly* confronted this audience.

> i. When Peter spoke of sin, he used the word **you** several times. In the sermon on the day of Pentecost it is recorded that he only used it once (Acts 2:23).

> - **You** *delivered up and denied.*
> - **You** *denied the Holy One and the Just.*
> - [You] *asked for a murderer to be granted to you.*
> - [You] *killed the Prince of Life.*

f. **And killed the Prince of life**: Of course, **the Prince of life** could not remain in the grave, and the apostles were united **witnesses** of the fact of His resurrection.

3. (16) How the man was healed.

And His name, through faith in His name, has made this man strong, whom you see and know. Yes, the faith which *comes* through Him has given him this perfect soundness in the presence of you all.

a. **And His name, through faith in His name, has made this man strong**: Peter said that it was in the **name** of Jesus that this man has been made whole. This means more than Peter said, "in Jesus name." It means that Peter consciously did this in the authority and power of Jesus, not in the authority and power of Peter. Peter would not even take credit for the *faith* that was exercised in the healing (**yes, the faith which comes through Him has given him this perfect soundness**).

> i. "In Semitic thought, a name does not just identify or distinguish a person, it expresses the very nature of his being. Hence the power of the person is present and available in the name of the person." (Longenecker)

b. **Through faith in His name**: When God's people really do good in this world, they do it **through faith in His name**. The temptation is always to do things trusting in something or someone else.

- To trust in good intentions.
- To trust in talents and gifts.

- To trust in material resources.
- To trust in reputation and prior success.
- To trust in hard work or smart work.

> i. Instead, we must always trust in and do good **through faith in His name**.

4. (17-18) Explaining the sufferings of Jesus.

Yet now, brethren, I know that you did *it* **in ignorance, as** *did* **also your rulers. But those things which God foretold by the mouth of all His prophets, that the Christ would suffer, He has thus fulfilled."**

a. **Yet now, brethren**: Though Peter spoke boldly to them about their sin, he didn't hate them. He didn't say, "Yet now, you filthy disgusting wretches." He still connected to them as **brethren**. Notice that twice Peter had accused them of *denying* Jesus (3:13, 14) – something Peter had himself done.

b. **I know that you did it in ignorance**: Peter recognized they called for the execution of Jesus in ignorance of God's eternal plan. This did not make them innocent, but it did carefully define the nature of their guilt. If we sin in ignorance, it is still sin; but it is different from sin done with full knowledge.

c. **He has thus fulfilled**: Despite all the evil they did to Jesus, it did not change or derail God's plan. God can take the most horrible evil and use it for good. Joseph could say to his brothers, "*you meant evil against me; but God meant it for good.*" (Genesis 50:20) The same principle was at work in the crucifixion of Jesus and is at work in our lives (Romans 8:28).

5. (19-21) Peter calls them to repentance.

Repent therefore and be converted, that your sins may be blotted out, so that times of refreshing may come from the presence of the Lord, and that He may send Jesus Christ, who was preached to you before, whom heaven must receive until the times of restoration of all things, which God has spoken by the mouth of all His holy prophets since the world began.

a. **Repent therefore**: As he did in his first sermon (Acts 2:38), Peter called upon the crowd to **repent**. He told them to turn around in their thinking and actions.

> i. Peter spoke boldly to them about their sin, but he didn't just want to make them feel bad. That wasn't the goal. The goal was to encourage them to repent and believe.

ii. Repentance does not describe being sorry, but describes the act of *turning around*. And as he used it in chapter two, here also Peter made **repent** a word of *hope*. He told them that they had done wrong; but that they could turn it around and become right with God.

b. **And be converted**: Peter knew the necessity of *conversion*, of God's work of bringing new life to us. Being a Christian is not "turning over a new leaf," it is being a *new creation in Christ Jesus* (2 Corinthians 5:17).

i. Boice says that **be converted** is better translated, "turn to God" – or, even better, "flee to God." Boice connects this with the imagery of the cities of refuge in the Old Testament, and thinks Peter told them to flee to Jesus as their place of refuge.

c. **That your sins may be blotted out**: This was the first *benefit* of repentance Peter presented to them. The one who repents and is converted is forgiven their sins, and the record itself is erased.

i. **Blotted out**: This has the idea of wiping ink off of a document. Ink in the ancient world had no acid content and didn't "bite" into the paper. It could almost always be wiped off with a damp cloth. Peter said that God would wipe away our record of sin just like that.

d. **So that times of refreshing may come from the presence of the Lord**: This was the second benefit of repenting and turning to God. In speaking of "**times of refreshing**," Peter referred to the time when Jesus will return and rule the earth in righteousness. Peter went so far as to say, "**that He may send Jesus Christ**," thus implying that if the Jewish people as a whole repented, God the Father would send Jesus to return in glory.

i. Peter made it clear that Jesus will remain in heaven **until the times of restoration of all things**, and since the repentance of Israel is one of the **all things**, there is some sense in which the return of Jesus in glory will not happen until Israel repents.

ii. Peter essentially offered Israel the opportunity to hasten the return of Jesus by embracing Him on a national level, something that must happen before Jesus will return (as in Matthew 23:37-39 and Romans 11:25-27).

iii. One may raise the hypothetical question, *if* the Jews of that day had received the gospel as a whole, would *then* Jesus had returned way back then? Hypothetically, this may have been the case, but there is no point in speculating about something that *didn't happen*!

iv. In a lesser (though glorious) sense, God sends **times of refreshing** to His people today. We should pray for and believe God for seasons of revival and **refreshing**.

6. (22-26) Peter warns of the danger of rejecting Jesus.

For Moses truly said to the fathers, 'The LORD your God will raise up for you a Prophet like me from your brethren. Him you shall hear in all things, whatever He says to you. And it shall be *that* every soul who will not hear that Prophet shall be utterly destroyed from among the people.' Yes, and all the prophets, from Samuel and those who follow, as many as have spoken, have also foretold these days. You are sons of the prophets, and of the covenant which God made with our fathers, saying to Abraham, 'And in your seed all the families of the earth shall be blessed.' To you first, God, having raised up His Servant Jesus, sent Him to bless you, in turning away every one *of you* from your iniquities."

a. **For Moses truly said to the fathers**: The Jewish people of Peter's day were aware of this prophecy of Moses (recorded in Deuteronomy 18:15 and 18:18-19), but some thought that the **Prophet** would be someone different than the *Messiah*. Peter made it clear that they are one and the same.

b. **Every soul who will not hear that Prophet shall be utterly destroyed**: The destruction promised in the prophecy would become the legacy of this generation of Jews. Many of this generation (certainly not all) rejected Jesus twice over.

i. This is the third blessing that comes from repenting and turning to God – being *spared* this promised judgment.

c. **And of the covenant which God made with our fathers, saying to Abraham**: Hidden in the idea of the promise to Abraham (**all the families of the earth shall be blessed**) and in the words **to you first** is the undeveloped theme of the extension of the gospel to all the world - even to the Gentiles.

d. **Sent Him to bless you, in turning away every one of you from your iniquities**: This is the fourth blessing that comes from repenting and turning to God. Jesus blesses us from heaven, and does this by **turning us away** from our sins. God's desire to bless us and to do good for us also includes His desire to turn us all away from our sins.

i. The lame man at the Beautiful Gate wanted something; but God wanted to give him something much greater. The same was generally true of the Jewish people Peter preached to. They expected the Messiah *in a certain way*, but God wanted to give them something much greater. They looked for a political and military Messiah, and not so much one to turn **every one of you from your iniquities**. It shows how important it is for us to expect the right things from God.

Acts 4 - Peter and John Face the Sanhedrin

A. Peter preaches to the Jewish leaders.

1. (1-4) The arrest of Peter and John.

Now as they spoke to the people, the priests, the captain of the temple, and the Sadducees came upon them, being greatly disturbed that they taught the people and preached in Jesus the resurrection from the dead. And they laid hands on them, and put *them* in custody until the next day, for it was already evening. However, many of those who heard the word believed; and the number of the men came to be about five thousand.

a. **The captain of the temple**: This refers to the police force of the temple precincts. The **captain**, together with the **priests** and the **Sadducees**, all came together to arrest Peter and John.

i. **Came upon them**: Boice says that the emphasis in the original indicates that they stopped and seized Peter and John *suddenly*. "They must have said, 'Enough of this,' grabbed them, and taken them away." (Boice)

b. **Being greatly disturbed**: The **Sadducees** *would* be **greatly disturbed** that Peter and John **taught the people and preached in Jesus the resurrection from the dead**; they did not believe in the afterlife or the resurrection at all.

i. We can say that they were arrested on suspicion of teaching dangerous ideas – such as that Jesus was raised from the dead, *and* for healing a man who had been crippled his entire life.

c. **Put them into custody until the next day**: Normally, this would be an intimidating experience for Peter and John. Suddenly arrested, **greatly disturbed** officials, handled roughly (**laid hands on them**), threats made against them (Acts 4:21 implies this), thrown into jail. The entire atmosphere was intended to make them *afraid*.

i. Acts 4:21 mentions *further* threats. If there were *further* threats, there must have been prior threats. "If you keep preaching we will arrest you and beat you." "If you keep preaching we will harm your family." *"Remember what we did to Jesus."*

ii. By all outward measures, Christianity – the movement of the followers of Jesus – was very weak at this early point.

- They were few in numbers.
- They were inexperienced in leadership.
- They were commanded to not fight back; they were not militant.
- They were opposed by institutions that had existed for hundreds of years.

iii. Boice notes that Acts 4:1-6 lists no less than 11 different groups or individuals opposing these followers of Jesus.

- *Groups*: Priests and the Sadducees (Acts 4:1); Rulers, elders, scribes (Acts 4:5); and others from the family of the high priest (Acts 4:6).
- *Individuals*: The captain of the temple (Acts 4:1); Annas the high priest, Caiaphas, John, and Alexander (Acts 4:6).

iv. "They were declaring: We have the power. If you are allowed to preach, as you have been preaching, it is because we have permitted you to do it.... Anytime we want, we can arrest you and carry you off to jail." (Boice)

d. **The number of the men came to be about five thousand**: Despite the opposition coming against the gospel, the number of Christians kept increasing, growing to 5,000 from 3,000 at last count (Acts 2:41). Opposition did not slow the church down at all.

i. Acts 4:4 shows that the power plays, the threats, the intimidation was all ineffective. More people started following Jesus, not less.

ii. In the Western world, Christians rarely face persecution. Satan instead has attacked us with worldliness, selfish pride, a need for acceptance, and status. The martyr can impress unbelievers with his courage and faith; the self-centered, compromising Christian is despised by the world.

2. (5-7) Peter and John are brought before the Sanhedrin.

And it came to pass, on the next day, that their rulers, elders, and scribes, as well as Annas the high priest, Caiaphas, John, and Alexander, and as many as were of the family of the high priest, were gathered together at

Jerusalem. And when they had set them in the midst, they asked, "By what power or by what name have you done this?"

a. **Rulers, elders, and scribes... were gathered together**: This was a scene of power and intimidation. This same group of leaders had recently condemned Jesus to death, and they wanted them to know that they had the power to do the same thing to Peter and John.

b. **By what power or by what name have you done this?** The ideas behind **by what power** and **by what name** are virtually the same. In their thinking, the **power** resided in the **name**, because the **name** represented the character of the person.

i. We can say that in itself, this was a legitimate inquiry. These were the guardians of the Jewish faith; they naturally were concerned about what was taught on the temple mount. *How* they did it their investigation may be faulted (with pressure and intimidation); also what they did with the results of their investigation.

3. (8-12) Peter boldly preaches to the Jewish leaders.

Then Peter, filled with the Holy Spirit, said to them, "Rulers of the people and elders of Israel: If we this day are judged for a good deed *done* to a helpless man, by what means he has been made well, let it be known to you all, and to all the people of Israel, that by the name of Jesus Christ of Nazareth, whom you crucified, whom God raised from the dead, by Him this man stands here before you whole. This is the 'stone which was rejected by you builders, which has become the chief cornerstone.' Nor is there salvation in any other, for there is no other name under heaven given among men by which we must be saved."

a. **Peter, filled with the Holy Spirit**: He was instantly **filled with the Spirit** again, evident by his supernatural boldness and ability to speak the gospel directly to the heart of the matter.

i. The filling of the Holy Spirit Peter experienced in Acts 2:4 (along with other disciples) was not a one-time event. It was something God wanted to continue doing in their lives.

b. **If we this day are judged for a good deed done to a helpless man**: The tone of Peter's reply shows that he was not intimidated by this court, though humanly speaking, he should have been intimidated by the same court that sent Jesus to crucifixion.

i. **For a good deed**: Peter's logic was piercing - why are we on trial for a **good deed**?

c. **By the name of Jesus Christ of Nazareth**: Peter preached **Jesus**, the Jesus *they* **crucified**, the Jesus **God raised from the dead**, the Jesus who healed this man.

d. **This is the 'stone which was rejected by you builders'**: The quotation from Psalm 118:22 was appropriate. Jesus was rejected by men – by those leaders – but was exalted by His Father.

e. **Nor is there salvation in any other**: Peter didn't merely proclaim Jesus as *a way* of salvation, but as the *only way* of salvation. The idea that there is **no salvation in any other**, and that there **is no other name under heaven given among men by which we must be saved** is hard to accept for many, but is plainly stated.

> i. "Oh, how the world hates such statements! If you want to be laughed at, scorned, hated, even persecuted, testify to the exclusive claims of Jesus Christ." (Boice)

> ii. Instinctively, man responds: "Isn't there *some way* that I can save myself? Isn't Jesus just for those ones who can't save themselves?" *No.* If you are going to be rescued; if you are going to be made right with God, *Jesus is going to do it.*

> iii. Does this mean that everyone must make a personal decision for Jesus Christ to be rescued from eternal peril? What about the infant who dies? What about the person who has never heard about Jesus? We can say that God will deal with them fairly and justly, and those who are saved will be rescued by the work of Jesus done on their behalf, even if they lacked a full knowledge of Jesus. *But what about you who have heard and perhaps reject?*

> iv. If someone wishes to believe that all are saved or that there are many roads to heaven or that one can take the best of all faiths and blend them into one; fine. Believe so and bear the consequences; *but please do not* claim this is the teaching of the Bible.

B. The Jewish rulers react to Peter's sermon.

1. (13) What they saw in Peter and John's character.

Now when they saw the boldness of Peter and John, and perceived that they were uneducated and untrained men, they marveled. And they realized that they had been with Jesus.

a. **They were uneducated and untrained men**: In a sense, we should probably disagree with the opinion of the Jewish leaders judging Peter and John. Certainly they were **uneducated** in one sense – they, like Jesus, had no formal rabbinic education according to the customs and standards of that time. Yet they *were* educated in two more important ways: they knew the Scriptures, and **they had been with Jesus.**

i. The greater importance of these two things – more important than formal education – has been proven in the lives of God's servants again and again. It has been proven true through such servants of God as Charles Spurgeon, D.L. Moody, William Carey, D. Martyn Lloyd-Jones, Hudson Taylor.

ii. Yet it is helpful to remember that God has used many who were greatly educated. Moses, Daniel, and Paul are all Biblical examples. Augustine, Martin Luther, and Billy Graham are just a few historical examples. It's just as wrong to think that formal education *disqualifies* someone for effective service as it is to think that it automatically *qualifies* someone for effective service.

iii. "Men are too anxious to be ranked with scholars; and so when error, however deadly, wears the glittering serpent-skin of scholarship, it insinuates itself into the very chair of the teacher, and the pulpit of the preacher, and no one seems to dare to smite it with a bold blow!" (Pierson)

b. **They saw the boldness of Peter and John**: Because they had **been with Jesus**, they were naturally bold. When one is a servant of the all-powerful God, they have nothing to fear from the judgment of men.

i. "A few men unarmed, furnished with no garrisons, do show forth more power in their voice alone, than all the world, by raging against them." (Calvin)

ii. "The word *boldness* means lucid and daring statement. In the Greek the word is *parresia*, telling it all'." (Ogilvie)

iii. "No one attribute is more needful to-day for Christ's witness than Holy Spirit boldness due to Holy Spirit fullness." (Pierson)

iv. It is interesting to note what the Jewish leaders did *not* do: they did not make any attempt to disprove the resurrection of Jesus. If it were possible to do, *this* was the time to do it; yet they could not. "Had it seemed possible to refute them on this point, how readily would the Sanhedrin seized the opportunity! Had they succeeded, how quickly and completely the new movement would have collapsed!" (Bruce)

c. **They realized that they had been with Jesus**: This means that the bold exclusivism of Acts 4:12 was coupled with a radiant love characteristic of Jesus. If we will preach *no other name* we should also make it evident that we have **been with Jesus.**

i. Sadly, when Christians became strong and powerful, and when Christianity became an institution – then too often *Christians* were those whoe arresting people and told them to be quiet, threatening them with violence and sometimes carrying it out against them. That is not evidence that one has **been with Jesus**.

ii. People *should* go to Jesus directly, but often they won't. The only Jesus they will see is what shines through us. We must work to make the fact that we have **been with Jesus** as obvious in our lives as it was in theirs.

2. (14) What they saw in the man who was healed.

And seeing the man who had been healed standing with them, they could say nothing against it.

a. **They could say nothing against it**: This miracle was examined by doubters and stood up as a genuine miracle. This was not a case where the healing was "lost" in a few hours, as some claim happens today.

b. **Nothing against it**: Previously this man was completely lame, having to be carried wherever he went (Acts 3:2). Now he was completely healed. This contrasts many who get up out of wheelchairs at modern "healing services" who come with a limited ability to walk, but are able for a few moments to walk much better because of the hype, emotion, and adrenaline. Yet they tragically leave the arena in the wheelchair, having "lost" their healing.

3. (15-18) Taking counsel, the Jewish leaders command Peter and John to stop preaching Jesus.

But when they had commanded them to go aside out of the council, they conferred among themselves, saying, "What shall we do to these men? For, indeed, that a notable miracle has been done through them *is* evident to all who dwell in Jerusalem, and we cannot deny *it*. But so that it spreads no further among the people, let us severely threaten them, that from now on they speak to no man in this name." And they called them and commanded them not to speak at all nor teach in the name of Jesus.

a. **They conferred among themselves**: Luke probably found out what the Sanhedrin discussed among themselves because a member of that Sanhedrin later became a Christian: Saul of Tarsus. Acts 26:10 gives us reason to believe Paul (Saul) was a member of the Sanhedrin to *cast his vote* against the early Christians.

i. If this is true, we can say that Peter and John had no idea they were preaching to a future apostle and the greatest missionary the church would ever see. It is an example of the truth that we have no idea how greatly God can use us.

b. **We cannot deny it**: The corruption of their hearts was plain. They acknowledged that a miracle had genuinely happened; yet they refused to submit to the God who worked the miracle.

c. **So that it spreads no further among the people**: Their fear of the preaching of Jesus was rooted in their own sinful self-interest, not in any desire to protect the people.

4. (19-20) Peter and John respond to the command to stop preaching Jesus.

But Peter and John answered and said to them, "Whether it is right in the sight of God to listen to you more than to God, you judge. For we cannot but speak the things which we have seen and heard."

a. **Whether it is right in the sight of God to listen to you more than to God, you judge**: It was self-evident that they should listen to God instead of man. Peter made an effective appeal to this truth.

b. **We cannot but speak**: Peter and John *must* speak of the **things which** they had **seen and heard**. They had to, not only because of the inner compulsion of the Holy Spirit, but also because of the command of Jesus: *You shall be witnesses to Me in Jerusalem* (Acts 1:8).

c. **Speak the things which we have seen and heard**: They did not originate this message; they merely relayed it as reliable eyewitnesses.

5. (21-22) Peter and John are released with threats of future punishment.

So when they had further threatened them, they let them go, finding no way of punishing them, because of the people, since they all glorified God for what had been done. For the man was over forty years old on whom this miracle of healing had been performed.

a. **Finding no way of punishing them, because of the people**: The Jewish leaders were completely unmoved by an obvious miracle from God, yet they responded to public opinion. This proves they cared far more about man's opinion than God's opinion.

b. **They all glorified God for what had been done**: This whole situation started out looking pretty bad. Peter and John were on trial before the same court that sent Jesus to Pilate for crucifixion. It was meant for great evil, but when it was all over, see what God did:

- 2,000 more people came to believe on Jesus.
- Peter was filled with the Holy Spirit again.
- Peter got to preach Jesus to the leaders of the Jews.

- Hostile examiners confirmed a miraculous healing.
- The enemies of Jesus were confused.
- Peter and John were bolder for Jesus than ever before.
- God was glorified.

C. The early church prays for boldness.

1. (23-24) Introduction: They acknowledge their God.

And being let go, they went to their own *companions* and reported all that the chief priests and elders had said to them. So when they heard that, they raised their voice to God with one accord and said: "Lord, You *are* God, who made heaven and earth and the sea, and all that is in them.

a. **Reported all that the chief priests and elders had said**: Peter and John had good news to report. We can picture them saying, "We got to tell them about Jesus! They realized we were like Jesus! They told us not to tell others about Jesus!"

i. In response, the early Christian community – **their own companions**, probably the apostles and some others – had a prayer meeting. Important events moved them to prayer.

b. **They raised their voice**: They prayed *vocally*. It is certainly possible to pray silently in our minds, but we focus our thoughts more effectively when we speak out in prayer.

i. **Voice** is in the singular. This means that they did not all pray individually, speaking at the same time. One person prayed and all agreed with that one, so that they were really praying with one **voice**.

ii. "With one accord they lift up their voice to God. This does not mean that they all prayed at once. That would have been confusion. Disorder in meetings, a number of people talking at the same time in a boisterous way with outward demonstrations, is an evidence that the Holy Spirit is not leading, for God is not a God of disorder." (Gaebelein)

c. **With one accord**: They prayed in *unity*. There was no strife or contention among them. There wasn't one group saying, "We should pray for this" and another saying, "we should pray for that." They had the same mind when they prayed.

d. **Lord, You are God**: They began by reminding themselves *who they prayed to*. They prayed to the **Lord** of all creation, the **God** of all power.

i. This word **Lord** is not the usual word for Lord in the New Testament; it is the Greek word *despotes*. It was a word used of a slave owner or ruler who has power that cannot be questioned. They prayed with power and confidence because they knew God was in control.

ii. When we pray, we often forget just who it is we pray to; or worse yet, we pray to an imaginary God of our own ideas. The disciples had power in prayer because they knew *who they prayed to*.

2. (25-28) They pray in light of the Scriptures.

Who by the mouth of Your servant David have said:

'Why did the nations rage,
And the people plot vain things?
The kings of the earth took their stand,
And the rulers were gathered together
Against the Lord and against His Christ.'

"For truly against Your holy Servant Jesus, whom You anointed, both Herod and Pontius Pilate, with the Gentiles and the people of Israel, were gathered together to do whatever Your hand and Your purpose determined before to be done.

a. **By the mouth of Your servant David have said**: Peter, speaking for all the disciples (remember they prayed *with one accord*), recognized that words of the Old Testament (Psalm 2 to be exact) were really the words of God. God was speaking **by the mouth of** [His] **servant David**.

i. It's an important point. Peter believed that the words of King David, recorded in Psalm 2, were *actually the words of the Lord God*, said **by the mouth** of King David. Peter had a high view of the Holy Scriptures.

b. **Why did the nations rage, and the people plot vain things?** Peter quoted Psalm 2 because he and the other disciples understood what happened by seeing what the Bible said about it. From Psalm 2, they understood that they should expect this sort of opposition and not be troubled because of it because God was in control of all things.

i. Psalm 2 expresses complete confidence in God and His victory. "He is the King. He is ruler in Zion. Servants you can bind, but the Word of God is not bound. And that unleashed, unbound, powerful Word of the gospel reached out from Jerusalem, that remote city of the Roman Empire, to permeate and eventually transform the entire world." (Boice)

ii. When we pray, we must see our circumstances in light of God's Word. For example, when we are in conflict, perhaps we need to know *we do not wrestle against flesh and blood, but against principalities, against powers, against the rulers of the darkness of this age* (Ephesians 6:12).

iii. Seeing our circumstances in light of God's Word also means seeing when there is a sin problem. Then, we should say with the Psalmist, "*When I kept it all inside, my bones turned to powder, my words became daylong groans. The pressure never let up; all the juices of my life dried up.*" (Psalm 32:3-4, Peterson). Perhaps we are in the same place the Psalmist was, in sin and needing to confess and be made right with God.

iv. We also use Scripture in prayer to pray the promises of God. When we need strength, we can pray according to Ephesians 3:16: *That He would grant you, according to the riches of His glory, to be strengthened with might through His Spirit in the inner man.* God's Word will speak to our situation.

c. **Do whatever Your hand and Your purpose determined before to be done**: Because they saw their circumstances in light of God's Word, they could recognize that the wrath of man never operated outside of the sphere of God's control; these enemies of Jesus could only **do whatever** the hand of God allowed.

i. This brings real peace, knowing that whatever comes my way has passed through God's hand first, and He will not allow even the most wicked acts of men to result in permanent damage.

3. (29-30) They ask for more boldness, more power, and for more trouble.

Now, Lord, look on their threats, and grant to Your servants that with all boldness they may speak Your word, by stretching out Your hand to heal, and that signs and wonders may be done through the name of Your holy Servant Jesus."

a. **Grant to Your servants that with all boldness they may speak Your word**: This request is consumed with God's cause and glory, not the comfort and advancement of the disciples. They ask for things that will lead to *more* confrontation, not less.

b. **By stretching out Your hand to heal**: They did not ask to do miracles themselves. They understood that Jesus heals by His hand; and that He does it from heaven through His people.

i. It is a snare to long to be used to do miraculous things. It is often rooted in the pride that wants everyone to see just how greatly God can use *me*. I should be delighted in the power of God, not because He has used *me* to display it.

4. (31) Their prayer is answered.

And when they had prayed, the place where they were assembled together was shaken; and they were all filled with the Holy Spirit, and they spoke the word of God with boldness.

a. **The place where they were assembled together was shaken**: They were given an earthquake as a unique emblem of God's pleasure. We don't know the extent of the shaking; it may have been confined to the house itself.

i. "The presence of the Holy Spirit was so wonderfully manifested that even dead walls felt the power of the Spirit of life – matter responded to spirit." (Pierson) Those walls didn't change, nor did that become a special holy place where the Spirit of God always dwelt. In a similar way, a person can be *shaken* by the Holy Spirit without being transformed or indwelt by the Spirit of God.

b. **They were all filled with the Holy Spirit**: They were filled with the Holy Spirit, *again*. The experience on Pentecost was not a one-time experience. For Peter, this counts as the *third* time he is specifically said to be **filled with the Holy Spirit**.

i. The idea that we are "Spirit filled" only at an experience known as the "Baptism of the Holy Spirit" is wrong, though there may be a wonderful and first yielding to the Spirit's power. We must be continually filled with the Holy Spirit, and make our "immersion" in Him a constant experience.

c. **They spoke the word of God with boldness**: They received the **boldness** they asked for. "The word *boldness* means lucid and daring statement. In the Greek the word is *parresia*, 'telling it all.'" (Ogilvie)

i. This **boldness** is necessary today; we need to *tell it all*. We often deliberately hide the work of God in our life from others who would actually benefit from hearing about it.

ii. Their **boldness** was a gift from God, received through prayer. It was not something that they tried to work up in themselves.

D. The sharing heart of the early church.

1. (32) Their attitude towards each other and towards material possessions.

Now the multitude of those who believed were of one heart and one soul; neither did anyone say that any of the things he possessed was his own, but they had all things in common.

a. **Those who believed were of one heart and one soul; neither did anyone say that any of things he possessed was his own**: This unity was a wonderful evidence of the work of God's Spirit among them. Because of their unity, they regarded *people* more important than *things*.

i. "This unity is not conformity, where everybody is exactly alike. It is not organizational, where everyone must be forced into the same denomination. The worst times in the history of the church have been when everyone has been part of one large organization. It is not that kind of a unity." (Boice)

b. **They had all things in common**: They recognized God's ownership of everything; it all belonged to God and His people. Because God had touched their lives so deeply, they found it easy to share **all things in common**.

c. **All things in common**: It isn't accurate to see this as an early form of communism. Communism is not *koinonia*. "Communism says, 'What is yours is mine; I'll take it.' *Koinonia* says, 'What is mine is yours, I'll share it.'" (LaSor)

i. "The Greek here does not mean that everyone sold their property at once. Rather, from time to time this was done as the Lord brought needs to their attention." (Horton)

ii. There was also probably immediate reason for this significant sharing of **all things in common**. Since Pentecost there was a large number of **those who believed** and many of them were from distant lands. Without permanent homes and jobs in Jerusalem and Judea, those who stayed in Jerusalem to learn more about being followers of Jesus needed special support from the Christian community.

iii. Some think that this radical sharing of possessions among the early church was a mistake. They say it was based on the wrong idea that Jesus was returning immediately, and that it led to much poverty in the Jerusalem church later on.

2. (33) The effective witness of the apostles.

And with great power the apostles gave witness to the resurrection of the Lord Jesus. And great grace was upon them all.

a. **With great power**: This is both the *result* and the *root* of the attitude in the previous verse. Acts 4:32 shows they put God first, people second, and material things a distant third.

b. **Gave witness to the resurrection**: Notice again the central place the resurrection of Jesus held in the message of the first Christians. They preached a resurrected Jesus.

c. **Great grace was upon them all**. Grace is God's favor, His smile from heaven, and it **was upon them all**. God's favor was evident everywhere.

i. **Great grace**: Hughes says this is literally *mega grace*. **Great power** is *mega power*.

3. (34-37) Examples of early giving.

Nor was there anyone among them who lacked; for all who were possessors of lands or houses sold them, and brought the proceeds of the things that were sold, and laid *them* at the apostles' feet; and they distributed to each as anyone had need. And Joses, who was also named Barnabas by the apostles (which is translated Son of Encouragement), a Levite of the country of Cyprus, having land, sold *it*, and brought the money and laid *it* at the apostles' feet.

a. **All who were possessors of lands or houses sold them**: This radical giving was absolutely necessary to meet the needs of this rapidly growing church. Remember, many of these Jerusalem Christians lived as refugees from abroad, having responded to the gospel on Pentecost.

b. **All who were possessors of lands**: People didn't wait for others to give. When a need arose, they gave what they had to help others.

c. **They distributed to each as anyone had need**: Unfortunately, this generosity of the early Christians soon began to be abused. Later the Apostle Paul taught regarding who should be helped and how they should be helped. Paul's directions were that:

- The church must discern who the truly needy are (1 Timothy 5:3).
- If one can work to support himself, he is not truly needy and must provide for his own needs (2 Thessalonians 3:10-12, 1 Timothy 5:8, 1 Thessalonians 4:11).
- If family can support a needy person, the church should not support them (1 Timothy 5:3-4).
- Those who are supported by the church must make some return to the church body (1 Timothy 5:5, 10).
- It is right for the church to examine moral conduct before giving support (1 Timothy 5:9-13).
- The support of the church should be for the most basic necessities of living (1 Timothy 6:8).

d. **Joses, who was also named Barnabas**: One man named **Barnabas** was a notable example of this giving spirit. Joses was known for more being generous with more than material things; he was so generous with **encouragement** that they called him **Barnabas**, meaning "**Son of Encouragement**."

Acts 5 - The Church Grows Despite Opposition

A. The lie of Ananias and Sapphira.

1. (1-2) What Ananias and Sapphira did.

But a certain man named Ananias, with Sapphira his wife, sold a possession. And he kept back *part* of the proceeds, his wife also being aware *of it,* and brought a certain part and laid *it* at the apostles' feet.

a. **But a certain man named Ananias, with Sapphira his wife, sold a possession**: After they saw the great generosity of Barnabas and how well he was respected (Acts 4:36-37), Ananias and Sapphira decided they wanted to receive the same respect.

b. **He kept back part of the proceeds**: They sold the **possession**, and gave only a *portion* to the church, while *implying* that they sacrificially gave it all to the church.

i. The ancient Greek word for **kept back** is *nosphizomai*, which means "to misappropriate." The same word was used of Achan's theft in the Greek translation of the Old Testament (Joshua 7:21). The only other time *nosphizomai* is used in the New Testament, it means to steal (Titus 2:10).

ii. "The story of Ananias is to the Book of Acts what the story of Achan is to the book of Joshua. In both narratives an act of deceit interrupts the victorious progress of the people of God." (Bruce)

c. **His wife also being aware of it**: Clearly, both husband and wife were partners in the deception. They both wanted the image of great generosity, without actually being remarkably generous.

i. "There may indeed be the further implication that Ananias and Sapphira had vowed to give the whole proceeds of the sale to God, but then changed their mind and handed over only part." (Bruce)

ii. "Once the love of money takes possession of a person, there is no evil that he cannot or will not do." (Horton)

iii. According to Calvin, these are the "evils packed under" the sin of Ananias, beyond the mere attempt to deceive God and the church:

- The contempt of God.
- Sacrilegious defrauding.
- Perverse vanity and ambition.
- Lack of faith.
- The corrupting of a good and holy order.
- Hypocrisy.

2. (3-4) Peter confronts Ananias.

But Peter said, "Ananias, why has Satan filled your heart to lie to the Holy Spirit and keep back *part* of the price of the land for yourself? While it remained, was it not your own? And after it was sold, was it not in your own control? Why have you conceived this thing in your heart? You have not lied to men but to God."

a. **Ananias, why has Satan filled your heart**: God apparently gave Peter supernatural knowledge of what Ananias had done. This spiritual gift, called *the word of knowledge*, is mentioned in 1 Corinthians 12:8.

i. When Peter said this, Ananias must have been crushed. Certainly he expected praise for his spectacular gift, but was rebuked instead. Peter saw that **Satan** was at work, even through a man numbered among believers like Ananias.

ii. Because his sin was lusting after public praise for his generosity, it was appropriate that the sin be exposed publicly. "It is a good general rule that secret sins should be dealt with secretly, private sins privately, and only public sins publicly." (Stott)

b. **Why has Satan filled your heart to lie to the Holy Spirit**: Peter did not accuse Ananias of lying to the church or to the apostles, but to the **Holy Spirit** Himself.

i. Peter clearly believed that the **Holy Spirit** was a *Person*, because one can only lie to a person. He also believed the Holy Spirit is God (**You have not lied to men but to God**).

c. **While it remained, was it not your own? And after it was sold, was it not in your own control?** Peter freely acknowledged that the land and its value belonged to Ananias alone; he was completely free to do with it what he wanted. His crime was not in withholding the money, but in deceptively implying that he gave it all.

i. Of course, his sin was greed (in keeping the money); but his greater sin was *pride*, in wanting everyone to consider him so spiritual that he "gave it all" – when he had not.

ii. Their sin is imitated in many ways today. We can create or allow the impression that we are people of Bible reading or prayer when we are not. We can create or allow the impression that we have it all together when we do not. We can exaggerate our spiritual accomplishments or effectiveness to appear something we are not. It is too easy to be happy with the *image* of spirituality without the *reality* of spiritual life.

iii. Their great sin was rooted in *pride*. Pride corrupts the church more quickly than anything else.

d. **While it remained, was it not your own? And after it was sold, was it not in your own control?** This shows how unnecessary their sin was. Ananias was free to use the money for whatever he wanted, *except* as a way to inflate his spiritual image and pride.

e. **Why have you conceived this thing in your heart?** Satan had **filled** the heart of Ananias, yet Peter could ask why he had **conceived this thing in your heart.** Satan can influence the life of a believer, even a spirit-filled believer, but he can't do your sinning for you. Ananias had to conceive it in his heart.

3. (5-6) The death of Ananias.

Then Ananias, hearing these words, fell down and breathed his last. So great fear came upon all those who heard these things. And the young men arose and wrapped him up, carried *him* out, and buried *him.*

a. **Then Ananias, hearing these words, fell down and breathed his last**: Peter did not pronounce a death sentence on Ananias. He simply confronted him with his sin and Ananias fell down dead. It isn't the business of the *church* to pronounce a death sentence on anyone.

i. Peter was probably more surprised than anyone else when Ananias fell down dead. "Observe that Peter said no word to Ananias about his death. The sentence was not calling down upon a man of a curse at the caprice of an ecclesiastical official. The death of Ananias was the act of God." (Morgan).

b. **Fell down and breathed his last**: This was a harsh penalty for a sin that seems to be common today. Some wonder if God was not excessively harsh against Ananias.

i. The greater wonder is that God delays His righteous judgment in virtually all other cases. Ananias received exactly what he deserved; he simply *could not* live in the atmosphere of purity that marked the church at that time.

ii. The physical means for the death of Ananias was perhaps a heart attack caused by sudden shock or terror. He lived in a time and among a people who really believed there was a God in heaven we must all answer to. It frightened him to have his sin exposed and to know he was accountable before God for it. He didn't yawn or debate when confronted with his sin; he **fell down and breathed his last**.

iii. What Ananias did also must be seen in the context of its time. This was a critical juncture for the early church and such impurity, sin, scandal and satanic infiltration could have corrupted the entire church at its root. "The Church has never been harmed or hindered by opposition from without; it has been perpetually harmed and hindered by perils from within." (Morgan)

iv. We can surmise that one reason we don't see the same remarkable judgment of God in this way today is because God's church has so many branches. Even if the entire body of Christ in the United States was to become corrupt through scandal or sin, there is plenty of strength in other parts of the tree.

v. "The Church's administration to-day is not what it was, or there might be many dead men and women at the end of some services." (Morgan)

c. **Fell down and breathed his last**: The shock of being exposed was too much for Ananias. For many Christians in compromise, their greatest fear is not in sinning itself, but in being found out.

i. As much as anything, the lesson of Ananias and Sapphira is that we presume greatly on God when we assume that there is always time to repent, time to get right with God, time to get honest with Him. Any such time given by God is an undeserved gift that He owes no one; we should never assume it will always be there.

ii. "We must not infer from the rarity of such judgments in this word, or from their solitariness, that God's mind has changed as to the exceeding sinfulness and hatefulness and ill desert of the sin he has thus rebuked. The solitary example must stand as a lasting and terrible monument of what God thinks of that sin." (Pierson)

d. **So great fear came upon all those who heard these things**: God's purpose was accomplished in the church as a whole. This was evidence of a great work of God among His people.

i. Dr. J. Edwin Orr's last sermon was titled *Revival is Like Judgment Day*. In it, he describes how the coming of revival is almost always marked by a radical work of God in dealing with the sins of believers.

ii. "Now, put this in a modern context. If this had happened today, we would have had a cover-up committee. Don't let it get out to the public. You can take heart, this may be a surprise to you, when God exposes things… one of the outcomes was that when God was vindicated, the work gained strength again." (Orr)

iii. "William Castle, from Sichuan in China, said, 'Revival means judgment day.' That's what happened in Shantung. Judgment on missionaries, pastors, people, and then fear fell on the world and God's name was glorified. And people have such a wrong idea of what revival means… They think of revival as something triumphant and, shall we say, an overflow of great blessing. It's judgment day for the church. But after the judgment, and after things are settled, it's blessing abounding." (Orr)

4. (7-9) Peter confronts Sapphira.

Now it was about three hours later when his wife came in, not knowing what had happened. And Peter answered her, "Tell me whether you sold the land for so much?" She said, "Yes, for so much." Then Peter said to her, "How is it that you have agreed together to test the Spirit of the Lord? Look, the feet of those who have buried your husband *are* at the door, and they will carry you out."

a. **How is it that you have agreed together to test the Spirit of the Lord?** Sapphira was a knowing and willing participant in the sin, as well as the blatant cover-up. God's judgment of her was just as righteous as His judgment of Ananias.

b. **You have agreed together**: We don't know if Ananias and Sapphira had a good or a bad marriage, if they agreed often or fought often. We do know that they at least **agreed together to test the Spirit of the Lord**. They should have found agreement *for* the Lord, instead of *against* Him.

i. We don't know if Ananias suggested this or if Sapphira did or they came to the idea together. But if Ananias thought of it and pressured Sapphira to go along, he was wrong to do so and she was wrong to go along. The concept of submission does not extend to submitting unto sin.

5. (10-11) The death of Sapphira.

Then immediately she fell down at his feet and breathed her last. And the young men came in and found her dead, and carrying *her* out, buried *her* by her husband. So great fear came upon all the church and upon all who heard these things.

a. **Then immediately she fell down at his feet and breathed her last**: Fittingly, the same judgment came upon Sapphira as came upon her husband Ananias. Since they shared the same sin, it was fitting that they shared the same reaction to being found out – shock and horror.

i. Ananias and Sapphira both died, but it doesn't necessarily mean that they did not go to heaven. It is impossible to say for certain, for only God knows. But we can see that it is possible for a Christian to *sin unto death* (1 John 5:16-17), and we have New Testament examples of saved Christians being judged by being "brought home" in death (1 Corinthians 11:27-32). "True Christians do not lose their salvation by sinning. The punishment of Ananias and Sapphira, though extreme, was for this life only." (Boice)

ii. In noticing the comparison between the incident of Ananias and Sapphira and Achan in the Book of Joshua, it is interesting also to look at the contrasts. In Joshua, God expected the people of God themselves to execute the judgment upon the offender. But in Acts, God took this type of judgment out of the church's hand and did it Himself. This shows that the church has no place in administering such punishment itself or in having civil authorities do so for them.

b. **Great fear came upon all the church**: The name Sapphira means, *Beautiful* in Aramaic. The name Ananias means *God is Gracious* in Hebrew. It might seem that their names contradicted their lives, but we see the beauty and graciousness of God in two significant ways.

i. If Ananias and Sapphira were actually heaven-bound, it shows that God was beautiful and gracious enough to not deny them salvation even for a grievous sin.

ii. The beauty and graciousness of God was seen in the continued blessing of God upon the church. He protected it not only against outside attack, but also against itself. If Ananias and Sapphira were filled with grace, *this would have pleased them*. "Oh Lord, take us to heaven now if You must; but let Your work continue and let Your name be glorified."

iii. This is the first use of the word **church** in the Book of Acts. "The Christian *ekklesia* was both new and old - new, because of its relation and witness to Jesus as Lord and to the epoch-making events of his death exaltation and the sending of the Spirit; old, as the continuation of the 'congregation of the Lord' which had formerly been confined within the limits of one nation, but now, having died and risen with Christ, was to be open to all believers without distinction." (Bruce)

B. Continuing power in the church.

1. (12) Power shown through miracles and unity.

And through the hands of the apostles many signs and wonders were done among the people. And they were all with one accord in Solomon's Porch.

a. **Many signs and wonders were done**: In Acts 4:30, we read that these early Christians prayed that God would continue to do **signs and wonders** *through the name of Your holy Servant Jesus*. This shows that this prayer was answered, and these remarkable **signs and wonders** continued.

i. We aren't told what these **signs and wonders** were. Presumably they were like what we see in other places in Acts and in the Gospels – healings, deliverance from demonic powers, unusual blessings.

b. **They were all with one accord**: Often, the fact that God's people are together **all with one accord** is a greater display of the power of the Holy Spirit than any particular sign or wonder. Our selfish hearts and stubborn minds can be harder to move than any mountain.

c. **Through the hands of the apostles**: Seemingly, God chose to do these miraculous works **through the hands of the apostles** and not mainly through others. Yet God wisely chooses which hands will bring a miracle. He had a purpose in doing it **through the hands of the apostles**.

d. **Solomon's Porch**: The second temple was a massive compound, with extensive colonnades and covered areas. No doubt, the early Christians gathered together in a particular area of the temple complex, in an area open to all.

2. (13-14) The church's reputation and growth.

Yet none of the rest dared join them, but the people esteemed them highly. And believers were increasingly added to the Lord, multitudes of both men and women.

a. **None of the rest dared join them**: The community of Christians had a marvelous reputation for integrity, and everybody knew it was a serious thing to be a follower of Jesus. An Ananias and Sapphira incident would reduce the level of casual commitment.

b. **And believers were increasingly added to the Lord**: Yet, the church kept growing. Though people knew it was a serious thing to be a Christian, the Spirit of God kept moving with power.

c. **Increasingly added to the Lord**: New believers were added: **Added to the Lord**, not to a "church" or to a person or even to a movement, but to God Himself. They were added in **multitudes**.

> i. The mention of **multitudes of both men and women** is Luke's way of reminding us that the cleansing of the church connected with Ananias and Sapphira did no lasting damage.

3. (15-16) The expectation of miracles among the early Christians.

So that they brought the sick out into the streets and laid *them* on beds and couches, that at least the shadow of Peter passing by might fall on some of them. Also a multitude gathered from the surrounding cities to Jerusalem, bringing sick people and those who were tormented by unclean spirits, and they were all healed.

a. **They brought the sick out into the streets**: People were so convinced of the reality and power of what the Christians believed, they thought they could be healed by the mere touch of Peter's shadow.

> i. **That at least the shadow of Peter passing by might fall on some of them**: Our text does not specifically say people were healed by Peter's shadow; it merely tells us people thought it would, and they took action based on this belief. We don't know for certain if people were actually healed when **the shadow of Peter** passed over them.

b. **That at least the shadow of Peter passing by might fall on some of them**: Assuming people were healed, apparently, even **the shadow of Peter** became a point of contact where people released faith in Jesus as healer. It seems that people well understood what Peter said in Acts 3:12-16: That Jesus heals, even if He does His healing work through His apostles.

> i. It may sound crazy that one could be healed by the touch of a shadow, but we know a touch of Jesus' clothing healed a woman (Luke 8:44). There wasn't anything magical in the garment, but it was a way that her faith was released. In the same, there was no power in Peter's **shadow** itself, but there was power when a person believed in Jesus to heal them, and the passing of Peter's shadow may have helped some to believe.

> ii. "It may be significant that the verb *episkiazo*, which Luke chooses, meaning 'to overshadow', he has used twice in his Gospel of the overshadowing of God's presence." (Stott)

iii. "The idea that shadows had magical powers, both beneficent and malevolent, was current in the ancient world and explains the motivation of the people." (Marshall)

iv. However, we can trust that Luke is not merely recording legends. "From what we know of physicians, even in those days, we cannot assume that Luke would gullibly accept stories of 'miraculous healing' without investigating them." (LaSor)

c. **They were all healed**: However God chose to bring the healing, there is no doubt that a remarkable work of healing was present. We shouldn't miss the connection between the purity preserved in the first part of the chapter (with the death of Ananias and the fear of God among the Christians) and the power displayed here. God blessed a pure church with spiritual power.

d. **A multitude gathered from the surrounding cities to Jerusalem**: This is the first mention of the work extending beyond Jerusalem. People came there instead of the apostles going to them. This was exciting, but not exactly according to the command of Jesus. He told the disciples to go out to *Jerusalem, and in all Judea and Samaria, and to the end of the earth* (Acts 1:8). The apostles didn't leave Jerusalem until they were forced to by persecution (Acts 8:1, 12:1-2).

C. The apostles are imprisoned by the Jewish rulers.

1. (17-18) The arrest and imprisonment of the apostles.

Then the high priest rose up, and all those who *were* with him (which is the sect of the Sadducees), and they were filled with indignation, and laid their hands on the apostles and put them in the common prison.

a. **Then the high priest rose up**: The meeting of Peter and John with the religious leaders in Acts 4:5-22 ended well for the early followers of Jesus. Yet that was not the end of the matter, and the religious establishment again pushed against them.

i. "Luke alternates between a picture of the church by itself...and a portrait of the church as it exists in its relationship to the world. The second portrait increasingly deals with persecution." (Boice)

b. **They were filled with indignation**: The apostles, like Jesus whom they represented, were persecuted because their good works and popularity were a threat to those who had an interest in the status quo of the religious establishment. Sadly, the religious establishment of that day left the people worse off, not better.

c. **Put them in the common prison**: Seemingly, this included all the apostles (**on the apostles**). It wasn't the first time that Peter and John had been imprisoned (Acts 4:3).

2. (19-20) Angelic intervention frees the apostles.

But at night an angel of the Lord opened the prison doors and brought them out, and said, "Go, stand in the temple and speak to the people all the words of this life."

a. **An angel of the Lord opened the prison doors**: This was easy for God to arrange. Angels are *all ministering spirits sent forth to minister for those who will inherit salvation* (Hebrews 1:14). God sent forth this angel *to minister for* the apostles. Locked doors are nothing for God or those who He uses.

b. **An angel of the Lord**: Possibly, they only understood this was an angel in retrospect. Angels often come in human appearance, and it may not always be easy to recognize an angel (Luke 24:3-7, Hebrews 13:2).

i. "There is some divine humor here, too, because the Sadducees [Acts 5:17] did not believe in angels." (Hughes)

c. **Go, stand in the temple and speak to the people all the words of this life**: Their rescue from prison was wonderful, but for a purpose – so they could continue their work. God didn't set them free primarily for their safety or comfort. They were set free for a reason; and after this they were not always delivered.

i. The later history of these apostles – and others associated with them in the early church – shows that sometimes God delivers by a miracle, sometimes He does not. According to fairly reliable church history and tradition, miraculous angels did not always deliver them.

- Matthew was beheaded with a sword.
- Mark died in Alexandria after being dragged through the streets of the city.
- Luke was hanged on an olive tree in Greece.
- John died a natural death, but they unsuccessfully tried to boil him in oil.
- Peter was crucified upside-down in Rome.
- James was beheaded in Jerusalem.
- James the Less was thrown from a height then beaten with clubs.
- Philip was hanged.

- Bartholomew was whipped and beaten until death.
- Andrew was crucified and preached at the top of his voice to his persecutors until he died.
- Thomas was run through with a spear.
- Jude was killed with the arrows of an executioner.
- Matthias was stoned and then beheaded – as was Barnabas.
- Paul was beheaded in Rome.

ii. This reminds us that we should trust God for miraculous things and wish to see them more and more; but knowing that He also has a purpose when He does *not* deliver with a miraculous hand. We also see that we, like the apostles, are set free for a purpose – not merely to live for ourselves.

iii. "The angel of the Lord opened the prison door and set free the preachers, but might not be a preacher himself. He might give the ministers their charge, but he had no charge to preach himself." (Spurgeon)

3. (21-23) The apostles resume their work and are discovered to be missing from prison.

And when they heard *that*, they entered the temple early in the morning and taught. But the high priest and those with him came and called the council together, with all the elders of the children of Israel, and sent to the prison to have them brought. But when the officers came and did not find them in the prison, they returned and reported, saying, "Indeed we found the prison shut securely, and the guards standing outside before the doors; but when we opened them, we found no one inside!"

a. **They entered the temple early in the morning and taught**: This was remarkable obedience and boldness. If they were not sure if God wanted them to continue their public teaching work, the word from the angel at Acts 5:20 made it clear that they were to continue.

i. They went to the most public place they could (**the temple**), and as soon as they could (**early in the morning**). When they were thought to be in the prison, they were obediently teaching God's word to the common people.

b. **They returned and reported**: There is humor in all of this. The religious establishment solemnly gathers to deal with the troublemakers who teach about Jesus. They intimidate them with a prison stay, and bring them to **the council** to put them in the proper place. Yet when the officers looked they saw the prison door as it should be, the guards as they should be, but no apostles in the cell.

4. (24-26) The apostles are found and arrested again.

Now when the high priest, the captain of the temple, and the chief priests heard these things, they wondered what the outcome would be. So one came and told them, saying, "Look, the men whom you put in prison are standing in the temple and teaching the people!" Then the captain went with the officers and brought them without violence, for they feared the people, lest they should be stoned.

a. **They wondered what the outcome would be**: At this point the religious leaders had to wonder just what they were dealing with. There was the repeated evidence of supernatural power at work with the followers of Jesus.

i. Following Luke's story to this point, we understand why **they wondered what the outcome would be**. Yet we, as readers of the account, don't wonder. We know God's work will continue.

b. **The captain went with the officers and brought them without violence**: The apostles were soon arrested again. It was perhaps tempting for them to think that since they were miraculously released that God would keep them from being arrested again, but that wasn't the case.

i. When the apostles went back into custody, they knew how easy it would be for God to release them again if it pleased Him to do so. Their past experience of the power of God had filled them with faith for the present.

c. **Brought them without violence**: Significantly, the apostles did not appeal to popular opinion for protection against the religious leaders. They could have incited the crowd by shouting, "Are you going to let them take us away?" But their trust was in God and God alone. A carnal solution to their problem was available, but they did not use it.

d. **For they feared the people**: The hearts of the religious leaders was again exposed. They **feared the people**, but they did not fear God who clearly showed that He was at work among the disciples.

5. (27-28) The accusation against the apostles.

And when they had brought them, they set *them* before the council. And the high priest asked them, saying, "Did we not strictly command you not to teach in this name? And look, you have filled Jerusalem with your doctrine, and intend to bring this Man's blood on us!"

a. **They set them before the council**: This was another attempt to intimidate the apostles with the trappings of the council's institutional authority. The apostles, knowing how God protected them, were probably not intimidated or even overly impressed.

b. **Did we not strictly command you not to teach in this name?** They had commanded Peter and John to no longer teach in the name of Jesus (Acts 4:17-18). Yet Peter and John openly told them that they would continue, in obedience to God (Acts 4:19-20).

c. **You have filled Jerusalem with your doctrine**: The accusation of the high priest was a wonderful testimony to the effectiveness of the message preached by the apostles. Their message had **filled Jerusalem**.

d. **Intend to bring this Man's blood on us**: By calling Jesus **this Man**, the religious leaders were obviously avoiding the name *Jesus*, but they could not avoid the power of Jesus; it stared them right in the face.

> i. The charge that the apostles did **intend to bring this Man's blood upon us** is interesting. The high priest no doubt meant that the apostles intended to hold the Jewish leaders responsible, in some measure, for the execution of Jesus (as in Acts 2:23). Yet, we know that the apostles must have desired for the high priest and the other Jewish leaders to come to faith in Jesus, even as some other priests did (Acts 6:7). For certain, the apostles wanted to **bring** the covering, cleansing blood of Jesus upon the high priest and others in the council.

D. The resolution of their case before the Jewish rulers.

1. (29-32) The testimony of the apostles before the Sanhedrin.

But Peter and the *other* apostles answered and said: "We ought to obey God rather than men. The God of our fathers raised up Jesus whom you murdered by hanging on a tree. Him God has exalted to His right hand *to be* Prince and Savior, to give repentance to Israel and forgiveness of sins. And we are His witnesses to these things, and *so* also *is* the Holy Spirit whom God has given to those who obey Him."

a. **We ought to obey God rather than men**: This was a testimony of *great boldness*, in contrast to the Sanhedrin, who were more concerned about man's opinion than God's opinion.

> i. The apostles' response to the council was not a defense, nor was it a plea for mercy; it was a simple explanation of action. In general, the New Testament teaches that we should submit to those in authority over us. Yet submission on the human level is never absolute, and never is more important than submission to God.

ii. We should obey rulers, but not when they contradict God: "Therefore, if a father, being not content with his own estate, do essay to take from God the chief honour of a father, he is nothing else but a man. If a king, or ruler, or magistrate, do become so lofty that he diminisheth the honour and authority of God, he is but a man. We must also thus think of pastors." (Calvin)

b. **The God of our fathers raised up Jesus**: This was a testimony *faithful* to the foundation of the Christian faith. Peter spoke of:

• Man's guilt (**Jesus whom you murdered**).

• Jesus' death (**hanging on a tree**).

• Jesus' resurrection (**Him God exalted to His right hand**).

• Man's responsibility to respond (**to give repentance to Israel and forgiveness of sins**).

> i. Peter referred to the cross as a **tree** because he drew an association from Deuteronomy 21:22-23, where it says that a person hanged from a tree is cursed by God. Peter brought attention to the magnitude of their rejection of Jesus, pointing out that they killed Him in the worst way possible, both from a Roman perspective (the cross) and a Jewish perspective (the **tree** association).

> ii. "While *xylon* [tree] was used in antiquity and in the LXX variously for 'a tree,' 'wood' of any kind, 'a pole,' and various objects made of wood, including 'a gallows,' it is also used in the NT for the cross of Jesus." (Longenecker)

c. **We are His witnesses to these things, and so also is the Holy Spirit**: This was a *reliable* testimony, because it was based on eyewitness testimony, which was also confirmed by God.

2. (33) The council's strong reaction.

When they heard *this*, they were furious and plotted to kill them.

a. **They were furious**: Peter and the apostles had clearly and briefly explained to them (again) the core ideas of who Jesus was, what He did for all of us on the cross, and how we should respond to who Jesus is and what He did. Their reaction was **furious** anger.

> i. "Luke graphically describes them as 'being sawn asunder (in heart).'" (Williams)

> ii. We can imagine what went through their minds. "Who are you to tell us to repent?" "We don't need this forgiveness." "Don't blame us for the death of Jesus." "Don't you know who we are?"

b. **And plotted to kill them**: Right then, the death of the apostles was set in motion. We had not previously read that they wanted to **kill them**, but now it is clear.

    i. "Since they were unable to contend with the disciples on the level of truth, they resorted to naked authority and force. First, threats. Second, a beating. Ultimately, death." (Boice)

3. (34-39) Gamaliel's advice to the Sanhedrin.

Then one in the council stood up, a Pharisee named Gamaliel, a teacher of the law held in respect by all the people, and commanded them to put the apostles outside for a little while. And he said to them: "Men of Israel, take heed to yourselves what you intend to do regarding these men. For some time ago Theudas rose up, claiming to be somebody. A number of men, about four hundred, joined him. He was slain, and all who obeyed him were scattered and came to nothing. After this man, Judas of Galilee rose up in the days of the census, and drew away many people after him. He also perished, and all who obeyed him were dispersed. And now I say to you, keep away from these men and let them alone; for if this plan or this work is of men, it will come to nothing; but if it is of God, you cannot overthrow it—lest you even be found to fight against God."

a. **A Pharisee named Gamaliel**: This was the grandson of the esteemed Hillel, the founder of Israel's strongest school of religion. **Gamaliel** was given the title *Rabban* ("our teacher"), which was a step above the title *Rab* ("teacher") or *Rabbi* ("my teacher").

    i. The Mishnah wrote of **Gamaliel**: "Since Rabban Gamaliel the elder died there has been no more reverence for the law; and purity and abstinence died out at the same time."

    ii. Significantly, Gamaliel was a **Pharisee**. Though the Sadducees had more political power (Acts 5:17), it was politically foolish for the Sadducees to ask the Romans to execute the apostles without support from the Pharisees.

b. **Some time ago Theudus rose up**: Josephus, the Jewish historian, mentioned a **Theudas** who led a rebellion, but at a later point than this. It could be that Josephus had his dates mixed up or that this was a different **Theudas** (it was a common name). Josephus did describe a **Judas of Galilee** (*Antiquities*, 18.1.1,2,6 and 20.5.2) who may be the same one mentioned here.

c. **If this plan or this work is of men, it will come to nothing; but if it is of God, you cannot overthrow it; lest you even be found to fight**

against God: Gamaliel spoke for himself and not for God. There are many movements that may be considered successful in the sight of man, but are against God's truth. Success is not the ultimate measure of truth.

i. Gamaliel was really a fence sitter. He spoke as if they should wait and see if Jesus and the apostles were really from God. But what greater testimony did he need, beyond Jesus' resurrection and the apostles' miracles? He took a "wait-and-see" attitude when there was plenty of evidence.

ii. Gamaliel proposed the test of time, and that is an important test, but more important than the test of time is the test of *eternity*.

iii. "We should not be too ready to credit Gamaliel with having uttered an invariable principle... the Gamaliel principle is not a reliable index to what is from God and what is not." (Stott)

4. (40-42) After a beating, the apostles resume preaching with joy.

And they agreed with him, and when they had called for the apostles and beaten *them*, they commanded that they should not speak in the name of Jesus, and let them go. So they departed from the presence of the council, rejoicing that they were counted worthy to suffer shame for His name. And daily in the temple, and in every house, they did not cease teaching and preaching Jesus *as* the Christ.

a. **When they had called for the apostles and beaten them**: The leaders thought they could intimidate and discourage the apostles with a beating. Instead, they left **rejoicing**. They were not **rejoicing** that they suffered, but that they **were counted worthy to suffer shame for His name**. It was a privilege to be associated with Jesus in any circumstance, even to **suffer shame**.

i. **Beaten** can also be translated *skinned*; the beating they received stripped the skin off of their backs. "It was no soft option; people were known to die from it, even if this was exceptional. It was meant to be a serious lesson to offenders." (Marshall)

ii. "Because of Gamaliel's rational entreaty a compromise was reached and the apostles were let off easy – easy, that is, if we think thirty-nine stripes is easy." (Hughes)

b. **They did not cease teaching and preaching Jesus as the Christ**. Whatever beating or shameful treatment the Sanhedrin gave them, it did absolutely no good. The disciples didn't stop preaching for a moment.

i. This challenges each of us as followers of Jesus. They continued where we may have stopped. We often find the threat of social rejection enough to make us keep quiet about who Jesus is and what He did for us. We need to have the apostles' courage and determination to stand firm for Jesus Christ.

ii. Spurgeon spoke of this kind of bold heart: "Now, I charge every Christian here to be speaking boldly in Christ's name, according as he has opportunity, and especially to take care of this tendency of our flesh to be afraid; which leads practically to endeavours to get off easily and to save ourselves from trouble. Fear not; be brave for Christ. Live bravely for him who died lovingly for you."

iii. Spurgeon also challenged the cowardly heart: "Yet you are a coward. Yes, put it down in English: you are a coward. If anybody called you so you would turn red in the face; and perhaps you are not a coward in reference to any other subject. What a shameful thing it is that while you are bold about everything else you are cowardly about Jesus Christ. Brave for the world and cowardly towards Christ!"

Acts 6 - The Appointment of Deacons and the Arrest of Stephen

A. The appointment of deacons.

1. (1) A dispute about the distribution of assistance to widows.

Now in those days, when *the number of* the disciples was multiplying, there arose a complaint against the Hebrews by the Hellenists, because their widows were neglected in the daily distribution.

> a. **There arose a complaint against the Hebrews by the Hellenists**: To this point in the Book of Acts, Satan's attacks on the church came on many different fronts. He attempted many forms of direct opposition and intimidation, and he tried to corrupt the church from within. These strategies were all unsuccessful in stopping or slowing the work of the church. Now Satan hoped to "divide and conquer" by raising one group of Christians against another.

> > i. We can say that with Acts 5 and 6, the good old days were over for the earliest Christians. They now had to deal with internal corruption, and now disputes and potential divisions. *How* they dealt with those things made all the difference.

> > ii. **When the number of disciples was multiplying** indicates that the work of God's kingdom through the early Christian community was still highly successful, and they dealt with the problems well.

> > iii. The mention of growth again reminds us that the early church was organized. They knew how many were saved; they met together at specific places and specific times. Money and goods were collected and distributed to those in need. Sin was confronted and dealt with. All these indicate at least some level of organization.

> b. **Against the Hebrews by the Hellenists**: The **Hebrews** were those Jews more inclined to embrace Jewish culture and were mostly from Judea. The

Hellenists were those Jews more inclined to embrace Greek culture and mostly were from the *Diaspora* (from all over the Roman Empire).

i. To oversimplify, **Hebrews** tended to regard **Hellenists** as unspiritual compromisers with Greek culture, and **Hellenists** regarded **Hebrews** as holier-than-thou traditionalists. There was already a natural suspicion between the two groups, and Satan tried to take advantage of that standing suspicion.

ii. It's important to remember that though the titles **Hebrews** and **Hellenists** are used, *these were Christians, followers of Jesus.* They were all from a Jewish background, but they had all embraced Jesus as their Messiah.

c. **The daily distribution**: The early church took its responsibility to help support **widows** seriously because they often had no other support; but they also expected these widows to serve the church faithfully (1 Timothy 5:3-16).

i. There is the hint here of a growing division between the religious leaders and the early followers of Jesus. The care of widows and orphans was an important part of Jewish life, and normally the temple authorities organized the distribution to the needy. Yet it seems that the Christian widows were not cared for by the Jewish leaders; probably because they didn't like the fact that the apostles kept preaching Jesus when they were told to stop.

d. **Because their widows were neglected in the daily distribution**: Apparently, some of the Christians from a Hellenistic background believed that the widows among the Hebrew Christians received better care.

i. "It is not suggested that the oversight was deliberate... more probably the cause was poor administration or supervision." (Stott)

ii. "In a congregation of that size, it was inevitable that someone's needs would be overlooked." (MacArthur)

iii. Satan loves to use an unintentional wrong to begin a conflict. The **Hebrews** were right in their *hearts*, and the **Hellenists** were right in their *facts*. These were perfect conditions for a church-splitting conflict.

2. (2-4) The apostles arrange for deacons to be nominated.

Then the twelve summoned the multitude of the disciples and said, "It is not desirable that we should leave the word of God and serve tables. Therefore, brethren, seek out from among you seven men of *good* reputation, full of the Holy Spirit and wisdom, whom we may appoint

over this business; but we will give ourselves continually to prayer and to the ministry of the word."

a. **It is not desirable that we should leave the word of God and serve tables**: The apostles explained that they should remain faithful to their central calling, which was **prayer and to the ministry of the word**. It was wrong for them to spend their time administrating the practical needs of the widows.

i. Some believe that this is evidence of a superior attitude among **the twelve**; that they considered themselves above such work. This was probably not so, and they were wise in delegating these responsibilities. God did not call these apostles to be *everything* for the church. God has and will raise up others to serve in other ways.

ii. A pastor should not have his time consumed in tasks that are essentially *serving tables*. Yet there is something wrong with a pastor who considers such work beneath him.

iii. This didn't concern the actual serving of food and cleaning of dining tables for these widows. This speaks of handling the practical administration of the financial and practical details relevant to caring for the widows. "A 'table' at that time meant a place where a money changer did his collecting or exchanging of money. The deacons were elected to oversee the distribution of monies and provisions to the needy among the fellowship." (Ogilvie)

b. **We will give ourselves continually to prayer and to the ministry of the word**: The fact that the apostles busied themselves with **prayer** and **the ministry of the word** shows how energetically they did those things and how consuming it is to preach and pray rightly.

i. The ministry is a lot of work, even apart from administrative headaches. A young man said to Donald Grey Barnhouse, "I'd give the world to be able to teach the Bible like you." Looking him straight in the eye, Dr. Barnhouse replied: "Good, because that's exactly what it will cost you."

ii. **We will give ourselves continually to prayer**: They gave themselves to more than **the ministry of the word**. "Therefore, pastors must not think that they have so done their duty that they need to do no more when they have daily spent some time in teaching." (Calvin)

c. **Seek out from among you**: The apostles (**the twelve**) spoke to the general group of believers (**the multitude of the disciples**) and pursued the solution with a lot of communication and input from among the people.

They even asked those – probably especially those who felt wronged – to suggest men of good character to do this work.

i. This was a wonderful way to solve the problem. They didn't throw the complainers out. They didn't divide into two congregations. They didn't shun the unhappy people. They didn't form a committee and discuss the problem to death.

ii. No doubt, someone suggested that the apostles themselves give more direct attention to the distribution of help to the widows. Instead, they delegated and brought more people into doing work of ministry. Meeting unmet needs is a great way to bring more people into ministry.

d. **Of good reputation, full of the Holy Spirit and wisdom**: The qualifications described by the apostles focused the *character* of the men to be chosen. The apostles were far more concerned with the internal quality of the men than their outward appearance or image.

i. The idea behind **full of the Holy Spirit and wisdom** is that these men were to be both *spiritually* minded and *practically* minded. This can be a hard combination to find.

ii. **Seven men**: Possibly they chose **seven** so that one could oversee the needs of the widows a different day of the week.

e. **Whom we may appoint**: The final decision rested with the apostles. They asked the congregation to nominate the men (**seek out from among you**), but the decision really rested with the apostles. This was not an exercise of congregational government, though the apostles wisely wanted and valued the input from the congregation.

f. **Whom we may appoint over this business**: Seven men were to be chosen to **serve tables**. It was simple, practical service that they are appointed to; yet they must be well qualified in a spiritual sense, especially because of the danger of division.

i. Therefore, the men need to be **of good reputation**. They had to be men the church family felt confident in.

ii. "The apostles were not trying to protect their own rights. They were not even protecting their own point of view. They simply wanted to solve the problem." (Boice)

3. (5-7) The selection of deacons.

And the saying pleased the whole multitude. And they chose Stephen, a man full of faith and the Holy Spirit, and Philip, Prochorus, Nicanor, Timon, Parmenas, and Nicolas, a proselyte from Antioch, whom they

set before the apostles; and when they had prayed, they laid hands on them. Then the word of God spread, and the number of the disciples multiplied greatly in Jerusalem, and a great many of the priests were obedient to the faith.

a. **And the saying pleased the whole multitude**: We can't say this was a good decision only because the people liked it. Yet, God confirmed the wisdom of the apostles through agreement among the people. The apostles were led of the Lord, not popular opinion. Yet, because they were all in basic agreement, they agreed on how the Lord was leading the apostles.

b. **Stephen... Philip, Prochorus**: The seven men all had Greek names, indicating that they were probably Hellenists themselves. The people (and the apostles) showed great sensitivity to the offended Hellenists by appointing Hellenists to take care of the widows' distribution.

i. "I would imagine there were more Aramaic-speaking Christians in the church than there were Greek-speaking Christians, but the church as a whole said, Let's elect Greek-speaking leaders." (Boice)

c. **Whom they set before the apostles; and when they had prayed, they laid hands on them**: In this case, the people nominated the men, and the apostles approved them by laying hands on them, after praying for God's guidance and approval.

i. It was important to lay **hands on them** even if their service was mainly for the practical needs of the widows. Practical service is spiritual service. The same Greek word is used for both *distribution* (Acts 6:1) and *ministry* (Acts 6:4). The idea behind the word in both places is *service*, whether in practical ways or spiritual ways.

ii. People should count it a privilege to serve the Lord in these basic, practical ways, instead of seeing it as an "unspiritual" burden. Apart from the cross, Jesus showed the ultimate measure of love by simply washing His disciples' feet (John 13:1-5).

iii. Nowhere in this chapter of Acts are these men called *deacons*, but most consider they were the first to fulfill the office of deacon as described in 1 Timothy 3:8-13. The word *deacon* simply means "servant," and these men were certainly servants. They could claim the same promise for faithful service that Paul specifically made to deacons in 1 Timothy 3:13: *For those who have served well as deacons obtain for themselves a good standing and great boldness in the faith which is in Christ Jesus.*

d. **Then the word of God spread, and the number of the disciples multiplied greatly in Jerusalem**: Considering all that could have gone wrong when Satan tried to attack through division, everyone involved deserves much credit.

> i. *Those with the complaint*, the Hellenists, did the right thing: They made the need known, instead of complaining and whining, and they trusted the solution of the apostles.

> ii. *Those of the other party*, the Hebrews, did the right thing: They recognized that the Hellenists had a legitimate need and they trusted the solution of the apostles.

> iii. *The seven* chosen men did the right thing: They accepted the call to unglamorous service.

> iv. *The apostles* did the right thing: They responded to the need without distracting themselves from their central task.

e. **And the word of God spread**: Because this situation was handled with wisdom and sensitivity to those who were offended, a potentially divisive issue was defused, and the gospel continued to go forth. Even **a great many of the priests** came to faith in Jesus.

> i. "The church gave Holy Ghost *deacons* and got converted *priests*… The disciples chose Holy Ghost deacons, and got Holy Ghost martyrs and evangelists."

> ii. "Men were chosen to serve tables – to do common things; but they were found doing uncommon things – working signs and wonders among the people."

> iii. Satan's strategy failed. He tried to divide the church, and it did not work. But Satan's second strategy also failed. The apostles were not distracted from the focus of ministry God had for them – to focus on the word of God and on prayer.

B. Stephen's witness and arrest.

1. (8-10) Stephen's witness for God.

And Stephen, full of faith and power, did great wonders and signs among the people. Then there arose some from what is called the Synagogue of the Freedmen (Cyrenians, Alexandrians, and those from Cilicia and Asia), disputing with Stephen. And they were not able to resist the wisdom and the Spirit by which he spoke.

a. **Stephen, full of faith and power, did great wonders and signs among the people**: God did **great wonders and signs** through the apostles; but also through others like Stephen, one of the servants chosen to help the widows. God used Stephen because he was **full of faith and power**.

i. There is a small textual dispute as to whether Luke's original text said that Stephen was **full of faith and power** or **full of** *grace* **and power**. The meaning is substantially the same, because to live in faith is walk in God's grace.

b. **Disputing with Stephen**: Stephen debated with Jews from **the Synagogue of the Freedmen**. Empowered by the Holy Spirit, he showed greater wisdom than his opponents (**they were not able to resist the wisdom and the Spirit by which he spoke**).

i. There is no indication that Stephen – in himself – was smarter, better educated, or a better debater than these Jews. We should attribute his upper hand in the debate to **the Spirit by which he spoke**.

ii. **Those from Cilicia**: "The mention of Cilicia suggests this may have been Paul's synagogue before he was converted. He came from Tarsus in Cilicia." (Lovett)

2. (11-14) The opposing Jews, defeated in debate, induce false accusations against Stephen.

Then they secretly induced men to say, "We have heard him speak blasphemous words against Moses and God." And they stirred up the people, the elders, and the scribes; and they came upon *him*, seized him, and brought *him* to the council. They also set up false witnesses who said, "This man does not cease to speak blasphemous words against this holy place and the law; for we have heard him say that this Jesus of Nazareth will destroy this place and change the customs which Moses delivered to us."

a. **They secretly induced men to say**: The opponents of Stephen could not win a fair fight, so they used lies and secret strategies to shape popular opinion against Stephen.

i. Normally, Luke would not know what the opponents of Stephen **secretly induced men to say**. Possibly he knew it because a man named Saul of Tarsus was among the opponents. Some of them were from Paul's home region of Cilicia. Saul (who became known as Paul the apostle) may have told Luke about this incident.

b. **They stirred up the people**: The opponents of Stephen could do nothing against the followers of Jesus until they got popular opinion on their side. Previously, persecution against the apostles had been limited because popular opinion was with them (Acts 2:47, 5:26).

i. Popular opinion can be easily shaped. The same crowds that praised Jesus (Luke 19:35-40) soon called for His crucifixion (Luke 23:18-23). The crowds that loved the apostles (Acts 2:47, 5:26) cry out against

Stephen. This is why we should never let popular opinion shape the vision or focus of the church, but let it rest on God's eternal Word.

c. **We have heard him speak blasphemous words against Moses and God…this man does not cease to speak blasphemous words against this holy place and the law… Jesus of Nazareth will destroy this place and change customs**: These were the accusations against Stephen. Significantly, many of the same false accusations were leveled against Jesus (Matthew 26:59-61). It is a good thing to be accused of the same things Jesus was accused of.

i. They accused him of these things because Stephen clearly taught that:

- Jesus was greater than Moses (**blasphemous words against Moses**).
- Jesus was God (**blasphemous words against… God**).
- Jesus was greater than the temple (**blasphemous words against this holy place**).
- Jesus was the fulfillment of the law (**blasphemous words against …the law**).
- Jesus was greater than their religious customs and traditions (**Jesus of Nazareth will destroy this place and change customs**).

ii. Of course, Stephen never taught **against Moses and God**, but his glorification of Jesus was twisted. Stephen never spoke **blasphemous words against this holy place** (the temple), but he would not make it an idol as many Jewish people in that day did. Stephen had his words twisted, and false accusations were brought against him.

iii. "Whatever form of words Stephen used which gave rise to the accusation that he said Jesus would destroy the temple, he certainly grasped and expounded the inner meaning of Jesus' own words." (Bruce).

iv. Several commentators imply or directly state that the thrust of Stephen's message - that Jesus supersedes the temple and its localized worship - was a doctrine that the apostles themselves must have shied away from proclaiming. This is unwarranted speculation. The demonstrated boldness of the apostles is undeniable proof that they withheld no truth from fear that it might be too controversial – or dangerous.

3. (15) Stephen's countenance when accused.

And all who sat in the council, looking steadfastly at him, saw his face as the face of an angel.

a. **All who sat in the council, looking steadfastly at him**: Stephen was on trial before the highest religious court he could face; examined by honored, educated, and powerful men. He had been falsely accused and seemed to have lost popular support.

b. **His face as the face of an angel**: Stephen's face did not have that mild, soft, angelic look that we see in so many paintings; nor was it a look of stern judgment and wrath. Instead, his face reflected the perfect peace and confidence of one that knows and trusts his God. His face had the same reflected glory that Moses had as he beheld God intimately.

i. "The description is of a person who is close to God and reflects some of His glory as a result of being in his presence (Exodus 34:29ff)." (Marshall)

c. **The face of an angel** also means that Stephen was at perfect peace. His face was not filled with fear or terror, because he knew his life was in God's hands and that Jesus never forsakes His people.

Acts 7 - Stephen's Response to the Council

A. The story of Israel from the time of Abraham.

1. (1) The High Priest invites Stephen to speak.

Then the high priest said, "Are these things so?"

a. **Then the high priest said**: The **high priest** mentioned here was probably still Caiaphas, the same one who presided over the trial of Jesus (Matthew 26:57).

b. **Are these things so?** The high priest invited Stephen to explain himself in light of the accusations recorded in Acts 6:11-14. Stephen was accused to speaking *blasphemous words against Moses and God*, and *against this holy place* [the temple] *and the law*. Additionally, they accused him of saying that Jesus would destroy both the temple and the customs delivered by Moses.

i. In his response Stephen gave a panorama of Old Testament history. We shouldn't think Stephen instructed the Sanhedrin on points of Jewish history they were ignorant of. Instead, Stephen emphasized some things in Jewish history they may not have considered: That God never confined Himself to one place (like the temple), and that the Jewish people had a habit of rejecting those God sends to them.

ii. This really was not a *defense*. Stephen wasn't interested in defending himself. He simply wanted to proclaim the truth about Jesus in a way people could understand. He was "Apparently not making a special defense at all or with one syllable referring to his accusers and their false witnesses, he is yet utterly refuting them and making the most effective defense." (Lenski)

iii. "Stephen seems to have perceived...that the old order of things was passing away and a new order was coming. This becomes particularly clear when he talks about the temple. It was cherished by the Jews. But it was destined to pass away, and Stephen seemed to have sensed that.

His speech is a transition speech that paves the way for presenting the gospel to the Gentiles, which begins in the very next chapter of Acts." (Boice)

iv. "Such a speech as this was by no means calculated to secure an acquittal before the Sanhedrin. It is rather a defense of pure Christianity as God's appointed way of worship." (Bruce)

2. (2-5) God's promise to Abraham.

And he said, "Brethren and fathers, listen: The God of glory appeared to our father Abraham when he was in Mesopotamia, before he dwelt in Haran, and said to him, 'Get out of your country and from your relatives, and come to a land that I will show you.' Then he came out of the land of the Chaldeans and dwelt in Haran. And from there, when his father was dead, He moved him to this land in which you now dwell. And *God* gave him no inheritance in it, not even *enough* to set his foot on. But even when *Abraham* had no child, He promised to give it to him for a possession, and to his descendants after him.

a. **The God of glory appeared to our father Abraham when he was in Mesopotamia**: At the very beginning, Stephen emphasized that the **God of glory appeared to** Abraham *before he even came into the Promised Land.*

i. Not only was the temple unnecessary for this revelation of **the God of glory**; the Promised Land itself was not necessary. God was greater than either, and this explained how Stephen was falsely accused of speaking against the temple. Stephen wasn't defending; he simply explained.

ii. "A single thread runs right through the first part of his defence. It is that the God of Israel is a pilgrim God, who is not restricted to any one place…If he has any home on earth, it is with his people that he lives." (Stott)

iii. "So it is not as if Abraham was in Mesopotamia and God, perhaps from Mount Zion many hundreds of miles away, shouted to him, 'Abraham, come over here. I want you to come to Palestine.' Rather God appeared to him right there in Mesopotamia in all his glory." (Boice)

b. **Get out of your country and from your relatives, and come to a land that I will show you**: God said this to Abraham when **he was in Mesopotamia**. Yet Stephen explained that Abraham did not immediately go to Canaan (he **dwelt in Haran**) and he did not immediately leave his relatives (his father came with him to **Haran**).

i. Abraham's partial obedience did not take God's promise away. Instead, it meant the promise was on hold until Abram was ready to do what the Lord said. The fulfillment of the promise didn't progress until Abraham left Haran and his father behind and went to the place God wanted him to go.

ii. Abraham will certainly become a giant of faith, even being the father of the believing (Galatians 3:7); yet he did not start there. Abraham is an example of one who *grew* in faith and obedience.

c. **God gave him no inheritance... no child**: Abraham was promised both the land and descendants, but had no outward proof of either. He could only trust God for the fulfillment of these things.

i. With this, Stephen emphasized a relationship with God on the basis of faith and not outward evidences like a temple or the structure of institutional religion and its customs.

ii. Even when Abraham was in the land, he was a pilgrim. He didn't make an idol out of the blessings God had either given or promised. This was a rebuke to the religious leaders Stephen spoke to, because many among them had stopped being pilgrims and they made idols out of the blessings of the temple and the land.

3. (6-8) God warned Abraham and gave him the covenant.

But God spoke in this way: that his descendants would dwell in a foreign land, and that they would bring them into bondage and oppress *them* four hundred years. 'And the nation to whom they will be in bondage I will judge,' said God, 'and after that they shall come out and serve Me in this place.' Then He gave him the covenant of circumcision; and so *Abraham* begot Isaac and circumcised him on the eighth day; and Isaac *begot* Jacob, and Jacob *begot* the twelve patriarchs.

a. **His descendants would dwell in a foreign land...into bondage**: The promise would not be easy or light for Abraham or his descendants. Yet, God promised to judge the nation that put Israel into bondage.

i. Stephen here suggested the idea that *God knows how to take care of and protect His people*. He rested in that assurance himself, and challenged the council to have the same assurance.

b. **He gave him the covenant of circumcision...Isaac begot Jacob, and Jacob begot the twelve patriarchs**: Circumcision became the sign of the covenant for Israel, and the covenant was passed down through these descendants of Abraham.

4. (9-16) God's faithfulness through Joseph.

"And the patriarchs, becoming envious, sold Joseph into Egypt. But God was with him and delivered him out of all his troubles, and gave him favor and wisdom in the presence of Pharaoh, king of Egypt; and he made him governor over Egypt and all his house. Now a famine and great trouble came over all the land of Egypt and Canaan, and our fathers found no sustenance. But when Jacob heard that there was grain in Egypt, he sent out our fathers first. And the second *time* Joseph was made known to his brothers, and Joseph's family became known to the Pharaoh. Then Joseph sent and called his father Jacob and all his relatives to *him,* seventy-five people. So Jacob went down to Egypt; and he died, he and our fathers. And they were carried back to Shechem and laid in the tomb that Abraham bought for a sum of money from the sons of Hamor, *the father* of Shechem.

a. **God was with him**: Again, Stephen emphasized the *spiritual* presence of God with Joseph all the time. Joseph did not need to go to the temple to be close to God - there was no temple. Instead, **God was with him** all the time.

b. **Becoming envious, sold Joseph:** Stephen mentioned the story of Joseph because he is a picture of Jesus, in that the sons of Israel rejected Joseph, who later became a savior to them (and the *only possible* savior).

c. **Seventy-five people**: Genesis 46:27 says there were 70 altogether of the family of Israel, when Stephen in Acts 7:14 said it was 75. Stephen quoted from the Septuagint version of the Old Testament, which says 75. The number in the Septuagint is not wrong, just arrived at in a different way, specifically adding five more sons (or grandsons) of Joseph born in Egypt.

d. **The tomb that Abraham bought**: The only land that Abraham ever actually possessed in Canaan was this burial plot. The rest was received only by faith.

B. The story of Israel from the time of Moses.

1. (17-22) The early life of Moses.

"But when the time of the promise drew near which God had sworn to Abraham, the people grew and multiplied in Egypt till another king arose who did not know Joseph. This man dealt treacherously with our people, and oppressed our forefathers, making them expose their babies, so that they might not live. At this time Moses was born, and was well pleasing to God; and he was brought up in his father's house for three months. But when he was set out, Pharaoh's daughter took

him away and brought him up as her own son. And Moses was learned in all the wisdom of the Egyptians, and was mighty in words and deeds.

a. **At this time Moses was born, and was well pleasing to God**: Moses was also like Jesus in that he was favored by God from birth and preserved in childhood. As well, he was **well pleasing to God** without the temple or the customs of institutional religion.

b. **Was mighty in words and deeds**: Moses was also like Jesus who would come after him, in that he was wise, skillful with words, and a man of **mighty…deeds**.

2. (23-29) Israel rejects Moses.

"Now when he was forty years old, it came into his heart to visit his brethren, the children of Israel. And seeing one of *them* suffer wrong, he defended and avenged him who was oppressed, and struck down the Egyptian. For he supposed that his brethren would have understood that God would deliver them by his hand, but they did not understand. And the next day he appeared to two of them as they were fighting, and *tried to* reconcile them, saying, 'Men, you are brethren; why do you wrong one another?' But he who did his neighbor wrong pushed him away, saying, 'Who made you a ruler and a judge over us? Do you want to kill me as you did the Egyptian yesterday?' Then, at this saying, Moses fled and became a dweller in the land of Midian, where he had two sons.

a. **When he was forty years old, it came into his heart to visit his brethren**: At an appointed time, Moses came down from his royal throne out of care and concern for **his brethren**. This was another way that Moses was like Jesus who would come after him.

b. **He supposed that his brethren would have understood that God would deliver them by his hand, but they did not understand**: When Moses offered deliverance to Israel, he was rejected and rejected with spite. Israel denied that he had any right to be a **ruler and a judge** over them.

i. Stephen's message was plain: "You have rejected Jesus, who was like Moses yet greater than him, and you deny that Jesus has any right to be **a ruler and a judge** over you."

3. (30-34) God appeared to Moses at Mount Sinai.

"And when forty years had passed, an Angel of the Lord appeared to him in a flame of fire in a bush, in the wilderness of Mount Sinai. When Moses saw *it*, he marveled at the sight; and as he drew near to observe, the voice of the Lord came to him, *saying,* 'I *am* the God of your fathers–the God of Abraham, the God of Isaac, and the God of

Jacob.' And Moses trembled and dared not look. Then the LORD said to him, "Take your sandals off your feet, for the place where you stand is holy ground. I have surely seen the oppression of my people who are in Egypt; I have heard their groaning and have come down to deliver them. And now come, I will send you to Egypt.'"

> a. **An Angel of the Lord appeared to him… in the wilderness of Mount Sinai**: Stephen again emphasized one of the main points of his reply to the council – that God, His glory, and His work was not confined to the temple. God **appeared** to Moses **in the wilderness**, before there ever was a temple.

> b. **I will send you to Egypt**: Stephen emphasized that God both called and commissioned Moses.

4. (35-36) Moses was Israel's deliverer, despite Israel's previous rejection.

"This Moses whom they rejected, saying, 'Who made you a ruler and a judge?' is the one God sent *to be* a ruler and a deliverer by the hand of the Angel who appeared to him in the bush. He brought them out, after he had shown wonders and signs in the land of Egypt, and in the Red Sea, and in the wilderness forty years.

> a. **This Moses whom they rejected**: Even though Israel had rejected Moses and his leadership, God appointed Moses with unmistakable signs, including the burning bush in the wilderness.

> b. **He brought them out**: Though Israel rejected Moses at what might be called his "first coming," he still remained God's chosen deliverer for Israel.

5. (37-41) Israel's repeated rejection of Moses.

"This is that Moses who said to the children of Israel, 'The LORD your God will raise up for you a Prophet like me from your brethren. Him you shall hear.' This is he who was in the congregation in the wilderness with the Angel who spoke to him on Mount Sinai, and *with* our fathers, the one who received the living oracles to give to us, whom our fathers would not obey, but rejected. And in their hearts they turned back to Egypt, saying to Aaron, 'Make us gods to go before us; *as for* this Moses who brought us out of the land of Egypt, we do not know what has become of him.' And they made a calf in those days, offered sacrifices to the idol, and rejoiced in the works of their own hands.

> a. **This is that Moses who said to the children of Israel**: Moses promised that there would come after him another **Prophet** and warned that Israel should take special care to listen to this coming **Prophet**. But just like Israel rejected Moses, so they were rejecting Jesus, who is the **Prophet** Moses spoke of.

i. Each individual should consider for themselves how they should *accept* Jesus, and not reject Him. They should receive Him as their Deliverer, the One who can rescue.

b. **This is he who was in the congregation…who received the living oracles**: Moses, like Jesus, led the **congregation** of God's people, enjoyed special intimacy with God and brought forth the revelation of God.

c. **They made a calf in those days… and rejoiced in the works of their own hands**: When ancient Israel rejected Moses and God's work through him, they replaced him with their own man-made religion. Stephen applied the same idea to the council he spoke to.

i. The phrase **and rejoiced in the works of their own hands** is especially meaningful. One of the accusations against Stephen was that he blasphemed the temple. It wasn't that Stephen spoke against the temple, but against the way Israel worshipped the temple of God instead of the God of the temple. Just as Israel worshipped the calf in the wilderness, so now they were worshipping **the works of their own hands**.

6. (42-43) God's response to the repeated rejection of His messengers.

Then God turned and gave them up to worship the host of heaven, as it is written in the book of the Prophets:

'Did you offer Me slaughtered animals and sacrifices *during* forty years in the wilderness,
O house of Israel?
You also took up the tabernacle of Moloch,
And the star of your god Remphan,
Images which you made to worship;
And I will carry you away beyond Babylon.'

a. **Then God turned and gave them up to worship the host of heaven**: In their rejection of Moses and the God who sent him, Israel turned instead to corrupt idols, bringing upon themselves the judgment described in the passage quoted from Amos 5:25-27.

i. Stephen took the passage from Amos and changed it slightly to bring the point to his listeners. Amos said, "*beyond Damascus*" (Amos 5:27), but Stephen changed it to "**beyond Babylon**."

ii. Boice explains: "Stephen, who quotes the text, alters it, because he is not talking to the people of the northern kingdom but to the leaders of Israel in the south. It is their history that he has in mind."

b. **God turned and gave them up to worship the host of heaven**: The idea here is both important and awesome. Paul later built on the thought of God giving man over to his sinful desires in Romans 1:24-32.

i. It makes each of us consider the question: If we reject Jesus, what will we be given up to?

7. (44-50) Even as Israel rejected God, they still had the tabernacle, and later the temple.

"Our fathers had the tabernacle of witness in the wilderness, as He appointed, instructing Moses to make it according to the pattern that he had seen, which our fathers, having received it in turn, also brought with Joshua into the land possessed by the Gentiles, whom God drove out before the face of our fathers until the days of David, who found favor before God and asked to find a dwelling for the God of Jacob. But Solomon built Him a house. However, the Most High does not dwell in temples made with hands, as the prophet says:

'Heaven *is* My throne,
And earth *is* My footstool.
What house will you build for Me? says the LORD,
Or what *is* the place of My rest?
Has My hand not made all these things?'

a. **Our fathers had the tabernacle... Solomon built Him a house**: Stephen's point was that the presence of the tabernacle or the temple did not keep them from rejecting God and His special messengers.

b. **However, the Most High does not dwell in temples made with hands**: Stephen confronted their idolatry of the temple. In doing so, they tried to confine God within the temple. Yet God is too big to fit in any temple man could make.

i. On a more subtle level, many Christians do the same thing. It may not be the worship of a church building (though certainly that does take place from time to time), but it is the confinement of God to one place. In other words, the only place they meet God is at the church. As far as they are concerned, God is absent from the rest of their lives. In the minds and lives of some today, God might as well only live at the church.

8. (51-53) Stephen applies the sermon to his listeners.

"*You* stiff-necked and uncircumcised in heart and ears! You always resist the Holy Spirit; as your fathers *did*, so *do* you. Which of the prophets did your fathers not persecute? And they killed those who foretold the coming of the Just One, of whom you now have become the betrayers

and murderers, who have received the law by the direction of angels and have not kept *it*."

a. **You always resist the Holy Spirit; as your fathers did, so do you**: One can imagine the angry whispering among the Sanhedrin as Stephen's history lesson began to make sense. Stephen saw this and knew they were rejecting again the One God sent, just as before.

> i. "He takes the sharp knife of the Word and rips up the sins of the people, laying open the inward parts of their hearts, and the secrets of their soul…He could not have delivered that searching address with greater fearlessness had he been assured that they would thank him for the operation; the fact that his death was certain had no other effect upon him than to make him yet more zealous." (Spurgeon)

b. **You stiff-necked and uncircumcised in heart and ears!** Drawing on concepts from the Old Testament, Stephen rebuked those who rejected Jesus as **stiff-necked** (as Israel is described in passages like Exodus 32:9), and as **uncircumcised in heart and ears** (as Israel is described in passages like Jeremiah 9:26).

> i. In using the two phrases together, he may have in mind a passage like Deuteronomy 10:16: *Therefore circumcise the foreskin of your heart, and be stiff-necked no longer.*

> ii. Almost 20 times in the Old Testament, God calls Israel **stiff-necked**. These religious leaders were acting just as their forefathers acted.

> iii. Israel prided itself on the sign of circumcision because it separated them from the Gentiles. Stephen essentially said, "You are just like the Gentiles in your rejection of the Lord."

c. **You now have become the betrayers and murderers**: Stephen's main point was unmistakable: "As Israel was in its history, so you are today. God gave you the law, but you **have not kept it**."

d. **Who have received the law by the direction of angels and have not kept it**: This accusation must have outraged the members of the council. They prided themselves on their obedience to the law, even as the Apostle Paul would later claim of his pre-Christian thinking: *concerning the righteousness which is in the law, blameless* (Philippians 3:6).

> i. Though it must have offended the council, Stephen's message was true. First, *God is no respecter of places*; that is, though the temple was a wonderful gift from God, it was wrong to overemphasize it as "the house of God." Second, *Israel at that time was guilty of what they had often been guilty of: rejecting God's messengers.*

ii. Jesus said that it is impossible for old wineskins to hold new wine (Matthew 9:17). Through Stephen, the Holy Spirit showed how the old traditions of Judaism (especially the over-emphasis on the temple) could not contain the new wine of Christianity.

iii. God used Stephen's coming martyrdom to send the church out into the entire world, but God also used Stephen's message to show that there was no *theological* reason to prevent the gospel from going to the Gentiles.

iv. The whole idea behind a permanent, stationary temple is "you come to me." This is why Israel, though they were a light to the nations, mainly thought in terms of the world coming to *them* for salvation. Through the church, God would show a different heart: "I will come to you," including to the Gentiles.

C. The council's reaction to the sermon of Stephen.

1. (54) They **were cut to the heart**, and convicted by the Holy Spirit.

When they heard these things they were cut to the heart, and they gnashed at him with *their* teeth.

a. **They were cut to the heart**: The council was angry, but because Stephen's message had hit the target. They could not dismiss or ignore what he said. The Sanhedrin reacted with rage instead of submission to the Holy Spirit.

b. **They gnashed at him with their teeth**: It is remarkable to think of this response from men who were dignified, respected leaders in Israel. This would as if a group of senators ground their teeth in anger in response to the testimony of a witness at a hearing.

i. The idea of **gnashing at him with their teeth** can't help but remind us of the imagery of Hell. Seven different times, Jesus described Hell as a place of *weeping and gnashing of teeth* (Matthew 8:12). These men were prominent, successful, and appeared to be religious; yet they were rejecting God and associating themselves with hell, not heaven.

ii. They didn't start **gnashing** when Stephen finished his speech. "All they could do in their frenzy was to gnash with their teeth. It was not a sudden outburst but the tense rather shows that it was prolonged." (Gaebelein)

2. (55-56) Stephen's vision of Jesus.

But he, being full of the Holy Spirit, gazed into heaven and saw the glory of God, and Jesus standing at the right hand of God, and said, "Look! I see the heavens opened and the Son of Man standing at the right hand of God!"

a. **But he, being full of the Holy Spirit**: This was a great contrast to the behavior of the council. The fact that Stephen was **full of the Holy Spirit** shows the source of his courage, wisdom, and power in preaching.

> i. J.B. Phillips' translates thus: *Stephen, filled through all his being with the Holy Spirit*. This is how we should be filled with the Holy Spirit.

b. **Saw the glory of God, and Jesus standing at the right hand of God**: It is difficult to describe exactly what Stephen saw. We can't say if this was a personal vision or if some sort of "window to heaven" was opened, but going beyond the plain description of the text is pure speculation.

c. **Jesus standing at the right hand of God**: It is significant to note Jesus is **standing**, as opposed to the more common description of *sitting* in heaven (Matthew 26:64, Colossians 3:1), at the right hand of God the Father.

> i. We can suppose that **Jesus** was **standing** here in solidarity and sympathy with Stephen at this moment of crisis.

> ii. We might also consider that Jesus stood to give a standing ovation to Stephen, whose fate made him unique among believers. Among all the followers of Jesus, Stephen was the first martyr.

> iii. Jesus said, *Therefore whoever confesses Me before men, him I will also confess before My Father who is in heaven* (Matthew 10:32). Jesus may have also stood to plead Stephen's case before God the Father, assuring that though he was found guilty and punished on earth, he was found righteous and rewarded in heaven.

> iv. "Stephen has been confessing Christ before men, and now he sees Christ confessing his servant before God." (Bruce)

3. (57-58) The execution of Stephen by stoning.

Then they cried out with a loud voice, stopped their ears, and ran at him with one accord; and they cast *him* out of the city and stoned *him*. And the witnesses laid down their clothes at the feet of a young man named Saul.

a. **Then they cried out with a loud voice**: When Stephen declared that he saw Jesus *standing at the right hand of God*, it was too much. The Sanhedrin reacted quickly, violently, and together. When Jesus, before this same body of men, declared that He would sit at the right hand of God, they had the same reaction and sealed his death as a blasphemer (Matthew 26:64-66).

> i. "For Stephen to suggest that the crucified Jesus stood in a position of authority at the right hand of God must have ranked as blasphemy in the thinking of those who knew that a crucified man died under the divine curse." (Bruce)

b. **They cried out with a loud voice, stopped their ears, and ran at him with one accord**: These were distinguished, older men who did this. The reaction of the Sanhedrin seems extreme, but is typical of those who reject God and are lost in spiritual insanity. They wailed in agony and covered their ears at the revelation of God, which they regarded as blasphemy.

i. It is a dangerous thing to be religious apart from a real relationship with Jesus Christ. This fulfills what Jesus warned about in John 16:2-3: *Yes, the time is coming that whoever kills you will think that he offers God service. And these things they will do to you because they have not known the Father nor Me.*

c. **Ran at him**: This uses the ancient Greek word *hormao*. This is the same word used to describe the mad rush of the herd of swine into the sea (Mark 5:13). This was an out-of-control mob rushing at Stephen.

d. **They cast him out of the city and stoned him**: The extent of their rage was shown by their execution of Stephen, which was done without regard for Roman law, and which was performed according to traditional Jewish custom (stoning).

i. The second-century Jewish writing *Mishnah*, described the practice of stoning: "When the trial is finished, the man convicted is brought out to be stoned…When ten cubits from the place of stoning they say to him, 'Confess, for it is the custom of all about to be put to death to make confession, and every one who confesses has a share in the age to come'…Four cubits from the place of stoning the criminal is stripped…The drop from the place of stoning was twice the height of a man. One of the witnesses pushes the criminal from behind, so that he falls face downward. He is then turned over on his back. If he dies from this fall, that is sufficient. If not, the second witness takes the stone and drops it on his heart. If this causes death, that is sufficient; if not, he is stoned by all the congregation of Israel." (Cited in Bruce)

e. **And the witnesses laid down their clothes at the feet of a young man named Saul**: Saul stood there as the supervisor of the operation. As a member of the Sanhedrin, he had also approved of Stephen's execution.

i. **Young man** literally means, "a man in his prime." It certainly does not mean that Saul wasn't old enough to be a member of the Sanhedrin. In Acts 26:10, Paul says *I cast my vote against them*, and the plain implication was that he had a vote as a member of the Sanhedrin.

4. (59-60) Stephen's last words.

And they stoned Stephen as he was calling on *God* and saying, "Lord Jesus, receive my spirit." Then he knelt down and cried out with a loud

voice, **"Lord, do not charge them with this sin." And when he had said this, he fell asleep.**

a. **They stoned Stephen as he was calling on God and saying, "Lord Jesus, receive my spirit."** Stephen's life ended in the same way it had been lived: In complete trust in God, believing that Jesus would take care of him in the life to come.

i. "The fires… in the olden days never made martyrs; they revealed them. No hurricane of persecution ever creates martyrs; it reveals them. Stephen was a martyr before they stoned him. He was the first martyr to seal his testimony with his blood." (Morgan)

b. **Lord, do not charge them with this sin**: God answered Stephen's prayer, and used it to touch the heart of a man who energetically agreed with his stoning - even though the man didn't know the prayer was being answered. When we get to heaven, we should thank Stephen for every blessing brought through the ministry of Saul of Tarsus.

i. God heard Stephen's prayer, and Paul is the evidence of it. We have no idea how greatly God can use us in our times of suffering.

ii. Augustine said, "If Stephen had not prayed, the church would not have had Paul."

c. **Cried out with a loud voice, "Lord, do not charge them with this sin"**: Stephen displayed the same forgiving attitude that Jesus had on the cross (Luke 23:34). He asked God to forgive his accusers, and he made the promises loudly and publicly.

i. If the gospels contain that which Jesus *began* to do and to teach, they also only contain that which Jesus *began* to suffer. There was a sense in which Jesus suffered along with Stephen as he was martyred.

d. **He fell asleep**: The text describes the passing of Stephen as tenderly as possible. Instead of saying simply that he died, it says that he merely **fell asleep** – with the idea that he woke up in a much better world.

i. If Stephen **fell asleep**, the church had to wake up. "If there had been any rose-colored optimism about quickly winning the Jewish people to their Messiah, that was gone. The Church could not expect triumph without a bloody battle." (LaSor)

ii. Stephen wasn't a superman, but he was a man filled through all his being with the Holy Spirit. Many have little idea of how greatly they can be used of God as they walk in the power of the Holy Spirit.

Acts 8 - Philip and the Samaritans

A. Saul persecutes the church.

1. (1) The church is persecuted and scatters.

Now Saul was consenting to his death. At that time a great persecution arose against the church which was at Jerusalem; and they were all scattered throughout the regions of Judea and Samaria, except the apostles.

a. **Now Saul was consenting to his death**: In Philippians 3:6, Paul said of his life before Jesus that he was so zealous in his religious faith that he persecuted the church. Saul's supervision of the execution of Stephen was just one example of this persecution.

i. **Consenting** describes Saul's attitude, but the English translation probably isn't strong enough. The idea behind the ancient Greek word *suneudokeo* is "to approve, to be pleased with." Some people are reluctant persecutors, but Saul wasn't one of these; he took *pleasure* in attacking Christians.

ii. Saul of Tarsus – whom most of us know by his Roman name, Paul – later came to deeply regret this persecution of the church. He later wrote, *For I am the least of the apostles, who am not worthy to be called an apostle, because I persecuted the church of God* (1 Corinthians 15:9).

iii. Acts 26:11 described what perhaps Paul regretted most: *And I punished them often in every synagogue and compelled them to blaspheme; and being exceedingly enraged against them, I persecuted them even to foreign cities.* Paul may have suffered many sleepless nights thinking about those whom he *compelled…to blaspheme.*

b. **A great persecution arose against the church**: Stephen's death was only the beginning. The floodgates of persecution were now open against the Christians. Saul was only one of many persecutors of Christians.

104

i. This was the first persecution of the Christians as a whole. Before, the apostles had been arrested and beaten and persecuted; here, every believer was threatened with violence and perhaps death.

ii. On Sunday, January 8, 1956, on the shores of a lonely river deep in the jungles of Ecuador, natives murdered five missionaries who came to tell about Jesus. To many, this death seemed like a senseless tragedy. Many could only see five young missionaries who had their careers cut short or the five widows and fatherless children. But God did an amazing work through those five men, even in their deaths, and the blessing still reverberates through people like Elisabeth Elliot - one of the five women whose husband was murdered.

iii. In the same way, Stephen's death might seem sort of meaningless at first glance. His young ministry of power and eloquence was cut abruptly short. His ministry also seemed to end in failure - no one was immediately brought to faith, and all that came forth was more persecution against the church. But as always has been the case, the blood of the martyrs became the seed of the church.

c. **They were scattered throughout the regions**: Now the Christians were forced to do what they had been reluctant to do - get the message of Jesus out to the surrounding **regions**.

i. **Scattered**: According to Boice, there are two different words in the ancient Greek language for the idea of "scattered." One has the idea of scattering in the sense of making something disappear, like scattering someone's ashes. The other word has the idea of scattering in the sense of planting or sowing seeds. This is the ancient Greek word used here.

ii. In Acts 1:8 Jesus clearly told His followers to look beyond Jerusalem and bring the gospel to Judea, Samaria, and the whole world. But to this point, Jesus' followers had not done this.

iii. The resulting good of the spread of the gospel leads some to see this persecution as being the will of God. God can and will use pressing circumstances to guide us into His will. Sometimes we have to be shaken out of our comfortable state before we do what God wants us to do.

2. (2) The burial of Stephen.

And devout men carried Stephen *to his burial*, and made great lamentation over him.

a. **And devout men**: Seemingly, these Jews were horrified at Stephen's murder. Perhaps this was Luke's way of reminding us that not *all* Jewish people of that time were enemies of Christianity.

b. **Made great lamentation over him**: Since Jewish law prohibited open mourning for someone that had been executed, Luke's record suggests that these **devout men** publicly repented of Stephen's murder.

3. (3-4) Saul continues his persecution.

As for Saul, he made havoc of the church, entering every house, and dragging off men and women, committing *them* to prison. Therefore those who were scattered went everywhere preaching the word.

a. **He made havoc**: This uses an ancient Greek word that could refer to an army destroying a city or a wild animal tearing at its meat. He viciously attacked Christians, including **women**.

i. "Not only did he not spare the women, but he did not stop short of seeking - and securing - his victims' death (9:1; 22:4; 26:10)." (Stott)

ii. "The tense of that verb, whether 'ravage' or 'destroy,' is imperfect, which means that he ravaged it and kept on ravaging it." (Boice)

b. **Those who were scattered went everywhere preaching the word**: The end result was for the glory of God, because the persecution simply served to spread the message. We shouldn't think that those who left Jerusalem left as formal preachers. Most were "accidental missionaries" who talked about Jesus wherever they went.

i. "The statement that they *preached the word* is misleading; the Greek expression does not necessarily mean more than *shared the good news*." (Stott)

ii. We can be just like these early Christians. We can share the good news of what Jesus has done in our lives. Most people don't come to Jesus through a professional preacher or an evangelist; they come to Jesus through people just like us.

iii. "In every church where there is really the power of the Spirit of God, the Lord will cause it to be spread abroad, more or less. He never means that a church should be like a nut shut up in a shell; nor like ointment enclosed in a box. The precious perfume of the gospel must be poured forth to sweeten the air." (Spurgeon)

B. Philip preaches to the Samaritans.

1. (5-8) Philip brings the gospel to the Samaritans.

Then Philip went down to the city of Samaria and preached Christ to them. And the multitudes with one accord heeded the things spoken by Philip, hearing and seeing the miracles which he did. For unclean spirits, crying with a loud voice, came out of many who were possessed;

and many who were paralyzed and lame were healed. And there was great joy in that city.

a. **Philip**: Like Stephen, he was one of the men chosen to serve the church family in practical ways when the dispute regarding Hellenist widows arose (Acts 6:5). He was one of those forced to flee persecution (Acts 8:1), ending up in Samaria.

b. **Preached Christ to them**: After the Jews had rejected the gospel again, we see God extending the offer of salvation in Jesus out to other peoples, beginning with the Samaritans.

c. **The city of Samaria**: 600 years before this, the Assyrians conquered this area of northern Israel and deported all the wealthy and middle-class Jews from the area. Then they moved in a pagan population from afar. These pagans intermarried with the lowest classes of remaining Jews in northern Israel, and from these people came the Samaritans.

i. Generally speaking, the Jews of that day hated the Samaritans. They considered them compromising half-breeds who corrupted the worship of the true God. "There was deep-seated prejudice, amounting almost to hatred, standing between the Jews and the Samaritans." (LaSor)

ii. James and John (and the other disciples as well) once thought that the Samaritans were only good for being burned by God's judgment (Luke 9:51-56).

iii. Jesus' experience with the Samaritan woman at the well (John 4) and His story about the kindness of a Samaritan (Luke 10:25-37) illustrate the natural tension between the Jews and Samaritans of that time.

iv. Yet, Philip **preached Christ to them**. Because Jesus had worked in him there was no room for this kind of prejudice in his heart or mind. He wasn't a racist towards the Samaritans.

d. **Hearing and seeing the miracles which he did**: Philip came presenting the gospel, with signs and wonders following as an impressive confirmation. When the people found Jesus, **there was great joy in that city**.

i. Undoubtedly, one reason there was such fruit was that Jesus had sown the seed in Samaria during His ministry (John 4:1-26). Now Philip reaped the harvest.

ii. The **great joy in that city** came from great sorrow and pain in Jerusalem. It came from the reality of spiritual power (**the miracles which he did**). But it especially came as Philip **preached Christ to them**.

iii. "Beloved friends, I delight to preach to you all the doctrines which I find in God's Word; but I desire always to preach the person of Christ above the doctrine; the doctrine is but the chair in which Christ sits as a Prophet to instruct us." (Spurgeon)

2. (9-13) Simon the Sorcerer believes.

But there was a certain man called Simon, who previously practiced sorcery in the city and astonished the people of Samaria, claiming that he was someone great, to whom they all gave heed, from the least to the greatest, saying, "This man is the great power of God." And they heeded him because he had astonished them with his sorceries for a long time. But when they believed Philip as he preached the things concerning the kingdom of God and the name of Jesus Christ, both men and women were baptized. Then Simon himself also believed; and when he was baptized he continued with Philip, and was amazed, seeing the miracles and signs which were done.

a. **A certain man called Simon**: This Simon had a fair degree of local fame. He was honored as one who didn't only *have* the power of God; they said of him **"This man *is* the great power of God."**

b. **Who previously practiced sorcery**: In the Bible **sorcery** is associated with occult, magical practices – and often with the taking of mind and mood altering drugs. Whatever *real* power Simon had, it was from Satan, not God.

i. The specific wording indicates that Simon was a *magi*. In the ancient world there was a class of astronomers and scientists known as magi (Matthew 2:1), but local wizards and sorcerers also took the title. They used it to prey on the ignorance and superstitions of the common people.

ii. "Ramsay describes the magi (esp. the lower sort who appealed to the widespread superstition of the ancient world) as the strongest influence that existed in that world and one that must either destroy or be destroyed by Christianity." (Williams)

c. **And they heeded him because he had astonished them with his sorceries**: The Samaritans wrongly assumed that because Simon had *real* spiritual power, it was from God – yet that simply wasn't the case.

d. **But when they believed Philip as he preached the things concerning the kingdom of God and the name of Jesus Christ**: Those who had previously been **astonished** by Simon and **his sorceries** now **believed Philip** and what he preached. He brought the message of the gospel and they believed it.

i. Those who believed proclaimed their faith when they **were baptized**. "There is no hint of any deficiency in their faith. Certainly Philip recognized none, else he would not have baptized them." (Williams)

e. **Amazed, seeing the miracles and signs which were done**: Simon was convinced by Philip's preaching and amazing miracles, to the point where he declared belief, was baptized, and **continued with Philip**. Simon became a follower of Philip and his ministry.

i. At this point – up to Acts 8:13 – there is nothing to indicate that Simon's belief was false or insincere. Yet it will be tested by his conduct and response over time.

3. (14-17) The Samaritans receive the Holy Spirit as Peter and John lay hands upon them.

Now when the apostles who were at Jerusalem heard that Samaria had received the word of God, they sent Peter and John to them, who, when they had come down, prayed for them that they might receive the Holy Spirit. For as yet He had fallen upon none of them. They had only been baptized in the name of the Lord Jesus. Then they laid hands on them, and they received the Holy Spirit.

a. **They sent Peter and John to them**: When Jesus gave unto Peter (and the other apostles) the *keys of the kingdom of heaven* (Matthew 16:19) it was really for this purpose. Here they officially welcomed those (the Samaritans) who had previously been excluded from the people of God into the kingdom of God.

b. **For as yet He had fallen upon none of them**: Obviously, there was a subsequent experience with the Holy Spirit that these Samaritan believers did not know until the apostles came and ministered to them.

c. **They laid hands on them**: Often, the empowering and filling of the Holy Spirit is received as hands are laid on a person and prayer is offered for them (Acts 9:17, 1 Timothy 4:14, 2 Timothy 1:6). We should always be ready to receive whatever special graces and gifts God has to give us through the laying on of hands.

d. **They received the Holy Spirit**: We don't know exactly how this was evident. Perhaps certain spiritual gifts were manifested (1 Corinthians 12:7-10).

e. **Received the Holy Spirit**: The fact that these Christians received the Holy Spirit in what seems to be a subsequent experience to their salvation has caused much controversy; there have been different explanations offered.

i. Some say they were never truly born again (converted) under Philip's preaching. When Peter and John came, they really trusted in Jesus and then received the Holy Spirit.

ii. Some say they were truly born again. Then, in a subsequent experience, they received the Holy Spirit in a pattern that believers should follow today.

iii. Some say they were converted in response to Philip's preaching; yet God, in a unique move, withheld the gift of the Holy Spirit until Peter and John could bestow it on them. God's purpose in this was to ensure continuity between the church in Jerusalem and the new church in Samaria, guarding against division.

iv. Some say they were really born again and did really receive the Holy Spirit at the time of conversion, but were given special gifts and graces of the Holy Spirit at the laying on of hands by Peter and John.

v. The last option seems to best explain what happened. Whatever the Samaritans experienced, it seems to have been more than the "regular" bestowal of the Holy Spirit at salvation. This is a filling of the Holy Spirit we should always desire and seek.

4. (18-19) Simon's selfish request.

And when Simon saw that through the laying on of the apostles' hands the Holy Spirit was given, he offered them money, saying, "Give me this power also, that anyone on whom I lay hands may receive the Holy Spirit."

a. **When Simon saw that through the laying on of the apostles' hands the Holy Spirit was given**: Simon noticed that when Peter and John laid hands on the Samaritans and prayed for them, something happened. He was impressed by that something.

b. **He offered them money**: Simon thought that the Holy Spirit was merely a power that could be bought or sold. He wanted to control the working of the Spirit, and regarded the Holy Spirit as a power he could use as he wanted, instead of a *Person* who ruled his life.

i. *Simony* is the word for the sin of buying or selling church offices or privileges, because it is done in the same spirit as this **Simon**. This sin is sometimes practiced today; but more commonly people simply think that *blessing follows money* instead of *money following blessing*.

c. **That anyone on whom I lay hands may receive the Holy Spirit**: Simon did not really desire the Holy Spirit for himself, but the ability to impart the power of the Holy Spirit to others at his will. This would give him much spiritual authority.

> i. "The sin was a desire to possess spiritual power for personal ends." (Morgan)

5. (20-23) Peter's response to Simon.

But Peter said to him, "Your money perish with you, because you thought that the gift of God could be purchased with money! You have neither part nor portion in this matter, for your heart is not right in the sight of God. Repent therefore of this your wickedness, and pray God if perhaps the thought of your heart may be forgiven you. For I see that you are poisoned by bitterness and bound by iniquity."

a. **You thought the gift of God could be purchased with money!** Of course, Simon was wrong in this thought. The gifts of God are received freely from Him, by faith.

> i. As it says in Isaiah 55:1: *Ho! Everyone who thirsts, come to the waters; And you who have no money, come, buy and eat. Yes, come, buy wine and milk without money and without price.*

> ii. What we receive from God will effect what we do with our money; but we can't **purchase** the gifts of God with money.

b. **Your money perish with you**: Simon was *so* wrong that he deserved this strong rebuke. Phillips translates the phrase **your money perish with you** like this: *To hell with you and your money.*

> i. Peter's bold discernment must have been difficult or awkward to watch. Few today would rebuke what seemed to be a young Christian so strongly. Yet Peter was willing to tell Simon the truth in love, though it was hard for Simon and those standing by to hear it.

c. **You have neither part nor portion in this matter, for your heart is not right in the sight of God**: Peter's rebuke to Simon doesn't exactly answer an important and interesting question – was Simon a true Christian, genuinely born again?

> i. Simon gave many evidences of conversion – at least to outward observation.

> - Simon expressed belief in the preaching of Philip (Acts 8:13).
> - Philip received Simon as a kind of follower (Acts 8:13).
> - Simon attended meetings of Christians (Acts 8:18).

> ii. For all these reasons, Philip regarded Simon as a Christian – a follower of Jesus – and baptized him (Acts 8:13). Like us today,

Philip could not actually see into Simon's spiritual heart and know with complete certainty that he was sincere in his faith; but he had demonstrated enough to make his proclamation of faith credible.

iii. Yet, it is possible to take Peter's statement "**You have neither part nor portion in this matter, for your heart is not right in the sight of God**" as evidence that Simon was not a true convert with repentance and sincere faith. His case is then "a warning to anybody who thinks that just because he or she has made a profession of faith or has gone through certain motions expected of Christians that he or she is right with God for that reason. That is not the case." (Boice)

iv. "Men may come very near, they may be intellectually convinced of the supremacy of Jesus; they may even decide that they will adopt His ethical ideal; they may go so far as to determine that they will imitate the perfection of His example. But these things do not make men Christians." (Morgan)

v. At the same time, Boice observed: "When Peter says, 'You have no part or share in this ministry,' it is interesting that he employs the same words Jesus used for him when Peter had objected to Jesus' washing his feet in the Upper Room. Jesus said, 'Unless I wash you, you have no part with me' (John 13:8). Strong words. Still Peter was not an unbeliever; he was just out of the will of God." (Boice)

vi. Without doubt, Simon was headed in the wrong direction, so he needed this rebuke. One could say that he was headed towards hell, from the phrase "**Your money perish with you.**"

d. **Poisoned by bitterness and bound by iniquity**: This accurately described Simon's heart. Yet Peter didn't attempt to cast a demon of bitterness or iniquity out of him. Instead, Peter called him to repentance (**Repent therefore**), to prayer (**pray God**), and to righteousness (dealing with **the thought of your heart**).

i. Perhaps *pride* prevented Simon from a genuine belief in Jesus. Before the coming of Philip and the gospel, Simon was an admired holy man in the region, and had been admired *for a long time* (Acts 8:11), so much so that people declared, "*This man is the great power of God*" (Acts 8:10). A proud person might give an outward display of faith because it is the "right" thing to do in the eyes of others, but in the secret place of their heart, they may fail to submit to Jesus Christ.

6. (24-25) Simon's reply and a summary of the work in Samaria.

Then Simon answered and said, "Pray to the Lord for me, that none of the things which you have spoken may come upon me." So when

they had testified and preached the word of the Lord, they returned to Jerusalem, preaching the gospel in many villages of the Samaritans.

a. **Pray to the Lord for me, that none of these things come upon me**: Instead of actually humbling his heart before God, Simon asked Peter to pray he would be spared the consequences of his sin. This shows Simon felt a true conviction of the Holy Spirit, but was not yet willing to humble his own heart before God. Peter couldn't humble Simon's heart for him.

> i. As bad as Simon's case was, he could still *repent therefore of this your wickedness, and pray God if perhaps the thought of your heart may be forgiven you* (Acts 8:22). The door of repentance and getting the heart right with God was open to Simon if he would only take it – but Peter could not do it for him.

> ii. "His words were what we would call in colloquial English 'a cop out.' He was refusing to do what he had been told he should do and was passing the buck to Peter." (Boice)

> iii. The preacher can't believe for you, nor can he repent for you; he has enough repenting to do all on his own. The preacher can pray for you, but you better also pray for yourself – as Peter told Simon to do.

> iv. We don't know what became of Simon. We don't know if he followed through on the conviction of heart evident in Acts 8:24. Church tradition says he went off the deep end, and became a dangerous false teacher among the early Christians. It is possible that he did repent and get his heart right with God.

b. **When they had testified and preached the word of the Lord, they returned to Jerusalem**: Peter and John had a successful, fruitful ministry in Samaria. Yet they **returned to Jerusalem** instead of continuing to reach out beyond that city.

C. Philip preaches to the Ethiopian.

1. (26-28) Philip, led by the Holy Spirit, is directed to an Ethiopian government official.

Now an angel of the Lord spoke to Philip, saying, "Arise and go toward the south along the road which goes down from Jerusalem to Gaza." This is desert. So he arose and went. And behold, a man of Ethiopia, a eunuch of great authority under Candace the queen of the Ethiopians, who had charge of all her treasury, and had come to Jerusalem to worship, was returning. And sitting in his chariot, he was reading Isaiah the prophet.

a. **Arise, and go toward the south**: We might have thought that Philip would object to leaving the great success of the work in Samaria to go out to the desolate desert, but God had a plan in it all. Philip submitted to God's plan.

    i. "Philip was the front-line man. He seemed to be utterly indispensable. Yet it was at precisely this moment when God called him to leave the area." (Boice)

    ii. If one heard the call to leave such a blessed, fruitful ministry, one likely would think it was the devil speaking and not the Lord. One might think, "Not now" or "Not me" or "Not there."

b. **This is desert**: Leaving fruitful ministry to go to a **desert** is foolish from man's perspective, but wise if directed by God. What could be more foolish than to leave a place of prospering ministry and go to a desert road?

    i. "There were two roads from Jerusalem to Gaza, and the Spirit commands Philip to take the one that was seldom used." (MacArthur)

    ii. "If Christ is hindered, it is because some Philip is not willing to go!" (Morgan)

    iii. "We have seen him, from the day of Pentecost on, moving on *multitudes*; we now trace his motions in the *individual*, and see him in his individual dealing and leading – observing how he guides *one believer* and leads *one inquirer*." (Pierson) Philip wasn't the only one being led by the Spirit. The man of Ethiopia was also, though he didn't yet know it.

c. **A man of Ethiopia…had come to Jerusalem to worship**: On the desert road, Philip encountered an Ethiopian proselyte to Judaism returning from Jerusalem - reading the Bible!

    i. This **Ethiopia** – much larger than modern-day Ethiopia – was the land where the Queen of Sheba came from, who saw the glory of Solomon's kingdom and professed faith in the God of Israel. It's possible that pieces of the Jewish faith were passed on through the centuries to men like this servant of the queen.

    ii. "He was a noble man on a noble search." (Hughes) We can't say if the Ethiopian found God in his visit to Jerusalem, but he certainly found the Word of God – and reading the Word of God would lead him to God.

d. **Of great authority…who had charge of all her treasury**: The Ethiopian was a successful man. Yet his success obviously didn't answer all the questions in his life. He knew he needed some real spiritual answers in his life, and he was seeking God.

i. **Candace** was the title for certain female royalty in Ethiopia.

e. **He was reading Isaiah the prophet**: The Ethiopian was hungry for God's Word. Typically, the scroll would cost him a lot of money, so it showed that he really wanted to read and know God's word.

2. (29-31) The Ethiopian invites Philip to explain the Bible.

Then the Spirit said to Philip, "Go near and overtake this chariot." So Philip ran to him, and heard him reading the prophet Isaiah, and said, "Do you understand what you are reading?" And he said, "How can I, unless someone guides me?" And he asked Philip to come up and sit with him.

a. **The Spirit said to Philip**: It took real boldness for Philip to go right up to the Ethiopian's chariot and speak to him, but that is what the Holy Spirit told him to do.

i. The Ethiopian was a rich man, a man of power, and at least in some way a celebrity. Yet Philip knew he needed Jesus just a much as anyone else. We should never fear speaking to those who are considered to be important people about Jesus.

ii. We often shrink back from speaking boldly about Jesus, and the world lets us know we shouldn't talk about such things. But the world does not hesitate to impose its own message on us. We should be just as bold to the world about Jesus as the world is bold to us about sin.

b. **Heard him reading**: It was common in the ancient world to read aloud. Philip knew what the Ethiopian was reading by listening as he read.

c. **Heard him reading the prophet Isaiah**: Philip knew at that moment that God had given him an open door, a prepared heart. Plainly, God had arranged this meeting between Philip and the Ethiopian; this is a wonderful example of how God opens doors for evangelism. God directed Philip because God had already arranged an open door.

i. One of our greatest jobs in preaching the gospel is to simply pray for open doors. Then, having prayed for open doors, we must keep alert to the opportunities God presents.

ii. Philip was effective as an evangelist because he knew how to flow with what the Holy Spirit wanted to do. He was truly led by the Spirit, not by his own whims and feelings.

d. **Do you understand what you are reading?** It was good for the Ethiopian to read the Bible, but unless **understanding** was brought to him, there was little benefit from his reading. But God had brought someone (Philip) to bring understanding.

i. "It was a good question – inoffensive, yet a subtle but gracious offer to explain the passage if the Ethiopian official was interested in receiving one." (Boice)

ii. **How can I, unless someone guides me?** This is the proper question of anyone who wants to understand the Bible. We should never feel bad if we need to be taught before we can understand many things.

iii. It is wonderful when we come to understand the great truths of Bible on our own, but God also has a place and a purpose for teachers among the followers of Jesus.

iv. To get more understanding from our Bibles, we must plunge in. Butterflies wander over the flowers in the garden and accomplish nothing, but bees plunge right down into the flower, and carry away essential food. We won't get anything if we just hover over our Bibles; we have to dive right in.

3. (32-35) Starting at the Isaiah passage, Philip preaches Jesus to the Ethiopian.

The place in the Scripture which he read was this:

"He was led as a sheep to the slaughter;
And as a lamb before its shearer *is* silent,
So He opened not His mouth.
In His humiliation His justice was taken away,
And who will declare His generation?
For His life is taken from the earth."

So the eunuch answered Philip and said, "I ask you, of whom does the prophet say this, of himself or of some other man?" Then Philip opened his mouth, and beginning at this Scripture, preached Jesus to him.

a. **He was led as sheep to the slaughter**: In God's wonderful planning, the Ethiopian was reading the amazing and specific prophecies in Isaiah 53 describing the sacrificial, sin-bearing work of the Messiah to come.

b. **I ask you, of whom does the prophet say this, of himself or of some other man?** Regarding this passage from Isaiah 53:7-8, the Jews of that day had different ways they understood the identity of this suffering servant.

• Some thought the suffering servant was the nation of Israel itself, as Israel had suffered greatly in wars, exile, and persecution.

• Some thought the suffering servant was Isaiah writing about himself.

- Some thought the suffering servant was the Messiah, but they found this hard to accept, because they didn't want to think of the Messiah suffering.

c. **Beginning at this Scripture**: Philip talked about more than this passage from Isaiah, but he started there. He began at common ground with the Ethiopian, but made his way to talking about Jesus. It was easy to talk about Jesus **beginning at this Scripture**.

i. Because the whole Bible points to Jesus in one way or another, we really can begin at any passage and find where it leads to Jesus.

d. **Preached Jesus to him**: Philip's effective preaching consisted in explaining *who Jesus was* (**like a lamb... preached Jesus**) and *what He has done for us* (**He was led as a sheep to the slaughter**). Explaining who Jesus is and what He has done for us is the essence of the gospel.

i. Too many preachers today focus on what we must do for God, but the gospel begins with and is founded upon what God has done for us in Jesus Christ.

ii. Philip preached Christ in Samaria (Acts 8:5) and he **preached Jesus to** this Ethiopian. We can be sure it was the same Jesus he preached in Jerusalem. He didn't need a different Jesus or a different message for different audiences.

4. (36-38) The Ethiopian believes and is baptized.

Now as they went down the road, they came to some water. And the eunuch said, "See, *here is* water. What hinders me from being baptized?" Then Philip said, "If you believe with all your heart, you may." And he answered and said, "I believe that Jesus Christ is the Son of God." So he commanded the chariot to stand still. And both Philip and the eunuch went down into the water, and he baptized him.

a. **And the Eunuch said**: The Ethiopian himself was ready to respond to the gospel. This was a work of the Holy Spirit, not a tribute to Philip's salesmanship.

b. **See, here is water. What hinders me from being baptized?** This shows that the Ethiopian did in fact believe, and that he wanted to be baptized to declare his belief. He saw the truth of God and knew that it was *for him*.

i. "Maybe Philip even ended his explanation of the gospel with an appeal for baptism like Peter did at Pentecost." (Hughes)

c. **If you believe with all your heart, you may**: Philip insisted that the Ethiopian **believe with all his heart** before being baptized. In a nutshell, this describes how we should respond to the gospel: **Believe with all your heart**.

i. The devil himself has the faith of the head, but he hates the truth in his heart. God wants His truth not only in our heads, but also in our hearts. We may intellectually know that Jesus died for the sins of the world, but do we know in our hearts that He died to cleanse *our* sins?

d. **I believe that Jesus Christ is the Son of God**: This confession of faith, taken in all that it means, is the essential belief for anyone who will come to God. We must believe in the *person* of **Jesus**, in all that He is and has done as **Christ**. We must believe that He is the Divine **Son**, and that He is the **Son of God** sent from the Father to accomplish the salvation of all those who will believe with all their hearts.

i. When the Ethiopian said "**Jesus Christ**," he confessed that Jesus is the Messiah (**Christ**). He agreed with his mind and heart that Jesus is the sin-bearing servant that Isaiah described and Jesus fulfilled.

e. **Went down into the water**: Clearly, Philip immersed the Ethiopian in baptism. This was not sprinkling, but immersion.

5. (39-40) Philip's mysterious departure.

Now when they came up out of the water, the Spirit of the Lord caught Philip away, so that the eunuch saw him no more; and he went on his way rejoicing. But Philip was found at Azotus. And passing through, he preached in all the cities till he came to Caesarea.

a. **The Spirit of the Lord caught Philip away, so that the eunuch saw him no more... Philip was found at Azotus**: Suddenly, the Spirit of the Lord carried Philip away as he and the Ethiopian came out of the water. He was then transported supernaturally in some way to the former Philistine city of **Azotus** (also known as Ashdod).

i. This is a strange, perhaps unprecedented event in the Scriptures. But a similar thing happened when the disciples' boat came immediately to its destination (John 6:15-21), and a similar thing will also happen when the church is *caught up together with Him* at the rapture (1 Thessalonians 4:15-18).

b. **He went on his way rejoicing**: The joy of the Ethiopian, even after Philip's strange departure, shows that his faith was firmly rooted in God, not in Philip.

i. The Coptic Christians – greatly persecuted today in Egypt – trace their spiritual heritage back to this Ethiopian official.

c. **Passing through, he preached in all the cities till he came to Caesarea**: This shows that Philip started preaching not only to Samaritan cities, but also the Gentile cities – such as Caesarea. This is the very beginning of the gospel's spread to the end of the earth – as Jesus commanded in Acts 1:8.

i. No wonder Philip is the only one in the New Testament specifically given the title, "The Evangelist" (Acts 21:8). Acts 21:8 finds him still in **Caesarea**, doing his work of evangelism there.

Acts 9 - The Conversion of Saul of Tarsus

A. Saul on the road to Damascus.

1. (1-2) Saul's purpose in traveling to Damascus.

Then Saul, still breathing threats and murder against the disciples of the Lord, went to the high priest and asked letters from him to the synagogues of Damascus, so that if he found any who were of the Way, whether men or women, he might bring them bound to Jerusalem.

a. **Then Saul**: We last saw Saul in Acts 8:3, where it says that *he made havoc of the church, entering every house, and dragging off men and women, committing them to prison*. Here he continued and expanded this work to the city of **Damascus** (about 130 miles or 210 kilometers northeast of Jerusalem; a six-day journey altogether).

i. **Still breathing threats and murder against the disciples of the Lord**: The picture is of an angry, violent man absolutely convinced of his own righteousness. Saul *hated* the **disciples of the Lord**. He wasn't seeking Jesus when Jesus sought him. We might say that Saul was decided *against* Jesus when Jesus decided *for* Saul.

ii. Of course, we don't know what **Saul** looked like. An old apocryphal book, dating to the end of the first century, described Paul like this: "A man of moderate stature, with crisp hair, crooked legs, blue eyes, large knit brows, and long nose, at times looking like a man, at times like an angel." (Cited in Gaebelein)

b. **Went to the high priest**: Saul did his persecuting work under the direct approval of the highest religious authorities. He **asked** and received **letters from** the high priest authorizing his mission.

i. The high priest mentioned here was Caiaphas. In December 1990 an ossuary (something like a burial urn; essentially a bone box) was discovered in Jerusalem. The ossuary was inscribed with the name of this Caiaphas and positively dated to this period. Inside were discovered some of the remains of a 60-year-old man, whom many researchers believe was this same Caiaphas. If true, these are the first physical remains (such as bones or ashes) of a specific person mentioned in the New Testament.

c. **Still breathing threats and murder**: Even after Saul became a Christian, he remembered his days as a persecutor. In Philippians 3, he made mention of this background, saying he was *circumcised the eighth day, of the stock of Israel, of the tribe of Benjamin, a Hebrew of the Hebrews; concerning the law, a Pharisee; concerning zeal, persecuting the church; concerning the righteousness which is in the law, blameless.*

i. In Galatians 1:13, Paul added more regarding his background: *For you have heard of my former conduct in Judaism, how I persecuted the church of God beyond measure and tried to destroy it. And I advanced in Judaism beyond many of my contemporaries in my own nation, being exceedingly zealous for the traditions of my fathers.*

ii. Saul of Tarsus – this highly educated man – thought that Christianity was both wrong and deceptive. Perhaps he took his example from Phineas, who in the Book of Exodus killed an immoral man and woman with a spear, and God honored his action by halting a plague. Maybe Saul thought he was trying to stop a plague of false religion.

d. **If he found any who were of the Way**: Here, Christianity is referred to as **the Way**. This seems to be the earliest name for the Christian movement, and a fitting one - used five times in Acts.

i. The name **the Way** means that Christianity is more than a belief or a set of opinions or doctrines. Following Jesus is a *way* of living as well as believing.

ii. It is significant to see that there was a Christian community large enough in Damascus for Saul to be concerned about. Christianity – **the Way** – was spreading everywhere.

2. (3-6) God meets Paul on the road to Damascus.

As he journeyed he came near Damascus, and suddenly a light shone around him from heaven. Then he fell to the ground, and heard a voice saying to him, "Saul, Saul, why are you persecuting Me?" And he said, "Who are You, Lord?" Then the Lord said, "I am Jesus, whom you are persecuting. It *is* hard for you to kick against the goads." So he, trembling and astonished, said, "Lord, what do You want me to do?" Then the Lord *said* to him, "Arise and go into the city, and you will be told what you must do."

a. **Suddenly a light shone around him from heaven... and heard a voice**: Somewhere outside of Damascus, this **suddenly** happened. This spectacular event must be regarded as unusual. God does not *normally* confront sinners with a heavenly light and an audible voice from heaven.

i. In Acts 22:6 Paul revealed that this happened at mid-day, when the sun shines at its brightest. Yet Paul said that this light was *brighter than the sun* (Acts 26:13).

b. **Then he fell to the ground**: Saul's reaction was simply to fall **to the ground**. This wasn't because of honor or reverence for God, it was simply a reaction of survival - he was terrified at the heavenly light.

i. In the minds of many or most people, Saul fell from a horse that he rode. Yet this account in Acts 8, nor the telling in Acts 22:3-11, nor the account of Acts 26:12-20 make any mention of a horse or of Saul riding any kind of animal. It *may be* that he rode, but the text does not specifically say so.

ii. "Many persons suppose he was on horseback, and painters thus represent him; but this is utterly without foundation. Painters are, in almost every case, wretched commentators." (Clarke)

iii. "It is significant in so short a book attempting to cover the expansion of Christianity from its small beginnings in Jerusalem to a religion that filled whole empire that the tale of one man's conversion should be so greatly emphasized." (Boice)

c. **And heard a voice saying to him**: According to F.F. Bruce, the rabbis of Saul's day mostly believed that God no longer spoke to man directly, as He did in the days of the prophets. However, they believed that one could hear the "echo" of God's voice, what they called "the daughter of the voice of God." Here, Saul learned that one can hear God directly.

d. **Saul, Saul**: When God repeats a name twice, it is to display deep emotion, but not necessarily anger (as in the *Martha, Martha* of Luke 10:41 and the *Jerusalem, Jerusalem* of Matthew 23:37).

e. **Why are you persecuting Me?** As the heavenly light overwhelmed him, Saul was confronted by the true nature of his crime: He persecuted *God*, not *man*.

i. Saul thought that he was serving God in viciously attacking Christians, but he discovered that he was fighting God.

ii. This has been sadly true through history. Often those who are convinced they are doing God a favor do much of the worst persecution and torture ever practiced.

iii. We shouldn't only emphasize the "**Me**" in the phrase "**why are you persecuting Me**." We should also notice the "**why**" and see that Jesus asked "*why* **are you persecuting Me?**" That is, "Saul, why are you doing such a futile thing?"

f. **I am Jesus**: Though Jesus was a fairly common name in that day, the ascended Jesus of Nazareth needed no further identification. When He said, "**I am Jesus**," Saul knew *exactly* which Jesus spoke. In all probability, Saul heard Jesus teach in Jerusalem; and as a likely member of the Sanhedrin, Saul sat in judgment of Jesus in the trial before His crucifixion.

i. "Unless Saul was hallucinating, the appearance of Jesus proved that Jesus was alive and that Jesus was God." (Boice)

g. **Who are You, Lord?... Lord, what do You want me to do?**: Saul responded with two of the most important questions anyone can (and must) ask.

i. Most everyone has questions they would like to ask God. A Gallup Survey from the 1990s asked people to choose three questions they would most like to ask God. The top five responses were:

- "Will there ever be lasting world peace?"
- "How can I be a better person?"
- "What does the future hold for my family and me?"
- "Will there ever be a cure for all diseases?"
- "Why is there suffering in the world?"

It is strange that people would want to ask God these questions when they are already answered in the Bible. But they really aren't the most important questions for us to ask. Saul asked the *right* questions.

ii. **Who are You, Lord?** We must ask this question with a humble heart, and ask it to God. Jesus showed us exactly who God is, and He can answer this question. Paul spent the rest of his life wanting to know more completely the answer to this question (Philippians 3:10).

iii. **What do You want me to do?** Few dare to really ask God this question, but when we ask it, we must ask it with submission and determined obedience.

iv. Saul's question was *personal*. He asked the question with a "**me**": "**Lord, what do You want me to do?**" We often are quite interested in what God wants others to do. But the surrendered heart asks, "**Lord, what do You want *me* to do?**"

h. **It is hard for you to kick against the goads**: This statement from Jesus was actually a small parable regarding Saul and his life.

i. The insertion of **it is hard for you to kick against the goads** and **Lord, what do You want me to do?** in Acts 9:5-6 is accurate, but not in Luke's original text. They were added by scribes, based on Acts 22:10 and 26:14, who thought they were doing God a favor by putting it in here.

ii. A goad was a long, extremely sharp stick used to get an ox going the way you wanted when plowing. One jabbed the hind legs of the ox with the goad until the ox cooperated.

iii. Essentially, Saul was the ox; Jesus was the farmer. Saul was stupid and stubborn - yet valuable, and potentially extremely useful to the Master's service. Jesus goaded Saul into the right direction, and the goading caused Saul pain. Yet instead of submitting to Jesus, Saul kicked against the goad - and only increased his pain.

iv. It is not too much to say that if we will not ask these two great questions and obediently listen to God's answers to these questions, then we are acting like stupid oxen.

v. We may complain that God compares us to oxen, and indeed it is an unfair comparison. After all, what ox has ever rebelled against God as we have? God almost owes an apology to oxen!

vi. Something was goading his conscience. Despite all his outward confidence, there was something bothering him inside. He kicked against it to be sure, but it was still there. The unease may have started with Stephen's prayer (Acts 7:57-60).

i. **It is hard for you**: This shows the great love of Jesus. He was the persecuted one, yet His concern was for the effect it had on Saul. What a tender heart Jesus has!

j. **So he, trembling and astonished**: The fact that Saul was **trembling and astonished** by all of this reminds us that it is not always pleasant to encounter heaven dramatically. Saul was terrified by this experience; not oozing with warm, gushy feelings.

i. In Acts 9, we are only given the briefest account of what happened here. We know more from what Paul says about this experience in Acts 22:3-11, Acts 26:12-18, 1 Corinthians 9:1 and 15:8. We also know more from what Barnabas said about Saul's experience in Acts 9:27 and from what Ananias said about Saul's experience in Acts 9:17. From these accounts, we learn that Jesus appeared to Saul *personally* in this blinding vision.

ii. In response to this light, Saul undoubtedly shut his eyes as tight as he could; yet, Jesus still appeared before him. After the same pattern, Jesus has often had to appear to us even though we shut our eyes.

iii. In this encounter with Jesus, Saul learned the gospel that he would preach his whole life. He insisted in Galatians 1:11-12, *that the gospel which was preached by me is not according to man. For I neither received it from man, nor was I taught it, but it came through the revelation of Jesus Christ.*

k. **Lord, what do You want me to do?** When Saul asked this question, Jesus only told him what to do right at that moment.

i. This is often the character of God's direction in our lives. He directs us one step at a time instead of laying out the details of the grand plan all at once.

3. (7-9) Saul immediately after the Damascus road.

And the men who journeyed with him stood speechless, hearing a voice but seeing no one. Then Saul arose from the ground, and when his eyes were opened he saw no one. But they led him by the hand and brought *him* into Damascus. And he was three days without sight, and neither ate nor drank.

a. **The men who journeyed with him stood speechless**: The experience was incomprehensible to Saul's companions, but as Saul opened his eyes (presumably shut tight in a terrified reaction to the heavenly light), he still could not see (**when his eyes were opened he saw no one**).

i. We can almost hear God saying to Saul, "You shut your eyes against My light and My Savior. Fine! Spend a few days as blind physically as you have been blind spiritually!"

b. **And he was three days without sight, and neither ate nor drank**: It seems that Saul was so shaken by the experience that he was unable to eat or drink for three days. All Saul could do was simply sit in a blind silence. This was a humbling experience, and a time when Saul must have challenged all his previous ideas about who God was and what pleased God.

i. In the **three days** of blindness and deprivation, Saul was dying to himself. It would only be after the **three days** of dying that he would receive resurrection life from Jesus.

B. God ministers to Saul through Ananias.

1. (10-12) God's message to Ananias.

Now there was a certain disciple at Damascus named Ananias; and to him the Lord said in a vision, "Ananias." And he said, "Here I am, Lord." So the Lord *said* to him, "Arise and go to the street called Straight, and inquire at the house of Judas for *one* called Saul of Tarsus, for behold, he is praying. And in a vision he has seen a man named Ananias coming in and putting *his* hand on him, so that he might receive his sight."

a. **Now there was a certain disciple at Damascus named Ananias**: We don't know anything about Ananias from either before or after this meeting with Saul. We don't know how he came to **Damascus**, or what happened to him afterward. From what we do know we can think of him as an average follower of Jesus – **a certain disciple**.

i. Ananias was an ordinary man - not an apostle, a prophet, a pastor, an evangelist, an elder, or a deacon. Yet God used him because he was an ordinary man. If an apostle or a prominent person had ministered to Saul, people might say Paul received his gospel from a man instead of Jesus. In the same way, God *needs* to use the **certain disciple** - there is a special work for them to do.

ii. In theory, it wasn't absolutely necessary that God use a man like Ananias for this work in Saul's life. Being simply **a certain disciple**, we can say that God simply used **Ananias** because because God loves to use people, and Ananias was a willing servant. Ananias asked Saul's question, *"Lord, what do You want me to do?"* (Acts 9:6) by the way he lived his life.

b. **To him the Lord said in a vision**: God spoke to Ananias in a completely different way than He spoke to Saul. Saul had a bold, almost violent confrontation from God, but Ananias heard the voice of God sweetly in a vision, where God called and Ananias obediently responded. To say, **"Here I am, Lord"** is a perfect response to God.

i. We shouldn't be surprised if people like Saul receive the God's Word with initial resistance and questioning. Yet we should expect disciples of Jesus to receive God's Word like Ananias did.

ii. In the case of Ananias, the vision from God was specific. God told him about:

- A specific street (**the street called Straight**).
- A specific house (**the house of Judas**).
- A specific man (**one called Saul of Tarsus**).
- A specific thing the man was doing (**he is praying**).

- A specific vision the man had (**in a vision he has seen a man named Ananias**).

This specificity was necessary and important, because God asked Ananias to do something bold and dangerous in meeting Saul, the great persecutor. He needed confirmation along the way that God was guiding him, and God gave him ways to confirm this.

c. **Arise and go**: God's instructions to Ananias were clear, but curiously, God told Ananias about Saul's vision in Ananias' own vision.

d. **Behold, he is praying**: This indicated a true change of heart in this man famous for persecuting the disciples of Jesus. One might say that Saul had never *really* prayed before; he merely repeated formal prayers. Before this:

- His prayers were more mechanical than spiritual.

- He had never prayed with Jesus as mediator.

- He had never prayed in Jesus' name.

- He had not prayed with a humble heart, near to God.

Saul had said many prayers, but he had never truly *prayed*.

2. (13-16) God overcomes Ananias' objections.

Then Ananias answered, "Lord, I have heard from many about this man, how much harm he has done to Your saints in Jerusalem. And here he has authority from the chief priests to bind all who call on Your name." But the Lord said to him, "Go, for he is a chosen vessel of Mine to bear My name before Gentiles, kings, and the children of Israel. For I will show him how many things he must suffer for My name's sake."

a. **Lord, I have heard from many about this man**: Certainly, Ananias had heard that this angry and violent persecutor named Saul of Tarsus was on his way from Jerusalem. The disciples in Damascus must have anxiously prepared for the coming persecution.

b. **I have heard from many about this man, how much harm he has done**: Ananias' objections were perfectly logical and well founded. However, they presumed that God needed instruction, or at best, counsel. Ananias almost asked, "God, do you know what kind of guy this Saul is?"

i. In fact, Ananias knew a great deal about the mission of Saul (**how much harm he has done to Your saints in Jerusalem…here he has authority from the chief priests to bind all who call on Your name**). It was apparently widely known.

c. **He is a chosen vessel of Mine to bear My name**: God had a call upon the life of Saul. At this time, God had not yet revealed that calling to Saul. He seems to have told Ananias first.

i. God considered Saul His **chosen vessel** long before there appeared anything worthy in Saul to choose. God knew what *He* could make of Saul, even when Saul or Ananias didn't know.

d. **To bear My name before Gentiles, kings, and the children of Israel**: This describes in broad outline the calling and future work of the broken, blind, afflicted man Ananias would soon meet. God called him to bring who He is and what He has done (**My name**) to **Gentiles**, to **kings**, and to **the children of Israel**.

i. We would not blame Ananias for a measure of disbelief – such a great, big calling for such an unlikely man.

e. **For I will show him how many things he must suffer for My name's sake**: This was a sobering addition to the great call God put upon the life of Saul. Saul would leave a life of privilege to embrace a higher call, but a call with much suffering.

3. (17-19) Ananias prays and Saul is healed and receives the Holy Spirit.

And Ananias went his way and entered the house; and laying his hands on him he said, "Brother Saul, the Lord Jesus, who appeared to you on the road as you came, has sent me that you may receive your sight and be filled with the Holy Spirit." Immediately there fell from his eyes *something* like scales, and he received his sight at once; and he arose and was baptized. So when he had received food, he was strengthened. Then Saul spent some days with the disciples at Damascus.

a. **Ananias went his way and entered the house**: This took great courage. In the centuries since, Christians have had to deal with those who make pretended conversions to infiltrate the followers of Jesus. Ananias had to overcome this fear or suspicion.

b. **Laying his hands on him he said, "Brother Saul"**: The act of **laying his hands** and the words **"Brother Saul"** powerfully communicated the love of God. Blind Saul could not see the love on Ananias' face, so he communicated it through his touch and his voice.

c. **Be filled with the Holy Spirit**: It seems that this is when Saul was actually born again. Here is where he received the Holy Spirit and was healed from his blindness, which was spiritual blindness as much as physical blindness.

i. **Be filled**: God did an effective job of breaking Saul, but it wasn't His intention to leave him broken. God wanted to break Saul so He could fill him and leave him filled.

ii. "It is often said that Saul was converted on the road to Damascus. Strictly speaking, this is not the fact. His conversion began in his encounter with the law but it was not accomplished until the gospel entered his heart by faith, and that did not occur on the road, but in Damascus." (Lenski)

d. **He received his sight at once; and he arose and was baptized**: When Saul could see – both physically and spiritually – he immediately wanted to identify with Jesus and with the disciples of Jesus by being **baptized**.

i. We are not told that Ananias told Saul about baptism. Perhaps he did; but it is just as likely (or even more likely) that Saul had seen Christian baptisms (such as on Pentecost, Acts 2:41). Especially, *God spoke directly to Saul* about many things during his time waiting for Ananias, including even the name of the man who would come and pray for him and restore his sight (Acts 9:12).

e. **When he had received food, he was strengthened**: Saul immediately began to be strengthened both physically and spiritually. God was concerned about both areas of need.

f. **Then Saul spent some days with the disciples at Damascus**: Saul was now numbered among the **disciples** of Jesus, and became friends with those he had previously tried to imprison or kill. This shows the remarkable, radical nature of his transformation.

i. Paul regarded his conversion experience as a pattern for all believers: *Although I was formerly a blasphemer, a persecutor, and an insolent man; but I obtained mercy because I did it ignorantly in unbelief… However, for this reason I obtained mercy, that in me first Jesus Christ might show all longsuffering, as a pattern to those who are going to believe on Him for everlasting life.* (1 Timothy 1:13,16).

ii. If Paul's conversion is a pattern, then we can share his experiences. First, Jesus must confront us with Himself, with our sin and rebellion against Him, even the sins done in ignorance. Then as we put our faith in Him, we must humbly wait for the work within us that only He can do.

iii. Saul's conversion reminds us that at its core, salvation is something God does in us. What we do is only a response to His work in us.

iv. Saul's conversion reminds us that God finds some who, by all appearance, are not looking for Him at all. Seeing how God reached

Saul encourages us to believe that God can reach the people in our life that we think are very far from Him. We often give up on some people and think they will *never* come to Jesus; but the example of Saul shows God can reach *anyone*.

v. Saul's conversion reminds us that God looks for people to cooperate in the conversion of others, even when they are not really necessary, except as a demonstration of the importance of the *family* of God.

vi. Saul's conversion reminds us that it isn't enough that we be broken before God, though that is necessary. God wants to only use brokenness as a prelude to filling.

C. Saul's initial ministry in Damascus and Jerusalem.

1. (20-22) Saul preaches powerfully in Damascus.

Immediately he preached the Christ in the synagogues, that He is the Son of God. Then all who heard were amazed, and said, "Is this not he who destroyed those who called on this name in Jerusalem, and has come here for that purpose, so that he might bring them bound to the chief priests?" But Saul increased all the more in strength, and confounded the Jews who dwelt in Damascus, proving that this *Jesus* is the Christ.

a. **Immediately he preached the Christ in the synagogues**: Because Saul was a skilled student of the great rabbi Gamaliel, he took advantage of the synagogue custom that invited any able Jewish man to speak from the Scriptures at synagogue meetings. He took advantage of this opportunity **immediately**.

b. **He preached the Christ**: The message of Saul was all about Jesus. He knew they needed to know Jesus in truth, **that He is the Son of God**.

i. Many people think when Jesus is called **the Son of God** it is a way of saying He is *not* God, but something less than God – only "the son of God." But in Jesus' day, everyone knew what this title meant. To be called the "son of" something meant you were totally identified with that thing or person, and their identity was your identity. When Jesus called Himself *the Son of God*, and when others called Him that, it was understood as a clear claim to His deity.

ii. In fact, on two occasions when Jesus called Himself *the Son of God*, He was accused of blasphemy, of calling Himself God (John 5:17-18, Matthew 26:63-65). Everybody knew what Jesus meant in calling Himself *Son of God*, and everyone knew what Saul meant when he preached that Jesus is the **Son of God**.

iii. To preach that Jesus **is the Son of God** is also to preach the perfection of His life, and especially His work for us on the cross. It is to preach how God saves us through the work of Jesus.

c. **Is this not he who destroyed those who called on this name**: People were genuinely amazed at Saul's conversion; it was hard to believe just how powerfully Jesus could change a life. Years later, Paul himself would write: *Therefore, if anyone is in Christ, he is a new creation; old things have passed away; behold, all things have become new.* (2 Corinthians 5:17) Paul *lived* that verse long before he *wrote* it.

d. **Saul increased all the more in strength**: Saul's early work for God so soon after his conversion should not surprise us. Often, that is the *best* time to serve the Lord, and especially to tell others about Jesus. When we are newly converted, we still understand the way people who don't yet know Jesus think.

i. It is true that young Christians shouldn't hastily be put in positions of authority in the church (1 Timothy 3:6), but you don't need a position of authority to serve God and to tell others about Jesus.

ii. Saul's willingness to serve the Lord was a contributing factor in the fact he **increased all the more in strength**. As we seek to serve others, God brings more strength to us.

e. **Proving that this Jesus is the Christ**: Saul, an expert in the Old Testament, could easily see how Jesus was the Messiah promised in the Hebrew Scriptures.

2. (23-25) Saul's escape from Damascus.

Now after many days were past, the Jews plotted to kill him. But their plot became known to Saul. And they watched the gates day and night, to kill him. Then the disciples took him by night and let *him* down through the wall in a large basket.

a. **After many days were past**: In Galatians 1:13-18, Paul explained more about what happened during these **many days**. He described how he went to Arabia for a period of time, and then returned to Damascus. After his return to Damascus, he went to Jerusalem. Paul spent a total of three years in Damascus and Arabia (Galatians 1:18); truly these were **many days**.

i. In 2 Corinthians 11:32-33, Paul refered to this incident and mentions it happened *under Aretas the king*. This means that this escape from Damascus happened between A.D. 37 and 39. So, taking into account the three years mentioned in Galatians 1:18, and that this incident happened at the end of those three years, we can surmise that Paul was converted sometime between A.D. 34 and 36.

b. **The Jews plotted to kill him**: This essentially began the *many things he must suffer for My name's sake* the Lord spoke of in Acts 9:16. Saul now was the *persecuted* instead of the *persecutor*.

c. **But their plot became known to Saul**: If Saul now knew what it was to be persecuted for his faith, he also knew the mighty deliverance of God. Saul enjoyed divine protection until his ministry was complete before God.

d. **The disciples took him by night and let him down through the wall in a large basket**: Saul indeed knew divine protection in the midst of persecution, but he also learned that God's deliverance often comes in humble ways. There is nothing triumphant about sneaking out of a city **by night** hiding in **a large basket**.

i. "It was the beginning of many escapes for Paul, and sometimes he didn't quite escape. Sometimes they caught him, imprisoned him, beat him. He did indeed have to suffer many things for Jesus' sake." (Boice)

3. (26-30) Saul with the Christians at Jerusalem.

And when Saul had come to Jerusalem, he tried to join the disciples; but they were all afraid of him, and did not believe that he was a disciple. But Barnabas took him and brought *him* to the apostles. And he declared to them how he had seen the Lord on the road, and that He had spoken to him, and how he had preached boldly at Damascus in the name of Jesus. So he was with them at Jerusalem, coming in and going out. And he spoke boldly in the name of the Lord Jesus and disputed against the Hellenists, but they attempted to kill him. When the brethren found out, they brought him down to Caesarea and sent him out to Tarsus.

a. **He tried to join the disciples; but they were all afraid of him**: It seems strange that Christians in Jerusalem were so suspicious of Saul even three years after his conversion. They perhaps thought that Saul was part of an elaborate and extended plot; they perhaps wondered why he went off by himself for a while in Arabia; or just as likely, they probably were reluctant to embrace such a dramatic conversion without seeing it with their own eyes. Simply, they **did not believe that he was a disciple**.

i. At this point, some people might turn their back on Jesus Christ. They might say, "I've been serving the Lord for three years, preaching Jesus Christ, enduring assassination attempts and death threats. Now you don't want to accept me as a Christian? This is the love of Jesus? Forget it!"

ii. But Saul had a greater heart of love for Jesus and Jesus' followers. It no doubt hurt, but he understood that the disciples in Jerusalem remembered the Christians Saul killed and persecuted. If the disciples in Jerusalem lacked a little in love, Saul added a little more love to make up for it.

b. **But Barnabas took him and brought him to the apostles**: Thank God for people like Ananias and Barnabas, who will welcome people into the family of God with simple friendship.

i. Barnabas simply extended the love of Jesus to Saul, and as Paul would write later, *love believes all things* (1 Corinthians 13:8).

c. **He was with them at Jerusalem, coming in and going out**: In Galatians 1:18, Paul wrote that in this first trip to Jerusalem, he stayed with Peter for fifteen days. He also wrote that he never had an audience with *all* the apostles, seeing only Peter and James, Jesus' brother.

i. This time with the apostles in Jerusalem was important, because it finally and certainly welcomed Saul into the family of the followers of Jesus. But Paul made a point of the limited nature of his time with the apostles in Jerusalem to show clearly that he did not receive his gospel from the other apostles. Though he was no doubt blessed and benefited from that time, he received his message by direct revelation from Jesus on the road to Damascus. Luke alluded to this when he wrote that Saul, speaking to the apostles, **declared to them…what He had spoken to him**. The apostles no doubt rejoiced that they and Saul and the exact same message from Jesus.

d. **He spoke boldly in the name of the Lord Jesus… but they attempted to kill him**: Saul again faced persecution and assassination attempts. This became a recurring pattern in his life.

i. The story of Saul's conversion begins with him leaving Jerusalem to persecute the followers of Jesus. It ends with him leaving Jerusalem as a persecuted follower of Jesus.

e. **They brought him down to Caesarea and sent him out to Tarsus**: For his own protection, the Christians in Jerusalem **sent him out to Tarsus**. Somewhere between 8 and 12 years passed in the life of Saul before he again entered into prominent ministry, being sent out as a missionary from the church at Antioch. At that time, it would also be **Barnabas** who reached out to Saul, remembering him and loving him.

i. He was Saul of Tarsus, the young, successful, energetic rabbi. Then he was Saul the Persecutor; then Saul the Blind. He became Saul the Convert and then Saul the Preacher. Yet before he became Paul the Apostle, he spent somewhere between 8 and 12 years as Saul the unknown. Those were not wasted years; they were good and necessary years.

ii. **Tarsus** was one of the great cities of the ancient world, with an excellent harbor and a strategic placement at trade routes. It was especially known as an university city, being one of the three great educational cities of the Mediterranean world. "Strabo speaks of the Tarsian university as even surpassing, in some respects, those of Athens and Alexandria (*Geography* 14.5.13). It was especially important as a center of Stoic philosophy" (Williams)

4. (31) The health of the churches in the whole region.

Then the churches throughout all Judea, Galilee, and Samaria had peace and were edified. And walking in the fear of the Lord and in the comfort of the Holy Spirit, they were multiplied.

a. **The churches throughout all Judea, Galilee, and Samaria**: Acts 9 began with a zealous man *breathing threats and murder against the disciples of the Lord* (Acts 9:1). But God was more than able to turn this terrible threat into a great blessing. Now Luke shows that God's work not only continued but it was *strong*, despite the great opposition that came against it.

b. **Galilee**: The Book of Acts tells us nothing about the planting of churches in Galilee. We don't know who started these churches, how they did it, or all the great works of God which took place in these young churches. This reminds us that Acts is only a *partial* history of God's work during this period.

c. **The churches... had peace**: This doesn't mean that all persecution had stopped; instead, it means that they had peace in the midst of persecution.

i. At the end of Acts 9:31, we reach an important historical crossroads in Acts and the events of the Roman Empire. In A.D. 37, Caiaphas was replaced as high priest, first by Jonathan, then by Theophilus. In the same year, Caligula succeeded Tiberius as Roman Emperor. Caligula was bitterly hostile against the Jews and was assassinated four years later.

d. **The churches... were edified**: The word **edified** has the idea of *being built up*. The churches were growing in numbers and strength.

e. **And walking in the fear of the Lord and in the comfort of the Holy Spirit, they were multiplied**: Whenever God's people are **walking in the fear of the Lord and in the comfort of the Holy Spirit**, you may expect that they will also see their numbers **multiplied**.

i. **The fear of the Lord...the comfort of the Holy Spirit**: Each of these are needed in the Christian walk. At any given moment a disciple of Jesus may more need **the fear of the Lord** or **the comfort of the Holy**

Spirit. Often, God wants the comfortable to be afflicted (gaining **the fear of the Lord**) and the afflicted to be comforted (by **the comfort of the Holy Spirit**).

ii. **In the comfort of the Holy Spirit**: Pierson points out that the word translated **comfort** here is essentially the same word translated *Helper* or *Comforter* in John 14:16 (*paraclesis*).

iii. "Is it not already but too evident that the church of our day has little or no conception of the pricelessness of blessing involved in this paraclesis of the Spirit? What if once more this lesson could be learned? What 'rest' would the church have from internal dissension and division, from heresy and schism! What edification, 'being built up' on the most holy faith! What holy 'walking in the fear of the Lord,' what rapid multiplication, and what world-wide evangelization! There is not an evil now cursing or threatening our church life which this 'comfort of the Holy Ghost' would not remedy and perhaps remove." (Pierson)

D. God works miracles through the apostle Peter.

1. (32-35) Peter heals Aeneas at Lydda.

Now it came to pass, as Peter went through all *parts of the country*, that he also came down to the saints who dwelt in Lydda. There he found a certain man named Aeneas, who had been bedridden eight years and was paralyzed. And Peter said to him, "Aeneas, Jesus the Christ heals you. Arise and make your bed." Then he arose immediately. So all who dwelt at Lydda and Sharon saw him and turned to the Lord.

a. **Peter went through all parts of the country**: The previous pattern of the apostles staying put in Jerusalem and those needing ministry coming from afar to them (as reflected in Acts 5:16) now shifted. Peter **went through all parts of the country** to do ministry, traveling the 35 miles (55 kilometers) from Jerusalem to **Lydda**.

i. Lydda is near modern day Lod, the site of Ben Gurion Airport outside of Tel Aviv.

b. **There he found a certain man**: Peter found a needy man God wanted to miraculously heal, and Peter found him as he was out ministering to others in the name of Jesus. If we will be like Peter, who **went through all parts of the country**, then we will also find opportunities for the miraculous power of God.

c. **Aeneas, Jesus the Christ heals you**: Peter clearly identified who healed – **Jesus the Christ**. Peter was only His instrument. Jesus healed with the power of Jesus, but Peter did not heal with the power of Peter. Peter relied solely on the power of Jesus.

i. The words of Peter – **"Arise and make your bed"** – were perhaps consciously an imitation of Jesus' healing of the paralytic man in Mark 2:10-12.

d. **So all who dwelt at Lydda and Sharon saw him and turned to the Lord**: The miraculous healing of Aeneas made many people turn **to the Lord** – presumably, with Peter preaching the gospel to them.

2. (36-38) Dorcas from Joppa dies.

At Joppa there was a certain disciple named Tabitha, which is translated Dorcas. This woman was full of good works and charitable deeds which she did. But it happened in those days that she became sick and died. When they had washed her, they laid *her* in an upper room. And since Lydda was near Joppa, and the disciples had heard that Peter was there, they sent two men to him, imploring *him* not to delay in coming to them.

a. **Named Tabitha, which is translated Dorcas**: Both the names **Dorcas** and **Tabitha** mean "deer." This woman was a beloved member of the Christian community in Joppa, because she **was full of good works and charitable deeds**.

i. Luke noted that Tabitha **was full of good works and charitable deeds which she did**. Some people are **full of good works and charitable deeds**, but they are only full of them in their minds and hearts. They don't actually do them as Tabitha did. This is why Luke added, **which she did**.

b. **Imploring him not to delay in coming to them**: Peter wasn't in Joppa when Tabitha died. Yet he wasn't far away, and the Christians in Joppa had heard that God was doing miraculous things through Peter in nearby Lydda. They begged Peter to come, perhaps asking when Dorcas was still alive or had just died.

3. (39-42) Dorcas is raised from the dead.

Then Peter arose and went with them. When he had come, they brought *him* to the upper room. And all the widows stood by him weeping, showing the tunics and garments which Dorcas had made while she was with them. But Peter put them all out, and knelt down and prayed. And turning to the body he said, "Tabitha, arise." And she opened her eyes, and when she saw Peter she sat up. Then he gave her *his* hand and lifted her up; and when he had called the saints and widows, he presented her alive. And it became known throughout all Joppa, and many believed on the Lord.

a. **Peter arose and went with them**: When the disciples from Joppa came to Peter in Lydda, they came with the hope that Peter would help her, or at least help the Christian community at that place work through their grief.

i. There is no indication in the Book of Acts that it was *common* or *popularly expected* that dead Christians would be resuscitated to life again. This miracle (and a few similar in Acts) is listed just because they were unusual and remarkable.

b. **All the widows stood by him weeping**: It may very well be that the expectation was that Peter would merely comfort these Christian widows and others in their grief over Dorcas' death. Yet Peter sensed a specific leading to do just as he had seen Jesus do as recorded in Mark 5:38-43 – he **put them all out**, in the anticipation that God would do for Tabitha what He did for the daughter of the ruler of the synagogue.

c. **Tabitha, arise**: Peter seemed to clearly remember what Jesus did in Mark 5:38-43 (or Luke 8:50-56). In that healing, Jesus said, "*Talitha, cumi.*" Peter said here (in the original language) "Tabitha cumi." Peter could hear Jesus' words in his head as he ministered.

i. Peter simply tried to do as Jesus did. Jesus was his leader. He wasn't trying to lead Jesus anymore, as he did when he told Jesus not to go the way of the cross in Matthew 16:22. Now Peter was letting Jesus lead him.

d. **And she opened her eyes, and when she saw Peter she sat up**: By all appearances, Tabitha was raised from the dead. She was dead and came back to life. These are remarkable, unusual miracles – yet things that have happened and still do (though one is wise to not gullibly accept every reported instance of such).

i. We should remind ourselves that Dorcas was not *resurrected*; she was *resuscitated* to her old life, where she would die again.

ii. The fact that the Lord raised Dorcas, yet Stephen (and later, James in Acts 12:2) remained dead, reflects on God's unknowable ways. After all, it certainly seemed that Stephen and James were more important to the church than Dorcas. Yet we must always trust God's greater wisdom and knowledge in all such things.

iii. Dorcas wasn't raised for her own sake. She would have enjoyed heaven better! She was raised for the sake of her ministry to others, which is the same reason we have *passed from death into life* (John 5:24).

e. **When he had called the saints and widows**: Acts 9:32 and 41 mention the **saints** in Lydda and Joppa. This is the first time Christians are called saints in Acts. When the Bible calls Christians **saints**, the idea isn't of a super-perfect people; the idea is of a people who are *different*. Saints are set apart from the world at large; they are distinctive.

4. (43) Peter stays with Simon, a tanner.

So it was that he stayed many days in Joppa with Simon, a tanner.

a. **He stayed many days in Joppa with Simon, a tanner**: This sentence would be somewhat shocking to an observant Jew of that time. According to their understanding of the law, it was strictly forbidden to associate with anyone who routinely worked with dead animals.

i. According to the laws of that time, a tanner had to live at least 75 feet (25 meters) outside a village because of his constant ritual uncleanness.

ii. "The trade of a tanner was held in such supreme contempt that if a girl was betrothed to a tanner without knowing that he followed that calling, the betrothal was void." (Morgan)

b. **He stayed many days in Joppa with Simon, a tanner**: Because of this, we see Peter was becoming less concerned about Jewish traditions and ceremonial notions than before. This work of God in Peter's heart laid groundwork for what God would do in Peter in the following chapter.

Acts 10 - Cornelius, Peter, and the Conversion of Gentiles

A. God speaks to Cornelius about Peter.

1. (1-2) Cornelius, a Gentile who served God.

There was a certain man in Caesarea called Cornelius, a centurion of what was called the Italian Regiment, a devout *man* and one who feared God with all his household, who gave alms generously to the people, and prayed to God always.

a. **A certain man in Caesarea**: Caesarea was a predominately Roman city on the shores of the Mediterranean in Judea. It was the headquarters of the Roman governor of the province of Judea. Archaeologists have discovered a stone from a building in Caesarea inscribed with the name *Pontus Pilate*.

b. **Cornelius, a centurion of what was called the Italian Regiment**: Cornelius was an officer in the Roman Army. A patriotic Jew of that day would naturally dislike or even hate him.

i. "Thirty-two such Italian cohorts were stationed in the different provinces of the empire. They were made up of Italian volunteers and were considered the most loyal Roman troops." (Lenski) Because he was such a loyal servant of the oppressors of Israel, most every patriotic Jewish person of that day would naturally be prejudiced against Cornelius.

c. **A devout man and one who feared God**: Yet, Cornelius was **a devout man**; a man **who feared God**, who **prayed to God always** and who **gave alms generously** to those who were in need.

i. "As a typical Roman he had been exposed to the Roman gods – Jupiter, Augustus, Mars, Venus, etc. – but found they had been exposed to the enlightened concepts of Judaism and had become devoutly monotheistic." (Hughes)

ii. Cornelius was in the category of what the Jews called *God-fearers* (**one who feared God**). These were Gentiles who loved the God of Israel; they were sympathetic to and supportive of the Jewish faith. Yet they stopped short of becoming full Jews in lifestyle and in circumcision.

iii. Jewish people of that time respected and appreciated these God-fearing Gentiles, but they could not really share their life and homes and food with them, because they were still in fact Gentiles and not full Jewish converts.

d. **And prayed to God always**: Because of the way the life and heart of Cornelius is described, we see a man who obviously had a real relationship with God. At the same time, he was not a part of the mainstream of Jewish life.

2. (3-6) God sends an angel to tell Cornelius to get Peter.

About the ninth hour of the day he saw clearly in a vision an angel of God coming in and saying to him, "Cornelius!" And when he observed him, he was afraid, and said, "What is it, lord?" So he said to him, "Your prayers and your alms have come up for a memorial before God. Now send men to Joppa, and send for Simon whose surname is Peter. He is lodging with Simon, a tanner, whose house is by the sea. He will tell you what you must do."

a. **About the ninth hour of the day he saw clearly in a vision**: We are not told specifically here that Cornelius was praying, but it was the **ninth hour** (3:00 in the afternoon). This was a customary time of prayer for Jews. Also, as Cornelius related the incident to Peter in Acts 10:30, he specifically said he was praying (*at the ninth hour I prayed in my house*).

b. **He saw clearly in a vision an angel of God**: This was not a dream, nor did it actually happen. This was **a vision** that came in the "mind's eye" of Cornelius. At the same time, it was so vivid that Cornelius would later say, *a man stood beside me in bright clothing* (Acts 10:30).

c. **Cornelius!** It is significant that God spoke to Cornelius directly, even calling him by name. It is also significant that Cornelius responded with a healthy fear of the heavenly and holy (**he was afraid**). This shows that Cornelius had a real relationship with God.

d. **Send for Simon whose surname is Peter**: Probably, Cornelius didn't even know who Peter was. But he knew that he should do what God told him to do, and he could trust that God was speaking to this one named **Peter** also (**He will tell you what you must do**).

e. **He will tell you what you must do**: God sent an angel in a vision to Cornelius, but He used a *man* to preach the gospel to him.

i. "Angels may help to connect men with God's appointed preachers, they are never allowed to do more." (Lenski)

3. (7-8) Cornelius obeys God's command and sends for Peter.

And when the angel who spoke to him had departed, Cornelius called two of his household servants and a devout soldier from among those who waited on him continually. So when he had explained all *these* things to them, he sent them to Joppa.

a. **Cornelius called two of his household servants and a devout soldier**: Apparently, the faith of Cornelius was contagious and there were those of his **household** and under his command who also honored the God of Israel.

B. Peter's vision of the great sheet.

1. (9-10) Peter on Simon the Tanner's housetop.

The next day, as they went on their journey and drew near the city, Peter went up on the housetop to pray, about the sixth hour. Then he became very hungry and wanted to eat; but while they made ready, he fell into a trance.

a. **As they went on their journey and drew near the city, Peter went up on the housetop to pray**: As God spoke to Cornelius, and as Cornelius sent the messengers to call Peter, God also spoke to Peter himself.

i. Typically, this is how God operates. He speaks to several people about a matter, not just one. Then confirmation is provided, and out of the mouth of two or three witnesses a word is established.

ii. "Two men are thirty miles apart. They must be brought together. In order that they may meet, while Joppa is busy with its trade, and Caesarea with its great shipping interests, and will know nothing of what is going on; God within the shadows keeping watch above His own, sends the angel to Caesarea, and grants the ecstatic trance in Joppa. They were thus brought together." (Morgan)

b. **Peter went up on the housetop to pray**: In that culture, the **housetop** was normally used as a sort of patio. There was nothing strange about Peter going **up on the housetop to pray**.

c. **Then he became very hungry**: This often happens during prayer; distractions in our body come as we try to direct ourselves to God. However, God used these very distractions to speak to Peter, as **he fell into a trance**.

2. (11-16) Peter's vision.

And saw heaven opened and an object like a great sheet bound at the four corners, descending to him and let down to the earth. In it were all kinds of four-footed animals of the earth, wild beasts, creeping things, and birds of the air. And a voice came to him, "Rise, Peter; kill and eat." But Peter said, "Not so, Lord! For I have never eaten anything common or unclean." And a voice *spoke* to him again the second time, "What God has cleansed you must not call common." This was done three times. And the object was taken up into heaven again.

a. **All kinds of four-footed animals of the earth, wild beasts, creeping things, and birds of the air**: Peter saw all sorts of kosher and non-kosher animals prominently displayed on a sheet-like background (**a great sheet bound at the four corners**). Then, Peter heard a command: **Rise, Peter, kill and eat**.

i. When Peter *became very hungry and wanted to eat* during prayer, he no doubt regarded it as a distraction. Yet, God used it by speaking to him through a vision regarding food. His hunger perhaps made him pay more attention!

b. **A voice came to him**: We don't know exactly what this was like for Peter. It is rare for God to speak in an audible voice. More often, God speaks to our inner man. As a vision can be "seen" by the "mind's eye," even so we can "hear" the voice of God with the "mind's ear."

i. "God does not need sound waves to fall on an ear drum to speak to a man. When it pleases him to do so, he can speak directly to one's mind where all sound waves are finally interpreted." (Lovett)

c. **Rise, Peter, kill and eat**: This obviously went against Peter's commitment as a Jew, which was to never eat anything except kosher foods. Certainly, among the **all kinds of four-footed animals of the earth, wild beasts, creeping things, and birds of the air** there were non-kosher animals included.

d. **Not so, Lord!** Peter's response was both absurd and yet typical of us. He said *"no"* to his **Lord**. The only legitimate answer to a request from our **Lord** is *"yes."*

i. Peter had a bad habit of telling Jesus "no" (Matthew 16:22, John 13:8). Compare Peter's response to God (**Not so, Lord!**) with Cornelius' response to God (*What is it, Lord?*). On that day, it seemed that Cornelius was more responsive to God than Peter was.

ii. Peter had pretty much put God in a box of limitations, and now God was going to shake Peter up to change his thinking. He can do the same for us. "Shake yourself up a little, my brother. If you are too precise may the Lord set you on fire, and consume your bonds of red tape! If you have become so improperly proper that you cannot commit a proper impropriety, then pray God to help you be less proper, for there are many who will never be saved by your instrumentality while you study propriety." (Spurgeon)

iii. Peter was saved, Peter was filled with the Holy Spirit, and Peter had been greatly used by God. At the same time, Peter was still Peter. God didn't use him because he was perfect, but because he was in the right direction and he was available. We often fall into the trap of thinking that we must be perfected until God can really use us.

e. **And a voice spoke to him again the second time**: God responded clearly to Peter. **What God has cleansed** (declared clean) **you must not call common** (impure, unholy, unacceptable to God).

i. In Old Testament thinking, there was the *holy* and the **common**. The *holy* was made **common** when it came into contact with something common, and could only be made *holy* again through a ritual cleansing. When something was made holy it was called *consecration*; when it was made common it was called *desecration*.

ii. At this point, Peter believed that God spoke only about food. But shortly, God showed Peter that He was really getting at another point.

f. **This was done three times**: For deep emphasis, God repeated this vision three times. Peter was to regard this as important.

i. "By the time the drama had been acted out the third time, Peter must have begun to get the idea that God was trying to tell him something, even though he did not know exactly what it was." (Boice)

3. (17-20) God makes Peter aware of the arrival of the messengers from Cornelius.

Now while Peter wondered within himself what this vision which he had seen meant, behold, the men who had been sent from Cornelius had made inquiry for Simon's house, and stood before the gate. And they called and asked whether Simon, whose surname was Peter, was lodging there. While Peter thought about the vision, the Spirit said to him, "Behold, three men are seeking you. Arise therefore, go down and go with them, doubting nothing; for I have sent them."

a. **Now while Peter wondered within himself what this vision which he had seen meant**: When the vision ended, Peter did not have it all figured out. That came in time, and it came as God spoke to Peter through the visitors just arriving at his door.

b. **The Spirit said to him**: Previously, in Acts 10:13 and 10:15, it was simply said that a *voice* spoke to Peter. Now, we are told that **the Spirit** spoke to Peter. This was God, in the person of the Holy Spirit, speaking to Peter.

c. **Three men are seeking you…go down and go with them, doubting nothing, for I have sent them**: At this point, God *has not* told Peter that his visitors were Gentiles. Normally, a godly Jew like Peter would not associate in this manner with Gentiles. Knowing this, and knowing Peter's previous resistance (*Not so, Lord!*), God simply surprised Peter with the knowledge that these men were Gentiles. All Peter needed to know was that the Spirit said, "**I have sent them.**"

4. (21-23) Peter goes with the messengers back to Caesarea to see Cornelius.

Then Peter went down to the men who had been sent to him from Cornelius, and said, "Yes, I am he whom you seek. For what reason have you come?" And they said, "Cornelius *the* centurion, a just man, one who fears God and has a good reputation among all the nation of the Jews, was divinely instructed by a holy angel to summon you to his house, and to hear words from you." Then he invited them in and lodged *them*. On the next day Peter went away with them, and some brethren from Joppa accompanied him.

a. **Then Peter went down to the men who had been sent to him from Cornelius**: Peter must have been shocked when he opened the door and saw two servants and a soldier (Acts 10:7) at his door. He would have known immediately that they were not Jews, and he would have wondered why God told him to go with them and why God had sent them.

   i. The idea that God could send and use Gentiles was entirely new to Peter. God was expanding Peter's mind and heart.

b. **To summon you to his house, and to hear words from you**: The messengers from Cornelius come with an invitation. Peter was to go to the house of Cornelius, who wants **to hear words from you**. Of course, this was an invitation Peter couldn't pass up - or could he?

   i. A Gentile - worse yet, an officer in the Roman army - wanted to hear the gospel from Peter. Peter never did anything like this before! How will he respond?

c. **Then he invited them in and lodged them**: We can see the change in Peter's heart by the way **he invited them in and lodged them**. **Lodged them** is literally "to entertain as a guest." Peter didn't just coldly give these Gentiles visitors a room; he entertained them as welcomed guests, and he did this against every custom of the Jewish people of that day.

i. "Normally a Jew would have said, 'Well, it is nice to meet you, but we need to stay out here in the street. You can't come inside.' Or he might have said, 'If you go down the street a little way, I think you'll find an inn where you can stay.' No orthodox Jew would have invited Gentiles into his house. He would not have sat down at the same table with them. He would not have had fellowship with them. It was forbidden." (Boice)

ii. By entertaining these Gentile guests, Peter went against the customs and traditions of Israel, but not against God's Word. Possibly, at this very moment, God flooded Peter's heart with an understanding that though the Old Testament said God's people were not to become like their pagan neighbors, it also said God wanted His people to become a light to their neighbors who didn't know the true God.

iii. "I think angels watched that house that night, with the despised tanner a fellow-disciple, the great apostle, the three Gentiles as they lodged there." (Morgan)

d. **On the next day Peter went away with them**: Peter reached out in love to his Gentile neighbors, in obedience to what God told him to do.

i. **Some brethren from Joppa accompanied him**: "I suppose he anticipated what was to happen and the misunderstanding and opposition that would result, and he judged that whatever God was leading him into it would be good to have some of the other Jews along to verify the outcome." (Boice)

ii. "Centuries ago another Jew had come to Joppa with a solemn message from his God, which he was commissioned to bear far hence to the Gentiles. Jonah, the prophet, took a ship from Joppa and refused obedience to the divine call." (Gaebelein)

iii. Jonah ran from God's call, thinking he could get away from the Lord, and he did not share God's heart for the lost. Peter was willing to re-examine his traditions and prejudices in light of God's word, and he shared God's heart for a lost world. Some are more like Peter, some more like Jonah.

C. The meeting between Cornelius and Peter.

1. (24-26) Peter comes to Cornelius' house.

And the following day they entered Caesarea. Now Cornelius was waiting for them, and had called together his relatives and close friends. As Peter was coming in, Cornelius met him and fell down at his feet and worshiped *him*. But Peter lifted him up, saying, "Stand up; I myself am also a man."

a. **Cornelius was waiting for them**: Cornelius had a lot of faith in God. He waited for Peter to come, knowing that since God motivated him to call Peter in the first place, God would bring the plan to completion.

i. Cornelius sent servants to get a man he had never met, so that he could meet this unknown man. He only knew that the man was a pious Jew, who by tradition would have nothing to do with a Gentile such as Cornelius. Despite all that, **Cornelius was waiting for them** in faith.

b. **Cornelius met him and fell down at his feet and worshipped him**: Cornelius didn't know Peter, but must have thought him to be a special man of God, so he **fell down at his feet and worshipped him**. This reaction was understandable, though wrong. Peter corrected Cornelius by saying, **"Stand up; I myself am also a man."** If Cornelius should not give such reverence to Peter, neither should Peter receive it.

i. Significantly, whenever in the Bible worship is offered to men or to angels (as in Revelation 19:10), it is refused. But Jesus received such worship freely (Matthew 8:2; 9:18; 14:33; 15:25; 28:9). This proves that Jesus is more than a man, and greater than any angel (Luke 4:8).

ii. In the great St. Peter's Cathedral in Rome, there is a huge statue of Peter, where people come and kiss the toe of the statue. This is undue and inappropriate reverence towards any man or angel. We might almost wish that Peter would visit the cathedral named after him and kindly correct such people.

iii. Peter and Cornelius honored each other. Peter honored Cornelius by coming all the way from Joppa to see him. Cornelius honored Peter by bowing low before him. They did just as Paul would later write, *in honor giving preference to one another* (Romans 12:10).

iv. "Peter refused both to be treated by Cornelius as if he were a god, and to treat Cornelius as if he were a dog." (Stott)

2. (27-29) Entering Cornelius' house, Peter explains why he came.

And as he talked with him, he went in and found many who had come together. Then he said to them, "You know how unlawful it is for a Jewish man to keep company with or go to one of another nation. But God has shown me that I should not call any man common or unclean. Therefore I came without objection as soon as I was sent for. I ask, then, for what reason have you sent for me?"

a. **He went in**: This is one of the shortest, yet most important passages of this section. Peter actually entered the house of a Gentile, something that Jewish customs and traditions strictly prohibited. By entering a Gentile's home, Peter showed that his heart and mind had changed, and that he had learned the lesson of the vision of the great sheet.

i. "The principle subject of this chapter is not so much the conversion of Cornelius as the conversion of Peter." (Stott)

b. **Then he said to them**: Peter had to explain why he, a godly Jew (who was also a Christian) had entered a Gentile's house. So, he explained the message he received in the vision, realizing that God wasn't only (or even primarily) talking about food in the vision (**I should not call any man common or unclean**).

i. In saying **"I should not call any man common or unclean,"** Peter understood that the vision was about people, not food. But the principle still relates to food. We understand believers are not under any obligation to keep a kosher diet. How we eat may be better or worse from a health perspective, but it doesn't make us any more right with God.

ii. Jesus spoke of this principle: *Do you not perceive that whatever enters a man from outside cannot defile him, because it does not enter his heart, but his stomach, and is eliminated, thus purifying all foods?* (Mark 7:19).

iii. Paul knew this principle: *I know and am convinced by the Lord Jesus that there is nothing unclean of itself* (Romans 14:14). Therefore he could conclude, *Therefore let no one judge you in food or in drink… which are a shadow of things to come, but the substance is of Christ* (Colossians 2:16-17).

iv. Yet the connection between unclean persons and unclean foods was important. The idea of unkosher *food* was closely connected to the idea of unkosher *people*. "It was largely because of their lack of scruples in food matters that Gentiles were ritually unsafe people for a pious Jew to meet socially." (Bruce)

c. **Therefore I came**: This confirmed it. If Peter had not received this vision, he would have never traveled with these Gentile messengers. God had to prepare Peter's heart with the vision before Peter would come.

3. (30-33) Cornelius explains why he sent for Peter.

So Cornelius said, "Four days ago I was fasting until this hour; and at the ninth hour I prayed in my house, and behold, a man stood before me in bright clothing, and said, 'Cornelius, your prayer has been heard, and your alms are remembered in the sight of God. Send therefore to Joppa and call Simon here, whose surname is Peter. He is lodging in the house of Simon, a tanner, by the sea. When he comes, he will speak to you.' So I sent to you immediately, and you have done well to come.

Now therefore, we are all present before God, to hear all the things commanded you by God."

a. **I prayed in my house**: Undoubtedly, Cornelius prayed either generally to draw closer to God, or specifically that God would send the Messiah. God would answer this prayer through the gospel Peter brought to Cornelius.

b. **I was fasting**: The *intensity* of his prayer was evident. He sought after God so intensely that for a time, food became less important. He sought God diligently and God revealed Himself to Cornelius.

c. **Cornelius, your prayer has been heard and your alms are remembered in the sight of God**: It is interesting to note that though Cornelius was not a Christian in the sense that he was not yet regenerated or born again, yet in this case God **heard** his prayers and **remembered** his generosity to others.

d. **Now therefore, we are all present before God, to hear all the things commanded you by God**: Peter was living a preacher's dream. His audience was attentive and well-prepared by the Holy Spirit.

i. The message Peter was about to preach had great *preparation*. Peter was prepared by the Holy Spirit, and those at Cornelius' house were prepared to hear the message Peter brought. Our blessing is greatly increased when we prepare ourselves to hear the word of God.

ii. "When you go to church, do you want to receive a good message? If so, the best way is to come with a prepared heart. I know that the preacher must be prepared too. But when God prepares the messenger as well as those who are to hear him, then tremendous things happen." (Boice)

4. (34-43) Peter's short sermon to the Gentiles at Cornelius' house.

Then Peter opened *his* mouth and said: "In truth I perceive that God shows no partiality. But in every nation whoever fears Him and works righteousness is accepted by Him. The word which *God* sent to the children of Israel, preaching peace through Jesus Christ–He is Lord of all–that word you know, which was proclaimed throughout all Judea, and began from Galilee after the baptism which John preached: how God anointed Jesus of Nazareth with the Holy Spirit and with power, who went about doing good and healing all who were oppressed by the devil, for God was with Him. And we are witnesses of all things which He did both in the land of the Jews and in Jerusalem, whom they killed by hanging on a tree. Him God raised up on the third day, and showed Him openly, not to all the people, but to witnesses chosen before by God, *even* to us who ate and drank with Him after He arose from the

dead. And He commanded us to preach to the people, and to testify that it is He who was ordained by God *to be* Judge of the living and the dead. To Him all the prophets witness that, through His name, whoever believes in Him will receive remission of sins."

a. **In truth I perceive that God shows no partiality**: This is the foundation for Peter's understanding that the gospel should now go forth to Gentiles. This statement goes completely against the prevailing Jewish thought at that time that God certainly *did* show partiality, towards the Jews and against the Gentiles. In essence, many Jews of Peter's day thought that God loved the Jews while hating the Gentiles.

i. According to William Barclay, it was common for a Jewish man to begin the day with a prayer thanking God that he was not a slave, a Gentile, or a woman. A basic part of the Jewish religion in the days of the New Testament was an oath that promised that one would never help a Gentile under any circumstances, such as giving directions if they were asked. But it went even as far as refusing to help a Gentile woman at the time of her greatest need - when she was giving birth - because the result would only be to bring another Gentile into the world.

ii. If a Jew married a Gentile, the Jewish community would have a funeral for the Jew and consider them dead. It was thought that to even enter the house of a Gentile made a Jew unclean before God. Ancient Jewish writings tell us of a Gentile woman who came to a rabbi. She confessed that she was a sinner and asked to be admitted to the Jewish faith. "Rabbi," she said, "bring me near." The Rabbi refused and simply shut the door in her face.

iii. But the Gentiles could give as bad as they got from the Jews. Gentiles despised Jews as weird traditionalists, and believed that they were evil plotters who worshipped pigs. After all, they thought, Jews refused to eat pork, so they must worship pigs!

iv. All of this changed with the spread of the gospel. Christianity was the first religion to disregard racial, cultural and national limitations.

v. When the Jews showed this kind of partiality they were not being faithful to God's heart as revealed in the Old Testament. The idea that God shows no partiality is also stated in Deuteronomy 10:17 and 2 Chronicles 19:7: *For the L*ORD *your God is God of gods and Lord of lords, the great God, mighty and awesome, who shows no partiality nor takes a bribe* (Deuteronomy 10:17).

b. **But in every nation whoever fears Him and works righteousness is accepted by Him**: Peter's point was not to imply that men like Cornelius were already right with God and don't need to become Christians. Instead, the point is that they need not feel excluded from God because of their national background.

> i. We often think God sees color; He only sees the heart. God does not see economic status; He only sees the heart. He doesn't see nationality or ethnic group; He only sees the heart.

c. **He is Lord of all**: This is a powerful phrase, showing the deity of Jesus. Peter could never say this if Jesus were not (and is not) God. Furthermore, **He is Lord of all** – meaning both Jew and Gentile.

d. **Whom they killed by hanging on a tree…Him God raised up on the third day**: Notably, Peter's preaching to the Gentiles was essentially the same as his preaching to the Jews. He presented the person and work of Jesus Christ, with an emphasis on the resurrection of Jesus and our responsibility before God in light of these things.

> i. Peter didn't have one sermon for one group and another sermon for another. *All* people needed to be saved by coming to a living faith in a living Jesus Christ.

> ii. Peter's sermon was a wonderful (if brief and perhaps condensed by Luke) explanation of the person and work of Jesus of Nazareth:

> * Jesus was baptized in identification with humanity.
> * Jesus was anointed with the Holy Spirit and with power.
> * Jesus went about doing good and healing, delivering those oppressed by the devil.
> * Jesus did this with the power of God, for God was with Him.
> * Jesus did these things in the presence of eyewitnesses.
> * Jesus was crucified.
> * Jesus rose from the dead, resurrected in view of many witnesses.
> * Jesus commanded His followers to preach the message of who He is and what He did.
> * Jesus is ordained by God to be Judge of the entire world.
> * Jesus is the one foretold by the prophets.

> iii. **Even to us who ate and drank with Him after He arose from the dead**: "Peter stresses eating and drinking with Christ because that is a way of saying that Christ's was a real resurrection." (Boice)

iv. **He commanded us to preach to the people, and to testify that it is He who was ordained by God to be Judge of the living and the dead**: "The apostle was not long in his address before he came to the doctrine of the judgment of all men by Jesus Christ. He says that he was commanded to preach it, and therefore he did preach it." (Spurgeon)

e. **Whoever believes in Him will receive remission of sins**: The brief sermon concluded with an understanding of the *broadness* of God's promise of salvation. Note it carefully: **Whoever believes**! Jew or Gentile; slave or free; white or black; good or wicked; rich or poor – **whoever believes**.

5. (44-48) God-fearing Gentiles are filled with the Holy Spirit and baptized.

While Peter was still speaking these words, the Holy Spirit fell upon all those who heard the word. And those of the circumcision who believed were astonished, as many as came with Peter, because the gift of the Holy Spirit had been poured out on the Gentiles also. For they heard them speak with tongues and magnify God. Then Peter answered, "Can anyone forbid water, that these should not be baptized who have received the Holy Spirit just as we *have*?" And he commanded them to be baptized in the name of the Lord. Then they asked him to stay a few days. *United Pentecostal Church*

a. **While Peter was still speaking these words**: Salvation came when each one of these Gentiles responded to Peter's message with believing faith in their hearts, so that they were actually born again as they listened and believed. "Oh that the Spirit of God would in the same manner interrupt us!" (Spurgeon)

i. While listening to Peter, these people made a *secret* and *invisible* transaction in their hearts with God, by setting their faith in Jesus Christ.

ii. The moment of a person's salvation isn't necessarily when they raise a hand or come forward at an evangelistic invitation. It is more likely at the moment they surrender to God and embrace with trust Jesus in the sincerity of their hearts.

iii. Peter allowed the Holy Spirit to interrupt his sermon. The Holy Spirit was doing the greater work in the hearts of those listening, and Peter went with the flow. He stopped and called for their baptism.

iv. These were likely not the first Gentiles to trust in Jesus and be born again. Gentiles had probably received salvation in the eight years since Pentecost (Acts 2). But those Gentiles were saved as they embraced

Judaism as well as Christianity. Gentiles may have received salvation before this, but they were saved as Jews, not as Gentiles.

v. All before this, a Gentile could certainly trust in Jesus as Messiah and receive the forgiveness of sins that Jesus won for them at the cross. Yet in doing so, he would first have to become a Jew – and then continue on in the Jewish ritual law. They would wear certain coverings for their head in church, they would eat only kosher foods, they would make pilgrimages to Jerusalem for the feasts, and they would observe dozens of ceremonial laws and rituals.

b. **The Holy Spirit fell upon all those who heard the word... they heard them speak with tongues and magnify God**: Their filling with the Holy Spirit was accompanied by the demonstration of spiritual gifts. This was a filling with the Holy Spirit in two senses: First, in the sense that He indwells and abides in every believer; second, in the sense of a special empowering with gifts and graces from the Holy Spirit.

i. When they spoke with tongues, it was to **magnify God**, not to teach men. The audience was God, not man, as is consistent with the principle of 1 Corinthians 14:2.

ii. This was unique. It was not common in the Book of Acts or in subsequent Christian experience for those who were not previously converted (born again) to instantly be born again and receive such evident spiritual gifts. Yet it was good and even necessary on this occasion, to show that they received *the exact same Spirit, the exact same blessing* as the apostles and first followers of Jesus did on the morning of Pentecost (Acts 2).

iii. "The Gentiles are brought into an exactly parallel position, not merely with normal Jews (or even Samaritans) who had believed on Jesus, but with the apostles themselves." (Boice)

c. **Those of the circumcision who believed were astonished**: The Jewish Christians present were amazed. They may have understood that God was now starting to love the Gentiles, but who would have thought God would fill Gentiles with the Holy Spirit in the same manner and degree as the Jews?

i. Peter made the point clearly when he noted that they **received the Holy Spirit just as we have**. It wasn't just that God loved or blessed the Gentiles that **astonished** them. It was that God loved and blessed the Gentiles just as He loved and blessed the Jews, and He did it *while they were still Gentiles*.

d. He commanded them to be baptized in the name of the Lord: This showed their full acceptance into the community of those who followed Jesus. Their baptism showed they were accepted as Gentile followers of Jesus.

> i. This entrance of Gentiles into the church was not a new plan, but something promised long before. The Old Testament looked for the day when a light would shine in the darkness of the Gentile world: *Arise, shine; for your light has come! And the glory of the LORD is risen upon you. For behold, the darkness shall cover the earth, and deep darkness the people; but the LORD will arise over you, and His glory will be seen upon you. The Gentiles shall come to your light, and kings to the brightness of your rising.* (Isaiah 60:1-3)

> ii. God promised Abraham and his descendants that the blessing that came through him would extend to all nations (Genesis 12:1-4). Here, we see Jesus - the greatest blessing from Abraham - extended to the nations.

> iii. Remember Jesus' promise of *other sheep, not of this fold* in John 10:16. Jesus also promised, *if I am lifted up from the earth, will draw all peoples to Myself* (John 12:32).

> iv. The first Gentile Jesus dealt with in His public ministry was a Roman centurion from Capernaum. When Jesus healed that centurion's servant, He declared *that many will come from east and west, and sit down with Abraham, Isaac, and Jacob in the kingdom of heaven* (Matthew 8:5-13).

> v. We should also see that Cornelius was an undoubtedly good man; yet he needed Jesus. Even good people, who are respectful towards God, still need to come to Jesus as their Lord and Savior, and put all their trust in who Jesus is and what He did for them.

Acts 11 – Defending Ministry to the Gentiles

A. A controversy in Jerusalem regarding ministry to the Gentiles.

1. (1-3) Peter hears objections to his association with Gentiles.

Now the apostles and brethren who were in Judea heard that the Gentiles had also received the word of God. And when Peter came up to Jerusalem, those of the circumcision contended with him, saying, "You went in to uncircumcised men and ate with them!"

a. **Now the apostles and brethren who were in Judea heard that the Gentiles had also received the word of God**: The greatness of the work among the Gentiles in Caesarea could not be kept hidden. There was no desire to hide it, even though many Jewish Christians (**those of the circumcision**) would be confused and offended.

b. **"You went in to uncircumcised men and ate with them!"** The charges against Peter were simple: "You, who are supposed to be a faithful Jew, associated with Gentiles and even ate with them." This offended these Christian Jews, so they **contended** with Peter.

i. **And ate with them**: Sharing a meal together was a special sign of fellowship in that time and culture. This was considered to be a significant compromise by these Jewish Christians.

ii. This reaction of the Christian Jews shows how significant the change was that God initiated in Acts 10. The change said, to the Gentiles, "You don't have to become Jews first, and put yourself under the Law of Moses first. Repent and believe, and you can come to Jesus." But it also said to the Jewish followers of Jesus, "Receive your Gentile brothers and sisters as full members of the family of God. They aren't inferior to you in any way."

iii. The objection of **those of the circumcision** was on the second point, not the first. They complained, **You went into uncircumcised**

men and ate with them! At first, they were more concerned with what Peter did than with what God was doing with the Gentiles.

c. **Those of the circumcision contended with him**: When we see what the reaction of the Jewish Christians in Jerusalem, we can see how wise it was of Peter to take six witnesses with him to Caesarea and his meeting with Cornelius (Acts 10:23 and 11:12).

2. (4-15) Peter explains his ministry to the Gentiles.

But Peter explained *it* to them in order from the beginning, saying: "I was in the city of Joppa praying; and in a trance I saw a vision, an object descending like a great sheet, let down from heaven by four corners; and it came to me. When I observed it intently and considered, I saw four-footed animals of the earth, wild beasts, creeping things, and birds of the air. And I heard a voice saying to me, 'Rise, Peter; kill and eat.' But I said, 'Not so, Lord! For nothing common or unclean has at any time entered my mouth.' But the voice answered me again from heaven, 'What God has cleansed you must not call common.' Now this was done three times, and all were drawn up again into heaven. At that very moment, three men stood before the house where I was, having been sent to me from Caesarea. Then the Spirit told me to go with them, doubting nothing. Moreover these six brethren accompanied me, and we entered the man's house. And he told us how he had seen an angel standing in his house, who said to him, 'Send men to Joppa, and call for Simon whose surname is Peter, who will tell you words by which you and all your household will be saved.' And as I began to speak, the Holy Spirit fell upon them, as upon us at the beginning."

a. **Peter explained it to them in order from the beginning**: This account is an obvious condensation from Acts 10:9-43. God emphasized the importance of these events by repeating the story.

i. "Peter did not flaunt his apostolic authority. Instead he began with a humble recitation of what happened. The Greek makes this particularly clear. It indicates that Peter began at the beginning and explained everything *precisely* – a very strong word – as it happened." (Boice)

b. **What God has cleansed you must not call common**: At first, Peter thought God spoke this about food. But Peter came to understand the vision of the sheet and kosher and unkosher animals had to do with people, not food (Acts 10:28: *God has shown me that I should not call any man common or unclean*).

i. There is a sense in which the sheet represents the church, having both "kosher" (Jews) and "unkosher" (Gentiles) on it, with no distinction or dividing line between the two (Ephesians 2:11-18).

c. **We entered the man's house**: This may have surprised Peter's questioners, because it seemed like an admission of guilt – Peter admitted entering the home of a Gentile, something prohibited by Jewish custom and tradition (though not by the Law of Moses.). Yet Peter was careful to add that before he ever **entered the man's house**, an **angel** had been **standing in his house**. If it was permitted for an angel of God to go into Cornelius' house, it must be permitted for Peter also.

d. **The Holy Spirit fell upon them, as upon us at the beginning**: This conclusion was important. It showed that God's stamp of approval was on this work towards the Gentiles. Peter's point to these Christian Jews (*those of the circumcision*, Acts 11:2) was clear: they could not withhold their acceptance when God had given His.

3. (16-18) Peter interprets these events by remembering the words of Jesus.

"Then I remembered the word of the Lord, how He said, 'John indeed baptized with water, but you shall be baptized with the Holy Spirit.' If therefore God gave them the same gift as *He gave* us when we believed on the Lord Jesus Christ, who was I that I could withstand God?" When they heard these things they became silent; and they glorified God, saying, "Then God has also granted to the Gentiles repentance to life."

a. **If therefore God gave them the same gift as He gave us when we believed on the Lord Jesus Christ, who was I that I could withstand God?** If God was reaching out to the Gentiles, who was Peter that he **could withstand God**? Peter recognized the importance of sensing where God is going and heading that same direction, instead of trying to persuade God to go *your* direction.

i. It is important also to note these Christians would see this was all in accord with the Scriptures. They had both the **word of the Lord** Jesus, recorded in Mark 1:8, and the Old Testament promises that Gentiles would come to the Lord through the Messiah (in passages such as Isaiah 49:6).

ii. There are many today who look at some work or another and say, "Look what God is doing." But activity alone isn't enough to validate a work of God. It must also be in line with God's Word. This work among the Gentiles passed both tests.

b. **They became silent**: The Jewish believers in Jerusalem (*those of the circumcision*, Acts 11:2) first reacted with a stunned silence. But then **they glorified God**, because they saw He was now at work among the Gentiles, also.

> i. This is a powerful passage, demonstrating that the hearts of the Jewish Christians in Jerusalem were soft enough to be guided and corrected by God. It is a glorious thing when God's people will allow their prejudices and traditions to be overcome by God's Word and God's work.

> ii. The church in Jerusalem embraced these Gentile believers at first, but it would be a long time until all the objections of *those of the circumcision* were answered.

B. The Church in Antioch.

1. (19-21) The church in Antioch grows as Gentiles turn to the Lord.

Now those who were scattered after the persecution that arose over Stephen traveled as far as Phoenicia, Cyprus, and Antioch, preaching the word to no one but the Jews only. But some of them were men from Cyprus and Cyrene, who, when they had come to Antioch, spoke to the Hellenists, preaching the Lord Jesus. And the hand of the Lord was with them, and a great number believed and turned to the Lord.

a. **Preaching the word to no one but the Jews only**: At first, Christians scattered over the Roman Empire preached only to Jews. But they eventually began to preach Jesus Christ to Gentiles as well.

b. **Some of them were men from Cyprus and Cyrene...spoke to the Hellenists, preaching the Lord Jesus**: These unnamed disciples from Cyprus and Cyrene are genuine heroes. They began the first mentioned "mission to the Gentiles" (here called **Hellenists**) in Antioch.

> i. In Antioch, we have the first example of Christians deliberately targeting Gentiles for evangelism, and this effort had great results (**a great number believed and turned to the Lord**).

c. **When they had come to Antioch**: Antioch was founded about 300 B.C. by Seleucus I, one of the inheritors of Alexander the Great's empire. He liked to make a city and name them after his father, Antioch, and he did this about fifteen times. This city of Antioch was called "Syrian Antioch" or "Antioch on the Orontes." In the first century it was a city of more than half a million people; today it is a Turkish city with a population of about 3,500.

i. **Antioch** was about 300 miles (480 kilometers) north of Jerusalem and about 20 miles (32 kilometers) inland from the Mediterranean Sea. Many considered Syrian **Antioch** the third greatest city in the Roman Empire, behind Rome and Alexandria. Antioch was known for its business and commerece, for its sophistication and culture, but also for its immorality.

ii. "The city's reputation for moral laxity was enhanced by the cult of Artemis and Apollo at Daphne, five miles distant, where the ancient Syrian worship of Astarte and her consort, with its ritual prostitution, was carried on." (Bruce)

iii. According to Hughes, when the ancient Roman senator Juvenal wanted to describe the decadence of Rome, he said that "The Orontes has flowed into the Tiber," flooding Rome with wickedness.

iv. One might say that Jerusalem was all about *religion*; Rome was all about *power*; Alexandria was all about *intellect*, and Athens was all about *philosophy*. Adding to that, one might say that Antioch was all about *business* and *immorality*.

v. When the Gospel came to Cornelius and he became a follower of Jesus, it came to a man who was already a *God-fearer*. He had a respect for the God of Israel and lived a moral life. When it came to Antioch, it came to an utterly pagan city.

d. **And the hand of the Lord was with them**: Because God was with them, their ministry was blessed and multiplied, the result was that **a great number believed and turned to the Lord**.

i. A ministry can't turn people to the Lord unless **the hand of the Lord** is with them.

- You can turn people to a personality without **the hand of the Lord**.
- You can turn people to a social club without **the hand of the Lord**.
- You can turn people to a church or an institution without **the hand of the Lord**.
- But you can't turn people **to the Lord** without **the hand of the Lord**.

ii. The phrase, "**believed and turned to the Lord**" is a good description of the work of both *faith* and *repentance*.

2. (22-24) The ministry of Barnabas in Antioch.

Then news of these things came to the ears of the church in Jerusalem, and they sent out Barnabas to go as far as Antioch. When he came and had seen the grace of God, he was glad, and encouraged them all that with purpose of heart they should continue with the Lord. For he was a good man, full of the Holy Spirit and of faith. And a great many people were added to the Lord.

a. **They sent out Barnabas**: The church in Jerusalem sent an able man in Barnabas, previously known for his generosity (Acts 4:36-37) and his warm acceptance of Saul of Tarsus after he was converted (Acts 9:26-28).

i. "News was always getting back to Jerusalem, and I suppose it is always that way. Whenever anything is done, there is always somebody who will run to those who are supposed to be important and say, 'Do you know what's going on?'" (Boice)

b. **When he came and had seen the grace of God, he was glad**: At the church in Antioch, when Barnabas **had seen the grace of God, he was glad**. There was something in the work and atmosphere among the followers of Jesus in Antioch that made Barnabas able to *see* the **grace of God**.

i. In whatever gathering of Christians we associate ourselves with, it is important that others be able to see **the grace of God** among us. They should not see an emphasis on self, on man-made rules, on human performance – but on the glorious **grace of God**. It will make them **glad**.

c. **Encouraged them all that with purpose of heart they should continue with the Lord**: Barnabas rightly focused on his main job as a leader of the congregation. He strengthened the church family itself, with the result that **a great many people were added to the Lord**.

i. This is the plan for church growth spoken of in Ephesians 4:11-16. Leaders in the church dedicate themselves to building strong, healthy Christians. As the saints are equipped for the work of the ministry, they grow into maturity, and do their ministry, and it *causes growth of the body*.

3. (25-26) Barnabas and Saul work together in Antioch.

Then Barnabas departed for Tarsus to seek Saul. And when he had found him, he brought him to Antioch. So it was that for a whole year they assembled with the church and taught a great many people. And the disciples were first called Christians in Antioch.

a. **Barnabas departed for Tarsus to seek Saul**: Barnabas remembered the precious brother Saul, and how he was sent to Tarsus for his own protection (Acts 9:28-30). Now Barnabas went and found him.

    i. It's not difficult to think of Barnabas being exhausted and overwhelmed by all the work and opportunities in Antioch, and then remembering Saul of Tarsus.

    ii. **To seek Saul** is more literally *to hunt him up*; Barnabas had to do some looking. MacArthur says the original word "suggests a laborious search on Barnabas' part." Saul was so valuable to Barnabas that it was worth it for him to leave the work in Antioch for a season and search hard to find him.

b. **So it was that for a whole year they assembled with the church and taught a great many people**. Together, Barnabas and Saul **taught a great many people**, making the church in Antioch strong.

    i. Saul had spent some twelve years in Tarsus since we last met him; these years were not wasted or lost, but spent in quiet ministry and preparation for future service.

    ii. In all this Antioch because a center for great teaching and preaching. Antioch "had the greatest preachers – in the first century Barnabas, Paul, and Peter; in the second Ignatius and Theophilus; in the third and fourth Lucian, Theodore, Chrysostom, and Theordoret." (Hughes)

    iii. But it also had great *informal* preaching, which is often the best kind. Acts 11:20 reminds us that they *spoke to the Hellenists, preaching the Lord Jesus*. This combination of great formal teaching/preaching and great informal teaching/preaching made the church community in Antioch something special and world-impacting.

c. **The disciples were first called Christians in Antioch**: It wasn't until these years at the Church in Syrian Antioch that the name *Christian* became associated with the followers of Jesus.

- They had been called disciples (Acts 1:15).
- They had been called saints (Acts 9:13).
- They had been called believers (Acts 5:14).
- They had been called brothers (Acts 6:3).
- They had been called witnesses (Acts 5:32).
- They had been called followers of the Way (Acts 9:2).
- They would be called Nazarenes (Acts 24:5).
- *Now* they would be called **Christians**.

i. In Latin, the ending *ian* meant "the party of." A *Christ-ian* was "of the party of Jesus." **Christians** was sort of like saying "Jesus-ites," or "Jesus People," describing the people associated with Jesus Christ. Boice thinks the idea was that they were called "Christ-ones."

ii. Also, soldiers under particular generals in the Roman army identifed themselves by their general's name by adding *ian* to the end. A soldier under Caesar would call himself a *Caesarian*. Soldiers under Jesus Christ could be called **Christians**.

iii. In Antioch, they probably first used the term **Christians** to mock the followers of Jesus. "Antioch was famous for its readiness to jeer and call names; it was known by its witty epigrams." (Gaebelein) But as the people of Antioch called the followers of Jesus the "Jesus People," the believers appreciated the title so much that it stuck.

iv. "Ironside says that when he was traveling in China years ago he was frequently introduced as 'Yasu-yan.' At first he did not know what the word meant, but he asked about it and learned that *Yasu* was the Cantonese word for Jesus, and *yan* was 'man.' So he was being introduced as a 'Jesus man.'" (Boice)

v. **First called Christians** can also have the idea that they were **called Christians** before they were called anything else. Their *first identity* was now to be called Christians. Today, Christians must be willing to take at least the idea of the title "Jesus People," and must also be *worthy* of the name. Instead of claiming any other title – Roman Catholic, Protestant, charismatic, whatever - we should be **first called Christians**.

vi. Eusebius, the famous early church historian, described a believer named Sanctus from Lyons, France, who was tortured for Jesus. As they tortured him cruelly, they hoped to get him to say something evil or blasphemous. They asked his name, and he only replied, "I am a Christian." "What nation do you belong to?" He answered, "I am a Christian." "What city do you live in?" "I am a Christian." His questioners began to get angry: "Are you a slave or a free man?" "I am a Christian" was his only reply. No matter what they asked about him, he only answered, "I am a Christian." This made his torturers all the more determined to break him, but they could not, and he died with the words "I am a Christian" on his lips. (Eusebius, *Church History*)

4. (27-30) A prophetic word announces a famine.

And in these days prophets came from Jerusalem to Antioch. Then one of them, named Agabus, stood up and showed by the Spirit that

there was going to be a great famine throughout all the world, which
also happened in the days of Claudius Caesar. Then the disciples,
each according to his ability, determined to send relief to the brethren
dwelling in Judea. This they also did, and sent it to the elders by the
hands of Barnabas and Saul.

a. **Showed by the Spirit that there was going to be a great famine
throughout all the world, which also happened in the days of Claudius
Caesar**: We don't know exactly how Agabus **showed by the Spirit** this
famine was on the way. But the Christians took the word seriously, and
generously prepared to meet the coming need.

i. "We know from other sources that Claudius's principate was marked
by a succession of bad harvests and consequent scarcity in various parts
of the empire - in Rome, Greece, and Egypt as well as in Judaea."
(Bruce)

b. **Then the disciples**: You can tell these were truly **disciples** and *Christians*,
because they gave generously to meet the need. They gave, **each according
to his ability**.

i. This means that they gave **according** to the **ability** of their resources;
those who had more gave more, probably referencing a proportional
giving. It also means that they gave **according** to the **ability** of their
faith, trusting that their gift to God's work was a worthy investment in
His kingdom, and not a loss.

ii. We also see they **determined** to give. If a person does not *determine*
to give, they often never do.

c. **Sent it to the elders by the hands of Barnabas and Saul**: The high
regard that Barnabas and Saul had among all was evident by the fact that
they were trusted with the relief fund.

i. "As far as I know, this is the first charitable act of this nature in all
recorded history – one race of people collecting money to help another
people. No wonder they were first called Christians at Antioch."
(Boice)

Acts 12 - James Is Martyred, Peter Is Set Free

A. James the apostle dies as a martyr.

1. (1) Herod harasses the church.

Now about that time Herod the king stretched out *his* hand to harass some from the church.

> a. **Herod the king**: This was Herod Agrippa I, the grandson of Herod the Great, who ruled in the days of Jesus' birth (Matthew 2:1-16). Herod Agrippa I was also the nephew of Herod Antipas, who had a role in the trial of Jesus (Luke 23:7-12).

> b. **Stretched out his hand to harass some from the church**: No doubt, this was done because it was politically popular for Herod. It pleased many of his citizens who didn't like Christians. Many political figures are ready to persecute Christians if it will make them politically popular.

2. (2) The death of the apostle James.

Then he killed James the brother of John with the sword.

> a. **Then he killed James the brother of John with the sword**: This was a new development in the history of the church. Of the twelve who followed Jesus, James was the first to be martyred.

> > i. Up to Acts 12, the church had been on a streak of success, experiencing one exciting conversion after another. First there was Saul of Tarsus, then the Gentile centurion Cornelius, then the highly successful work among Gentiles (and Jews) in Antioch. But in Acts 12, the ugly opposition inspired by Satan again raised its head.

> > ii. James was certainly not the first *Christian* to die in faithfulness to Jesus. Stephen (Acts 7:58-60) was martyred before this, and certainly others were also. But the death of James shattered the illusion that somehow, the twelve enjoyed a unique Divine protection.

b. **James the brother of John**: James, in particular, might have thought to have been protected. He was one of the special intimates of Jesus, often mentioned with his brother John and with Peter (Matthew 17:1, 26:37, Mark 5:37, 9:2, 14:33; Luke 5:37, 9:2, and 14:33).

> i. But Jesus promised no special protection for even His closest followers; He warned them to be ready for persecution (Matthew 10:16-26).

> ii. In Mark 10:35-40, John and his brother James came to Jesus and asked to be considered His two chief lieutenants. Jesus replied to them, *You do not know what you ask. Can you drink the cup that I drink, and be baptized with the baptism I am baptized with?* James and John, not really knowing what they were saying, replied by saying they could. Jesus promised them, *You will indeed drink the cup that I drink, and with the baptism I am baptized with you will be baptized.* This martyrdom was the fulfillment of that promise for James. John fulfilled it by a lifetime of devoted service to God despite repeated attempts to martyr him.

c. **With the sword**: Normally, this means that James was beheaded. Eusebius relates a story from Clement of Alexandria, who said the soldier guarding James before the judge was so affected by his witness that he declared himself a Christian also and was also willingly executed for Jesus along side of James (Eusebius, *Church History* 2.9.2-3).

> i. Significantly, there was no attempt to replace James, as there was to replace Judas (Acts 1). This was because James died as a faithful martyr, but Judas revealed his apostasy in betraying Jesus. There was no need for another man to take the office of James.

B. The release of Peter from prison.

1. (3-4) Herod imprisons Peter.

And because he saw that it pleased the Jews, he proceeded further to seize Peter also. Now it was *during* the Days of Unleavened Bread. So when he had arrested him, he put *him* in prison, and delivered *him* to four squads of soldiers to keep him, intending to bring him before the people after Passover.

a. **Because he saw that it pleased the Jews**: Seeing his increased popularity when he killed James, Herod sought to improve his ratings even more when **he proceeded further to sieze Peter also**.

> i. There was a significant difference between the persecution from Saul of Tarsus (Acts 8:1-3) and from Herod. Saul, wrong as he was, persecuted out of sincere (though misguided) religious conviction; Herod persecuted out of purely political motives.

b. **Intending to bring him before the people after Passover**: Herod decided to deal with Peter at a politically opportune time, fearing an unpredictable mob reaction when Passover pilgrims filled Jerusalem.

  i. Horton suggests three reasons for the delay in executing Peter: (1) Herod wanted to show how scrupulously he observed the Passover; (2) he wanted to wait until the pilgrim crowds went home, fearing a riot; (3) he wanted to wait until he had the full attention of the Jewish population.

c. **Delivered him to four squads of soldiers**: Knowing Peter (with the other apostles) had mysteriously escaped from prison before (Acts 5:17-21), Herod assigned a high-security detail to guard Peter.

  i. "Normally it was considered enough for a prisoner to be handcuffed to one soldier, but as a special precaution Peter had a soldier each side of him and both his wrists were manacled" (Stott)

  ii. "So there were always four soldiers guarding Peter. Extraordinary precautions were also taken by chaining him to two soldiers instead of one as usual (compare Seneca, Epistulae, 5:7). The other two soldiers kept watch outside the cell." (Hughes)

2. (5) The church prays for Peter.

Peter was therefore kept in prison, but constant prayer was offered to God for him by the church.

a. **Prayer was offered to God for him by the church**: In this contest, Herod had his soldiers and his prisons; but the church had the power of prayer. The outcome would soon be seen, and easily decided.

  i. **Peter was therefore kept in prison**, but the church was free to pray. When every other gate is shut and locked, the gate to heaven is wide open. We take advantage of that open gate through prayer.

b. **Constant prayer was offered to God for him**: The word **constant** also has the idea of *earnest*; literally, the word pictures someone *stretching out all they can for something*. "The verb *ektenos* is related to *ektenes*, a medical term describing the stretching of a muscle to its limits." (MacArthur)

  i. Luke uses this same word *ektenos* for the agonizing prayer of Jesus in the Garden of Gethsemane (Luke 22:44).

  ii. Much of our prayer is powerless because it lacks earnestness. Too often we almost pray with the attitude of wanting God to care about things we really don't care too much about.

  iii. *Earnest* prayer has power not because it in itself persuades a reluctant God. Instead, it demonstrates that our heart cares passionately about the things God cares about, fulfilling Jesus' promise *If you abide in Me and My words abide in you, you will ask what you desire and it shall be done for you* (John 15:7).

c. **Constant prayer was offered to God**: It is also important to see that the church prayed **to God**. It may seem obvious, but often our prayers are weak because we are not consciously coming into the presence of our great and holy God, offering our requests to Him.

3. (6-11) God sends an angel to free Peter from prison.

And when Herod was about to bring him out, that night Peter was sleeping, bound with two chains between two soldiers; and the guards before the door were keeping the prison. Now behold, an angel of the Lord stood by *him,* and a light shone in the prison; and he struck Peter on the side and raised him up, saying, "Arise quickly!" And his chains fell off *his* hands. Then the angel said to him, "Gird yourself and tie on your sandals"; and so he did. And he said to him, "Put on your garment and follow me." So he went out and followed him, and did not know that what was done by the angel was real, but thought he was seeing a vision. When they were past the first and the second guard posts, they came to the iron gate that leads to the city, which opened to them of its own accord; and they went out and went down one street, and immediately the angel departed from him. And when Peter had come to himself, he said, "Now I know for certain that the Lord has sent His angel, and has delivered me from the hand of Herod and *from* all the expectation of the Jewish people."

a. **That night Peter was sleeping**: Peter showed no signs of anxiety. He was able to sleep soundly on what seemed to be the last night before his execution. Remember, *He gives His beloved sleep* (Psalm 127:2).

b. **Bound with two chains between two soldiers…guards before the door**: The chains, the guards, the prison doors meant nothing to God and His appointed messengers; Peter was instantly set free.

c. **Did not know that what was done by the angel was real, but thought he was seeing a vision**: Peter obeyed without really knowing what was happening. He knew enough to sense that God was doing something and the explanation could come later.

d. **They came to the iron gate that leads to the city, which opened to them of its own accord**: The soldiers, the chains, the guard posts, the iron gate - were all nothing when God was with Peter and prayer was behind him.

i. Many of us worry about the **iron gate** before we ever get to it. A month beforehand, and we are anxious about the **iron gate**! But God will take care of it when we come to it. For Peter, it opened **of its own accord**. That phrase uses the ancient Greek word, *automate*. One could say that the gates opened automatically for Peter.

ii. F.F. Bruce relates the story of Sundar Singh, a Tibetan Christian who was likewise freed miraculously from a prison. For preaching of the gospel, he was thrown into a well, and a cover set over it and securely locked. He would be left in the well until he died, and he could see the bones and rotting corpses of those who had already perished in there. On the third night of his imprisonment, he heard someone unlocking the cover of the well and removing it. A voice told him to take hold of the rope that was being lowered. Sundar was grateful that the rope had a loop he could put his foot in, because he had injured his arm in the fall down into the well. He was raised up, the cover was replaced and locked, but when he looked to thank his rescuer he could find no one. When morning came, he went back to the same place he was arrested and started preaching again. News of the preaching came to the official who had him arrested, and Sundar was brought before him again. When the official said someone must have gotten the key and released him, they searched for the key - and found it on the official's own belt. God is still writing the Book of Acts!

e. **And has delivered me from the hand of Herod**: James was martyred (Acts 12:1-2) and Peter was rescued. The reasons God does such things, or does not do them, are often known only to Him. We do know that James, having graduated to glory, did not consider himself a loser in any way.

i. Simply, it wasn't time for Peter to go to his heavenly home yet. Until it was time, he was invulnerable. He couldn't be harmed. It was time for James; it was not time for Peter.

4. (12-17) Peter presents himself to the believers that prayed for him.

So, when he had considered *this*, he came to the house of Mary, the mother of John whose surname was Mark, where many were gathered together praying. And as Peter knocked at the door of the gate, a girl named Rhoda came to answer. When she recognized Peter's voice, because of *her* gladness she did not open the gate, but ran in and announced that Peter stood before the gate. But they said to her, "You are beside yourself!" Yet she kept insisting that it was so. So they said, "It is his angel." Now Peter continued knocking; and when they opened *the door* and saw him, they were astonished. But motioning to them with his hand to keep silent, he declared to them how the Lord had brought

him out of the prison. And he said, "Go, tell these things to James and to the brethren." And he departed and went to another place.

a. **He came to the house of Mary…knocked at the door of the gate**: Peter naturally went to where he knew Christians would be gathered and praying. They would want to know that their prayers had been answered.

b. **Because of her gladness she did not open the gate, but ran in and announced that Peter stood before the gate**: Rhoda was so excited to hear from Peter that she left him out at the gate! The natural, true-to-life feel of these accounts show the reliable historical character of the Book of Acts.

c. **But they said to her, "You are beside yourself!"** We are comforted (and amused) by the little faith of these Christians. Even while they prayed for Peter, they found it hard to believe God actually answered their prayer.

i. Their prayer was earnest (Acts 12:5), but their faith was not overwhelming. Little faith can accomplish great things if it is placed in the great God.

d. **It is his angel**: The Jews believed in the idea of guardian angels, and it seems that some among them may have believed that one's guardian angel bore some kind of resemblance to the human it was assigned to.

e. **Go, tell these things to James and the brethren**: The **James** that Peter told others to report to was not the James who was just martyred. It was probably James, the brother of Jesus, who was a prominent figure in the church at Jerusalem.

f. **And he departed and went to another place**: Except for a brief mention in Acts 15, this is the last Luke speaks of Peter. We know that Peter later met Paul in Antioch (Galatians 2:11-14), and later he wrote his two letters.

5. (18-19) The execution of the soldiers who guarded Peter.

Then, as soon as it was day, there was no small stir among the soldiers about what had become of Peter. But when Herod had searched for him and not found him, he examined the guards and commanded that *they* should be put to death. And he went down from Judea to Caesarea, and stayed *there*.

a. **There was no small stir**: This is one of the great understatements of the Bible. Herod was furious that his prized prisoner had escaped.

b. **He examined the guards and commanded that they should be put to death**: The execution of the guards was customary. In that day, if a guard's prisoner escaped, the guard was given the penalty due to the prisoner - in this case, death.

C. God judges a blaspheming Herod and blesses an obedient church.

1. (20-21) Herod gives a speech to the people of Tyre and Sidon, who are anxious to please Herod.

Now Herod had been very angry with the people of Tyre and Sidon; but they came to him with one accord, and having made Blastus the king's personal aide their friend, they asked for peace, because their country was supplied with food by the king's *country.* So on a set day Herod, arrayed in royal apparel, sat on his throne and gave an oration to them.

a. **They asked for peace**: The **people of Tyre and Sidon** wanted to make **peace** with Herod (Herod Agrippa I), the grandson of Herod the Great. Since Herod **had been very angry** with them, and they needed the **food** that came from Herod's **country**, the crowd was motivated to please Herod.

b. **Arrayed in royal apparel...gave an oration**: Dressed in impressive clothes, Herod spoke before an audience eager to please him.

2. (22-23) Herod receives the overstated praise of the people of Tyre and Sidon, and he receives the judgment of the God he refused to glorify.

And the people kept shouting, "The voice of a god and not of a man!" Then immediately an angel of the Lord struck him, because he did not give glory to God. And he was eaten by worms and died.

a. **The voice of a god and not of a man!** It is in human nature to look for political deliverers and messiahs, and the people of Tyre and Sidon seemed to praise Herod as if he were a god. For his part, Herod enjoyed it, taking the glory unto himself (**he did not give glory to God**).

b. **He was eaten by worms and died**: The manner of Herod's death was appropriate to his spiritual state; he was corrupted from the inside out. In writing to the Roman world, the ancient Jewish historian Josephus also described the death of Herod in gory detail.

i. "He put on a garment made wholly of silver, and of a contexture truly wonderful, and came into the theatre early in the morning; at which time the silver of his garment, being illuminated by the fresh reflection of the sun's rays upon it, shone out after a surprising manner, and was so resplendent as to spread a horror over those that looked intently upon him; and presently his flatterers cried out, one from one place, and another from another (though not for his good), that he was a god…A severe pain also arose in his belly, and began in a most violent manner…when he had been quite worn out by the pain in his belly for five days, he departed this life." (*Antiquities*, XIX.8.2)

3. (24-25) The work of God continues without hindrance.

But the word of God grew and multiplied. And Barnabas and Saul returned from Jerusalem when they had fulfilled *their* ministry, and they also took with them John whose surname was Mark.

a. **But the word of God grew and multiplied**: The contrast between Herod and the church was clear. Herod believed he had the upper hand against God's people, but God showed who was really in charge - Herod was judged, and the church was blessed.

i. Herod fought against God. He killed James but didn't defeat God's plan. He arrested Peter, but the earnestly praying church saw God rescue Peter and the apostle's work continue.

ii. History is filled with the stories of men who thought they could fight God and succeed; their ruined lives are evidence that it can't be done. Friedrich Nietsche was the philosopher who coined the idea that God was dead, and that Christianity was a despised religion of weaklings. Fighting God drove him insane, and he spent the last several years of his life in that condition. Sinclair Lewis won the Nobel Prize for literature, and fought against God in his book *Elmer Gantry*. The book was about an evangelist who was also an alcoholic and would sleep with any woman he could. Sinclair Lewis died a hopeless alcoholic in a clinic near Rome. Writer Ernest Hemingway lived his life of adventure and sin against God seemingly without consequences - until he shot himself in the head with a shotgun. Fighting against God just doesn't work.

b. **Barnabas and Saul returned from Jerusalem**: Coming back from their relief effort to Jerusalem (Acts 11:30), Barnabas and Saul brought John Mark with them back to the church at Antioch.

Acts 13 - Paul's First Missionary Journey Begins

A. Barnabas and Saul are called and sent by the Holy Spirit.

1. (1) The people at the church in Antioch.

Now in the church that was at Antioch there were certain prophets and teachers: Barnabas, Simeon who was called Niger, Lucius of Cyrene, Manaen who had been brought up with Herod the tetrarch, and Saul.

> a. **Now in the church that was at Antioch**: In Acts 12:25, we learn Barnabas, Saul, and John Mark were all at the church in Antioch, having returned from delivering a gift of support to the church in Jerusalem (Acts 11:27-30). Saul and Barnabas were among the teachers and prophets there, as were **Simeon**, **Lucius**, and **Manaen**.

> b. **Simeon who was called Niger**: Since **Niger** means *black*, he was presumably a black African among the congregation at Antioch, and possibly the same **Simeon** who carried Jesus' cross (Luke 23:26).

> c. **Manaen who had been brought up with Herod the tetrarch**: This **Manaen** mentioned here grew up with **Herod the tetrarch**. This was the same Herod who beheaded John the Baptist and presided over one of Jesus' trials (Luke 23:7-12).

>> i. Herod and Manaen grew up together, but went very different ways. One killed John the Baptist and presided over one of the trials of Jesus before His crucifixion. The other became a Christian, and a leader in the dynamic congregation at Antioch.

2. (2) The Holy Spirit calls Barnabas and Saul.

As they ministered to the Lord and fasted, the Holy Spirit said, "Now separate to Me Barnabas and Saul for the work to which I have called them."

> a. **As they ministered to the Lord**: This was part of what happened at the congregation in Antioch. Barnabas and others certainly ministered to the

congregation, and the congregation also ministered one to another. Yet they also **ministered to the Lord**.

> i. This is the first job of any servant of God, to minister unto the Lord. In doing this, they did the service of priests under the new covenant, offering their bodies as living sacrifices (Romans 12:1). Ministering to the Lord means doing what pleases Him and honors Him – worship, praise, prayer, listening to, honoring God.

> ii. "The word translated *worshipping* [*ministered*, NKJV] is that usually employed in the LXX for the service of priests and Levites in the temple." (Williams)

b. **They ministered to the Lord and fasted**: As part of their service to the Lord, they also **fasted**. Presumably, they fasted because they sensed a need to seek God in a special way.

> i. Judging from the calling described in the text, it is possible that they sought God about the need to spread the gospel to all the earth.

> ii. If we assume they fasted and prayed about the need of the world for Jesus, we can see how God answered their prayer - by using them. This is often how God moves, by sending the people who have it on their hearts to pray.

> iii. Many want to be "back seat drivers" in God's work. They hope to say, "I'll have the burden and you do the work." But God's typical way of working is to send the people who have the burden to do the work.

c. **The Holy Spirit said**: As they ministered unto the Lord, God spoke to them. This was a word of *calling* that would guide **Barnabas and Saul** into a specific work.

d. **The Holy Spirit said**: Presumably, the call came through the ministry of prophets in the church at Antioch, though it could have come simply through the inner witness of the Holy Spirit.

> i. "I do not for a moment imagine that the assembly heard a voice. That is the mistake we too often make. We try to force ourselves into ecstasies in order to hear the voice, then we imagine we hear it!" (Morgan)

e. **Separate to Me**: Before Barnabas and Saul could do anything significant for God, they first had to be separated to Him. If you will separate **to** God, it means you must separate from some other things.

> i. You can't really say "yes" to God's call on your life until you can say "no" to things that will keep you from that call.

f. **Separate to Me Barnabas and Saul for the work**: It is significant that the two men called to missionary service were – as far as we know – the two most gifted and able men in the congregation.

g. **For the work to which I have called them**: God had a specific **work** He had appointed to Barnabas and Saul to do. Paul would later write in Ephesians 2:10: *For we are His workmanship, created in Christ Jesus for good works, which God prepared beforehand that we should walk in them.* Here, God called Barnabas and Saul to those kind of good works.

> i. The calling God had for the life of Paul had already been stated in Acts 9:15-16: *He is a chosen vessel of Mine to bear My name before Gentiles, kings, and the children of Israel. For I will show him how many things he must suffer for My name's sake.* This was not a touchy-feely "feel good" call - it was a serious call to a serious ministry.

h. **Now separate to Me**: God gave a timetable - **now**. Before, God had told Paul through Ananias what his calling was, but not that it was **now**. **Now** meant there was to be no delay.

3. (3) The sending of Barnabas and Saul.

Then, having fasted and prayed, and laid hands on them, they sent *them* away.

> a. **Having fasted and prayed**: They were sent with fasting and prayer. This whole work required a substantial dependence on God, and fasting and prayer demonstrated that dependence.

> b. **And laid hands on them**: The laying on of hands was a formal commissioning to this work. Certainly Barnabas and Saul were "ordained" before this, but now they entered a different sphere of ministry.

> c. **They sent them away**: Notice that the church in Antioch *sent* Barnabas and Saul out. They were supported and sent by a specific congregation. As far as we know, this had never happened before in the history of the church. Many went out as "accidental missionaries" (as in Acts 8:4 and 11:19) but there was never a concerted and organized effort to win people to Jesus like this.

> > i. Being intentionally **sent** by the church in Antioch, many regard this as the first real known *missionary* effort of the church. "The word 'missionary' has to do with sending. The Latin word *mitto, mittere*, means 'to send'; 'mission' and 'missionary' come from the forms *missi* and *missum*." (Boice)

> > ii. They seem to have done this without a committee report, without a demographic analysis, without a marketing survey, without what is

sometimes called "spiritual mapping." Barnabas and Saul went out without any of these things, only with the call and power of the Holy Spirit.

B. Ministry in the cities of Seleucia, Salamis and Paphos.

1. (4) First stop: **Seleucia**.

So, being sent out by the Holy Spirit, they went down to Seleucia, and from there they sailed to Cyprus.

a. **So, being sent out by the Holy Spirit**: The Christians of the church at Antioch sent Barnabas and Saul; but more importantly, the **Holy Spirit** sent them. Any group of Christians can send someone, but if the **Spirit** doesn't send them, it won't amount to eternally effective ministry.

b. **Went down to Seleucia**: We aren't told of any specific work that took place in **Seleucia**, a city near Antioch. Saul and Barnabas may have gone there merely because it was the port city near Antioch, but it is hard to imagine them not doing *any* ministry there.

i. Since **Seleucia** wasn't far from Antioch, where there was a thriving church, it isn't difficult to assume there was already a group of Christians there in that city.

2. (5) On the island of Cyprus: The city of **Salamis**, on the east coast.

And when they arrived in Salamis, they preached the word of God in the synagogues of the Jews. They also had John as *their* assistant.

a. **When they arrived in Salamis**: We are not told *why* they went to Cyprus first, but we do know Barnabas grew up on that island (Acts 4:36).

b. **They preached the word of God in the synagogues**: This custom of the open synagogue gave Barnabas and Saul many opportunities to preach. This tradition invited any learned man to speak to the people of the synagogue at the Sabbath meeting.

c. **They also had John as their assistant**: This man, also known as *John Mark*, was mentioned previously in Acts 12:25. He traveled with Barnabas and Saul on this trip and was the same Mark who later wrote the Gospel that bears his name.

i. Mark was a valuable companion for Barnabas and Saul. He grew up in Jerusalem, and was an eyewitness of many of the events in the life of Jesus and could relate them with special power to Barnabas and Saul, and to others whom they preached to.

3. (6-7) Meeting the Roman proconsul in **Paphos**.

Now when they had gone through the island to Paphos, they found a certain sorcerer, a false prophet, a Jew whose name *was* Bar-Jesus, who was with the proconsul, Sergius Paulus, an intelligent man. This man called for Barnabas and Saul and sought to hear the word of God.

a. **Paphos**: This city on the west coast of Cyprus was known for its immorality. Here Barnabas and Saul faced a combination of immorality and spiritual darkness that was common across the pagan world of the Roman Empire.

i. "Paphos was infamous for its worship of Venus, the goddess of [sexual] love" (Barclay). "Athanasius styled its religion 'the deification of lust.' Neither men nor women could resort to the shrine of Venus without being defiled in mind and depraved in character." (Spurgeon)

b. **The proconsul, Sergius Paulus**: This was an important man. A Roman **proconsul** was responsible for an entire province and answered to the Roman Senate.

i. "All Roman provinces were divided into two classes, those that required troops and those that did not. The latter were administered by the Senate and ruled by proconsuls; the former were under the administration of the emperor." (Williams)

ii. "Sir William Ramsay reports that inscriptions bearing Sergius Paulus' name have been found on Cyprus confirming that he was a Christian and that his entire family became Christians." (Hughes)

c. **This man called for Barnabas and Saul and sought to hear the word of God**: While ministering in Paphos (presumably after the same fashion - going into the synagogues and presenting Jesus), an unexpected door opened – the proconsul wanted **to hear the word of God**.

4. (8-12) The resistance of Elymas the sorcerer.

But Elymas the sorcerer (for so his name is translated) withstood them, seeking to turn the proconsul away from the faith. Then Saul, who also *is called* Paul, filled with the Holy Spirit, looked intently at him and said, "O full of all deceit and all fraud, *you* son of the devil, *you* enemy of all righteousness, will you not cease perverting the straight ways of the Lord? "And now, indeed, the hand of the Lord *is* upon you, and you shall be blind, not seeing the sun for a time." And immediately a dark mist fell on him, and he went around seeking someone to lead him by the hand. Then the proconsul believed, when he saw what had been done, being astonished at the teaching of the Lord.

a. **Elymas the sorcerer (for so his name is translated)**: Paul was opposed by a man named **Elymas**. His real name was *Bar-Jesus* (Acts 13:6) which means "son of Jesus," and Luke couldn't bear to call him that. This **Elymas** (who was some kind of advisor to the proconsul) attempted to frustrate the missionary efforts of Barnabas and Saul.

i. We should not be surprised or shaken by opposition. "Wherever there is likely to be great success, the open door and the opposing adversaries will both be found. If there are no adversaries, you may fear that there will be no success. A boy cannot get his kite up without wind, nor without a wind which drives *against* his kite." (Spurgeon)

b. **Saul, who also is called Paul**: It was common for people in that day to have names that were similar yet different according to the language or culture they were in. Certainly, Saul's given name was **Saul**, a Jewish name after the first king of Israel. But his Roman name was **Paul** – which meant "Little" and sounded similar to "Saul."

i. "Saul's father gave the child a Roman and a Latin name because he was a Roman citizen with all the rights in the Roman Empire this implied. The child had both names from infancy. When his father called him he shouted, 'Saul, Saul!' but when the Greek boys with whom he played called him they shouted, 'Paul, Paul!'" (Lenski)

c. **Filled with the Holy Spirit...Said, "O full of all deceit and all fraud"**: Paul, using spiritual discernment and operating in the gift of faith, rebuked and pronounced the judgment of God upon Elymas (**you shall be blind**).

i. As Elymas was struck with blindness, we can't help but think Paul would remember his own experience with God. Paul was struck blind at his conversion on the road to Damascus (Acts 9:9). Certainly, those who resist God are blind spiritually, so God just gave Elymas a physical blindness that matched his spiritual blindness. Sadly, we never hear of Elymas repenting, as Paul did.

d. **Then the proconsul believed**: Paul was harsh in his confrontation against Elymas because the eternal destiny of the proconsul was at stake.

i. If one wants to commit spiritual suicide, that's one thing. But it is never right to bring others down also. If you want to give up on the things of God and grow bitter in your heart against Him, that's your choice. But it is a heavy sin to draw anyone else away with you, either with your words or your example.

ii. "The severest words of the Bible, Old and New Testaments, are reserved for those who stand between men and truth, for those who stand between men and God...It must be the heart that loves Sergius Paulus that speaks in anger to Elymas the sorcerer." (Morgan)

e. **When he saw what had been done**: Among other things, we can say that the proconsul saw something in Paul and something in Elymas.

i. He saw the *courage* of Paul. Here was a man of conviction, bold in his belief, and willing to make a stand for what he believed.

ii. He saw the *just result* of Elymas' sin, physical blindness corresponding to his spiritual blindness. When we see the trouble sin brings people into, it helps us pursue God more earnestly.

f. **Being astonished at the teaching of the Lord**: As amazing as the miracle of Elymas' sudden blindness was, the good news the proconsul heard from Paul was even more amazing. His astonishment is said to be at the **teaching of the Lord** (presumably, the doctrines of God's gracious gift to man in Jesus, through the cross) not the miraculous work before his eyes.

4. (13) From Paphos to Perga.

Now when Paul and his party set sail from Paphos, they came to Perga in Pamphylia; and John, departing from them, returned to Jerusalem.

a. **Now when Paul and his party set sail**: The missionary group is now described as "**Paul and his party.**" Previously – as recently as Acts 13:7 – the group was described as *Barnabas and Saul*. From this point on, Paul's leadership and prominence will be evident.

b. **They came to Perga**: They left the island of Cyprus, coming to Perga on the mainland of what is today Turkey.

c. **John, departing from them, returned to Jerusalem**: We don't know exactly why John Mark went home to Jerusalem. Perhaps he was homesick. Perhaps he was afraid of the tough and dangerous travel through the mountains ahead of them. Perhaps he resented that the team of his cousin *Barnabas and Saul* (Acts 12:25) had now become **Paul and his party**. Perhaps he lost confidence because Paul suffered poor health (according to Galatians 4:13).

i. As will be clear from Acts 15:36-41, Paul didn't appreciate the departure of John Mark here, and to some degree he seems to have lost confidence in him as a missionary companion, a member of the team. This reminds us that as great and godly as these men were, and as great as the work was that they did, they still had problems.

C. The sermon at Pisidian Antioch.

1. (14-15) The customary invitation in the synagogue gives Paul an opportunity to preach Jesus.

But when they departed from Perga, they came to Antioch in Pisidia, and went into the synagogue on the Sabbath day and sat down. And after the reading of the Law and the Prophets, the rulers of the synagogue sent to them, saying, "Men *and* brethren, if you have any word of exhortation for the people, say on."

a. **They departed from Perga, they came to Antioch in Pisidia: Perga** was a costal, harbor city, where the ship from Paphos came to the mainland. **Antioch in Pisidia** was about 135 miles (220 kilometers) inland, to the north. This general region was known as Galatia, and later Paul wrote a letter to these churches that is included in our New Testament library.

i. "Pisidian Antioch was in the mountains at an altitude of about 3,600 feet. Since Paul mentions in the letter to the Galatians that he had a bodily affliction at this time, some scholars have supposed that Paul caught a disease, perhaps malaria, while living in Pamphylia's lower coastal plains and that he had his party pressed on into the healthier mountain climate because of it." (Boice)

b. **Went into the synagogue on the Sabbath day and sat down. And after the reading of the Law and the Prophets**. A first-century synagogue service followed a general order. Opening prayers were offered, and then there was a reading from **the Law** (the first five books of the Old Testament). Then, a reading from **the Prophets**. Then, if there was an educated person present, they were invited to speak on subjects related to the readings.

c. **Men and brethren, if you have any word of exhortation for the people, say on**: The **rulers of the synagogue** gave Paul the customary invitation, and he was more than happy to use the opportunity.

2. (16-23) Paul begins his sermon in the synagogue, explaining how God's work in history leads up to Jesus.

Then Paul stood up, and motioning with *his* hand said, "Men of Israel, and you who fear God, listen: The God of this people Israel chose our fathers, and exalted the people when they dwelt as strangers in the land of Egypt, and with an uplifted arm He brought them out of it. Now for a time of about forty years He put up with their ways in the wilderness. And when He had destroyed seven nations in the land of Canaan, He distributed their land to them by allotment. After that He gave *them* judges for about four hundred and fifty years, until Samuel the prophet. And afterward they asked for a king; so God gave them Saul the son of Kish, a man of the tribe of Benjamin, for forty years. And when He had removed him, He raised up for them David as king, to whom also He gave testimony and said, 'I have found David the *son* of Jesse, a man

after My *own* heart, who will do all My will.' From this man's seed, according to *the* promise, God raised up for Israel a Savior; Jesus."

a. **Men of Israel and you who fear God**: Paul addressed both groups at the synagogue on a typical Sabbath; both Jews and "near Jews," those Gentiles who admired the Jewish religion but did not make a full commitment to Judaism.

b. **According to the promise, God raised up for Israel a Savior; Jesus**: In this survey of Israel's history, Paul noted important events - the choosing of the patriarchs, the deliverance from Egypt, the time in the wilderness, the conquest of Canaan, the time of the Judges, the creation of a monarchy - but it all led up to Jesus.

i. This survey of Israel's history demonstrates that God has a plan for history, and we need to sense a connection to that plan. Jesus is the goal of history, and as we are in Jesus, we are in the flow of God's great plan of redemption.

3. (24-29) Using the examples of John the Baptist and the Jewish rulers, Paul shows how people both received and rejected Jesus.

"After John had first preached, before His coming, the baptism of repentance to all the people of Israel. And as John was finishing his course, he said, 'Who do you think I am? I am not *He*. But behold, there comes One after me, the sandals of whose feet I am not worthy to loose.' Men *and* brethren, sons of the family of Abraham, and those among you who fear God, to you the word of this salvation has been sent. For those who dwell in Jerusalem, and their rulers, because they did not know Him, nor even the voices of the Prophets which are read every Sabbath, have fulfilled *them* in condemning *Him*. And though they found no cause for death *in Him*, they asked Pilate that He should be put to death. Now when they had fulfilled all that was written concerning Him, they took *Him* down from the tree and laid *Him* in a tomb."

a. **As John was finishing his course, he said**: John the Baptist responded to Jesus the right way. He prepared the hearts of others for Jesus, and he saw Jesus as who He really was. John knew Jesus was the One greater than all others. He knew Jesus was more than a teacher; He was the Lord God we must all answer to.

i. **The sandals of whose feet I am not worthy to loose**: This statement shows that John knew Jesus was high above him. In that day, it was not uncommon for a great teacher to have disciples follow him, and it was expected that the disciples would serve the teacher in various ways. This arrangement came to be abused, so the leading rabbis established certain things that were too demeaning for a teacher to expect of his disciple. It was decided that for a teacher to expect his disciple to undo the strap of his sandal was too much; it was too demeaning. Here, John insisted he wasn't even worthy to do this for Jesus.

b. **For those who dwell in Jerusalem, and their rulers, because they did not know Him**: Those who didn't know the Scriptures rejected Jesus, and delivered Him to Pilate to be executed. This was true even though they lived **in Jerusalem** and were **rulers** among the Jews. Therefore Jesus was executed and laid in a tomb.

c. **They took Him down from the tree**: In calling the cross a **tree**, Paul drew on the idea from Deuteronomy 21:22-23. In that passage, it says that God curses a person who is hanged from a tree. Paul wanted to communicate the idea that Jesus was cursed so that we could be blessed (Galatians 3:13).

4. (30-37) Paul preaches the resurrected Jesus.

But God raised Him from the dead. He was seen for many days by those who came up with Him from Galilee to Jerusalem, who are His witnesses to the people. And we declare to you glad tidings; that promise which was made to the fathers. God has fulfilled this for us their children, in that He has raised up Jesus. As it is also written in the second Psalm:

**'You are My Son,
Today I have begotten You.'**

And that He raised Him from the dead, no more to return to corruption, He has spoken thus:

'I will give you the sure mercies of David.'

Therefore He also says in another *Psalm*:

'You will not allow Your Holy One to see corruption.'

"For David, after he had served his own generation by the will of God, fell asleep, was buried with his fathers, and saw corruption; but He whom God raised up saw no corruption.

a. **But God**: These are wonderful words. Man did his best to fight against God - even to kill Him - **but God** was greater than man's sin and rebellion, and Jesus rose from the grave, winning over sin and death.

b. **But God raised Him from the dead**: Here, the fact was simply stated. Yet, evidence from eyewitnesses was also offered (**He was seen for many days by those who came up with Him**).

i. We should not miss an emphasis on *events* in Paul's preaching here; it is so evident that it can be missed. He focused on things that actually happened, not on philosophy or even theology. "Christianity is not just a philosophy or a set of ethics, though it involves these things. Essentially Christianity is a proclamation of facts that concern what God has done." (Boice)

c. **God has fulfilled this for us their children**: Then Paul applied the truth of Jesus' resurrection. The resurrection means that Jesus truly is the unique Son of God (Psalm 2:7), and it proves that He was utterly holy even in His work on the cross (Psalm 16:10).

5. (38-41) With a promise and a warning, Paul applies the truth of who Jesus is and what He did for us.

Therefore let it be known to you, brethren, that through this Man is preached to you the forgiveness of sins; and by Him everyone who believes is justified from all things from which you could not be justified by the law of Moses. Beware therefore, lest what has been spoken in the prophets come upon you:

'Behold, you despisers,
Marvel and perish!
For I work a work in your days,
A work which you will by no means believe,
Though one were to declare it to you.'"

a. **Through this Man is preached to you the forgiveness of sins**: The promise is that, because of who Jesus is and what He did for us, **forgiveness** is offered to us freely in Jesus. We may be **justified from all things from which you could not be justified by the law of Moses**.

i. We can never justify ourselves before God. To think so assumes God grades on a curve, a measure that bends according to human weakness. To think so also gives us the glory for our own salvation instead of simply saying, "*For by grace you have been saved through faith, and that not of yourselves; it is the gift of God, not of works, lest anyone should boast.*" (Ephesians 2:8-9)

ii. Some refuse to embrace the salvation of Jesus in the secret place of their heart, because they want a salvation of their *own* making. They want to be saved the old-fashioned way - they want to *earn* it.

iii. Only a few months after this Paul, wrote a letter to these churches in Galatia, dealing with these same themes of being justified by God's grace, and not by keeping the law.

b. **Everyone who believes is justified**: Jesus does not only forgive us, but we are also **justified** by Him. Forgiveness takes care of the debt of sin, but justification puts a positive credit on our account before God.

c. **Beware, therefore**: The warning is that if we do not embrace the person and work of Jesus with our whole lives, we are **despisers** who will **perish**. In this warning, Paul quoted a passage from Habakkuk regarding the judgment that came upon Jerusalem. If God judged them, He will also judge those who refuse and reject His offer of forgiveness through the work of Jesus.

i. "Although ours is an age of great grace, God is nevertheless also a God of great judgment, and sin must be judged if it is not atoned for by the work of Christ." (Boice)

ii. Some commentators complain that Paul here preached too much like Peter did on Pentecost. It is a strange complaint. This shows us that Peter and Paul preached the same gospel, and the same gospel was preached some fifteen years after Pentecost as was preached on that first day.

iii. Others note similarities between Paul's sermon here and the sermon of Stephen in Acts 7. That was a sermon that Paul heard when he still hated the name of Jesus. Perhaps the sermon of the first martyr of the church still rang in the ears of the man who presided over his execution.

D. The Response to the sermon at Pisidian Antioch.

1. (42-43) Many people, both Jews and Gentiles, express interest in Paul's message.

So when the Jews went out of the synagogue, the Gentiles begged that these words might be preached to them the next Sabbath. Now when the congregation had broken up, many of the Jews and devout proselytes followed Paul and Barnabas, who, speaking to them, persuaded them to continue in the grace of God.

a. **When the Jews went out of the synagogue, the Gentiles begged that these words might be preached to them the next Sabbath**: Both Jews and Gentiles at the synagogue responded positively, yet Luke noted an even greater response from the **Gentiles** present.

i. We should assume that many of these believed for two reasons.

- First, because **many of the Jews and devout proselytes followed Paul and Barnabas**. There was a continuing interest in their message.

- Second, because Paul and Barnabas **persuaded them to continue in the grace of God**. This means they had already started to trust in the grace of God.

b. **Persuaded them to continue in the grace of God**: *Continuing* in grace is as important as beginning in grace; we must never leave it as the basic principle of our relationship with God. Far too many only think of **grace** as the introduction to the Christian life, but God wants **grace** to remain as the foundation for our life with Him.

2. (44-45) On the next Sabbath, envy creates opposition.

On the next Sabbath almost the whole city came together to hear the word of God. But when the Jews saw the multitudes, they were filled with envy; and contradicting and blaspheming, they opposed the things spoken by Paul.

a. **On the next Sabbath almost the whole city came together to hear the word of God**: The scene is easy to picture. The whole city was ready to hear the gospel from Paul on the next Sabbath.

i. "In our day, people are overwhelmed with information. We have radio, television, newspapers, magazines. People did not have any of this in that day. So when somebody came through from another city, the person was a source of precious information and people naturally thronged about him. The missionaries were proclaiming something new." (Boice)

ii. Yet there was not merely the power of novelty; there was more notably the power of **the word of God**. *This* was the primary power that attracted people, and Luke emphasized it in his account.

- *The whole city came together to hear the word of God* (Acts 13:44).
- Paul and Barnabas spoke *the word of God* to them first (Acts 13:46).
- The Gentiles responded to *the word of the Lord* (Acts 13:48).
- The *word of the Lord* spread through the region (Acts 13:49).

b. **But when the Jews saw the multitudes, they were filled with envy**: The dramatic response made the leaders of the synagogue envious. This is inevitable for those who are more concerned about being popular than serving God. When someone else is more popular, they become **filled with envy**. We can't all be popular to the same degree, but we can all serve and please God to the same degree in Jesus Christ.

c. **Contradicting and blaspheming, they opposed the things spoken by Paul**: Suddenly, Paul's preaching was opposed as if he were conducting a debate, with his opponents **contradicting** him and **blaspheming** God.

i. The blasphemy mentioned probably has to do with abusive and degrading language directed towards Jesus, whom Paul preached.

d. **They opposed the things spoken by Paul**: It seems strange that these religious people who waited so long for their Messiah would now reject Him when Jesus was presented to them. One great reason was they wanted to keep the division between Jew and Gentile, and if Jesus was to be the Messiah of all men, they wanted no part of Him.

> i. "They simply could not accept a teaching that opened such floodgates. For themselves and their adherents they could accept a message as God-sent and tolerate some change in their teaching and practice, but they could not endure that the Gentiles should be made equal with God's ancient people." (Williams)

> ii. "The Jews could not endure that the Gentiles should be equal to them, being as much concerned against the Gentiles being exalted, as against their own being depressed." (Poole)

> iii. Some people end up rejecting Jesus because of the way He changes our relationship with other people. Some would rather hold on to their bitterness and animosity towards others than turn to Jesus and be reconciled.

3. (46-48) Paul and Barnabas respond to the Jewish opposition.

Then Paul and Barnabas grew bold and said, "It was necessary that the word of God should be spoken to you first; but since you reject it, and judge yourselves unworthy of everlasting life, behold, we turn to the Gentiles. For so the Lord has commanded us:

**'I have set you as a light to the Gentiles,
That you should be for salvation to the ends of the earth.'"**

Now when the Gentiles heard this, they were glad and glorified the word of the Lord. And as many as had been appointed to eternal life believed.

a. **Then Paul and Barnabas grew bold**: They had wonderful zeal for the things of God. They wouldn't let this challenge go unanswered, because they really believed the truth about Jesus.

b. **Since you reject it, and judge yourselves unworthy of everlasting life, behold, we turn to the Gentiles**: They rebuked those who rejected Jesus, letting the Jews know that it was a privilege that this message should come to them first, a privilege they were now rejecting.

> i. When you want to tell others about Jesus, begin with your own group. But if they don't receive it, or when they start to reject it, don't stop telling others about Jesus. Just find others to tell, others who will listen.

c. **Now when the Gentiles heard this, they were glad and glorified the word of the Lord. And as many as had been appointed to eternal life believed**: They also responded with more evangelism to open hearts, now directing their efforts to the Gentiles, in obedience to God's command (Romans 1:16) and in fulfillment of prophecy (the quotation from Isaiah 49:6).

i. The Gentiles responded to Paul's invitation with enthusiastic belief, learning with joy that God *does not* hate Gentiles, but offered them salvation in Jesus.

ii. Paul showed wisdom in not spending all his time trying to persuade hardened hearts. We know that even after he made Gentiles the focus of his evangelistic efforts, he still prayed earnestly for the salvation of Israel (Romans 10:1), but he spent his missionary time ministering to more open hearts.

4. (49-50) Blessing and opposition.

And the word of the Lord was being spread throughout all the region. But the Jews stirred up the devout and prominent women and the chief men of the city, raised up persecution against Paul and Barnabas, and expelled them from their region.

a. **And the word of the Lord was being spread**: It was being spread through the efforts of Paul and Barnabas, but especially through the lives of these people being brought to Jesus Christ.

i. It's remarkable to think that this church was born in a little more than a week. On one Sabbath Paul and Barnabas preached in the synagogue and there was a wonderful response. The following Sabbath there was a mixed response, some very hostile and some very receptive. They took the receptive ones and started a church that was lasted for hundreds of years and through that church, **the word of the Lord was being spread throughout all the region** (Acts 13:49).

ii. Sometimes remarkable works of God happen quite quickly. We should be happy for such seasons of rapid progress in God's work.

b. **But the Jews stirred up the devout and prominent women and the chief men of the city, raised up persecution against Paul and Barnabas, and expelled them from their region**: Wherever there is revival, the second group to be revived is the Devil. Jewish opposition was strong enough to force Paul and Barnabas to leave the area.

5. (51-52) Paul and Barnabas react to their expulsion from the city of Pisidian Antioch.

But they shook off the dust from their feet against them, and came to Iconium. And the disciples were filled with joy and with the Holy Spirit.

a. **But they shook off the dust from their feet against them**: In doing this, Paul and Barnabas treated the city as if it were a God-rejecting Gentile city.

i. If Jewish people had to go in or through a Gentile city, when leaving the city they shook the dust off their feet as a gesture saying, "We don't want to take anything from this Gentile city with us." In this sense, Paul said "I don't want to take anything with me from you Jesus-rejecting religionists."

ii. This rejection did not make Paul and Barnabas think there was anything wrong with *themselves*. They knew the problem is with their opposition, not themselves.

b. **And came to Iconium**: They carried on the work, going next to **Iconium**. All too often, rejection and opposition for the sake of the gospel makes us want to give up. But Paul and Barnabas responded with appropriate determination.

c. **Filled with joy and with the Holy Spirit**: Being filled with joy and being filled with the Holy Spirit go together. Paul and Barnabas had joy that contradicted their circumstances.

i. Paul is a great example of his own command to *be constantly being filled with the Holy Spirit* (Ephesians 5:18).

ii. "The happiness of a genuine Christian lies far beyond the reach of earthly disturbances, and is not affected by the changes and chances to which mortal things are exposed. The martyrs were more happy in the *flames* than their persecutors could be on their beds of down." (Clarke)

Acts 14 – The Conclusion of the First Missionary Journey

A. In the city of Iconium.

1. (1) Paul and Barnabas have evangelistic success in Iconium.

Now it happened in Iconium that they went together to the synagogue of the Jews, and so spoke that a great multitude both of the Jews and of the Greeks believed.

a. **They went together to the synagogue of the Jews**: The leaders of the synagogue in Antioch had just expelled Paul and Barnabas from that city. Yet when they came to **Iconium**, they again began their evangelistic efforts by preaching in the **synagogue**. It was still a good way to start.

b. **So spoke that a great multitude both of the Jews and of the Greeks believed**: Paul and Barnabas had success among the Jews and the Greeks, presenting the same gospel to both. The fact that **Jews and… Greeks believed** shows that Paul preached the same thing to both groups: That salvation is in Jesus, and we appropriate it by our belief (trust in, reliance on) in Him.

i. The success is refreshing, because they had just been kicked out of Pisidian Antioch, after much success there (Acts 13:50).

ii. On other occasions Paul was inclined to stay in a region for an extended period of time, strengthening the churches and working where evangelistic efforts had already borne fruit. Therefore, it may be best to see the persecution Paul had in Pisidian Antioch as God's way of moving him on to Iconium and other places.

iii. **And so spoke**: Paul and Barnabas presented the gospel in a way that invited belief. The way they preached encouraged people to believe in the message of who Jesus is and what He had done for them.

2. (2-6) Successful ministry creates opposition, forcing Paul and Barnabas out of Iconium.

But the unbelieving Jews stirred up the Gentiles and poisoned their minds against the brethren. Therefore they stayed there a long time, speaking boldly in the Lord, who was bearing witness to the word of His grace, granting signs and wonders to be done by their hands. But the multitude of the city was divided: part sided with the Jews, and part with the apostles. And when a violent attempt was made by both the Gentiles and Jews, with their rulers, to abuse and stone them, they became aware of it and fled to Lystra and Derbe, cities of Lycaonia, and to the surrounding region.

a. **Unbelieving Jews stirred up the Gentiles and poisoned their minds against the brethren**: Luke made it clear that it was not all the Jews of Iconium who did this, because many believed (Acts 14:1). Yet some not only rejected the message, but **stirred up** others to reject the message and the messengers (**against the brethren**).

b. **Therefore they stayed a long time**: They stayed as long as they could, despite the opposition, leaving only when it was absolutely necessary. They did this because they knew that these Christians in Iconium needed all the grounding they could get to stand strong in a city with much opposition.

i. "It took a long time, however, for the opposition to become serious, and the missionaries continued to preach the gospel freely and boldly." (Bruce)

c. **Speaking boldly in the Lord**: Despite the opposition, Paul and Barnabas continued to preach boldly, **bearing witness to the word of His grace** and touching others with the power of Jesus.

i. **Granting signs and wonders to be done by their hands**: "For no apostle could work a miracle by himself; nor was any sign or wonder wrought even by the greatest apostle, but by a special grant or dispensation of God. This power was not resident in them at all times." (Clarke)

d. **Bearing witness to the word of His grace**: The miraculous works done confirmed this message they preached - **the word of His grace**. That is the only word by which both Jews and Gentiles could be saved on an equal basis.

i. "The gospel is here called *the message of his grace* because divine grace is its subject matter." (Bruce)

e. **A violent attempt was made by both the Gentiles and Jews, with their rulers, to abuse and stone them, they became aware of it and fled**:

When forced to, Paul and Barnabas left Iconium for Lystra (some twenty miles away) and Derbe. Their perseverance under the difficulty in Iconium didn't mean that it was time for them to become martyrs.

i. Acts 14:4 is the first time Paul and Barnabas are called **apostles** in the Book of Acts. The only other time the title is used for them in Acts is at 14:14. Paul often used the title of himself in his letters.

f. **Lystra and Derbe, cities of Lycaonia**: William Ramsay demonstrated that Lystra and Derbe were indeed together in the Roman province of Lycaonia, but only between A.D. 37 and 72, the exact period these events in Acts took place. This kind of accuracy persuaded Ramsay that the Biblical account was true, especially in an age when they were all thought to be fables and made-up stories.

B. In the cities of Lystra and Derbe.

1. (7-10) In Lystra, a lame man is healed.

And they were preaching the gospel there. And in Lystra a certain man without strength in his feet was sitting, a cripple from his mother's womb, who had never walked. *This* man heard Paul speaking. Paul, observing him intently and seeing that he had faith to be healed, said with a loud voice, "Stand up straight on your feet!" And he leaped and walked.

a. **And they were preaching the gospel there**: Paul and Barnabas did many miraculous works, one of which is recorded in the following passage. Yet they did not travel as miracle workers. Their focus was always **preaching the gospel**.

i. "The apostles did not go into these cities to do miracles, and then to preach. Rather, it was the other way around: They went to preach; then sometimes there were healings." (Boice)

b. **This man heard Paul speaking**: The crippled man heard Paul preach about Jesus. When he heard about Jesus, his face and manner showed that he believed Jesus could touch *his* life; he **had faith to be healed**.

i. This **certain man without strength in his feet** made the important transition from hearing about the work of Jesus to believing that it was for him. Not everyone makes this same transition, but they should.

c. **Paul, observing him intently and seeing that he had faith to be healed**: There was something about this man's faith that was evident, and it is likely that God gave Paul the gift of discernment, so much so that Paul knew God intended to heal the man at that moment.

i. "That this lame man had faith was made plain by his ready obedience to Paul's command to stand up." (Bruce)

2. (11-13) The excited crowd in Lystra declares Paul and Barnabas to be Greek gods, visiting the earth.

Now when the people saw what Paul had done, they raised their voices, saying in the Lycaonian *language,* "The gods have come down to us in the likeness of men!" And Barnabas they called Zeus, and Paul, Hermes, because he was the chief speaker. Then the priest of Zeus, whose temple was in front of their city, brought oxen and garlands to the gates, intending to sacrifice with the multitudes.

a. **The gods have come down to us in the likeness of men!** These people saw a stupendous miracle happen before their eyes, yet their idea of *who God is* had not changed. Therefore it seemed logical to them to consider Paul and Barnabas gods.

i. The miracle merely attracted attention, and in a way, it was unwanted attention. The miracle itself saved no one.

b. **Barnabas they called Zeus, and Paul, Hermes, because he was the chief speaker:** In Greek mythology, it was common for the gods to come to earth in human form, though they did not always do so for the good of man.

i. The people of Lystra had a legend that once Zeus and Hermes visited their land disguised as mortals, and no one gave them any hospitality except for one older couple. In their anger at the people, Zeus and Hermes wiped out the whole population, except for the old couple. This may help explain why the Lystrians were so quick to honor Paul and Barnabas.

c. **And Paul, Hermes:** He was known as the messenger of the gods, so it made sense to the Lystrians that Paul (the more talkative one) was **Hermes, because he was the chief speaker.** Barnabas apparently had an air of authority about him, so they regarded him as **Zeus.**

i. Their adoration of Paul and Barnabas progressed because they praised them **in the Lycaonian language.** "The crowd's use of Lycaonian explains why Paul and Barnabas did not grasp what was afoot until the preparations to pay them divine homage were well advanced." (Bruce)

ii. But when Paul and Barnabas saw **the priest of Zeus,** with **oxen and garlands... intending to sacrifice,** they knew things had gone too far. This was far more than honoring guests to the city.

3. (14-18) Paul appeals to the crowd, asking them to recognize the true God instead of worshipping Paul and Barnabas.

But when the apostles Barnabas and Paul heard this, they tore their clothes and ran in among the multitude, crying out and saying, "Men, why are you doing these things? We also are men with the same nature as you, and preach to you that you should turn from these useless things to the living God, who made the heaven, the earth, the sea, and all things that are in them, who in bygone generations allowed all nations to walk in their own ways. Nevertheless He did not leave Himself without witness, in that He did good, gave us rain from heaven and fruitful seasons, filling our hearts with food and gladness." And with these sayings they could scarcely restrain the multitudes from sacrificing to them.

a. **They tore their clothes**: They did this to show that they were completely human, just as the Lystrians. They also did it out of an instinctively Jewish reaction to blasphemy. For Paul and Barnabas, it wasn't just *inconvenient* that they were called gods; it was *blasphemy*.

b. **That you should turn from these useless things**: These were strong words from Paul to people who took their pagan worship seriously, but Paul wasn't afraid to confront this mob with the truth, and the truth was that their idolatry was wrong. They had to **turn** from it.

i. As Paul told them more about Jesus and what He has done, he especially wanted them to **turn from these useless things to the living God**. Jesus could not merely be added to their pagan ways.

c. **To the living God, who made the heaven, the earth, the sea, and all things that are in them**: Paul called the Lystrian crowd to consider the real God, the One who stands behind all creation, not one of the lesser (and imaginary) Greek gods.

i. The things Paul mentions in Acts 14:17 (**He did good... gave us rain from heaven... and fruitful seasons... filling our hearts with food and gladness**) were just the kind of things these people would think that Zeus gave them. Paul told them these blessings come from the true God who lives in heaven, not from Zeus.

ii. God's kindness to all men (in giving rain and fruitful crops) should be seen as a witness of His love and power, something theologians sometimes call *common grace*.

iii. Paul did not preach to these pagan worshippers the same way he preached to Jews or those acquainted with Judaism. He did not quote the Old Testament to them, but instead appealed to natural revelation, to the things that even a pagan could understand by looking at the world around them.

d. And with these sayings they could scarcely restrain the multitudes from sacrificing to them: Even with all this, Paul and Barnabas had an extremely difficult time challenging the wrong conceptions of God held by the Lystrians.

4. (19-20a) Persecution follows Paul.

Then Jews from Antioch and Iconium came there; and having persuaded the multitudes, they stoned Paul *and* dragged *him* out of the city, supposing him to be dead. However, when the disciples gathered around him, he rose up and went into the city.

a. **Then Jews from Antioch and Iconium came**: These opponents were not content to kick Paul out of their own region (Acts 14:5-6); they followed him and brought their persecution with them.

i. Some of these persecuting **Jews from Antioch and Iconium** traveled more than one hundred miles just to make Paul miserable. They were dedicated adversaries of Paul.

b. **Having persuaded the multitudes**: They incited the people of Lystra against Paul and Barnabas, and instigated the stoning of Paul. This was obviously an attempt to execute Paul and Barnabas - with the rocks being thrown by the same people who wanted to worship them shortly before.

i. This is a dramatic demonstration of how fickle a crowd can be. Their admiration of the miracle and desire to honor Paul and Barnabas as gods did not last long.

ii. It is dangerous for any spiritual leader to cultivate or allow a kind of hero-worship. The same people who give this honor will feel terribly betrayed when the leader is shown to be human.

c. **They stoned Paul and dragged him out of the city, supposing him to be dead. However, when the disciples gathered around him, he rose up and went into the city**: Paul was miraculously preserved here. Some think that he was even actually killed and raised to life again, because stoning was usually reliable form of execution.

i. When Paul later wrote, *I bear in my body the marks of Jesus* (Galatians 6:17), he may have had in mind the scars from this incident. He certainly later referred to this stoning in 2 Corinthians 11:25.

ii. It has been suggested that the heavenly vision described by Paul in 2 Corinthians 12 took place at this attack. This is possible, but only conjecture.

iii. It's reasonable to think that Paul remembered Stephen when he was being stoned, and how he had been a part of Stephen's execution (Acts 7:58-8:1).

d. **He rose up and went into the city**: When Paul was revived, he did not flee the city that stoned him. Instead he immediately went back into it. He had been driven out of Antioch and Iconium by this traveling mob, and he was determined to leave Lystra on his own terms.

i. In Acts 16:1, we learn of a young Christian in Lystra and his mother - Timothy. Perhaps Timothy saw all this and was inspired to the high call of the gospel by noticing Paul's courage and power in ministry.

5. (20b-21a) Paul leaves Lystra for the city of Derbe, where they find more evangelistic success.

And the next day he departed with Barnabas to Derbe. And when they had preached the gospel to that city and made many disciples.

a. **When they had preached the gospel to that city and made many disciples**: Despite the persecution in Lystra, the work of God continued - just in a different place, **Derbe**. Yet Paul and Barnabas continued their work: preaching the **gospel** and making **disciples**.

C. The return trip home to Syrian Antioch.

1. (21b-22) The message of Paul and Barnabas on the return trip.

They returned to Lystra, Iconium, and Antioch, strengthening the souls of the disciples, exhorting *them* to continue in the faith, and *saying*, "We must through many tribulations enter the kingdom of God."

a. **Strengthening the souls of the disciples, exhorting them to continue in the faith**: As Paul and Barnabas decided to head back home to Antioch, they passed through the cities they had visited before, to strengthen and encourage the Christians in those cities. Paul and Barnabas wanted to do far more than gain conversions; they had a passion to make **disciples**.

i. Many Christians need **strengthening** in their **souls**. Many need **exhorting... to continue in the faith**. It is no small thing to walk with the Lord, year after year, trial after trial. It takes a strong soul and an encouraged faith.

b. **We must through many tribulations enter the kingdom of God**: This was the message that helped strengthen and exhort these disciples. This was a simple message, proved in Paul's personal experience. Paul could *preach* that message because he had *lived* that message.

i. This is for many a forgotten message today. They consider any kind of tribulation completely counter-productive to Christian living, failing to note the significant place suffering has in God's plan.

2. (23) The work of Paul and Barnabas on the way home to Syrian Antioch.

So when they had appointed elders in every church, and prayed with fasting, they commended them to the Lord in whom they had believed.

a. **So when they had appointed elders in every church**: Paul and Barnabas were committed to not just making new Christians, but in establishing new *churches*, places where these new Christians could grow and be established in the Lord.

i. "The apostles had left behind only a tiny core of believers, and these had hardly been taught anything, since the apostles had been there at best for only a few weeks. How could this little group survive? It survived because the work was actually being done by God. The church was his church." (Boice)

b. **When they had appointed elders in every church**: Paul and Barnabas knew that these churches must have proper administration, so they appointed elders in every city where there were Christians.

i. "It has more than once been pointed out that more recent missionary policy would have thought it dangerously idealistic to recognize converts of only a few weeks' standing as leaders in their churches; perhaps Paul and Barnabas were more conscious of the presence and power of the Holy Spirit in the believing communities." (Bruce)

c. **And prayed with fasting**: Paul and Barnabas demonstrated their great concern for the health of these churches by their prayer and fasting.

d. **They commended them to the Lord in whom they had believed**: But in the end, they can only trust in God's ability to keep these churches healthy, having **commended them to the Lord**. It was in the Lord **they had believed**, not in Paul or Barnabas or the elders. The church belongs to Jesus.

3. (24-26) The itinerary of Paul and Barnabas on the way home.

And after they had passed through Pisidia, they came to Pamphylia. Now when they had preached the word in Perga, they went down to Attalia. From there they sailed to Antioch, where they had been commended to the grace of God for the work which they had completed.

a. **After they had passed through Pisidia**: On the continent, they returned pretty much the same way they came. They did not stop on the island of Cyprus, but **sailed to Antioch**, returning to their home congregation.

b. **For the work which they had completed**: They beautiful words were only partially true. Although the immediate mission was accomplished, the work of planting new churches and strengthening existing ones has never ended. This would be merely the first of several missionary journeys.

4. (27-28) Paul and Barnabas arrive back in Antioch.

Now when they had come and gathered the church together, they reported all that God had done with them, and that He had opened the door of faith to the Gentiles. So they stayed there a long time with the disciples.

a. **They reported all that God had done with them, and that He had opened the door of faith to the Gentiles**: Their success with evangelism among the Gentiles, and the blessing of God that it demonstrated, showed that what God did in Antioch was not unique. God wanted to replicate this work all over the world.

i. "In saying that the missionaries *reported* these things, Luke has used the verb in the imperfect. This may mean that the report was repeated as the two met with different groups scattered throughout the city. But the word *church* is in the singular. There may have been a number of groups meeting separately, but there was only one church." (Williams)

b. **He had opened the door of faith**: The trip was a great success, though not without great obstacles: The difficulty of travel itself, the confrontation with Elymas on Cyprus, the quitting of John Mark, being driven out of the cities of Antioch and Iconium, the temptation to receive adoration, and being stoned in Lystra. Yet Paul and Barnabas would not be deterred from the work God had them to do.

i. It can and should be asked of each follower of Jesus, "What will it take for you to back down from doing God's will? What kind of temptation or obstacle or opposition will do it?" Nothing stopped Jesus from doing God's will on our behalf; as we look to Him, we won't be stopped either.

ii. Paul later expressed this drive in a letter to a congregation: *I press on, that I may lay hold of that for which Christ Jesus has also laid hold of me. Brethren, I do not count myself to have apprehended; but one thing I do, forgetting those things which are behind and reaching forward to those things which are ahead, I press toward the goal for the prize of the upward call of God in Christ Jesus.* (Philippians 3:12-14)

c. **So they stayed there a long time with the disciples**: Back at their home church in Syrian Antioch, we can assume that Paul and Barnabas took a long break and found plenty of ministry to do back there.

Acts 15 - The Jerusalem Council

A. The dispute between the men from Judea and Paul and Barnabas.

1. (1) The men **from Judea** state their case.

And certain *men* came down from Judea and taught the brethren, "Unless you are circumcised according to the custom of Moses, you cannot be saved."

> a. **Certain men came down from Judea and taught the brethren, "Unless you are circumcised according to the custom of Moses, you cannot be saved."** These Jewish Christians (often called "Judaizers") came to the congregation in Antioch and taught that Gentiles may become Christians, but only after first becoming Jews, and submitting to all Jewish rituals, including circumcision.
>
>> i. It was very difficult for some Jewish Christians to accept that Gentiles could be brought into the church as equal members without first coming through the Law of Moses. "It was one thing to accept the occasional God-fearer into the church, someone already in sympathy with Jewish ways; it was quite another to welcome large numbers of Gentiles who had no regard for the law and no intention of keeping it." (Williams)
>
> b. **Came down from Judea and taught the brethren**: These Christians were **from Judea**, and were not content to keep their beliefs to themselves, but felt compelled to persuade other Christians. They **taught the brethren**, coming all the way to Antioch to preach this message.
>
>> i. By their teaching, these **certain men from Judea** made a negative judgment on all of Paul and Barnabas' missionary endeavors. On their recent missionary journey, they founded churches among the Gentiles *without* bringing them under the Law of Moses. These **certain men from Judea** said Paul and Barnabas were all wrong in doing this.

196

ii. When in the city of Antioch in Pisidia, Paul preached this message: *And by Him* [Jesus] *everyone who believes is justified from all things from which you could not be justified by the law of Moses* (Acts 13:39). These **certain men…from Judea** would have objected, saying "Jesus saves us, but only after we have done all we can do to keep the Law of Moses." But Paul taught a man could only be right with God on the basis of what Jesus had done.

c. **You cannot be saved**: This was not a side issue; it had to do with salvation itself – how one is made right with God. This was not a matter where there could be disagreement among believers, with some believing you must be under the law, and some believing it wasn't important. This was an issue that went to the core of Christianity, and it had to be resolved.

i. We can just imagine how Satan wanted to take advantage of this situation. First, he wanted the false doctrine of righteousness by works to succeed. But even if it didn't, Satan wanted a costly, bitter doctrinal war to completely split and sour the church. This may be the greatest threat to the work of the gospel yet seen in the Book of Acts.

2. (2-4) Paul and Barnabas respond to the teaching of the men from Judea.

Therefore, when Paul and Barnabas had no small dissension and dispute with them, they determined that Paul and Barnabas and certain others of them should go up to Jerusalem, to the apostles and elders, about this question. So, being sent on their way by the church, they passed through Phoenicia and Samaria, describing the conversion of the Gentiles; and they caused great joy to all the brethren. And when they had come to Jerusalem, they were received by the church and the apostles and the elders; and they reported all things that God had done with them.

a. **Paul and Barnabas had no small dissension and dispute with them**: Their first response was to persuade. We can imagine there was **no small dissension and dispute with them** indeed. These two who saw God work so powerfully through the Gentiles would not abandon that work easily.

i. In this, Paul and Barnabas showed the hearts of true shepherds: To confront and dispute with those who insist on promoting false doctrines in the church.

b. **They determined that Paul and Barnabas and certain others of them should go up to Jerusalem**: When persuasion did not end the issue, Paul and Barnabas went to Jerusalem to have the matter settled by **the apostles and elders**. They couldn't just agree to disagree on this issue, because it was at the core of what meant to be a follower of Jesus.

i. Who were the ones **who determined that Paul and Barnabas** should go to Jerusalem to determine this question? It seems to speak of the church collectively in Antioch, where this false teaching was promoted. The statement that they were **sent on their way by the church** suggests this.

c. **They caused great joy to all the brethren**: As Paul and Barnabas went to Jerusalem, they found plenty of other Christians who rejoiced at what God did among the Gentiles. This was in contrast to the certain men from Judea.

3. (5) The men from Judea re-state their teaching.

But some of the sect of the Pharisees who believed rose up, saying, "It is necessary to circumcise them, and to command *them* to keep the law of Moses."

a. **Some of the sect of the Pharisees who believed rose up**: Many of those who opposed Paul and Barnabas were Christians who had been **Pharisees**. The **Pharisees** were well known for their high regard for the law, and their desire to obey the law in the smallest details.

i. If the Pharisees believed anything, they believed one could be justified before God by keeping the law. For a Pharisee to really be a Christian, it would take more than an acknowledgment that Jesus was Messiah; he would have to forsake his attempts to justify himself by the keeping of the law and accept the work of Jesus as the basis of his justification.

ii. In Lystra, Paul and Barnabas did not allow the pagans to merely add Jesus to their pantheon of Roman gods. They commanded that they had to turn from their vain gods to the true God (Acts 14:14-15). These Pharisees who had become Christians had to do the same thing: Turn from *their* efforts to earn their way before God by keeping the law, and look to Jesus. You can't just add Jesus and now say "Jesus helps me to justify myself through keeping the law."

iii. Paul himself was a former Pharisee (Philippians 3:5) who became a Christian. But he came to know that Jesus didn't help him do what a Pharisee did, only better. He knew that Jesus *was* his salvation, not *the way* to his salvation. Paul wrote: *knowing that a man is not justified by the works of the law but by faith in Jesus Christ, even we have believed in Christ Jesus, that we might be justified by faith in Christ and not by the works of the law; for by the works of the law no flesh shall be justified.* (Galatians 2:16)

b. **It is necessary to circumcise them, and to command them to keep the law of Moses**: These former Pharisees taught two things. First, Gentile converts must be *initiated* into Judaism through circumcision. Second, that Gentile converts must *live under* **the law of Moses** if they were to be right with God and embraced into the Christian community.

i. Basically, their teaching was: "Gentiles are free to come to Jesus. We welcome them and want them to come to Jesus. But they have to come through the Law of Moses in order to come to Jesus. Paul and Barnabas, among others, have allowed Gentiles to come to Jesus without first coming through the Law of Moses."

c. **It is necessary to circumcise them, and to command them to keep the law of Moses**: We can imagine how they would have even made a case from the Old Testament for this teaching. They might have said Israel has *always* been God's chosen people and that Gentiles must become part of Israel if they want to be part of God's people.

i. Passages **the Pharisees who believed** might quote in defense of their position are Exodus 12:48-49 and Isaiah 56:6. These passages might be quoted to say that the covenant the Gentiles were invited to join was a covenant of circumcision.

B. The Jerusalem council.

1. (6-11) In the midst of a great dispute, the apostle Peter speaks to the issue.

Now the apostles and elders came together to consider this matter. And when there had been much dispute, Peter rose up and said to them: "Men and brethren, you know that a good while ago God chose among us, that by my mouth the Gentiles should hear the word of the gospel and believe. So God, who knows the heart, acknowledged them by giving them the Holy Spirit, just as *He did* to us, and made no distinction between us and them, purifying their hearts by faith. Now therefore, why do you test God by putting a yoke on the neck of the disciples which neither our fathers nor we were able to bear? But we believe that through the grace of the Lord Jesus Christ we shall be saved in the same manner as they."

a. **Now the apostles and elders came together to consider this matter**. These leaders came together to decide the issue. They didn't just let the issue sit, nor leave it up to the conscience of each believer. The **matter** was too important for that.

i. The question raised by the Jerusalem council was immense: Are Christians made right with God by faith alone, or by a *combination* of faith and obedience of the Law of Moses? Is the work of Jesus by itself enough to save the one who trusts in Jesus, or must we add our work to Jesus' work in order to be made right with God?

ii. With significant doctrinal issues today, perhaps this sort of public "trial" of doctrine would be beneficial.

b. **And when there had been much dispute**: This would have been amazing to see. Christians serious enough about the truth to **dispute** for it! In the midst of this, Peter, as one of the leading apostles, **rose up** to make his opinion known on the matter.

c. **Men and brethren, you know that a good while ago**: Peter began with a history lesson, recounting the work God had already done. He then made the point that **God** had fully received the Gentiles apart from their being circumcised (**God, who knows the heart, acknowledged them by giving them the Holy Spirit, just as He did to us**). If God had **acknowledged** these Gentiles as full partners in His work, then why shouldn't the church? If God received them, so should the church!

i. In saying, "**Made no distinction between us and them**," Peter made an important observation. It came straight from his vision of the clean and unclean animals, from which God taught him this principle: *God has shown to me that I should not call any man common or unclean* (Acts 10:28). Those *of the sect of the Pharisees who believed* thought that the Gentiles were inherently "common" or "unclean" (in the sense of unholy) and had to be made holy and clean by submitting to the Law of Moses.

d. **Purifying their hearts by faith**. Peter showed *how* the heart is purified: **by faith**, not by keeping of the law. If they were purified by faith, then there was no need to be purified by submitting to ceremonies found in the Law of Moses. Christians are not only *saved* by faith; they are also *purified* by faith.

e. **Why do you test God by putting a yoke on the neck of the disciples which neither our fathers nor we were able to bear?** Peter wisely answered another objection. One might ask, "What is the *harm* in bringing Gentiles under the Law of Moses?" Peter was correct when he observed that the law was **a yoke** which **neither our fathers nor we were able to bear**.

i. This is demonstrated by a survey of Israel's history. At the birth of the nation at Mount Sinai, they broke the law by worshipping the golden calf. At the end of Old Testament history, they still broke the law by disregarding the Sabbath and marrying pagan women (Nehemiah 13). From beginning to end, Israel could not bear the **yoke** of the law.

ii. Those *of the sect of the Pharisees who believed* made a critical mistake. They looked at Israel's history under the law with eyes of nostalgia, not truth. If they had carefully and truthfully considered Israel's failure under the law, they would not have been so quick to also put Gentiles under the law.

iii. Paul made the same argument in Galatians 3:2-3. If the law does not save us, why would we return to it as the principle by which we live? In light of the finished work of Jesus, it offends God to go back to the law. This is why Peter asked, "**why do you test God?**"

f. **But we believe that through the grace of the Lord Jesus Christ we shall be saved in the same manner as they**. Peter concluded with the observation that it is **through grace** that all are saved - both Jew and Gentile – and not by obedience to the law. If we are made right with God by grace, then we are not saved by grace *and* law-keeping.

i. Peter also insisted there is only one way of salvation: **We** [Jews] **shall be saved in the same manner as they** [Gentiles]. Jewish Christians were not saved, even in part, by their law-keeping; they were made right with God the same way Gentiles were: **Through the grace of the Lord Jesus Christ**.

ii. "Peter, the Jew, would normally have said it the other way around. He would have said, 'We believe that they can be saved by grace through faith, *just like us.*' That is, *they can be like us.*" (Boice) Yet Peter turned it around and noted that all are saved by grace alone through faith alone, Gentiles and Jews.

2. (12) Paul and Barnabas tell of their work among the Gentiles, supporting Peter's claim that God is doing a work among them.

Then all the multitude kept silent and listened to Barnabas and Paul declaring how many miracles and wonders God had worked through them among the Gentiles.

a. **Then all the multitude kept silent and listened**: This shows that even though *there had been much dispute*, these men were all of an honorable heart. They were willing to listen, and to be persuaded if wrong.

b. **Declaring how many miracles and wonders God had worked through them among the Gentiles**: Barnabas and Paul confirmed Peter's previous point. Essentially they said, "*God* has accepted the Gentiles, should not we as well?"

3. (13-21) James, the brother of Jesus, speaks to the issue, supporting what Peter and Paul had said.

And after they had become silent, James answered, saying, "Men *and* brethren, listen to me: Simon has declared how God at the first visited

the Gentiles to take out of them a people for His name. And with this the words of the prophets agree, just as it is written:

'After this I will return
And will rebuild the tabernacle of David, which has fallen down;
I will rebuild its ruins,
And I will set it up;
So that the rest of mankind may seek the LORD,
Even all the Gentiles who are called by My name,
Says the LORD who does all these things.'

"Known to God from eternity are all His works. Therefore I judge that we should not trouble those from among the Gentiles who are turning to God, but that we write to them to abstain from things polluted by idols, *from* sexual immorality, *from* things strangled, and *from* blood. For Moses has had throughout many generations those who preach him in every city, being read in the synagogues every Sabbath."

a. **After they had become silent**: This is more evidence of the honorable hearts of the men who had opposed Paul and Barnabas. They were willing to be convinced. They didn't endlessly argue the issue and were willing to admit they were wrong.

b. **James answered, saying, "Men and brethren, listen to me"**: This James was *not* the apostle James, whose martyrdom is recorded in Acts 12:2. This was the one traditionally known as James the Just - the half-brother of Jesus (Matthew 13:155), the brother of Jude (Jude 1), and the author of the book of James (James 1:1).

i. Bruce on the leadership of James: "The church's readiness to recognize his leadership was due more to his personal character and record than his blood relationship with the Lord."

ii. "Interestingly enough, James was the chairman of the council, not Peter." (Boice)

c. **God at the first visited the Gentiles to take out of them a people**: James began by insisting God had a **people** among the Gentiles. This would amaze most religious Jews of that time.

i. The ancient Greek word for **Gentiles** (it could also be translated *nations*) is *ethne*. The ancient Greek word for **people** in this passage is *laos*. The Jews considered themselves a *laos* of God, and never among the *ethne*. For them *ethne* and *laos* were contrasting words. So, it was a challenge for them to hear that **God at the first visited the Gentiles** (*ethne*) **to take out of them a people** (*laos*).

ii. "The paradox inherent in the contrast between *Gentiles* (or *nations*) and *people* is striking, since the latter term was often used of the Jews as the people of God in contrast to the Gentiles. Now it is being urged that God's people includes the Gentiles." (Marshall)

d. **With this the words of the prophets agree, just as it is written**: James judged this new work of God by the way any work of God should be judged. James looked to what **is written**, to the Bible.

i. **Even all the Gentiles who are called by My name**: In the passage James quoted (Amos 9:11-12), it actually says that salvation will come to the Gentiles. This demonstrates that what God did among the Gentiles had a *Biblical* foundation.

ii. Today, many things are considered *Biblical* if they simply don't contradict something in the Bible, even though they may have no root in the Scriptures. For James and the rest, an outside authority would settle this debate. The outside authority was God's Word.

iii. "Councils have no authority in the church unless it can be shown that their conclusions are in accord with Scripture." (Stott)

e. **I will return and will rebuild the tabernacle of David, which has fallen down**: When James quoted the prophecy in Amos 9:11-12 about rebuilding the fallen tabernacle of David, he remembered that the Judaism of his day had **fallen down** in the sense that it had rejected its Messiah. Now God wanted to rebuild that work, focusing on a church made up of both Jew and Gentile.

i. **All the Gentiles who are called by My name**: When God said there were Gentiles who are called by His name, He said they stay Gentiles. They were not Gentiles who had been made Jews. Therefore, Gentiles do not need to become Jews and come under the law to become right with God.

f. **Therefore I judge**: This phrasing implies that James had a position of high authority in the church. He was probably respected as the leader or senior pastor of the church at Jerusalem.

ii. The ancient Greek phrases it even more strongly as "I determine" or "I resolve" (Expositor's). In addition, when the decision of James was published, it was presented as the mutual decision of all present (Acts 15:25: I*t seemed good to us*). Clearly, James' leadership was supported by everyone present.

iii. "The rest either *argued* on the subject, or gave their *opinion*; James alone pronounced the *definitive sentence*." (Clarke)

g. **We should not trouble those from among the Gentiles who are turning to God**: James essentially said, "Let them alone. They **are turning to God**, and **we should not trouble** them." At the bottom line, James decided that Peter, Barnabas, and Paul were correct, and that those *of the sect of the Pharisees who believed* were wrong.

> i. "The Protestant Reformers wisely and insistently pointed out that councils have erred and do err. They have erred throughout history, and they continue to err today…But God blessed it nevertheless, and he has often done with the formal meetings of sinful human beings who nevertheless gather to seek God's will in a matter." (Boice)

h. **But that we write to them to abstain from things polluted by idols, from sexual immorality, from things strangled, and from blood**: James' decision that Gentile believers should not be under the Mosaic Law was also given with practical instruction. The idea was that it was important that Gentile believers did not act in a way that would offend the Jewish community **in every city** and destroy the church's witness among Jews.

> i. If the decision was that one did not have to be Jewish to be a Christian, it must also be said clearly that one did not need to *forsake* the Law of Moses to be a Christian.

i. **To abstain from things polluted by idols… from things strangled, and from blood**: These three commands had to do with the eating habits of Gentile Christians. Though they were not bound under the Law of Moses, they were bound under the Law of Love. The Law of Love told them, "Don't unnecessarily antagonize your Jewish neighbors, both in and out of the church."

j. **To abstain from… sexual immorality**: When James declared that they forbid the Gentile Christians to **abstain from… sexual immorality**, we shouldn't think that it simply meant sex outside of marriage, which all Christians (Jew or Gentile) recognized as wrong. Instead, James told these Gentiles living in such close fellowship with the Jewish believers to observe the specific marriage regulations required by Leviticus 18, which prohibited marriages between most family relations. This was something that would offend Jews, but most Gentiles would think little of.

k. **To abstain from**: Gentile Christians had the "right" to eat meat sacrificed to idols, to continue their marriage practices, and to eat food without a kosher bleeding, because these were aspects of the Mosaic Law they definitely were not under. However, they were encouraged (required?) to law down their rights in these matters as a display of love to their Jewish brethren.

i. "All four of the requested abstentions related to ceremonial laws laid down in Leviticus 17 and 18, and three of them concerned dietary matters which could inhibit Jewish-Gentile common meals." (Stott)

4. (22) Sending Paul, Barnabas, Judas, and Silas with news of the council's decision.

Then it pleased the apostles and elders, with the whole church, to send chosen men of their own company to Antioch with Paul and Barnabas, *namely,* Judas who was also named Barsabas, and Silas, leading men among the brethren.

a. **It pleased the apostles and elders, with the whole church**: Much credit goes to the *certain men* of Acts 15:1, who allowed themselves to be convinced by the evidence from the Scriptures and by the confirmation of the Holy Spirit. They all agreed!

i. We can almost admire the *certain men* of Acts 15:1, because they boldly stated their convictions, even though their convictions were wrong. But even more admirable is the way they are willing to be taught and shown they are wrong. A teachable spirit is a precious thing.

b. **To send chosen men of their own company to Antioch**: The Jerusalem council wisely sent two members of its own community (probably Jewish Christians themselves) with Paul and Barnabas back **to Antioch**, the place where the whole dispute arose.

5. (23-29) A letter of decision is drafted.

They wrote this *letter* by them:
The apostles, the elders, and the brethren,
To the brethren who are of the Gentiles in Antioch, Syria, and Cilicia: Greetings.
Since we have heard that some who went out from us have troubled you with words, unsettling your souls, saying, *"You must be circumcised and keep the law"*–to whom we gave no *such* commandment–it seemed good to us, being assembled with one accord, to send chosen men to you with our beloved Barnabas and Paul, men who have risked their lives for the name of our Lord Jesus Christ. We have therefore sent Judas and Silas, who will also report the same things by word of mouth. For it seemed good to the Holy Spirit, and to us, to lay upon you no greater burden than these necessary things: that you abstain from things offered to idols, from blood, from things strangled, and from sexual immorality. If you keep yourselves from these, you will do well.
Farewell.

a. **They wrote this letter by them**: The letter gives the express decision of the Jerusalem council, that Gentiles should consider themselves under no obligation to the rituals of Judaism, except the sensitivity which love demands, so as to preserve the fellowship of Jewish and Gentile believers.

b. **To the brethren who are of the Gentiles in Antioch, Syria, and Cilicia**: This letter was written specifically to these churches where Jews and Gentiles mixed together with the potential of tension and conflict. It was not addressed to every Gentile congregation.

c. **For it seemed good to the Holy Spirit, and to us**: James voiced the decision of the council (Acts 15:19), but the unity behind the decision was one of several evidences that it was the work of **the Holy Spirit**. The Holy Spirit spoke through James and confirmed it through others.

> i. So much so that they could really say that the decision was made in cooperation with the Holy Spirit – **it seemed good to the Holy Spirit, and to us**. "They boldly treat the Holy Spirit *as one of their number* – a fellow-counselor, who unites with them in the announcement of a joint conclusion; as though he, the Spirit of God, had sat with them in their deliberations." (Pierson)

d. **Farewell**: Therefore, the issue is settled here in the infancy of Christianity, and for all time: We are saved by grace, through faith in Jesus Christ, not by any conformity to the law, and such obedience comes as a result of true faith, *after* the issue of salvation has been settled.

> i. "Here is a lesson for all ages on the *true character of church councils*. What we call a 'court of Jesus Christ' has too often been more like an assembly of unbelievers, if not like a 'synagogue of Satan.'" (Pierson)

C. Paul and Barnabas return to Antioch.

1. (30-31) A joyful reception among the Gentile Christians at the church of Antioch.

So when they were sent off, they came to Antioch; and when they had gathered the multitude together, they delivered the letter. When they had read it, they rejoiced over its encouragement.

a. **When they had gathered the multitude together, they delivered the letter**: We can imagine how these Gentile Christians felt, wondering how the decision might come forth. Would the council in Jerusalem decide that they really were not saved after all because they had not submitted to circumcision and the Law of Moses?

b. **When they had read it, they rejoiced over its encouragement**: How relieved they were to see that the principle of grace had been preserved! They heard that they *were* saved and right with God after all.

2. (32-35) The work of the gospel continues in Antioch.

Now Judas and Silas, themselves being prophets also, exhorted and strengthened the brethren with many words. And after they had stayed *there* for a time, they were sent back with greetings from the brethren to the apostles. However, it seemed good to Silas to remain there. Paul and Barnabas also remained in Antioch, teaching and preaching the word of the Lord, with many others also.

a. **Judas and Silas**: These two served well in Antioch as visiting ministers from Jerusalem. Then **Judas** returned, leaving **Silas** in Antioch for future ministry.

b. **Teaching and preaching the word of the Lord, with many others also**: The *certain men* who had come from Judea to Antioch (Acts 15:1) had the potential to ruin the work of God in Antioch and beyond. But because the situation was handled correctly, the brethren were strengthened and the word of God continued to go forth.

D. The contention over John Mark.

1. (36) Paul suggests that he and Barnabas return to all the cities where they planted churches in the first missionary trip.

Then after some days Paul said to Barnabas, "Let us now go back and visit our brethren in every city where we have preached the word of the Lord, *and see* how they are doing."

a. **Let us now go back and visit our brethren**: Paul did much pioneer evangelism, where he preached in places where there was yet no Christian community. Yet, he also understood the importance of strengthening and encouraging those who were already Christians. That was the initial motivation for this second missionary venture.

i. Paul had the heart of both an obstetrician (bringing people into the body of Christ) and a pediatrician (growing people up in the body of Christ).

b. **And see how they are doing**: This shows Paul had a real pastor's heart. He was not content to merely plant churches without seeing them carefully nurtured and growing in the faith.

2. (37-41) Paul and Barnabas divide over the issue of taking John Mark with them.

Now Barnabas was determined to take with them John called Mark. But Paul insisted that they should not take with them the one who had departed from them in Pamphylia, and had not gone with them to the work. Then the contention became so sharp that they parted from one another. And so Barnabas took Mark and sailed to Cyprus; but Paul chose Silas and departed, being commended by the brethren to the grace of God. And he went through Syria and Cilicia, strengthening the churches.

a. **John called Mark**: John Mark had previously left the missionary party under what seemed to be less than honorable circumstances (Acts 13:13). This probably made Paul unwilling to trust him on future endeavors.

b. **Barnabas was determined... But Paul insisted**: Luke did not give us a clue as to who was right and who was wrong in the dispute between Paul and Barnabas. But it is never good when personal disputes flare up among those serving in the ministry.

i. **Then the contention became so sharp**: Wherever there is **sharp... contention**, *someone* is wrong, and usually there is wrong on both sides. There could be no way that *both* Paul and Barnabas were each walking in the Spirit on this issue.

ii. Earlier in this chapter there was *dispute* and *no small dissention* (Acts 15:2) and *much dispute* (Acts 15:7) over an important doctrinal matter. Here the sharp contention seemed less important and more personal.

iii. The relationship between Paul and Barnabas was probably also strained when Barnabas sided with the Judaizers in Antioch when Peter came to visit (Galatians 2:13).

c. **Barnabas took Mark and sailed to Cyprus**: Since Barnabas was John Mark's cousin (Colossians 4:10), and because Barnabas had such an encouraging, accepting character (Acts 4:36, 9:26-27), it is easy to see why he would be more understanding towards John Mark.

d. **They parted from one another**: So, Paul (accompanied by Silas) and Barnabas (accompanied by Mark) split, each going out to different fields of ministry.

i. It is hard to know if their personal relationship was strained for a prolonged period. As Christians, we are commanded to resolve relationship problems with others before we present ministry to God (Matthew 5:23-24). It is always wrong to step over people in the name of ministry, and when it happens it must be made right.

ii. There is no doubt God used this division; but this can never be casually used as an excuse for carnal division. God can redeem good out of evil, yet we are all held accountable for the evil we do, even if God ends up bringing good out of the evil. Either Paul or Barnabas - probably both - had to get this right with God and each other.

iii. "But this example of God's providence may not be used as an excuse for Christian quarreling." (Stott)

iv. Later, Paul came to minister with John Mark and to value his contributions to the work of God (Colossians 4:10; Philemon 4:24; 2 Timothy 4:11). We don't know if it was Mark who changed or Paul who changed. Probably God had a work to do in both of them!

e. **Paul chose Silas**: Silas (also called *Silvanus* in several passages) became an important part of Paul's team in doing the work of the ministry.

- Silas was recognized as one of the *leading men among the brethren* (Acts 15:22).
- Silas was a prophet (Acts 15:32).
- Silas was a Roman citizen (Acts 16:37).
- Silas probably spoke Greek (comparing Acts 15:22 and 15:32).
- Silas wrote out one of Peter's letters (1 Peter 5:12) and maybe some of Paul's (1 Thessalonians 1:1; 2 Thessalonians 2:1).

f. **Strengthening the churches**: This was Paul's work, in addition to evangelism. New Christians needed strong churches to grow and mature in.

Acts 16 - *The Second Missionary Journey Begins*

A. From the city of Derbe to Troas.

1. (1-2) Paul meets Timothy in Lystra.

Then he came to Derbe and Lystra. And behold, a certain disciple was there, named Timothy, *the* son of a certain Jewish woman who believed, but his father *was* Greek. He was well spoken of by the brethren who were at Lystra and Iconium.

a. **Then he came to Derbe and Lystra**: Paul (and Silas) arrived in **Derbe**, where he had great success on his first missionary journey (Acts 14:20-21), and in **Lystra**, where a crowd tried to honor Paul and Barnabas as pagan gods on the first missionary journey (Acts 14:8-20).

   i. Paul began this missionary journey having come from Antioch. First, he did the work of *strengthening the churches* through the regions of Syria and Cilicia (Acts 15:40-41).

   ii. According to the estimate of William Barclay, the first missionary journey finished about five years before the events of this chapter. Paul was anxious to see for himself how the work of the Lord continued among these churches he founded five years before.

b. **A certain disciple was there, named Timothy**: In the time since Paul had been to Lystra, a young man **named Timothy** had been serving the Lord (**He was well spoken of by the brethren**). Timothy had a believing mother with a Jewish background (**son of a certain Jewish woman who believed**), and a (presumably) unbelieving **Greek** father.

   i. The last time Paul was in Lystra, they first worshipped him as a god and then tried to kill him by stoning (Acts 14:11-20). Paul's courage and wisdom in the face of these obstacles built a great legacy in people like Timothy.

2. (3-5) Timothy joins Paul and Silas, and their work continues.

Paul wanted to have him go on with him. And he took *him* and circumcised him because of the Jews who were in that region, for they all knew that his father was Greek. And as they went through the cities, they delivered to them the decrees to keep, which were determined by the apostles and elders at Jerusalem. So the churches were strengthened in the faith, and increased in number daily.

a. **Paul wanted to have him go on with him**: Paul was impressed enough with Timothy to ask him to join their missionary team. This shows God's provision, because John Mark and Barnabas just left Paul (Acts 15:36-41). No single worker in God's kingdom is irreplaceable. When a Barnabas leaves (for whatever reason), God has a Timothy to **go on with him**.

b. **And he took him and circumcised him because of the Jews in that region**: Paul had Timothy **circumcised**, not for the sake of his salvation (Paul would never do so) but so there would be less to hinder ministry among the Jews.

i. In Acts 15, Paul argued strongly that it was not necessary for Gentile converts to come under the Law of Moses for salvation (Acts 15:2 and 15:12). At the time Paul met Timothy, he was delivering the news of this decree that came out of the Acts 15 council (**as they went through the cities, the delivered to them the decrees to keep, which were determined by the apostles and elders at Jerusalem**).

ii. Yet, Paul did not contradict his belief or the findings of the council when he had Timothy circumcised. Paul did this not for Timothy's salvation or right standing with God, but so that Timothy status as a non-circumcised man from a Jewish mother would not hinder their work among the Jews and in synagogues. Paul did things for the sake of love that he would not do for the sake of trying to please God through legalism. Paul insisted that Titus, a Gentile co-worker, did *not* have to be circumcised (Galatians 2:3-5).

iii. "By Jewish law Timothy was a Jew, because he was the son of Jewish mother, but because he was uncircumcised he was technically an apostate Jew. If Paul wished to maintain his links with the synagogue, he could not be seen to countenance apostasy." (Bruce)

iv. "As Paul saw it, being a good Christian did not mean being a bad Jew." (Longenecker) The wording of Acts 16:3 implies that Paul *himself* performed the circumcision (**he took him and circumcised him**).

c. **So the churches were strengthened in the faith, and increased in number daily**: Paul, Silas, and Timothy together enjoyed great success in their work of strengthening and growing churches.

i. Their work was successful because their first interest was in strengthening the churches. Strong churches will naturally increase in number daily, without relying on man-centered and manipulative methods.

3. (6-8) The Holy Spirit forbids Paul to go towards the province of Asia Minor.

Now when they had gone through Phrygia and the region of Galatia, they were forbidden by the Holy Spirit to preach the word in Asia. After they had come to Mysia, they tried to go into Bithynia, but the Spirit did not permit them. So passing by Mysia, they came down to Troas.

a. **They were forbidden by the Holy Spirit to preach the word in Asia**: After strengthening the churches in the region, Paul sought to go next to the south-west, towards the important city of Ephesus. Yet, Paul was **forbidden by the Holy Spirit** to go there.

i. We note with interest that the Holy Spirit actually forbade Paul to do something we normally think of as *good* – preaching God's Word to those who need it. Yet the Spirit of God directed this work, and Paul wasn't the right person in the right place at the right time to begin bringing the gospel to the Roman Province of Asia Minor. There was certainly nothing wrong with Paul's *desire* to **preach the word in Asia**; but it wasn't God's timing, so this was **forbidden by the Holy Spirit**.

ii. It is difficult to say exactly how the Holy Spirit said *no*; it may have been through a word of prophecy, or by an inward speaking of the Holy Spirit, or by circumstances. One way or another, Paul and his company got the message. Ephesus would come later, not now.

iii. **Asia** does not refer to the Far East as we know it today. It refers to the Roman Province of Asia Minor, which is modern day Turkey.

b. **They tried to go into Bithynia, but the Spirit did not permit them**: After the attempt to go to Asia, Paul sought to go north into **Bithynia**, but was again prevented by the Holy Spirit. So, **they came down to Troas**.

i. Paul didn't set out to go to **Troas**. It was at least the third choice for him. But it was the Holy Spirit's plan to lead him there. Paul, beautifully responsive to the Holy Spirit, was willing to lay down his will and his plans for the direction that the Holy Spirit brings.

ii. Paul was guided by hindrance. The Holy Spirit often guides as much by the *closing* of doors as He does by the *opening* of doors.

iii. David Livingstone wanted to go to China, but God sent him to Africa. William Carey wanted to go to Polynesia, but God sent him to India. Adoniram Judson went to India, but God guided him to Burma. God guides us along the way, to just the right place.

4. (9-10) God directs Paul to the region of Macedonia.

And a vision appeared to Paul in the night. A man of Macedonia stood and pleaded with him, saying, "Come over to Macedonia and help us." Now after he had seen the vision, immediately we sought to go to Macedonia, concluding that the Lord had called us to preach the gospel to them.

a. **And a vision appeared to Paul in the night**: In Troas, God made Paul's direction clear. In **a vision**, Paul was invited to the region of Macedonia, westward across the Agean Sea.

i. This moved Paul and his missionary team from the continent of Asia to the continent of Europe; this was the first missionary endeavor to Europe.

ii. The wisdom and greatness of God's plan was beginning to unfold. In Paul's mind, he wanted to reach a few cities in his region. But God wanted to give Paul a *continent* to win for Jesus Christ.

b. **A man of Macedonia stood and pleaded with him, saying, "Come over to Macedonia and help us."** The Macedonian man wanted **help**. So Paul went to bring Macedonia the gospel – the best possible help.

i. The greatest help we can bring anyone is the life-changing gospel of Jesus Christ. It is good for us to bring other help along with the gospel, but without the gospel, little *real* help is given.

c. **Now after he had seen the vision, immediately we sought to go**: Paul did not hesitate to answer the call of the Macedonian man. Paul's missionary team did not hesitate to follow him on the basis of this call. This was a strong, godly man, leading a strong, godly team.

i. God still calls people to the mission field, and He may call through unusual ways. It's still possible for a type of Macedonian Man to give an unusual call to serve God in a distant place. When that happens, it's important to respond the way Paul and his team did.

d. **Immediately we sought to go**: The shift from *they* (*they came down to Troas*, Acts 16:8) to **we** in this verse probably means that Luke joined the band of missionaries in Troas. Perhaps he even came as Paul's personal doctor.

i. Now we see another reason why *they were forbidden by the Holy Spirit to preach the word in Asia*. We see another reason why *the Spirit did not permit them* to go into Bithynia. God wanted Paul and his team to go to Troas and pick up a doctor named Luke. Because God said "no" to Paul these two times, we have a gospel and a Book of Acts written by Doctor Luke.

ii. At the time, Paul probably had no idea of the greatness of God's purpose. God wanted to give him a continent for Jesus, to give him a personal doctor, and to give all of us the man whom God would use to write more of the New Testament than anyone else did. God knows what He is doing when he says, "No."

B. Paul's work in the Macedonian city of Philippi.

1. (11-12) Arrival in Philippi.

Therefore, sailing from Troas, we ran a straight course to Samothrace, and the next *day* came to Neapolis, and from there to Philippi, which is the foremost city of that part of Macedonia, a colony. And we were staying in that city for some days.

a. **Sailing from Troas**: Paul and his missionary team (now including Luke) had to sail across the Agean Sea, from the continent of Asia to the continent of Europe. This was a big step, perhaps bigger than Paul even knew.

i. "That they 'sailed straight for Samothrace' is quite revealing, because this is a nautical expression that means the wind was at their backs. So perfect were the winds that they sailed 156 miles in just two days, whereas returning the other way at a later time (Acts 20:6) it took five days." (Hughes)

b. **From there to Philippi, which is the foremost city of that part of Macedonia**: Paul here followed a plan to plant churches in the major cities. He knew that it was easier for the gospel to spread *from* these cities than *to* these cities.

i. Philippi was "the place where the armies of Mark Antony and Octavian defeated Brutus and Cassius in the decisive battle of the second Roman civil war in 42 B.C." (Hughes) Because of this, many Roman soldiers retired in the area, and Philippi was proud of its Roman connection.

2. (13-15) The conversion of Lydia.

And on the Sabbath day we went out of the city to the riverside, where prayer was customarily made; and we sat down and spoke to the women who met *there*. Now a certain woman named Lydia heard *us*. She was a seller of purple from the city of Thyatira, who worshiped God. The Lord opened her heart to heed the things spoken by Paul. And when she and her household were baptized, she begged *us*, saying, "If you have

judged me to be faithful to the Lord, come to my house and stay." So she persuaded us.

a. **On the Sabbath day we went out of the city to the riverside, where prayer was customarily made**: The fact that the Jews of Philippi had no synagogue and met by the river means that there were not many Jewish men in Philippi.

i. "Had there been ten Jewish men, they would have sufficed to constitute a synagogue. No number of women would compensate for the absence of even one man necessary to make up the quorum of ten." (Bruce)

b. **Lydia...was a seller of purple**: Anyone who **was a seller of purple** dealt in a valued, luxurious product. The dyes used for making purple were expensive and highly regarded. This woman was the first convert in Europe, and one might say that the Macedonian man turned out to be a woman.

i. **From the city of Thyatira**: Thyatira was well known as a center for this purple dye and fabric made from it. Later, there was a church in Thyatira also, and it was one of the seven churches addressed in Revelation (Revelation 2:18-29).

c. **The Lord opened her heart to heed the things spoken by Paul**: Before Lydia was converted (as demonstrated by her baptism), **the Lord opened her heart**. This is a work God must do in all who believe, because as Jesus said, *no one can come to Me unless the Father who sent Me draws him* (John 6:44).

i. Therefore, a most important element in evangelism is asking God through prayer to *open hearts*, for without this there can be no genuine conversion.

d. **She begged us, saying, "If you have judged me to be faithful to the Lord, come to my house and stay."** Immediately, Lydia set about doing good. Her hospitality was touching and wonderful example.

2. (16-17) A demon-possessed slave girl follows Paul.

Now it happened, as we went to prayer, that a certain slave girl possessed with a spirit of divination met us, who brought her masters much profit by fortune-telling. This girl followed Paul and us, and cried out, saying, "These men are the servants of the Most High God, who proclaim to us the way of salvation."

a. **A certain slave girl possessed with a spirit of divination...brought her masters much profit**: This girl, though demon possessed, was a source of money for her owners as a fortune teller. Presumably this was because demons gave her supernatural insight into the lives of others.

> i. "It actually says, 'She had a spirit of Pythona.' That does not mean much to most of us, which is why it is not translated literally. But 'pythona' was a certain kind of snake – a python. It is used here because the python was associated with the god Apollo…not far from Philippi, in this very area of Europe, there was a shrine to the Pythian Apollo." (Boice)

> ii. Today, much of what fortune-tellers and psychics do is only a money making sham. But when it is true and has a supernatural origin (as opposed to clever, insightful guessing), there is no doubt that it is inspired by demons. There are still those today who are **possessed with a spirit of divination**.

> iii. Because demons are created beings, not "gods" themselves, we suppose that they cannot read minds, nor actually foretell the future. But they can read and predict human behavior, and can attempt to steer events towards a previously predicted conclusion.

b. **This girl followed Paul and us, and cried out, saying, "These men are the servants of the Most High God, who proclaim to us the way of salvation."** The demon-possessed slave girl preached for Paul, giving a demonic testimony to their divine credentials and their message. She didn't do this only once, but for many days (Acts 16:18).

3. (18) Paul casts the demon out of the slave girl.

And this she did for many days. But Paul, greatly annoyed, turned and said to the spirit, "I command you in the name of Jesus Christ to come out of her." And he came out that very hour.

a. **But Paul, greatly annoyed:** Paul was **greatly annoyed**, and he did not appreciate the free advertising from the demon. He did not appreciate the source of the recommendation, and he didn't need demonic approval of his work.

> i. Paul knew that a man will be identified by both his friends and his enemies, and could do without a demonic letter of reference. In this, Paul was like Jesus, who often told demons to be silent, even when they told the truth about Him (Matthew 8:28-34, Mark 3:11-12).

b. **I command you in the name of Jesus Christ to come out of her:** Jesus cast out demons with His own authority. Paul was careful to speak to demons only in the authority of Jesus Christ, and he spoke beyond the afflicted girl to the demon itself with this authority of Jesus.

c. **And he came out that very hour**: The idea behind **that very hour** is that the demon came out immediately. Yet Jesus said that some demons would be more difficult to cast out than others (Matthew 17:21).

> i. Bruce translates the phrase, *It came out there and then*. He comments: "The words had scarcely left his lips when she was released from its power."

4. (19-24) Paul and Silas are arrested, beaten, and imprisoned for delivering the slave-girl from her demonic possession.

But when her masters saw that their hope of profit was gone, they seized Paul and Silas and dragged *them* into the marketplace to the authorities. And they brought them to the magistrates, and said, "These men, being Jews, exceedingly trouble our city; and they teach customs which are not lawful for us, being Romans, to receive or observe." Then the multitude rose up together against them; and the magistrates tore off their clothes and commanded *them* to be beaten with rods. And when they had laid many stripes on them, they threw *them* into prison, commanding the jailer to keep them securely. Having received such a charge, he put them into the inner prison and fastened their feet in the stocks.

a. **Her masters saw that their hope of profit was gone**: This explains why Paul and Silas were treated so badly. The masters of the demon possessed girl cared nothing for the girl herself, only for their ability to exploit her demonic possession for money. They were occult "pimps," prostituting her spiritually.

b. **They seized Paul and Silas**: Paul and Silas were singled out not only because there were the leaders of the evangelistic group, but also, by their appearance, they were the most obviously Jewish. This is indicated by how they began their accusation: "**These men, being Jews**."

> i. Luke was a Gentile, and Timothy was only half Jewish. Paul and Silas *looked* Jewish, and "Anti-Jewish sentiment lay very near the surface in pagan antiquity." (Bruce) The objection that these men were Jews is even more interesting knowing the Jewish community in Philippi was small.

c. **Exceedingly trouble our city; and they teach customs which are not lawful for us, being Romans, to receive or observe**. Their charges were vague, simply accusing Paul and Silas of being troublemakers. But those vague charges were enough, because both the **multitude** and the **magistrates** were biased against Paul and Silas. They were biased because of their Jewish appearance, and because they assumed Paul and Silas were not Roman citizens.

i. In the Roman Empire there were two very different laws: one for citizens of the Roman Empire, and one for those who were not citizens. Roman citizens had specific, zealously guarded civil rights. Non-citizens had no civil rights, and were subject to the whims of both the **multitude** and the **magistrates**.

ii. Since they assumed Paul and Barnabas were not Roman citizens, they were offended that these obviously Jewish men harassed Roman citizens with their strange religion of a crucified Savior. As well, the **multitude** and the **magistrates** felt free to abuse Paul and Silas because they assumed they were not Roman citizens.

iii. "There was great indignation that Roman citizens should be molested by strolling peddlers of an outlandish religion. Such people had to be taught to know their proper place and not trouble their betters." (Bruce)

d. **When they had laid many stripes on them, they threw them into prison**: After being severely beaten, Paul and Silas were imprisoned in maximum-security conditions (**commanding the jailer to keep them securely...the inner prison...fastened their feet in the stocks**).

i. Jewish legal tradition gave a maximum number of blows that could be delivered when beating a person, but the Romans had no such limit. We simply know Paul and Silas were severely beaten. Paul later wrote of his life: *In labors more abundant, in stripes above measure, in prisons more frequently, in deaths often.* (2 Corinthians 11:23)

ii. After such a bad beating, they were put in uncomfortable conditions (**fastened their feet in the stocks**). "These stocks had more than two holes for legs, which could thus be forced apart in a such a way as to cause the utmost discomfort and cramping pain." (Bruce)

iii. Even in their pain, God was not far from Paul and Silas. Tertullian said, "The legs feel nothing in the stocks when the heart is in heaven."

5. (25-32) Paul and Silas sing in prison.

But at midnight Paul and Silas were praying and singing hymns to God, and the prisoners were listening to them.

a. **But at midnight Paul and Silas were praying and singing hymns to God**: Though they were arrested, beaten, and imprisoned for doing good, Paul and Silas were filled with joy, and sang praises to God. It seemed as if nothing would make them stop praising God.

i. Anyone can be happy in pleasant circumstances, but real joy comes only from within, and is a gift available to Christians at all times. "Instead of cursing men, they blessed God." (Stott)

b. **And the prisoners were listening to them**: What a strange sound this was to the other **prisoners**! Prayers and praises unto God at midnight, in the midst of a brutal prison. Those prison walls had probably never heard such a sound.

6. (26-29) The great earthquake and its result.

Suddenly there was a great earthquake, so that the foundations of the prison were shaken; and immediately all the doors were opened and everyone's chains were loosed. And the keeper of the prison, awaking from sleep and seeing the prison doors open, supposing the prisoners had fled, drew his sword and was about to kill himself. But Paul called with a loud voice, saying, "Do yourself no harm, for we are all here." Then he called for a light, ran in, and fell down trembling before Paul and Silas.

a. **Suddenly there was a great earthquake**: This earthquake was clearly supernatural. This was not only because of its timing and location, but also in the way that **all the doors were opened and everyone's chains were loosed**.

b. **The keeper of the prison…was about to kill himself**: The jailer did this for a good reason. Under Roman law and custom, guards who allowed their prisoners to escape received the penalty of their escaped prisoners. Knowing this, **Paul called with a loud voice, saying, "Do yourself no harm, for we are all here."** He assured the jailer that no one had escaped.

i. It would have been easy for Paul and Silas to escape thinking God provided another miraculous jailbreak. But to them, the lives of others were more important than their own personal freedom and comfort.

ii. In not escaping, they showed tremendous discernment. The *circumstances* said, "escape." But love said, "Stay for the sake of this one soul." They were not guided merely by circumstances, but by what love compelled.

c. **Ran in, and fell down trembling before Paul and Silas**: This hardened keeper of the prison **fell down trembling**. This was as dramatic as it sounds. This man was more affected by the love and grace demonstrated by Paul and Silas than by the earthquake. As well, this may have even been the same guard who beat them a few hours earlier.

7. (30-32) The conversion of the Philippian jailer.

And he brought them out and said, "Sirs, what must I do to be saved?" So they said, "Believe on the Lord Jesus Christ, and you will be saved, you and your household." Then they spoke the word of the Lord to him and to all who were in his house.

a. **Sirs, what must I do be saved?** The jailer was so impressed by Paul and Silas - by the love they showed to him, and from their ability to take joy even in misery - that he instantly wanted the kind of life that Paul and Silas have.

i. This is how God wants our lives to be: Natural magnets drawing people to Him. Our Christianity should make others want what we have with God.

b. **Believe on the Lord Jesus Christ, and you will be saved**: Paul's answer to the keeper of the prison is a classic statement of the essence of the gospel. This is salvation by grace alone, received by faith alone.

i. Some have worried that Paul's invitation to salvation here is *too* easy, and would promote a too-easy faith or a cheap grace. Others refuse to preach repentance, claiming that this text says that it is not necessary.

ii. Paul never specifically called the keeper of the prison to repent because *he was already repenting*. We see the humble repentance of the jailer in that he *fell down trembling*, in the full idea of the word **believe** (*pistis*, which means to trust in, rely on, and cling to), and in the command to believe on the **Lord** Jesus Christ).

iii. For the Philippian jailer, Paul did not direct him to counseling. He did not give him a lecture on theology. He did not discuss the spiritual terminology of the jailer. He did not talk about sacraments or even churches. He pointed this obviously repentant man to faith in Jesus Christ.

iv. There was an old chaplain general of the British Army – Bishop John Taylor Smith – who used a unique test on candidates for the chaplaincy. He asked them to say how they would speak to a man injured in battle, who had three minutes to live, how to be saved and come to peace with God. If they couldn't do it within three minutes, they weren't fit for the chaplain's service. Paul would be qualified.

c. **You and your household**: This seems to be a specific promise for that Philippian jailer. Under inspiration by the Holy Spirit, Paul told the keeper of the prison that his household would trust Jesus just as he did.

i. This was a promise made specifically to the keeper of the prison. But it is a promise that the Holy Spirit may well make alive to us, helping us to trust Him for the salvation of our families.

ii. However, the jailer's household was not saved merely because he was; Paul came and **spoke the word of the Lord to him and to all who were in his house**. They were all saved because they all trusted the word of God and the Jesus revealed to us through the word.

8. (33-34) The Philippian jailer serves Paul and Silas.

And he took them the same hour of the night and washed *their* stripes. And immediately he and all his family were baptized. Now when he had brought them into his house, he set food before them; and he rejoiced, having believed in God with all his household.

a. **And he took them the same hour of the night and washed their stripes**: The same jailer who had punished them now cared for Paul and Silas, caring for their wounds and **he set food before them**. This shows how repentant he was and how he followed the example of love shown by Paul and Silas.

b. **And immediately he and all his family were baptized**: The jailer and his family saw no reason to delay baptism; they were baptized that very night, and all this began around midnight (Acts 16:25).

c. **And he rejoiced**: This man was carried from suicidal fear to abounding joy in just a few minutes. The Holy Spirit used the courageous praise of Paul and Silas in their terrible adversity.

9. (35-36) Paul and Silas return to the prison, and are set free by the magistrates the next day.

And when it was day, the magistrates sent the officers, saying, "Let those men go." So the keeper of the prison reported these words to Paul, saying, "The magistrates have sent to let you go. Now therefore depart, and go in peace."

a. **The magistrates sent the officers**: Paul and Silas left the prison (in the protective custody of the jailer) to minister to the jailer's household. Yet they returned to the prison willingly to spare the jailer certain death.

b. **Let those men go**: In societies that recognize few rights for their citizens it is common for one to be arrested, beaten, imprisoned – and then quickly and unexpectedly released. This sort of treatment effectively terrorizes the population into submission.

c. **The magistrates have sent to let you go. Now therefore depart, and go in peace**: If Paul and Silas were released the day after their beating, arrest, and imprisonment, why did God send the earthquake? We see that the earthquake had absolutely *nothing* to do with freeing Paul and Silas from prison. But it had everything to do with the salvation of a certain prison guard and his household.

10. (37-39) Paul and Silas reveal their Roman citizenship.

But Paul said to them, "They have beaten us openly, uncondemned Romans, *and* have thrown *us* into prison. And now do they put us out secretly? No indeed! Let them come themselves and get us out." And the officers told these words to the magistrates, and they were afraid when they heard that they were Romans. Then they came and pleaded with them and brought *them* out, and asked *them* to depart from the city.

a. **They have beaten us openly, uncondemned Romans**: Because Paul and Silas were Roman citizens, they *had* recognized civil rights, which were violated by the Philippian magistrates. Upon learning this, the magistrates were filled with fear, because it was a grave offense to treat Roman citizens as Paul and Silas had been treated.

i. Why didn't Paul and Silas reveal their Roman citizenship earlier? It is possible that they didn't have the opportunity, but it is more likely that the Holy Spirit directed them to not reveal it until a certain time.

ii. Our *rights* are not as important as our *obedience* to the will of God. God may ask us to lay down our rights for the good of another (in this case, for the good of the Philippian jailer).

iii. How could Paul and Silas prove their Roman citizenship? "They may each have carried a copy of his *professio* or registration of birth, in which his Roman status would have been recorded. These were convenient in size…To claim Roman citizenship falsely was punishable by death." (Williams)

b. **They came and pleaded with them and brought them out, and asked them to depart from the city**: The magistrates acted as politicians often act by instinct. They tried to make their problem go away quietly by sweeping it under the rug.

11. (40) Paul and Silas leave Philippi on their own terms.

So they went out of the prison and entered *the house of* Lydia; and when they had seen the brethren, they encouraged them and departed.

a. **When they had seen the brethren, they encouraged them**: Only after this did they agree to go. Paul and Silas would not be hurried out of town until they had brought their work there to a conclusion.

i. The great missionary David Livingstone summarized the spirit of Paul when he said, "I am prepared to go anywhere, so long as it is forward." (Cited in Barclay)

b. **They encouraged them and departed**: In Philippi, Paul and Silas left behind two notable converts: Lydia and the prison guard. Each of these two had their lives touched by Jesus in very different ways.

i. Lydia was a churchgoer; the guard was not. Lydia was prospering in business; the guard was about to kill himself. Lydia's heart was gently opened; the guard's heart was violently confronted. The guard had a remarkable sign - an earthquake, but all Lydia had was the move of the Holy Spirit in her heart. Both heard the gospel and believed, and through each of them their whole families were touched!

ii. It was a strange and wonderful church they left behind in Philippi: Lydia, perhaps the slave girl, the jailer and his household, and others. The use of "**they**" here suggests that Luke stayed behind in Philippi for at least a while, perhaps to care for this new congregation.

Acts 17 - Paul in Thessalonica, Berea, and Athens

A. God's work in Thessalonica.

1. (1-4) Paul preaches in Thessalonica over three Sabbaths.

Now when they had passed through Amphipolis and Apollonia, they came to Thessalonica, where there was a synagogue of the Jews. Then Paul, as his custom was, went in to them, and for three Sabbaths reasoned with them from the Scriptures, explaining and demonstrating that the Christ had to suffer and rise again from the dead, and *saying,* **"This Jesus whom I preach to you is the Christ." And some of them were persuaded; and a great multitude of the devout Greeks, and not a few of the leading women, joined Paul and Silas.**

a. **They came to Thessalonica**: This was an important port city, about 100 miles (160 kilometers) and a three-day walk from Philippi. Modern Thessalonika is still a large, thriving city.

b. **As his custom was**: Paul first went to the synagogue, and preached Jesus crucified and risen again to the Jews and God-fearing Gentiles there. There were several notable aspects to his presentation of Jesus.

i. Paul **reasoned with them from the Scriptures**; "The Greek word translated 'reasoned' is the root for our English word dialogue. There was exchange, questions and answers. He dialogued with them 'from the Scriptures.'" (Hughes)

ii. Paul did the work of **explaining**; "This word literally means 'opening'...Paul opened the Scriptures with clarity and simplicity." (Hughes)

iii. Paul did the work of **demonstrating that the Christ had to suffer and rise again from the dead**; "'Giving evidence' (NASB; 'proving,' NIV), which means 'to place beside' or 'to set before.'" (Hughes) The idea is of presenting persuasive evidence to listeners.

iv. Paul emphasized in all this who Jesus is (**This Jesus whom I preach to you is the Christ**) and what He did for them (**suffer and rise again from the dead**).

c. **Some of them were persuaded**: Among the hearers, there was a good response from **some**. Most of those – actually, **a great multitude** – were **devout Greeks**, but also many prominent Jewish women (**not a few of the leading women**). By all accounts, the work was a success: **a great multitude believed... not a few**.

i. When Paul was in Thessalonica, he received financial support from the Christians in Philippi (Philippians 4:15-16). They helped with this successful work among the Thessalonians.

2. (5-8) More mob violence against Paul and Silas.

But the Jews who were not persuaded, becoming envious, took some of the evil men from the marketplace, and gathering a mob, set all the city in an uproar and attacked the house of Jason, and sought to bring them out to the people. But when they did not find them, they dragged Jason and some brethren to the rulers of the city, crying out, "These who have turned the world upside down have come here too. Jason has harbored them, and these are all acting contrary to the decrees of Caesar, saying there is another king; Jesus." And they troubled the crowd and the rulers of the city when they heard these things.

a. **The Jews who were not persuaded, becoming envious, took some of the evil men from the marketplace, and gathering a mob, set all the city in an uproar**: As happened at Pisidian Antioch (Acts 13:45, 50), at Iconium (Acts 14:2, 5), and at Lystra (Acts 14:19) on the first missionary journey, here also Paul was opposed by a mob incited by **envious** people among the Jewish people.

b. **And attacked the house of Jason**: **Jason** was a Christian in Thessalonica whose house seems to have been a center for the church. When the **evil men from the marketplace** did not find Paul and Silas there, they attacked Jason himself, and **some brethren** who were with him.

c. **Crying out, "These who have turned the world upside down have come here too."** When accusing these Christians before **the rulers of the city**, the **evil men from the marketplace** gave an unintended compliment to the effectiveness of God's work through Paul and Silas. To complain that the Christians were **these who have turned the world upside-down have come here too** was to say, "these men have radically impacted our world and nothing seems the same."

i. God willing and blessing, people would say such things about the effectiveness of Christians today. One might say that Jesus did not come only to be our teacher, but to turn our world upside-down. Jesus turns the thinking and the power structures of this world around.

ii. Jesus gave a great example of this upside-down thinking when He spoke of a rich man who amassed great wealth, and all he could think about was building bigger barns to store all his wealth. We might make the man a civic leader or recognized him as a prominent man; Jesus turned it all upside down and called the man a fool, because he had done nothing to make his life matter for God's kingdom (Luke 12:16-21).

iii. Actually, God was working through Paul and Silas to turn the world *right side-up* again. But when you yourself are upside-down, the other direction appears to be upside-down!

d. **These are all acting contrary to the decrees of Caesar, saying there is another king; Jesus**: This was the serious accusation made by the **evil men from the marketplace**. The charge was serious enough that it **troubled the crowd and the rulers of the city when they heard these things**, because this raised the fear that their city might become known for opposition against Caesar and Rome.

i. Their fears were unfounded. Even though the gospel has definite political implications, it makes Christians *better* citizens than before, and their prayers for officials of government are more helpful than most people imagine.

ii. Even the unfounded accusation of political revolution had a compliment hidden inside. Even the **evil men from the marketplace** understood that Christians taught that Jesus was a **king**, that He had the right to rule over His people. This is a message that seems to be missed on many churchgoers today.

iii. "It may be for this reason that Paul avoided the use of 'kingdom' and 'king' in his letters to his converts, lest Gentile imperial authorities misconstrue them to connote opposition to the empire and emperor." (Longenecker)

3. (9-10a) Paul and Silas leave Thessalonica by night.

So when they had taken security from Jason and the rest, they let them go. Then the brethren immediately sent Paul and Silas away by night to Berea.

a. **When they had taken security from Jason and the rest, they let them go**. Jason and the others were released once they left a security deposit, to guarantee against any future riots.

i. In general, Roman officials did not care what the people believed. Yet when the public order was disrupted by riots, they came down with an iron hand. If things got out of hand, it wouldn't be long until the Emperor dispatched his legions to restore order, and no one wanted that. So Jason had to post the bond even though he did not start the riot.

b. **Then the brethren immediately sent Paul and Silas away by night to Berea**: Paul and Silas left Thessalonica quickly, not wanting to bring more persecution on the Christians there or to jeopardize Jason's security deposit.

i. Paul only spent a few weeks in Thessalonica (Acts 17:2) and it seems he wished he could have taught them more. He decided to teach them more in a written letter, and many believe that 1 Thessalonians was his first letter written to a congregation.

B. God's work in Berea.

1. (10b-12) More evangelistic success in the city of Berea.

When they arrived, they went into the synagogue of the Jews. These were more fair-minded than those in Thessalonica, in that they received the word with all readiness, and searched the Scriptures daily *to find out* whether these things were so. Therefore many of them believed, and also not a few of the Greeks, prominent women as well as men.

a. **When they arrived, they went into the synagogue of the Jews**: In Berea, they followed their familiar strategy, and found that their audience was **more fair-minded than those in Thessalonica**. Two things earned this compliment for the Bereans: first, **they received the word with all readiness**. Second, they **searched the Scriptures daily to find out whether these things were so**.

i. The Bereans heard the teaching of the most famous apostle and theologian of the early church, and the human author of at least 13 New Testament books. Yet, they **searched the Scriptures** when Paul taught, to see if his teaching was truly Biblical. They would not accept Paul's teaching without checking for themselves, so they could *know* if **these things were so**.

ii. When the Bereans heard Paul teach, their settled reaction wasn't "My, he's a fine speaker." It wasn't "I don't like the way he talks." It wasn't "What a funny preacher" Instead, the Bereans wanted to know,

"Are **these things…so**? Does this man teach the truth? We must search the Scriptures **daily to find out whether these things** are so."

iii. Their research was not casual; it had a certain character.

- They **searched** the Scriptures. It was worth it to them to work hard at it, and investigate what the Word of God said, and how Paul's teaching matched up with it.

- They also searched the Scriptures **daily** to find out. It wasn't a one-time, quick look. They made it a point of diligent, extended study.

- Also, they searched the Scriptures daily **to find out**. They believed they could understand and **find out** truth from the Bible. For them, the Bible was not just a pretty book of poetry or mystery or nice spiritual inspiration for thoughts-for-the-day. It was a book of *truth*, and that truth was there **to find out**.

iv. But with all their diligent searching and concern for the truth, the Bereans did not become skeptics. They **received the word with all readiness**. When Paul preached, they had open hearts; but also clear heads. Many people have clear heads but closed hearts, and never receive **the word with all readiness**. It was *both* of these things that made the Bereans **more fair-minded than those in Thessalonica**.

b. **Therefore many of them believed**: Paul had nothing to fear by the diligent searching of the Scriptures by the Bereans. If they were really seeking God and His Word, they would find out that what Paul was preaching was true. This is exactly what happened among the Bereans, and **therefore many of them believed**.

2. (13-15) Paul is forced to leave Berea.

But when the Jews from Thessalonica learned that the word of God was preached by Paul at Berea, they came there also and stirred up the crowds. Then immediately the brethren sent Paul away, to go to the sea; but both Silas and Timothy remained there. So those who conducted Paul brought him to Athens; and receiving a command for Silas and Timothy to come to him with all speed, they departed.

a. **The Jews from Thessalonica**: They were not satisfied to force Paul out of only their own city. They even followed Paul to Berea to disrupt his work there also.

b. **Stirred up the crowds**: The same had happened at Pisidian Antioch (Acts 13:45, 50), at Iconium (Acts 14:2, 5), at Lystra (Acts 14:19) and at

Thessalonica (Acts 17:5-8) This was the fifth city Paul was run out of by an angry mob, stirred up by envious Jewish leaders.

c. **Then immediately the brethren sent Paul away**: The Christians in Berea sent Paul away to Athens, fearing for his life and a total disruption of the work going on there. **But both Silas and Timothy remained there**, because Paul wanted to leave them behind to teach and take care of the new Christians in Berea.

> i. The fact that **both Silas and Timothy remained there** showed again that Paul had a passion for planting churches, not just making converts. It also showed that Paul didn't believe that he alone could do the work of teaching and strengthening Christians; men like **Silas and Timothy** also could.

C. God's work in Athens.

1. (16-17) Paul is provoked to preach in the city of Athens.

Now while Paul waited for them at Athens, his spirit was provoked within him when he saw that the city was given over to idols. Therefore he reasoned in the synagogue with the Jews and with the *Gentile* worshipers, and in the marketplace daily with those who happened to be there.

> a. **Now while Paul waited for them at Athens, his spirit was provoked within him**: The sense is that Paul would have preferred to wait until Timothy and Silas came from Berea before he began ministry in Athens. But **when he saw that the city was given over to idols**, he was compelled to preach the gospel immediately.

> > i. As Paul sailed to Athens from the sea near Berea, he came to a city he had probably never been to before, and like any tourist, he was ready to be impressed by this famous and historic city – which, hundreds of years before, was one of the most glorious and important cities in the world. But when Paul toured Athens, he was only depressed by the magnitude of the idolatry he saw all around.

> > ii. The idea behind **given over to idols** (*kateidolos*) is really *under* idols, or *swamped by idols*. Paul saw the beauty of Athens, having the best that Greek sculptors and architects could offer; but all that beauty did not honor God, so it did not impress him at all.

> b. **Therefore he reasoned in the synagogue…and in the marketplace daily**: Paul's practice was to preach wherever he could get an audience. Here it was both in the **synagogue** and in the **marketplace**.

c. **Those who happened to be there**: Paul faced a challenging audience in Athens. It was a cultured, educated city that was proud of its history. It was an intellectual center, much like Oxford or Cambridge. Paul spoke to a city perhaps different than any other city he had preached in.

> i. "Although Athens had long since lost the political eminence which was hers in an earlier day, she continued to represent the highest level of culture attained in classical antiquity." (Bruce)

> ii. "By now the greatest days of Athens were behind it, but it could still be fairly described as the intellectual capital of the Greco-Roman world and, at the same time, the religious capital of Greece." (Williams)

2. (18-21) The novelty of his message earns Paul an invitation to preach at the intellectual center of the city, the *Areopagus*.

Then certain Epicurean and Stoic philosophers encountered him. And some said, "What does this babbler want to say?" Others said, "He seems to be a proclaimer of foreign gods," because he preached to them Jesus and the resurrection. And they took him and brought him to the Areopagus, saying, "May we know what this new doctrine *is* of which you speak? For you are bringing some strange things to our ears. Therefore we want to know what these things mean." For all the Athenians and the foreigners who were there spent their time in nothing else but either to tell or to hear some new thing.

a. **Then certain Epicurean...philosophers encountered him**: The *Epicureans* pursued pleasure as the chief purpose in life, and valued most of all the pleasure of a peaceful life, free from pain, disturbing passions and superstitious fears (including the fear of death). They did not deny the existence of gods, but believed that they had nothing to do with man.

b. **Then certain...Stoic philosophers encountered him**: The *Stoics* were pantheists who put great emphasis on moral sincerity and a high sense of duty. They cultivated a spirit of proud dignity, and believed that suicide was better than a life lived with less dignity.

> i. The Stoics believed that everything was god, and god was in everything. So they believed that all things, good or evil, were from "god," and so nothing should be resisted, and they believed there was no particular direction or destiny for mankind.

c. **And some said**: Some mocked Paul because he did not speak with the philosophical niceties popular in Athens (**What does this babbler want to say?**). Others thought Paul was an exotic **proclaimer of foreign gods**.

d. **He preached to them Jesus and the resurrection**: Though Paul spoke in a different place, to a different kind of audience, his message did not change in Athens. He focused on **Jesus and the resurrection**.

e. **For all the Athenians and the foreigners who were there spent their time in nothing else but either to tell or hear some strange new thing**: It was the *novelty* of Paul's message that earned him the invitation to the **Areopagus**. These ancient Greeks loved a constant and always changing stream of news and information.

> i. In the early nineteenth century, Adam Clarke described the situation of his day, and it sounds like it is even truer of our own time. "This is a striking feature of the city of London in the present day. The itch for news, which generally argues a worldly, shallow, or unsettled mind, is wonderfully prevalent: even ministers of the Gospel, negligent of their sacred function, are become in this sense Athenians; so that the book of God is neither read nor studied with half the avidity and spirit as a *newspaper*…It is no wonder if such become political preachers, and their sermons be no better than husks for swine. To such *the hungry sheep look up, and are not fed.*"

3. (22-23) Paul begins to speak on Mars' Hill (the **Areopagus**).

Then Paul stood in the midst of the Areopagus and said, "Men of Athens, I perceive that in all things you are very religious; for as I was passing through and considering the objects of your worship, I even found an altar with this inscription: To THE UNKNOWN GOD. Therefore, the One whom you worship without knowing, Him I proclaim to you:

a. **Men of Athens, I perceive that in all things you are very religious**: Paul did not begin with an exposition of Scripture, which was his custom when dealing with Jews or Gentiles who were familiar with the Old Testament. Instead, Paul began with general references to religion.

b. **In all things you are very religious**: Many ancient observers noticed the religious character of Athens, and some thought that Athenians were the most religious of all people. But when Paul said this of the Athenians, he didn't necessarily mean it in a positive way. Religion can lead one away from God, and if we trust in a false religion, it is little credit to say of us that we are "religious."

c. **I even found an altar with this inscription: To THE UNKNOWN GOD**: Paul understood that in their extensive pantheon, the Greeks had an **UNKNOWN GOD**, who covered any god that may have been neglected. Paul wanted to reveal the identity of the **UNKNOWN GOD**.

i. Athens was filled with statues dedicated To THE UNKNOWN GOD. Six hundred years before Paul, a terrible plague came on the city and a man name Epimenides had an idea. He let loose a flock of sheep through the town, and wherever they lay down, they sacrificed that sheep to the god that had the nearest shrine or temple. If a sheep lay down near no shrine or temple, they sacrificed the sheep To THE UNKNOWN GOD.

4. (24-29) Paul tells the Athenians who God is.

God, who made the world and everything in it, since He is Lord of heaven and earth, does not dwell in temples made with hands. Nor is He worshiped with men's hands, as though He needed anything, since He gives to all life, breath, and all things. And He has made from one blood every nation of men to dwell on all the face of the earth, and has determined their preappointed times and the boundaries of their dwellings, so that they should seek the Lord, in the hope that they might grope for Him and find Him, though He is not far from each one of us; for in Him we live and move and have our being, as also some of your own poets have said, 'For we are also His offspring.' Therefore, since we are the offspring of God, we ought not to think that the Divine Nature is like gold or silver or stone, something shaped by art and man's devising.

a. **God, who made the world and everything in it, since He is Lord of heaven and earth**: Paul spoke about the God who created everything, yet is distinct from His creation. Paul told them that God was bigger than any temple men's hands could build (**does not dwell in temples made with hands**), and could not be represented by anything men could make with their hands (**Nor is He worshipped with men's hands**).

i. In explaining God to them, Paul started at the beginning: God is the Creator, and we are His creatures. "This view of the world is very different from either the Epicurean emphasis on a chance combination of atoms or the virtual pantheism of the Stoics." (Stott)

ii. Paul recognized that these philosophers had to change their ideas about God. They had to move from their own personal opinions to an understanding of who God is according to what He tells us about Himself in the Bible

b. **And He has made from one blood every nation of men**: Paul told them we are all descended from Adam through Noah, and that there is one God who created us all and to whom we all are obligated. Since God created us all, we **should seek the Lord…though He is not far from each one of us**.

c. **For in Him we live and move and have our being…For we are also His offspring**: These two quotations Paul used from Greek poets are attributed respectively to Epimenides the Cretan [600 B.C.] (who Paul quotes again in Titus 1:12) and Aratus [310 B.C.].

i. Paul did not quote these men because they were prophets or because all their teaching was of God. He quoted them because these specific words reflected a Biblical truth, and by using them he could build a bridge to his pagan audience.

d. **Therefore since we are the offspring of God, we ought not to think that the Divine Nature is like gold or silver or stone**: Paul told them of our responsibility to God because we are His **offspring**. Since we are His **offspring**, we are responsible to have right ideas about God, and therefore must reject the wrong idea that **gold or silver or stone** could represent God.

i. "The Athenians have acknowledged in their altar inscription that they are ignorant of God, and Paul has been giving evidence of their ignorance. Now he declares such ignorance to be culpable." (Stott)

5. (30-31) Paul tells the Athenians what they must do because of who God is.

Truly, these times of ignorance God overlooked, but now commands all men everywhere to repent, because He has appointed a day on which He will judge the world in righteousness by the Man whom He has ordained. He has given assurance of this to all by raising Him from the dead."

a. **Now commands all men everywhere to repent, because He has appointed a day on which He will judge the world in righteousness**: Paul went from knowing who God is (our Creator), to who we are (His offspring), to our responsibility before Him (to understand Him and worship Him in truth), to our accountability if we dishonor Him (judgment).

i. Paul didn't preach a "soft" gospel. He boldly confronted the wrong ideas the Athenians had about God, and confronted them with the reality of coming judgment.

b. **He will judge the world in righteousness by the Man who He has ordained**: Now, for the first time in his message to the Athenians, Paul referred to Jesus. His first mention of Jesus presented Jesus as a righteous judge.

i. Certainly, Paul did not want to leave the Athenians with the idea that Jesus was *only* a righteous judge. However, he was stopped short before he could tell them everything he wanted to about Jesus. Probably, all that Paul said before was introduction. He would now begin at what he really wanted to speak about: The person and work of Jesus.

c. **He has given assurance of this by raising Him from the dead**: The emphasis on the resurrection is important. Paul saw the resurrection of Jesus as the **assurance of this**; it demonstrated that Jesus Himself, His teaching, and His work were all perfectly approved by the Father.

i. Paul seemed unable to preach a sermon without focusing on the resurrection of Jesus. For him, none of the Christian life made sense without the triumph of Jesus' resurrection.

6. (32-34) The reaction of the listeners at Areopagus.

And when they heard of the resurrection of the dead, some mocked, while others said, "We will hear you again on this *matter.*" So Paul departed from among them. However, some men joined him and believed, among them Dionysius the Areopagite, a woman named Damaris, and others with them.

a. **When they heard of the resurrection of the dead, some mocked**: The resurrection was not a popular idea among Greek philosophers. Some though Paul foolish for even believing such a thing, and other wanted to hear more about this new teaching (**others said, "We will hear you again on this matter"**).

i. The Greeks were fond of the idea of the immortality of the soul, but not of the idea of the resurrection of the body. They felt that anything material was inherently evil, so there really could be no such thing as a glorified body. They thought the ultimate form of glory would be pure spirit.

ii. "All Greeks thought that man was composed of spirit (or mind), which was good, and matter (or body), which was bad. If there was to be a life to come, the one thing they certainty did not want it cluttered up with a body." (Boice)

b. **So Paul departed among them**: Paul wanted to talk about Jesus. He could have, if he wanted to, stayed there and discussed Greek philosophy all day long. But Paul was not interested in that; if he couldn't talk about Jesus, he didn't have much to say.

i. Without doubt, Paul was really just beginning his sermon. Far more than wanting to quote Greek poets, he wanted to tell them about Jesus. But as soon as he mentioned the resurrection, they stopped him short. Certainly, Paul discussed more with people one-on-one. But he was prevented from saying all he wanted to in his speech at the Areopagus.

c. **However, some men joined him and believed**: The results at the Areopagus seemed small, yet some did believe. Among those believing were a man named **Dionysius** (who must have been a regular participant at the Areopagus) and a woman named **Damaris**.

i. Some criticize Paul's sermon in Athens because there is no detailed reference to the cross or specific quotes from the Old Testament. Some think Paul compromised his message for an intellectual audience, and therefore there were few conversions.

ii. This idea continues, saying that when Paul went next to Corinth, he decided to preach the cross and the cross only, even if it seemed foolish (1 Corinthians 1:18-2:5). Because Paul preached this way in Corinth, the thinking goes, he saw much better results.

iii. Ramsay popularized the theory that Paul was disappointed by his "meager" results in Athens, and went on to Corinth preaching the gospel with a pure focus on the cross, and without any attempt at philosophical explanation.

iv. Yet Paul's sermon here *was* eminently Biblical. "Like the biblical revelation itself, his argument begins with God the creator of all and ends with God the judge of all...The speech as it stands admirably summarizes an introductory lesson in Christianity for cultured pagans." (Bruce)

v. As well, Paul *did* preach Christ crucified in Athens. In Acts 17:30-31 he specifically mentioned the resurrection, and how could he preach the resurrection without preaching the cross which came before it? This is obviously a short extract of Paul's speech on the Areopagus; what is recorded takes barely two minutes to say.

vi. "We learn from Paul that we cannot preach the gospel of Jesus without the doctrine of God, or the cross without the creation, or salvation without judgment." (Stott)

vii. In addition, it is dangerous to judge the content of the message by the magnitude of the response. "The reason the gospel did not take root there probably lay more in the attitude of the Athenians themselves than in Paul's approach or in what he said." (Longenecker)

Acts 18 - Paul in Corinth; the End of the Second Missionary Journey and Beginning of the Third

A. Paul in the city of Corinth.

1. (1-3) Paul arrives in Corinth and meets Aquila and Priscilla.

After these things Paul departed from Athens and went to Corinth. And he found a certain Jew named Aquila, born in Pontus, who had recently come from Italy with his wife Priscilla (because Claudius had commanded all the Jews to depart from Rome); and he came to them. So, because he was of the same trade, he stayed with them and worked; for by occupation they were tentmakers.

a. **And went to Corinth**: Corinth was a major city of the Roman Empire, at an important crossroads of trade and travel. It was also a city notorious for its hedonism and immorality.

i. In Paul's day, **Corinth** was already an ancient city. It was a commercial center with two harbors and had long been a rival to its northern neighbor, Athens. Corinth was a city with a remarkable reputation for loose living and especially sexual immorality. In classical Greek, to *act like a Corinthian* meant to practice fornication, and a *Corinthian companion* meant a prostitute. This sexual immorality was permitted under the widely popular worship of Aphrodite (also known as Venus, the goddess of fertility and sexuality). In 146 B.C. Corinth rebelled against Rome and was brutally destroyed by Roman armies. It lay in ruins for a century, until Julius Caesar rebuilt the city. It quickly re-established its former position as a center for both trade and immorality of every sort. One ancient writer described Corinth as a town where "none but the tough could survive." (Williams)

ii. "It is significant that it was from this city that Paul wrote his Roman letter; and when one reads his description of Gentile corruption in that

Roman letter, one has almost certainly a mirror of what he found in Corinth. (Romans 1:22-32)" (Morgan)

iii. Paul knew that because people from all over the Empire passed through Corinth, a strong church there could touch lives all over the Empire. He knew Corinth was a tough city, but he wasn't only interested in planting churches where he thought it was *easy*.

b. **And he found a certain Jew named Aquila…with his wife Priscilla … and he came to them**: It is implied, though not clearly stated, that Aquila and Priscilla were at this time Christians. But it is possible that Paul led them both to Jesus as they worked together as **tentmakers** (those who worked with leather).

i. This began one of the important friendships of the New Testament – Paul and **Aquila** and **his wife Priscilla**. Paul called them his *fellow workers* who had *risked their own necks for my life* (Romans 16:3-4).

ii. "*Priscilla* is a diminutive form of Prisca, which is one of the great families of Rome. She was probably related to this family in some way." (Hughes) In half the mentions of this New Testament married couple, Priscilla's name is written first – which is said to be unusual.

c. **For by occupation they were tentmakers**: Paul's tentmaking was an important part of his ministry. Though he recognized his right to be supported by those he ministered to (1 Corinthians 9:7-14), he voluntarily supported himself in his missionary and preaching work so that no one could accuse him of seeking converts for the sake of enriching himself (1 Corinthians 9:15-18).

ii. In the modern missions movement, people call any work that a missionary does to support himself on the mission field *tentmaking*.

iii. "In Judaism it was not considered proper for a scribe or a rabbi to receive payment for his teaching, so many of them practised a trade in addition to their study and teaching of the law." (Bruce)

d. **Because Claudius had commanded all the Jews to depart from Rome**: The Roman historian Suetonius wrote that **Claudius** banished Jews from Rome because they were "indulging in constant riots at the instigation of Chrestus." There have been many attempts to explain who *Chrestus* was, but a likely solution is that Suetonius referred to Jesus Christ, but writing some 70 years after the events, had the name somewhat mixed up. It seems that the expulsion had to do with "dissension and disorder within the Jewish community of Rome resulting from the introduction of Christianity into one or more of the synagogues of the city." (Bruce)

i. Chronology is often a tricky matter, but it seems that this expulsion of Jews from Rome occurred at about A.D. 49.

2. (4-5) Paul's ministry among the Jews and Gentiles of Corinth.

And he reasoned in the synagogue every Sabbath, and persuaded both Jews and Greeks. When Silas and Timothy had come from Macedonia, Paul was compelled by the Spirit, and testified to the Jews *that* Jesus *is* the Christ.

a. **And he reasoned in the synagogue every Sabbath**: Paul was effective as he **reasoned** (discussed, debated) among the Jews and Greeks. The **Greeks** present in the synagogue were Gentiles interested in and sympathetic with Judaism.

i. Paul later described the character of his bold preaching in Corinth in: *For I determined not to know anything among you except Jesus Christ and Him crucified* (1 Corinthians 2:1-16).

b. **When Silas and Timothy had come from Macedonia**: When Timothy came, he brought news about how the Christians in Thessalonica were remaining steadfast in the faith (1 Thessalonians 3:6-10). This brought Paul great joy, spurring him on in ministry (**Paul was compelled by the Spirit**). He answered back by writing 1 Thessalonians from Corinth.

i. According to 2 Corinthians 11:8-9, while Paul was in Corinth, financial support arrived from the Christians in Philippi, and he was able to put aside tentmaking for a while and concentrate more fully on the task of building the church in Corinth.

3. (6-8) Opposition rises against Paul in Corinth.

But when they opposed him and blasphemed, he shook *his* garments and said to them, "Your blood *be* upon your *own* heads; I *am* clean. From now on I will go to the Gentiles." And he departed from there and entered the house of a certain *man* named Justus, *one* who worshiped God, whose house was next door to the synagogue. Then Crispus, the ruler of the synagogue, believed on the Lord with all his household. And many of the Corinthians, hearing, believed and were baptized.

a. **But when they opposed him and blasphemed**: The blasphemy must have been directed against Jesus, because Paul preached Jesus as the Messiah (*testified to the Jews that Jesus is the Christ*, Acts 18:5). This is an indirect declaration of the deity of Jesus, because someone can only really blaspheme God.

b. **From now on I will go to the Gentiles**: Paul strongly sensed his responsibility to preach to the Jews first (Romans 1:16), but when his message was rejected, he wasted no time in going to the Gentiles.

i. Paul fulfilled the spirit of what Jesus said in Matthew 7:6: *Do not give what is holy to the dogs; nor cast your pearls before swine, lest they trample them under their feet, and turn and tear you in pieces.* When people are determined to reject the gospel, we shouldn't keep trying with them until the door is open again.

c. **He shook his garments**: Paul did this so that not a speck of dust from the synagogue would remain on his clothes, much less his sandals. This was a dramatic way of expressing *his* rejection of *their* rejection. Paul was certainly capable of dramatic and vivid demonstrations of his message.

d. **Crispus, the ruler of the synagogue, believed on the Lord with all his household**: This shows that Paul treated the Jews of Corinth with love and grace even after they rejected him and his message. He certainly did not forbid Jewish people from coming to Jesus; he merely switched the focus of his evangelism from the Jews to the Gentiles.

i. **Crispus** was one of the few in Corinth whom Paul personally baptized (1 Corinthians 1:14).

e. **Many of the Corinthians, hearing, believed and were baptized**: Paul told us what kind of people these Corinthians were in 1 Corinthians 1:26: *For you see your calling, brethren, that not many wise according to the flesh, not many mighty, not many noble, are called.*

4. (9-11) God's special encouragement to Paul in Corinth.

Now the Lord spoke to Paul in the night by a vision, "Do not be afraid, but speak, and do not keep silent; for I am with you, and no one will attack you to hurt you; for I have many people in this city." And he continued *there* a year and six months, teaching the word of God among them.

a. **Do not be afraid**: The implication behind this message was that Paul *was* afraid, fearing that here in Corinth his work would be cut short by either opposing Jews (as in Thessalonica and Berea) or by the highly-charged worldliness around him.

i. "There had been culture shock in Athens, and now Paul experienced moral shock in Corinth. Its sweat and perfume and grit smothered Paul's righteous soul, and he became depressed." (Hughes)

b. **But speak, and do not keep silent**: The solution to Paul's fear was for him to *obey* Jesus' command to not be afraid; and to **speak and not keep silent**, that is, to keep getting the Word of God out.

i. Jesus didn't tell Paul that his opponents wouldn't *try* to stop him, only that they would not be successful (**no one will attack you to hurt you**).

c. **For I am with you**: This promise was the *basis* for God's command to not be afraid and to keep preaching. When we understand what this means, and Who says it, this is enough.

i. Spurgeon considered the promise of Jesus, "**For I am with you.**" He thought it emphasized three things: The *presence* of Jesus, the *sympathy* of Jesus, and the *cooperation* of Jesus.

d. **For I have many people in this city**: This additional promise was a constant assurance to Paul, who must have often had doubts about the survival and health of the Corinthian church.

e. **And he continued there a year and six months**: Paul was in Corinth a year and a half, which seems to be longer than in any other city where he founded a church. His ministry at Corinth is described simply: **teaching the word of God among them**.

i. The duration of Paul's stay in Corinth shows where his heart was in ministry. He was no "in and out" evangelist, but a man committed to making disciples.

5. (12-17) The Jews of Corinth attempt (unsuccessfully) to convict Paul before the civil authorities.

When Gallio was proconsul of Achaia, the Jews with one accord rose up against Paul and brought him to the judgment seat, saying, "This *fellow* persuades men to worship God contrary to the law." And when Paul was about to open *his* mouth, Gallio said to the Jews, "If it were a matter of wrongdoing or wicked crimes, O Jews, there would be reason why I should bear with you. But if it is a question of words and names and your own law, look *to it* yourselves; for I do not want to be a judge of such *matters*." And he drove them from the judgment seat. Then all the Greeks took Sosthenes, the ruler of the synagogue, and beat *him* before the judgment seat. But Gallio took no notice of these things.

a. **When Gallio was proconsul of Achaia**: In approaching Gallio, the Jews of Corinth tried to stop Paul's preaching work in the entire province.

i. "If Gallio had accepted the Jewish charge and found Paul guilty of the alleged offense, provincial governors everywhere would have had a precedent, and Paul's ministry would have been severely restricted. As it was, Gallio's refusal to act in the matter was tantamount to the recognition of Christianity as a *religio licita*" (Longenecker)

b. **When Paul was about to open his mouth**: Before Paul could defend himself, Gallio did it for him. He correctly saw that the government has no role in attempting to decide religious matters, though government does have a legitimate role in matters of **wrongdoing or wicked crimes**.

c. **Then all the Greeks took Sosthenes, the ruler of the synagogue, and beat him before the judgment seat**: Gallio looked the other way when angry Gentiles beat **Sosthenes**, the leader of the synagogue. Probably, both the crowd and Gallio himself were more *against* the Jews than they were *for* Paul.

i. "It was his duty to let this good man alone, but it was not his duty to allow the Gentiles, on the other hand, to begin beating the Jews." (Spurgeon)

ii. Apparently, when *Crispus* trusted in Jesus, he was replaced as *ruler of the synagogue* (Acts 18:8) by **Sosthenes** - who later himself seems to have become a Christian (1 Corinthians 1:1).

B. The end of Paul's second missionary journey.

1. (18) Paul leaves the city of Corinth with Aquila and Priscilla.

So Paul still remained a good while. Then he took leave of the brethren and sailed for Syria, and Priscilla and Aquila *were* with him. He had *his* hair cut off at Cenchrea, for he had taken a vow.

a. **So Paul still remained a good while**: Unlike previous cities, Paul wasn't forced out of Corinth. He stayed there **a good while**, fulfilling the promise Jesus made to him in Acts 18:9-10.

b. **Priscilla and Aquila were with him**: Paul developed such a deep friendship and partnership with this married couple that they decided to go with him as decided to head east back to Jerusalem and then Antioch.

c. **He had his hair cut off at Cenchrea, for he had taken a vow**: The **vow** was almost certainly the vow of a Nazirite (Numbers 6). Usually this vow was taken for a certain period of time and when completed, the hair (which had been allowed to freely grow) was cut off and offered to the Lord at a special ceremony at the temple in Jerusalem.

i. The purpose of the vow of a Nazirite was to express a unique consecration to God, promising to abstain from all products from the grapevine, to not cut one's hair, and to never come near a dead body.

ii. Paul's performance of this vow shows that Jewish opposition to his preaching had not made him anti-Jewish. He never forgot that he was Jewish, His Messiah was Jewish, that Christianity is Jewish, and that Old Testament forms and rituals might still be used to good purpose. Apparently, though Paul was adamant that Jewish ceremonies and rituals must not be required of Gentiles, he saw nothing wrong with Jewish believers who wished to observe such ceremonies, presumably if their fulfillment in Jesus was also recognized.

iii. William Barclay suggests that Paul's motive was *gratitude*. "No doubt Paul was thinking of all God's goodness to him in Corinth and took this vow to show his gratitude." But the purpose of a Nazirite vow seems to be more of *consecration* than *thanksgiving*. Perhaps the intense worldliness of Corinth made Paul want to express his dedication and separation unto the Lord more than ever.

iv. By tradition, a Nazirite vow could only be fulfilled in Judea. Paul began this vow **at Cenchrea**, not in Judea. Paul's adoption of the vow out of the bounds dictated by Jewish tradition could indicate a desire to practice a more purely Biblical observance of Jewish rituals.

2. (19-21) Paul in the city of Ephesus.

And he came to Ephesus, and left them there; but he himself entered the synagogue and reasoned with the Jews. When they asked *him* to stay a longer time with them, he did not consent, but took leave of them, saying, "I must by all means keep this coming feast in Jerusalem; but I will return again to you, God willing." And he sailed from Ephesus.

a. **And he came to Ephesus**: Paul wanted to preach in Ephesus some two years earlier, but was prevented by the Holy Spirit (Acts 16:6). Now, the Holy Spirit gave him the liberty to preach in this important city, and great results were seen.

i. God has a special timing for everything in our lives. If Paul could have discerned it, the Holy Spirit was really saying, "wait" when he wanted to go to Ephesus, instead of "no." Sometimes God says, "wait" and He always knows what He's doing when He says it.

b. **And left them there**: Aquila and Priscilla stayed at Ephesus, seemingly at Paul's request. Something good started at Ephesus, and Paul wanted the work to continue with his trusted friends.

c. **They asked him to stay a longer time with them, he did not consent, but took leave of them, saying, "I must by all means keep this coming feast in Jerusalem"**: Paul could not stay long in Ephesus, wanting to present the offering of his Nazirite vow in Jerusalem at an upcoming feast.

3. (22) Landing at Caesarea, and going through Jerusalem, Paul returns to his home church at Antioch of Syria, concluding his second missionary journey.

And when he had landed at Caesarea, and gone up and greeted the church, he went down to Antioch.

> a. **Gone up and greeted the church**: When it says that Paul had **gone *up* and greeted the church**, it means he went **up** to Jerusalem and fulfilled his Nazirite vow in the temple.

> b. **He went down to Antioch**: Leaving Jerusalem, Paul returned to his home church in Syrian Antioch. They must have been pleased to have Paul return and tell of all his work over the previous three years or so.

C. Paul's third missionary journey begins in the regions of Galatia, Phyrgia, and the city of Ephesus.

1. (23) In the regions of Galatia and Phyrgia.

After he had spent some time *there*, he departed and went over the region of Galatia and Phrygia in order, strengthening all the disciples.

> a. **After he had spent some time there**: We don't know exactly how much time Paul spent back at his home congregation in Syrian Antioch. Luke wrote the account to give the sense of an immediate move on to Paul's next missionary journey.

> b. **Went over the region of Galatia and Phrygia in order**: Since Paul's first focus on this trip was **strengthening all the disciples**, he went back to the churches already founded on previous missionary works. This would include congregations in Tarsus, Derbe, Lystra, Iconium, and Pisidian Antioch.

> c. **Strengthening all the disciples**: Paul's passion for building disciples, not merely making converts, was again evident. This work was important to Paul.

> > i. If Paul were to visit one of our modern congregations, he would want to know: "How strong of a disciple are you? What can I do to strengthen your walk with Jesus Christ?" He would remind us all that it isn't enough to make a strong beginning with Jesus, but we must be always be growing in strength.

2. (24-26a) The ministry of Apollos in Ephesus.

Now a certain Jew named Apollos, born at Alexandria, an eloquent man *and* mighty in the Scriptures, came to Ephesus. This man had been instructed in the way of the Lord; and being fervent in spirit, he spoke and taught accurately the things of the Lord, though he knew only the baptism of John. So he began to speak boldly in the synagogue.

a. **A certain Jew named Apollos**: As Paul did his work in Galatia and Phrygia, this man named **Apollos** came from Alexandria to Ephesus. By many measures, he was a remarkable man.

- Apollos was **an eloquent man**.
- Apollos was **mighty in the Scriptures**.
- Apollos had been **instructed in the way of the Lord**.
- Apollos was **fervent in spirit**. Literally this means, "to boil in the spirit" with the idea of "bubbling over with enthusiasm." (Williams)
- Apollos **spoke and taught accurately the things of the Lord**.

i. It seems Apollos (like many in his day) was a missionary called by God alone, because we have no indication that he was sent or commissioned by any specific congregation or apostle. He simply **came to Ephesus**.

b. **Though he knew only the baptism of John**: We see again that the reputation and work of John the Baptist was widely known throughout the Jews of the Roman Empire, reaching here as far as Alexandria.

i. Because Apollos knew of the work of John the Baptist, it is likely that he preached that the Messiah had come and we must repent and respond to Jesus, but he probably had little knowledge of the *full* person and work of Jesus Christ.

ii. "Apollos was a well-educated and also a well-traveled man. We can imagine that in his youth he had gone to Jerusalem, especially if he had an interest in the Old Testament, and while there had come under the influence of the preaching of John the Baptist." (Boice)

c. **So he began to speak boldly in the synagogue**: Apollos didn't know much about Jesus, but what he did know was **taught accurately** – and with bold passion. He didn't know much about Jesus, but what he did know genuinely excited him.

i. "What is mentioned here is 'fervor,' and this means not merely skill on his part but conviction based on something deeply embedded in his heart." (Boice)

3. (26b-28) Aquila and Priscilla help Apollos.

When Aquila and Priscilla heard him, they took him aside and explained to him the way of God more accurately. And when he desired to cross to Achaia, the brethren wrote, exhorting the disciples to receive him; and when he arrived, he greatly helped those who had believed through grace; for he vigorously refuted the Jews publicly, showing from the Scriptures that Jesus is the Christ.

a. **Aquila and Priscilla**: Paul met this couple that shared his profession of tentmaking in Corinth (Acts 18:3). They went with him from Corinth to Ephesus, and Paul left them there while he continued eastward to Caesarea, Jerusalem, and Antioch (Acts 18:18-22).

b. **They took him aside and explained to him the way of God more accurately**: Aquila and Priscilla did something valuable for God's kingdom. They helped someone who had a passion for God and at least some power in serving Him; yet he had limited knowledge and therefore limited resources for truly effective ministry.

c. **The brethren wrote, exhorting the disciples to receive him**: With both instruction from Aquila and Priscilla and letters of reference from the church in Ephesus, Apollos served effectively in Achaia, especially among opposing Jews (**he vigorously refuted the Jews publicly**).

> i. When Apollos went to the region of **Achaia**, it probably means he went to the city of Corinth in the region of Achaia. From what Paul wrote in 1 Corinthians, he apparently had a remarkable ministry there. Apollos went to Corinth to water what Paul had planted.

> ii. Though some Corinthians fixated on Apollos in a divisive spirit (1 Corinthians 1:12, 3:4), there is no reason to believe that Apollos himself encouraged this. Paul regarded Apollos as a trusted colleague (1 Corinthians 3:5-7 and 16:12).

> iii. Apollos was Jewish, and is described as *eloquent* and *fervent in spirit* (Acts 18:24-25). He also **vigorously refuted the Jews**, and was able to demonstrate **from the Scriptures that Jesus is the Christ**. Because of these things, some scholars consider him the type of person who could have wrote the letter to the Hebrews.

Acts 19 - Paul in Ephesus

A. Ephesian disciples are baptized in the Holy Spirit.

1. (1-2) In Ephesus, Paul finds some disciples who had not yet received the Holy Spirit.

And it happened, while Apollos was at Corinth, that Paul, having passed through the upper regions, came to Ephesus. And finding some disciples he said to them, "Did you receive the Holy Spirit when you believed?" So they said to him, "We have not so much as heard whether there is a Holy Spirit."

> a. **Paul, having passed through the upper regions, came to Ephesus**: Paul was last in Ephesus on his way back from Corinth on his second missionary journey. Now he came from the east, arriving in Ephesus from the region of Phrygia. He came back to Ephesus as he had promised in Acts 18:21.

> b. **Did you receive the Holy Spirit when you believed?** Apparently there was something about these **disciples** that prompted this question from Paul. We don't have any indication that it was his custom to ask people if they had received the Holy Spirit when they believed.

> c. **We have not so much as heard whether there is a Holy Spirit**: By their reply, these Ephesian **disciples** showed they didn't know much about God's nature as revealed in Jesus. They knew enough to be saved and to be students of Jesus (they were called **disciples**), but they didn't know much about all Jesus did for us, especially in His promise to send the Holy Spirit when He ascended to heaven.

> > i. It may be that this was not the core group of disciples that Paul originally spoke to in Ephesus (Acts 18:19-21) and whom Aquila and Priscilla were left behind to serve. Aquila and Priscilla were with Paul for a year and a half in Corinth, and it seems from his letters to the

Corinthians that Paul taught them about the Person and the work of the Holy Spirit. These "**some disciples**" may have been new or young **disciples**, not the core group at Ephesus.

2. (3-4) Paul distinguishes between the baptism of John and baptism in the name of the Jesus.

And he said to them, "Into what then were you baptized?" So they said, "Into John's baptism." Then Paul said, "John indeed baptized with a baptism of repentance, saying to the people that they should believe on Him who would come after him, that is, on Christ Jesus."

a. **Into John's baptism**: These Ephesian disciples had only a basic understanding of the Messiah Jesus and His ministry, only what could be gained through the message of John the Baptist. They were in the same place as Apollos before Aquila and Priscilla explained *the way of God more accurately* (Acts 18:24-26).

i. They could have received **John's baptism** from the hands of John himself; or perhaps from some of John's disciples who continued on in his ministry after John's death.

b. **John indeed baptized with a baptism of repentance**: Paul points out that John's baptism was one of **repentance**, not necessarily faith unto salvation. John's message pointed to Jesus, but did not take men there itself.

i. One can imagine that these Ephesian disciples heard about the coming of the Messiah through John's message, and they heard their need to be ready through repentance to receive the Messiah. Yet they actually do not seem to have heard that the Messiah *had* in fact come, and had not heard of their need to trust in His specific person and work.

ii. Some have suggested that these Ephesian disciples were not actually Christians yet. The problem in this is that they are called *disciples*, which almost always refers to Christians, genuine followers of Jesus Christ. However, it must be said that the word *disciple* does have a broader understanding and application than its most frequent usage - describing a follower of Jesus.

iii. However, Bruce makes the point: "When the men are called *disciples* without further qualification, that…seems to mean that they were disciples of Jesus. Had Luke meant to indicate that they were disciples of John the Baptist… he would have said so explicitly."

3. (5-7) The twelve Ephesian disciples believe on Jesus, are baptized, and receive the Holy Spirit with His gifts.

When they heard *this*, they were baptized in the name of the Lord Jesus. And when Paul had laid hands on them, the Holy Spirit came upon them, and they spoke with tongues and prophesied. Now the men were about twelve in all.

a. **They were baptized in the name of the Lord Jesus**: Having been completely prepared by their response to the preaching of John the Baptist, they were ready to embrace Jesus fully, and were **baptized in the name of Jesus**.

b. **The Holy Spirit came upon them**: After they were baptized, **Paul…laid hands on them**, and they were filled with the **Holy Spirit**, and received His gifts.

i. Paul wrote the letters of 1 and 2 Corinthians during his stay in the city of Ephesus at this time, and 1 Corinthians has much to say about person and work of the Holy Spirit.

c. **Now the men were about twelve in all**: This reminds us that not the entire church in Ephesus had this incomplete understanding and embrace of Jesus' person and work, but only a small group.

i. An often-debated question is, "Were these 12 Ephesian disciples actually Christians before this remarkable filling of the Holy Spirit, or not?" On the one hand, they were called *disciples* - and appeared to part of the company of Christians in Ephesus, things that would not usually be said of them if they were not actually Christians. On the other hand, they knew so little about Jesus; and they were baptized in water again, this time in the name of Jesus. It is difficult to say with certainty if they were already Christians or not, but one can say with certainty that Paul perceived they lacked something of the Holy Spirit in their lives.

ii. It is fair for each Christian today to consider if someone were to look at their own life, would they notice a conspicuous absence of the Person and power of the Holy Spirit?

iii. These Ephesian disciples sensed their need to get right with God, and knew the answer was in God's Messiah - but they had gone no further than that. They need to go all the way, to trust in everything Jesus is and everything He had done, and to be filled with the power of the Holy Spirit.

iv. "Have ye then received the Spirit since you believed? Beloved, are you now receiving the Spirit? Are you living under his divine influence? Are you filled with his power? Put the question personally. I am afraid some professors will have to admit that they hardly know whether there be any Holy Ghost; and others will have to confess that though they have enjoyed a little of his saving work, yet they do not know much of his ennobling and sanctifying influence." (Spurgeon)

v. God always wants us to go deeper. We tend to sip where we could drink deeply; we drink deeply where we could wade in, and we wade in where we could plunge in and swim. Most of us need to be encouraged to go deeper and further into the things of the Holy Spirit.

vi. If someone doesn't seem to *know* if they have the power and presence of the Holy Spirit in their life, it's fair to assume that they *don't have it*. If you have it, you should know it. "Give a man an electric shock, and I warrant you he will know it; but if he has the Holy Ghost, he will know it much more." (Spurgeon) This isn't something to *hope* about; we can *know* - one can *know* they are filled with the Holy Spirit.

B. Paul's continuing ministry in the city of Ephesus.

1. (8-10) Paul eventually leaves the synagogue and begins teaching in a borrowed school building.

And he went into the synagogue and spoke boldly for three months, reasoning and persuading concerning the things of the kingdom of God. But when some were hardened and did not believe, but spoke evil of the Way before the multitude, he departed from them and withdrew the disciples, reasoning daily in the school of Tyrannus. And this continued for two years, so that all who dwelt in Asia heard the word of the Lord Jesus, both Jews and Greeks.

a. **He went into the synagogue and spoke boldly for three months**: Paul had an extended time of preaching in the synagogue, but eventually, the influence of the Jews who rejected the message drove him out. He then resumed his teaching in the hall of a Gentile teacher named Tyrannus (**reasoning daily in the school of Tyrannus**).

i. One ancient, though not inspired, writing says that Paul held his meetings at the school of Tyrannus from eleven in the morning to four in the afternoon. This was the time most people rested from work, including Paul, who worked to support himself while in Ephesus (Acts 20:34-35). These also may have been the "off hours" for the school of Tyrannus.

ii. Paul did this **daily**, meaning every day. Considering his extended time in Ephesus, this meant many hundreds of hours of teaching. It is no wonder that the work in Ephesus was so broad and effective.

b. **And this continued for two years**: Paul carried this on for two years, and his effective teaching equipped believers, who got the word of God out to **all who dwelt in Asia**.

i. By himself, there was no way that Paul could reach this region. But he could equip Christians to do the work of the ministry, just as he described in Ephesians 4:11-12.

2. (11-12) Unusual miracles in Ephesus.

Now God worked unusual miracles by the hands of Paul, so that even handkerchiefs or aprons were brought from his body to the sick, and the diseases left them and the evil spirits went out of them.

a. **Now God worked unusual miracles**: Luke states these were **unusual** miracles, and gives an example; that Paul's **handkerchiefs or aprons** (literally, "sweat-bands") could be laid on a person even without Paul present, and that person was healed or delivered from demonic possession.

i. It was unusual for God to use **handkerchiefs or aprons** in such a way. "The pieces of material were presumably those which Paul used in his tentmaking or leather-working - the sweat-rags for tying around his head and the aprons for tying around his waist." (Bruce)

b. **Handkerchiefs or aprons were brought from his body to the sick**: We don't really know how this worked, other than the same way that the shadow of Peter (Acts 5:15) or the hem of Jesus' garment (Matthew 14:36) might heal: the item became a point of contact by which a person released faith in Jesus as healer.

i. We can imagine this happening at first almost by accident – perhaps a person in need of healing took a handkerchief from Paul in a superstitious manner and was healed. But it became a pattern that others imitated. As we will see, the superstitious practice of magic and sorcery was prevalent in Ephesus. So, it should not surprise us that some took a quite superstitious view of the miracles done through Paul.

ii. God will stoop down to meet us even in our crude superstitions. This never means that God is pleased with our superstition, but that in His mercy He may overlook them to meet a need.

iii. I remember seeing what looked to be loosely rolled up newspapers on a pulpit in Bulgaria, being told they were pieces of fabric (wrapped in newspapers) that the pastor prayed over, and they were taken home to sick people. This was a common practice in these Bulgarian churches.

c. **God worked unusual miracles**: This phrase could be translated, *miracles not of the ordinary kind.* Even if we should expect miracles, these were the unexpected kind of miracles.

i. Note that these were *unusual* miracles; we should not expect that God would continue to use this method to bring healing.

ii. God seems to like doing things in new and different ways. Therefore we *receive* whatever is proven to be from the hand of God, but we *pursue* only that which we have a Biblical pattern for.

iii. Significantly, it does not say that *Paul* did these unusual miracles, but that **God worked** them **by the hands of Paul**.

3. (13-16) A rebuke to the seven sons of Sceva, the hopeful Jewish exorcists.

Then some of the itinerant Jewish exorcists took it upon themselves to call the name of the Lord Jesus over those who had evil spirits, saying, "We exorcise you by the Jesus whom Paul preaches." Also there were seven sons of Sceva, a Jewish chief priest, who did so. And the evil spirit answered and said, "Jesus I know, and Paul I know; but who are you?" Then the man in whom the evil spirit was leaped on them, overpowered them, and prevailed against them, so that they fled out of that house naked and wounded.

a. **Some of the itinerant Jewish exorcists**: At that time, there were Jewish exorcists who practiced their trade with a lot of superstition and ceremony. Here, a group of **itinerant Jewish exorcists** tried to imitate what they though was Paul's formula for success.

b. **We exorcise you by the Jesus whom Paul preaches**: The **Jewish exorcists** failed because they had no personal relationship with Jesus. They only knew that Jesus was the God of Paul, not their own God.

ii. We could say that the sons of Sceva did not have *the right* to use the name of Jesus, because they had no real personal connection to Him. In the same pattern, there are many people - many churchgoers - who will perish in hell because they have no personal relationship with Jesus Christ. They only know "the Jesus the pastor preaches" or "the Jesus my spouse believes in" instead of the Jesus of their own salvation.

c. **And the evil spirit answered and said, "Jesus I know, and Paul I know; but who are you?"** The evil spirit knew exactly who Jesus was, and knew exactly who Paul was. But they didn't know who the **seven sons of Sceva** were. Apparently, evil spirits know who their enemies are (in this case, **Jesus** and **Paul**), and they don't waste their effort knowing those who aren't a threat to them (in this case, the **seven sons of Sceva**).

d. **Then the man in whom the evil spirit was leaped on them, overpowered them, and prevailed against them**: Because the **seven sons of Sceva** had no real relationship with Jesus, they had no spiritual power against the **evil spirit**. They left the encounter **naked and wounded**. It was dangerous for them to take the reality of spiritual warfare lightly.

4. (17-20) Many in Ephesus renounce objects associated with the demonic.

This became known both to all Jews and Greeks dwelling in Ephesus; and fear fell on them all, and the name of the Lord Jesus was magnified. And many who had believed came confessing and telling their deeds. Also, many of those who had practiced magic brought their books together and burned *them* in the sight of all. And they counted up the value of them, and *it* totaled fifty thousand *pieces* of silver. So the word of the Lord grew mightily and prevailed.

a. **This became known both to all Jews and Greeks dwelling in Ephesus; and fear fell on them all**: The incident with the sons of Sceva impressed the people with the reality of the demonic realm. It made them fear the Lord and the demonic (both in healthy ways). As a result, **the name of the Lord Jesus was magnified**.

i. "Ephesus was a stronghold of Satan. Here many evil things both superstitious and satanic were practiced. Books containing formula for sorcery and other ungodly and forbidden arts were plentiful in that city." (Gaebelein)

b. **Many who had believed came confessing and telling their deeds**: Apparently, before the sons of Sceva incident, many believers did not *know* they were involved in the demonic. They saw their actions in a far more innocent light, until they knew the reality of demonic activity.

c. **Many of those who had practiced magic brought their books together and burned them in the sight of all**: The sons of Sceva incident also prompted Christians to renounce any remaining connection to the demonic. They renounced the demonic by **confessing** and by burning their magic books, disregarding whatever value they had.

i. It is significant that these practitioners of magic **came confessing and telling their deeds**. It was thought that the power of these magic spells was in their *secrecy*, which was renounced in the telling.

ii. These **books** and scrolls full of magic charms, amulets and incantations were well known in Ephesus, and they were valuable. The value of **fifty thousand pieces of silver** today has been estimated at anywhere between $1 million and $5 million.

iii. Christians must do this also today, removing books, images, computer files, statues, charms, games, or whatever else might have connection with demonic spirits. They should also destroy them so they are of no use to others.

iv. "You will have enough temptation in your own mind without going after these things. Is there any habit, any practice, that you have got that defiles your soul? If Christ loves you, and you come and trust in him, you will make short work of it. Have done with it, and have done with it forever." (Spurgeon)

d. **The word of the Lord grew mightily and prevailed**: This demonstrates that the end result was obviously worth it all. The work in Ephesus and the region of Roman Asia continued in a remarkable way.

C. The riot in Ephesus.

1. (21-22) Paul's companions leave him alone in Ephesus.

When these things were accomplished, Paul purposed in the Spirit, when he had passed through Macedonia and Achaia, to go to Jerusalem, saying, "After I have been there, I must also see Rome." So he sent into Macedonia two of those who ministered to him, Timothy and Erastus, but he himself stayed in Asia for a time.

a. **Paul purposed in the Spirit**: Guided by the Holy Spirit, Paul determined his itinerary. He decided to travel through Macedonia and Achaia, then to Jerusalem, then to Rome.

i. Luke doesn't mention it here, but we know that one reason why Paul wanted to go through Macedonia and Achaia, then to Jerusalem was to collect and deliver a fund he had been collecting from other churches to help out the church in Jerusalem (Romans 15:25-31; 1 Corinthians 16:1-4).

ii. **I must also see Rome** reflects Paul's passion to visit and serve the Christian community that was already there. That passion is also mentioned in Romans 1:8-15.

b. **So he sent into Macedonia two of those who ministered to him, Timothy and Erastus**: Paul sent Timothy and Erastus on ahead to Macedonia, while he stayed in Ephesus (**Asia**) for a time.

c. **Who ministered to him**: A significant part of the work of Timothy and Erastus was simply to help Paul. They were truly assistants to the apostle, helping Paul to maximize his ministry.

2. (23-28) Demetrius, a maker of idols, opposes Paul because his business has suffered.

And about that time there arose a great commotion about the Way. For a certain man named Demetrius, a silversmith, who made silver shrines of Diana, brought no small profit to the craftsmen. He called them together with the workers of similar occupation, and said: "Men, you know that we have our prosperity by this trade. Moreover you see and hear that not only at Ephesus, but throughout almost all Asia, this Paul has persuaded and turned away many people, saying that they are not gods which are made with hands. So not only is this trade of ours in danger of falling into disrepute, but also the temple of the great goddess Diana may be despised and her magnificence destroyed, whom all Asia and the world worship." Now when they heard *this*, they were full of wrath and cried out, saying, "Great *is* Diana of the Ephesians!"

a. **About that time there arose a great commotion about the Way**: When the work was going so well, and when Paul was thinking about leaving Epehsus, another **commotion** arose. Again, for the third time in Acts (and the second time in this chapter) the Christian movement is called **the Way**.

b. **This trade of ours in danger of falling into disrepute, but also the temple of the great goddess Diana may be despised and her magnificence destroyed**: This tremendous temple to Diana (also known as Artemis) in Ephesus was regarded as one of the seven wonders of the ancient world. It was supported by 127 pillars, each 60 feet high, and was decorated with great sculptures. It was lost to history until it was discovered in 1869, and its main altar was unearthed in 1965.

i. "The epicenter of Artemis worship was a black meteorite that either resembled or had been fashioned into a grotesque image of a woman. The lower part was wrapped like a mummy…the idol was covered with breasts, symbolizing fertility." (Hughes)

ii. "The Temple of Artemis was also a major treasury and bank of the ancient world, where merchants, kings, and even cities made deposits, and where their money could be kept safe under the protection of deity." (Longenecker)

iii. **Whom all Asia and the world worship**: The temple of Diana in Ephesus was indeed famous around the world. The trinkets and idols from it must have been a substantial trade, no matter how immoral the worship of the sex-goddess was.

c. **This Paul has persuaded and turned away many people, saying that they are not gods which are made with hands**: The opposition of Demetrius and the other idol makers was a great compliment to the effectiveness of Paul's work in the region. Paul was not on a campaign to close down the temple of Diana; he just did the Lord's work. As people came to Jesus, they naturally stopped worshipping Diana and buying shrines associated with the temple.

i. Christianity should affect the economy – not just personally, but in a community as well. This effect will not always be welcomed. In Ephesus, business was down at the pagan shrines because of the transforming work of the Jesus Christ. This happens again and again as Jesus does His work. For example, a Roman official named Pliny later wrote a letter to another official named Trajan, describing how people were not going to shrines anymore because of Christian influence. Pliny wanted to know what he should do about it.

ii. This is how we should endeavor to change society. "I wish the gospel would affect the trade of London; I wish it might. There are some trades that need affecting, need to be cut a little shorter…Not by an Act of Parliament! Let Acts of Parliament leave us alone. We can fight that battle alone. But may it come to an end by the spread of the gospel…I have no faith in any reformation that does not come through men's hearts being changed." (Spurgeon)

d. **Also the temple of the great goddess Diana may be despised and her magnificence destroyed, whom all Asia and the world worship**: Demetrius was clever in how he spoke to the crowd. He first appealed to them both on the basis of financial self-interest, and then on the basis of civic pride ("How dare Paul insult and despise our great temple!").

i. **Whom all Asia and the world worship** is the "everybody does it" argument. "Everybody does this" and "everybody thinks this" are not eloquent arguments, but they are powerful.

ii. Yet in Acts 19:37, the city clerk specifically said that Paul had *not* blasphemed the goddess Diana. Paul was on a pro-Jesus campaign more than an anti-everything else campaign.

3. (29-34) The riot builds momentum.

So the whole city was filled with confusion, and rushed into the theater with one accord, having seized Gaius and Aristarchus, Macedonians, Paul's travel companions. And when Paul wanted to go in to the people, the disciples would not allow him. Then some of the officials of Asia, who were his friends, sent to him pleading that he would not venture into the theater. Some therefore cried one thing and some another, for the assembly was confused, and most of them did not know why they had come together. And they drew Alexander out of the multitude, the Jews putting him forward. And Alexander motioned with his hand, and wanted to make his defense to the people. But when they found out that

he was a Jew, all with one voice cried out for about two hours, "Great *is* Diana of the Ephesians!"

a. **The whole city was filled with confusion, and rushed into the theater with one accord**: Considering Rome's iron-fisted attitude towards such civil disorder, things were rapidly getting out of hand.

> i. It has often happened in the history of Christianity that when God moves among His people and they become very serious about their Christianity, that it affects the livelihood of those who trade in vice or immorality. For example, in the early years of the Salvation Army, they were so effective that pimps and bar owners organized a "Skeleton Army" to oppose them with threats and violence – and even a few Salvation Army workers were murdered.

b. **They drew Alexander out of the multitude, the Jews putting him forward**: Alexander wanted to make sure that the mob knew that the Jews did not approve of Paul either; but he accomplished nothing before the angry crowd.

c. **Great is Diana of the Ephesians!** This repeated chant must have sent a chill up the backs of the Christians, including Paul who no doubt could hear it from outside the theater.

> i. "The noise must have been deafening. The acoustics of the theater are excellent even today and at that time were even better because of bronze and clay sounding vessels placed throughout the auditorium." (Williams)

> ii. For two hours they shouted, "**Great is Diana of the Ephesians!**" Think of how this echoes to our own time, and see the strangeness of our world. People say today, in words, actions, time or dollars spent:

> - "Great is my sports team!"
> - "Great is my political party!"
> - "Great is the consumer economy!"
> - "Great is internet porn!"
> - "Great is material wealth!"
> - "Great is getting drunk or getting high!"

And yet if one says, "Great is the Lord Jesus Christ" – *they* are regarded by many as strange.

> iii. For all the supposed greatness of Diana of the Ephesians, no one worships her today (at least directly). Yet there are millions and millions today who live for and worship Jesus Christ, and who would willingly

die for Him. Idols and false gods all have expiration dates – Jesus of Nazareth lives forever.

4. (35-41) The city clerk is able to calm the passion of the crowd.

And when the city clerk had quieted the crowd, he said: "Men of Ephesus, what man is there who does not know that the city of the Ephesians is temple guardian of the great goddess Diana, and of the *image* which fell down from Zeus? Therefore, since these things cannot be denied, you ought to be quiet and do nothing rashly. For you have brought these men here who are neither robbers of temples nor blasphemers of your goddess. Therefore, if Demetrius and his fellow craftsmen have a case against anyone, the courts are open and there are proconsuls. Let them bring charges against one another. But if you have any other inquiry to make, it shall be determined in the lawful assembly. For we are in danger of being called in question for today's uproar, there being no reason which we may give to account for this disorderly gathering." And when he had said these things, he dismissed the assembly.

a. **Therefore, since these things cannot be denied, you ought to be quiet and do nothing rashly**: The **city clerk** (something like the mayor of the city) spoke sensible words. Luke wanted to show that rational people saw nothing to fear or oppose in Christianity.

i. God worked mightily in Ephesus, but so did the devil. This may be one reason why Paul wrote so specifically about the spiritual battle each Christian faces against powers of spiritual darkness in his letter to the Ephesians (Ephesians 6:10-20).

ii. "This chapter teaches us all a permanent lesson: that when disciples have a true *revival*, society gets a *revolution*. When the Spirit moves mightily upon children of God we may look for other might mighty movements among unbelievers, and need not be surprised if the devil himself comes down, having great wrath, as though he knew that his time were short." (Pierson)

b. **He dismissed the assembly**: God used the city clerk to calm the mob and end the immediate threat to Paul and the other Christians. God had preserved His work, and His people, again.

i. **Assembly** in Acts 19:41 is the Greek word *ekklesia*, the same word used for "church." It was a non-religious term used to describe a gathering or association of people.

Acts 20 - Paul's Farewell to the Ephesian Elders

A. Paul in the region of Macedonia again.

1. (1) From Ephesus, Paul travels to Macedonia.

After the uproar had ceased, Paul called the disciples to *himself*, embraced *them*, and departed to go to Macedonia.

a. **After the uproar had ceased**: The rioting in Ephesus (Acts 19) had convinced Paul to move on, so he went westward across the Aegean Sea to Macedonia (modern Greece).

b. **Paul called the disciples to himself, embraced them, and departed**: Paul couldn't leave without this demonstration of love to his fellow followers of Jesus. He spent two very fruitful years in Ephesus, but it was now time to go.

2. (2-5) Travels through Greece and Macedonia.

Now when he had gone over that region and encouraged them with many words, he came to Greece and stayed three months. And when the Jews plotted against him as he was about to sail to Syria, he decided to return through Macedonia. And Sopater of Berea accompanied him to Asia—also Aristarchus and Secundus of the Thessalonians, and Gaius of Derbe, and Timothy, and Tychicus and Trophimus of Asia. These men, going ahead, waited for us at Troas.

a. **When he had gone over that region and encouraged them with many words**: Paul spent his time working with the churches he had already established, as recorded in Acts 16-17.

i. "One activity that especially concerned Paul at this time was collecting money for the relief of impoverished believers at Jerusalem...Paul viewed it as a symbol of unity that would help his Gentile converts realize their debt to the mother church in Jerusalem." (Longenecker)

ii. Paul's extended time in this region may help to explain a bit of a puzzle. In Romans 15:19, Paul made this claim: *So that from Jerusalem and round to Illyricum I have fully preached the gospel of Christ.* The puzzle is that the Book of Acts never specifically mentions a visit by Paul to Illyricum, but it may fit in here at Acts 20:2-3, where Paul **had gone over that region…and stayed three months**. Illyricum is due west from Thessalonica, and there was a famous Roman Road (the *Via Egnatia*) that went between Thessalonica and the Roman province of Illyricum. Today, the area of Illyricum is modern day Albania, on the eastern coast of the Adriatic Sea, with the mainland of Italy westward across the water.

iii. The mention of Illyricum in Romans 15:19 reminds us that the Book of Acts, as wonderful as it is, *is by no means a complete accounting* of all that God did through His people in the first century. There is much, even in the life of the Apostle Paul, that is not described – not to mention the life and work of many, many others.

b. **When the Jews plotted against him as he was about to sail to Syria, he decided to return through Macedonia**. From Greece, Paul had planned to take the long journey by sea directly back to Syria (where his sending church at Antioch was), but the plotting of some anti-Christian Jews made him take a more overland route back through Macedonia, accompanied by many companions.

i. "It may have been planned to attack him on board ship, especially if the vessel was crowded with Jewish pilgrims for Passover or Pentecost." (Williams)

c. **Sopater of Berea… Aristarchus and Secundus of the Thessalonians… Gaius of Derbe… Trophimus of Asia**: These traveling companions of Paul were probably representatives from other churches who had sent money with Paul to Jerusalem. They were also present as ambassadors from the churches Paul has founded among the Gentiles, and were there to vouch for Paul's good stewardship in regard to the collection destined for Jerusalem.

i. **Aristarchus** and **Secundus** both came from Thessalonica. **Aristarchus'** name was connected with *aristocracy*, the ruling class. It's likely that he came from a wealthy and powerful family. **Secundus** was a common name for a slave. It meant "Second." Slaves were often not called by their true names, and the first-ranking slave in a household would often be called *Primus*. The second-ranking slave was often called **Secundus**. It's nice to think of Christians from both high and low stations in life serving the Lord together, from Thessalonica and helping the Apostle Paul.

B. Back to Troas and the region of Asia Minor (modern day Turkey).

1. (6) Arrival at the city of Troas.

But we sailed away from Philippi after the Days of Unleavened Bread, and in five days joined them at Troas, where we stayed seven days.

a. **We sailed away from Philippi... joined them at Troas**: Paul sailed back across the Agean Sea, eastward towards the Roman province of Asia Minor.

b. **We sailed away... we stayed seven days**: Luke has resumed the **we** narrative He met Paul in Philippi and then sailed with Paul to Troas where they met Paul's other traveling companions. Paul had left Luke in Philippi in Acts 16:40.

2. (7-12) A long sermon and Eutychus raised from the dead.

Now on the first *day* of the week, when the disciples came together to break bread, Paul, ready to depart the next day, spoke to them and continued his message until midnight. There were many lamps in the upper room where they were gathered together. And in a window sat a certain young man named Eutychus, who was sinking into a deep sleep. He was overcome by sleep; and as Paul continued speaking, he fell down from the third story and was taken up dead. But Paul went down, fell on him, and embracing *him* said, "Do not trouble yourselves, for his life is in him." Now when he had come up, had broken bread and eaten, and talked a long while, even till daybreak, he departed. And they brought the young man in alive, and they were not a little comforted.

a. **Now on the first day of the week, when the disciples came together to break bread**: This is the first *certain* example we have of Christians making a practice to gather together on the first day of the week for fellowship and the word - though here, it seems they gathered in the evening, because Sunday was a normal working day for them.

b. **Spoke to them and continued his message until midnight**: Paul sensed the need to preach for a long time because he was **ready to depart the next day**. He knew he might never see these particular Christians again - so he preached for some six hours to them!

c. **A certain young man named Eutychus... fell down from the third story and was taken up dead**: The combination of the late hour, the heat, and perhaps the fumes from the oil lamps made the young man Eutychus fall asleep. His fall and death certainly would have put a sour note on the meeting.

i. It is comforting for any preacher to think that people might fall asleep during the preaching of even the Apostle Paul. Yet, Paul taught for many hours and after a long day of work for most of his audience. There is also some evidence that Eutychus *fought* the sleep the best he could: "The tenses of the Greek verbs portray poor Eutychus as being gradually overcome despite his struggle to remain awake." (Hughes)

ii. Yet in the end, sleep got the best of him: "The word translated 'sleep' is the word from which we derive our English word *hypnosis*." (Hughes)

d. **Do not trouble yourselves, for his life is in him**: Paul, again receiving the gift of faith from God, sensed that God would raise this boy from the dead - and God did.

i. "Paul's comment that the boy's *life* was *in him* refers to his condition after he had ministered to him. Luke would not have devoted space to the raising up of somebody who was merely apparently dead." (Marshall)

e. **Talked a long while, even till daybreak**: Paul, obviously getting their attention back, continued preaching until daybreak.

C. Paul's address to the Ephesian elders.

1. (13-17) Paul comes to Miletus and sends for the elders of the church in Ephesus to meet him there.

Then we went ahead to the ship and sailed to Assos, there intending to take Paul on board; for so he had given orders, intending himself to go on foot. And when he met us at Assos, we took him on board and came to Mitylene. We sailed from there, and the next *day* came opposite Chios. The following *day* we arrived at Samos and stayed at Trogyllium. The next *day* we came to Miletus. For Paul had decided to sail past Ephesus, so that he would not have to spend time in Asia; for he was hurrying to be at Jerusalem, if possible, on the Day of Pentecost. From Miletus he sent to Ephesus and called for the elders of the church.

a. **Intending himself to go on foot**: Paul apparently preferred to walk from Troas to Assos instead of sail with the rest of his group; but he sailed with them from Assos to Miletus (**we took him on board**).

i. Paul "stayed till the last possible moment, probably to be assured of Eutychus's complete restoration to consciousness and health, and then took a shortcut by land to join the ship at Assos." (Bruce).

b. **Paul had decided to sail past Ephesus**: Paul's intention wasn't to slight the church in Ephesus, but he knew that it would be impossible for him to have a *short* visit there, and he wanted to hurry so as to be **at Jerusalem, if possible, on the Day of Pentecost**.

c. **From Miletus he sent to Ephesus and called for the elders of the church**: Though Paul knew he couldn't make a *brief* visit to Ephesus, he still wanted to pour his heart into the leaders of the church at Ephesus. So, **from Miletus**, he **called for the elders of the church** to come for a special meeting.

2. (18-21) Paul begins his farewell to the elders of Ephesus by recounting his work among them.

And when they had come to him, he said to them: "You know, from the first day that I came to Asia, in what manner I always lived among you, serving the Lord with all humility, with many tears and trials which happened to me by the plotting of the Jews; how I kept back nothing that was helpful, but proclaimed it to you, and taught you publicly and from house to house, testifying to Jews, and also to Greeks, repentance toward God and faith toward our Lord Jesus Christ.

a. **And when they had come to him, he said to them**: Most of the time in Acts, we see Paul the evangelist; but here in Acts 20, we get a unique picture of Paul the pastor - what was important to him as a leader and shepherd of God's people.

i. "It is the only Pauline speech delivered to Christians which Luke has recorded, and it is not surprising to discover how rich it is in parallels to the Pauline letters (especially, in fact, to the later ones)." (Bruce)

b. **You know, from the first day that I came to Asia, in what manner I always lived among you**: Paul first calls attention to himself as an example. Not an example *instead* of Jesus, but an example as he followed Jesus. Paul didn't act like a religious celebrity and expect people to serve and honor him; he just wanted to be **serving the Lord with all humility**.

i. In a similar pattern, we can each be good examples of how to live the Christian life. There is no reason for us to not be so. Even the young, new Christian can be a good example of how a new Christian should follow Jesus.

c. **I kept back nothing that was helpful, but proclaimed it to you**: Paul could solemnly say before these elders of the Ephesian church that he **kept back nothing that was helpful**. He didn't only teach the topics that pleased him. He **proclaimed it** all.

i. **Testifying to Jews, and also to Greeks**: if Paul didn't limit his message, he didn't limit his audience either. He wanted to preach all the word of God to all people.

d. **From house to house**: This implies that the Ephesian church, lacking any central building, was organized logically in house-churches. Probably, each elder had charge over a particular house-church. These were much more like house-church pastors than what we think of today as a board of elders who presided over one large congregation.

3. (22-24) Paul speaks of his future.

And see, now I go bound in the spirit to Jerusalem, not knowing the things that will happen to me there, except that the Holy Spirit testifies in every city, saying that chains and tribulations await me. But none of these things move me; nor do I count my life dear to myself, so that I may finish my race with joy, and the ministry which I received from the Lord Jesus, to testify to the gospel of the grace of God.

a. **I go bound in the spirit to Jerusalem, not knowing the things that will happen to me there**: Paul didn't know what was ahead of him; he even had reason to believe it was bad. But that didn't trouble him. He could give it all over to God even when he didn't know what would happen. There should always be more Christians who will say, "**none of these things move me.**"

   i. *Uncertainty* did not move Paul. Even though he was "**not knowing the things that will happen to me there**," he would not be moved from his cause. Paul could sing this Psalm from his heart: *I have set the Lord always before me; because He is at my right hand I shall not be moved.* (Psalm 16:8)

b. **Holy Spirit testifies in every city, saying that chains and tribulations await me**: Paul recognized the dangerous road ahead of him; apparently he had received many words of prophecy telling him of this danger already. Yet he was not set off the track by danger, but was willing to lay down his life for **the gospel of the grace of God**.

   i. **Nor do I count my life dear to myself**: Paul thought of himself as an *accountant*, weighing carefully the credits and the expenses; and in the end, he does not count his own life dear to him, compared to his God and how he can serve him.

   ii. **So that I may finish my race with joy**: Paul thought of himself as a *runner* who had a race to finish, and nothing would keep Paul from finishing the race with joy. Additionally, Paul speaks of *my race* - he had his race to run, we have our own - but God calls us to finish it with joy.

   iii. This shows that even at this point, Paul had his death in mind. It would be many years until he actually died, but he considered that what he did with his life now was *worth dying for*. In the words of

Spurgeon, he preached *a gospel worth dying for*. It is a worthy challenge to any preacher: Is the gospel you preach worth dying for?

- The gospel of moral reform? Not worth dying for.
- The gospel of save yourself through good works? Not worth dying for.
- The gospel of social action and improvement? Not worth dying for.
- The gospel of religious traditions? Not worth dying for.
- The gospel of merely having spiritual conversations? Not worth dying for.
- The gospel of mystical mumbo-jumbo? Not worth dying for.
- The gospel seeking the church of true hipness? Not worth dying for.
- The gospel of self-esteem? Not worth dying for.
- The gospel of ecological salvation? Not worth dying for.
- The gospel of political correctness? Not worth dying for.
- The gospel of emergent church feel-goodism? Not worth dying for.

iv. "Yet there used to be a gospel in the world which consisted of facts which Christians never questioned. There was once in the church a gospel which believers hugged to their hearts as if it were their soul's life. There used to be a gospel in the world, which provoked enthusiasm and commanded sacrifice. Tens of thousands have met together to hear this gospel at peril of their lives. Men, to the teeth of tyrants, have proclaimed it, and have suffered the loss of all things, and gone to prison and to death for it, singing psalms all the while. Is there not such a gospel remaining?" (Spurgeon)

4. (25) Paul announces that he probably won't see the Ephesian elders again.

"And indeed, now I know that you all, among whom I have gone preaching the kingdom of God, will see my face no more.

a. **You all, among whom I have gone preaching the kingdom of God**: Paul did a lot in Ephesus. In that city God used him to work some amazing miracles.

- Acts 19:11 says that in Ephesus, the hands of Paul did *unusual miracles*.

- Acts 19:12 says that in Ephesus, handkerchiefs or aprons from Paul's body were brought to sick people and they were healed and delivered from demonic spirits.

- Acts 19:15 says that in Ephesus, demonic spirits said they knew Paul and his ministry

  i. With all that, Paul didn't say to the Ephesian elders here, "You all, among whom I did some awesome miracles." Or, "You all, among whom even the demons said they knew me." Instead Paul was always focused on the life-transforming power of the word of God, and he said "**You all, among whom I have gone preaching the kingdom of God.**"

  ii. It's as if Paul said, "This is what I do. Sure, I do a lot of other things, but at the core I'm a preacher, and I preach the kingdom of God."

b. **You all... will see my face no more**: Paul here showed great sadness, great compassion, and great courage. He told them something he hadn't told them before: that this would probably be the last time they saw him, and he saw them. This would be like a bombshell to these church leaders.

  i. Don't forget the great bond Paul had with these Ephesian leaders. He was in Ephesus for two years, and the ministry was so effective that Acts 19:10 says, *all who dwelt in Asia heard the word of the Lord Jesus, both Jews and Greeks.*

  ii. That amount of time and that kind of effective ministry builds bonds of fellowship and friendship that last.

  iii. It was hard for them to believe it. Maybe at first they thought he was joking. But they quickly understood that he wasn't and they understood why he asked them to walk 36 miles to meet with him.

c. **Will see my face no more**: In all of this, Paul's great love and concern for the leaders and the congregation in Ephesus was simply a reflection of Jesus' great love and concern for them. Paul followed Jesus in every way he could; since Jesus loved these believers so much, so did Paul.

  i. It's fascinating to think of how much this segment of Paul's life mirrored the life of Jesus.

  - Like Jesus, Paul traveled to Jerusalem with a group of his disciples.

  - Like Jesus, Paul was opposed by hostile Jews who plotted against his life.

- Like Jesus, Paul made or received three successive predictions of his coming sufferings in Jerusalem, including being handed over to the Gentiles.

- Like Jesus, Paul declared his readiness to lay down his life.

- Like Jesus, he was determined to complete his ministry and not be deflected from it.

- Like Jesus, he expressed his abandonment to the will of God.

ii. Would we expect any different? Is the servant greater than his Master? We too should expect to know *the fellowship of His sufferings* (Philippians 3:10).

5. (26-27) Paul's solemn declaration of his innocence before God.

Therefore I testify to you this day that I *am* innocent of the blood of all men. For I have not shunned to declare to you the whole counsel of God.

a. **Therefore**: There is much wrapped up in this simple word. It has the sense of, Because I probably won't see you again... because I love you so much...because I have invested so much of my heart and life among you all... you therefore need to know that.

b. **I testify to you this day that I am innocent of the blood of all men**: As if he were giving witness in a court of law, Paul declared that his heart was clear. He could leave these Christians to God's care with a good conscience, knowing that he had **not shunned to declare to** [them] **the whole counsel of God**.

i. We should have a greater appreciation of the value of a *clear conscience*. God helping us, we can have one – at least as clear as possible from this point forward.

c. **The whole counsel of God**: Paul could leave them with a clear conscience because he knew that he taught them **the whole counsel of God**.

i. Acts 19:9-10 tells us that Paul taught the Ephesians and those in the region for more than two years, using a rented room from *the school of Tyrannus*. There are some indications that Paul taught for several hours a day, and some six days a week. This means hundreds of hours of teaching time (probably well more than 1,500 hours).

ii. He had plenty of time to take them verse-by-verse through the books of the Hebrew Scriptures. They may have also studied the life of Jesus from some of the accounts of His life being written in that same period.

iii. Today, there should be more and more who will present **the whole counsel of God**. Paul later warned that in the last days, people would not endure sound doctrine, but would look for teachers who would tell them what they want to hear - teachers who would scratch their itching ears (2 Timothy 4:3).

iv. Many preachers today simply use a Bible text as a launching pad, and then go on to say what they want - what the people want to hear. Others throw in Bible quotations to illustrate their points, or to illustrate their stories. Yet the real calling of a preacher is to simply let the Bible speak for itself and let it declare its own power.

v. Taking Paul's testimony at full strength, we must say that those preachers who deliberately fail to **declare... the whole counsel of God** *are guilty* of the blood of all men. The preacher who preaches what his audience wants to hear, and not **the whole counsel of God**, hurts both his audience and himself!

6. (28) Encouraging them to take heed to themselves and to God's people.

Therefore take heed to yourselves and to all the flock, among which the Holy Spirit has made you overseers, to shepherd the church of God which He purchased with His own blood.

a. **Therefore**: This is Paul's second **therefore** in this section. The first *therefore* looked at his own life (*I testify to you that I am innocent of the blood of all men*). This second **therefore** instructs the leaders of the Ephesian Christians.

b. **Take heed to yourselves**: "Pay attention to your own life. You have a high standard to fulfill. The standard isn't perfection, but it is nevertheless high. You won't fulfill that high standard without paying attention to it, if you don't **take heed to yourselves**."

i. These words from Paul were all the more dramatic knowing the tension and the atmosphere of this meeting. These words mattered.

ii. The godly leader knows that effective leadership flows from a life, not just knowledge.

c. **Take heed... to all the flock**: "Pay attention to the people of God. Love them, look over them, care for them. Do it because **the Holy Spirit has made you overseers**."

d. **To shepherd the church of God**: Flock has the idea of *sheep*; **shepherd the church of God** continues that thought. He is telling them to be pastors, **to shepherd the church of God** – to serve their house-church congregations as faithful pastors.

i. The first idea behind being a shepherd is *feeding* God's people. "They are to *be shepherds* of God's church, *poimanino* meaning in general to *tend* a flock and in particular *to lead a flock to pasture and so to feed it*. This is the first duty of shepherds." (Stott)

ii. Shepherds don't only *feed*; they also *lead*. Under the guidance of the Chief Shepherd and in the community of God's people, they lead the people of God to where God wants them to be.

e. **Which He purchased with His own blood**: This is one important reason *why* they had to take heed to themselves and to the flock of God. They had to do it because *the church doesn't belong to them*, it belongs to Jesus who **purchased** it **with His own blood**.

i. Any responsible person is going to take greater care of something that belongs to someone else. Leaders need to remember that the church belongs to Jesus. Taken together, it's really a wonderful balance:

- The sheep need to remember that God has appointed shepherds to feed and lead them.

- The shepherds need to remember that the flock belongs to God, and not to them.

ii. Considering the greatness of the price, this calls leaders among God's people to be dedicated and godly: **His own blood**.

7. (29) Take heed to the flock because of danger from the outside.

For I know this, that after my departure savage wolves will come in among you, not sparing the flock.

a. **For I know this**: Paul presses the urgency here, warning these leaders that **savage wolves will come in among** them all. He knew that a pastor, a leader among God's people has to do more than only **feed** and **lead** – he also has to *protect*.

i. Paul doesn't say how he knew; only that he did **know**.

b. **Not sparing the flock**: These wolves would be vicious. They wouldn't hold back against the people of God, but take as many of them as they could.

8. (30) Take heed to the flock because of danger from the inside.

Also from among yourselves men will rise up, speaking perverse things, to draw away the disciples after themselves.

a. **Also from among yourselves men will rise up**: It is often easier for pastors to deal with the wolves that come from the outside - obviously false teachings and goofy winds of doctrine. But it is often very difficult to deal with those who rise up **from among yourselves**.

   i. Imagine how *these men listening to Paul* would have received this. It would be hard to believe, and like the disciples with Jesus, many of them would say, "Not me, Lord!"

b. **Speaking perverse things**: This is their *method* – they would *twist* what was good.

c. **To draw away the disciples after themselves**: This is their *motivation* – they wanted a following. Ego can make people do things that they *never* thought they would do.

9. (31) Further encouragement to watch.

Therefore watch, and remember that for three years I did not cease to warn everyone night and day with tears.

a. **Therefore watch**: This was Paul's third **therefore** in such a short section.

   • He gave one *therefore* about himself (his clear conscience, Acts 20:26).

   • He gave a second *therefore* about what they should do (take heed, Acts 20:28).

   • This third **therefore** is given after the urgency of taking heed has been explained.

b. **Remember that for three years I did not cease to warn everyone night and day with tears**: Paul asked them to have the same careful concern for the people of God that he himself had.

   • It was a long-term care (**for three years**).

   • It was a constant care (**did not cease**).

   • It was a watchful care (**to warn**).

   • It was a universal care (**everyone**).

   • It was a heart-felt care (**with tears**).

10. (32-35) Paul's conclusion: Remember a heart of sacrifice.

"So now, brethren, I commend you to God and to the word of His grace, which is able to build you up and give you an inheritance among all those who are sanctified. I have coveted no one's silver or gold or apparel. Yes, you yourselves know that these hands have provided for my necessities, and for those who were with me. I have shown you in every way, by laboring like this, that you must support the weak. And

remember the words of the Lord Jesus, that He said, 'It is more blessed to give than to receive.'"

a. **I commend you to God and to the word of His grace**: Though Paul gave his all for the Christians in Ephesus for some three years, at the bottom line, he could only **commend** [them] **to God and to the word of His grace**. Paul knew there was trouble ahead for him, and some trouble ahead for the Ephesian Christians. Yet **God** and **the word of His grace** would see them through.

i. Programs can't do it; the spirit of the age can't do it; slick marketing can't do it; entertainment can't do it; only **God** and the **word of His grace** can **build you up and give you an inheritance** in heaven.

b. **I have coveted no one's silver or gold or apparel**: Paul concludes by trying to communicate his heart, his *motive* in ministry. He wasn't in it for himself, but for God's glory and for the building up of God's people. **Laboring like this** means that Paul was a hard worker for God's glory.

c. **It is more blessed to give than to receive**: His parting words, taken from a quote of Jesus' unrecorded in the gospels, are perfect for all who would minister to God's people. Leaders must be more concerned about what they can give their flock than concerned about what their flock can give them.

i. Without a heart of *sacrifice* there can be no real effective, eternal ministry – and it should be a *glad sacrifice*, knowing the blessedness of it all.

ii. "**It is more blessed to give than to receive**" is the best beatitude of all. In the Sermon on the Mount, Jesus told us how to be blessed; here, He tells us how to be **more** blessed!

iii. It should not stumble us to consider that Jesus taught many things unrecorded in the gospels; John said as much in John 21:25. But we can trust that God has preserved all that is *necessary* of the teaching of Jesus.

11. (36-38) Paul's tearful good-bye to the Ephesian elders.

And when he had said these things, he knelt down and prayed with them all. Then they all wept freely, and fell on Paul's neck and kissed him, sorrowing most of all for the words which he spoke, that they would see his face no more. And they accompanied him to the ship.

a. **He knelt down and prayed with them all. Then they all wept freely**: This reminds us that Paul was not a cold dispenser of doctrine, but a warm, pastoral man who loved his people greatly and won great love from them.

b. **That they would see his face no more**: They part with prayer, tears, and a sending-off party, believing they would only meet again in eternity.

i. Given the strength of Paul's warning to these leaders, it is fair to wonder how the Christian community in Ephesus fared after this. Some 30 to 40 years later, Jesus sent a letter to this church in Ephesus, found in Revelation 2. He complimented them on many things:

- Their hard work for the kingdom of God.

- Their endurance through difficult times.

- Their dealing with those who are evil, and with false apostles.

- Not giving up when they were weary.

ii. Yet despite it all, Jesus gave them a severe warning: they had left their first love (Revelation 2:4). Unless things changed in a hurry, Jesus wouldn't even be present among them anymore.

iii. It may well be that in their zeal to fight against false doctrine – which they seemed to do well – they left their love for Jesus and their love for one another behind. It's a great illustration of the principle that the devil doesn't care which side of the boat we fall out of, just as long as we're in the water and not in the boat.

Acts 21 - Paul Arrives in Jerusalem

A. Events on the way from Asia Minor to Jerusalem.

1. (1-2) Leaving Miletus and the meeting with the Ephesian elders.

Now it came to pass, that when we had departed from them and set sail, running a straight course we came to Cos, the following *day* to Rhodes, and from there to Patara. And finding a ship sailing over to Phoenicia, we went aboard and set sail.

> a. **When we had departed from them**: More literally, this is *tore ourselves away from them* (Bruce). This was not an easy parting. Paul poured his life and love into these leaders from Ephesus, and they loved him deeply in return.

2. (3-4) Paul is warned again in the city of Tyre.

When we had sighted Cyprus, we passed it on the left, sailed to Syria, and landed at Tyre; for there the ship was to unload her cargo. And finding disciples, we stayed there seven days. They told Paul through the Spirit not to go up to Jerusalem.

> a. **Landed at Tyre… and finding disciples**: We are not told how a church was planted in Tyre, but there were **disciples** there. This reminds us that the Book of Acts gives only a partial picture of the early church's activity.

> b. **They told Paul through the Spirit not to go up to Jerusalem**: Apparently, among the disciples at Tyre, some prophesied of the danger that awaited Paul in Jerusalem, something that he had been warned about before in several other places (Acts 20:22-23).

> > i. It would seem that the specific warning **not to go up to Jerusalem** was a human interpretation of the Holy Spirit's prophecy of the danger that awaited Paul. Otherwise it is difficult to see why Paul would have gone against the Holy Spirit's direction – unless he was in direct rebellion, which some commentators believe is so.

3. (5-6) Departing from Tyre, on the way to Jerusalem.

When we had come to the end of those days, we departed and went on our way; and they all accompanied us, with wives and children, till *we were* out of the city. And we knelt down on the shore and prayed. When we had taken our leave of one another, we boarded the ship, and they returned home.

a. **We departed and went on our way**: Despite the heartfelt pleas of the Christians of Tyre, Paul and his group did not turn away from going to Jerusalem. He was persuaded it was God's will, so they continued.

b. **They all accompanied us... till we were out of the city**: The practice of walking with a traveler to the outskirts of the city was traditional; yet the practice of kneeling on the shore together for prayer was uniquely Christian (**we knelt down on the shore and prayed**).

4. (7) Arrival in Ptolemais.

And when we had finished *our* voyage from Tyre, we came to Ptolemais, greeted the brethren, and stayed with them one day.

a. **We came to Ptolemais, greeted the brethren, and stayed with them one day**: It must have been wonderful for Paul and his companions to find Christians in virtually every city they stopped. This showed the expansion and the deepening of the Christian movement across the Roman Empire. *Christians were everywhere*, it seemed.

5. (8-9) Arrival at Caesarea and the home of Philip the evangelist.

On the next *day* we who were Paul's companions departed and came to Caesarea, and entered the house of Philip the evangelist, who was *one* of the seven, and stayed with him. Now this man had four virgin daughters who prophesied.

a. **Philip the evangelist, who was one of the seven**: Acts 8:40 tells us that after Philip's work in bringing the Ethiopian eunuch to faith, he preached through the costal region and ended up in Caesarea. Many years later he was still there.

i. It's a wonderful title: **Philip the evangelist**. He was known by the good news he presented to other people, the good news about who Jesus is and what He did for us.

b. **Now this man had four virgin daughters who prophesied**: It's interesting that with these four daughters who had the gift of prophecy, none of them seemed to tell Paul anything about his upcoming time in Jerusalem. The Holy Spirit *could* have used them, but He chose to use someone else.

i. According to ancient records, "The daughters, or at least some of them, lived to a great age, and were highly esteemed as informants on persons and events belonging to the early years of Judean Christianity." (Bruce)

6. (10-14) Agabus warns Paul at Caesarea.

And as we stayed many days, a certain prophet named Agabus came down from Judea. When he had come to us, he took Paul's belt, bound his *own* hands and feet, and said, "Thus says the Holy Spirit, 'So shall the Jews at Jerusalem bind the man who owns this belt, and deliver *him* into the hands of the Gentiles.'" Now when we heard these things, both we and those from that place pleaded with him not to go up to Jerusalem. Then Paul answered, "What do you mean by weeping and breaking my heart? For I am ready not only to be bound, but also to die at Jerusalem for the name of the Lord Jesus." So when he would not be persuaded, we ceased, saying, "The will of the Lord be done."

a. **A certain prophet named Agabus came down from Judea**: In the spirit of Old Testament prophets, Agabus acted out his message to Paul - that certain danger awaited him at Jerusalem.

b. **So shall the Jews at Jerusalem bind the man who owns this belt, and deliver him into the hands of the Gentiles**: The prophecy of Agabus was true, and genuinely from the Holy Spirit. But to this true word, they added a human application (they **pleaded with him not to go up to Jerusalem**). That additional word was not of the Lord, otherwise Paul would have been disobedient to go to Jerusalem.

i. Acts 21:12 shows that *even Luke and Paul's traveling companions* tried to persuade Paul not to go to Jerusalem (**both we and those from that place pleaded with him**).

ii. Paul had received several prophetic words on this very topic. This is God's custom with such a remarkable prophecy, that there should be a great deal of confirmation, as there was in Macedonia (Acts 20:22-23), in Tyre (Acts 21:4) and now in Caesarea.

c. **For I am ready not only to be bound, but also to die at Jerusalem for the name of the Lord Jesus**: Paul's insistence on going to Jerusalem despite the dangers predicted by the Holy Spirit was not a result of rebellion, but an obedient response to the command of the Holy Spirit in his heart. He was *bound in the spirit* to go to Jerusalem (Acts 19:21 and 20:22).

i. The warnings from the Holy Spirit were intended to *prepare* Paul, not to *stop* him.

ii. "To choose to suffer means that there is something wrong; to choose God's will even if it means suffering is a very different thing. No healthy saint ever chooses suffering; he chooses God's will, as Jesus did, whether it means suffering or not." (Chambers, cited in Hughes)

iii. Think about the *Savior* Paul was willing to pay this price for; think about the *message* that brought this willingness.

d. **The will of the Lord be done**: Paul companions – including Luke – came to the understanding that God's will would be done. They came to trust that even if Paul was probably right, and even if he was wrong, God would use it.

i. Again, the warnings of *danger* came from the Holy Spirit and were meant to prepare Paul. The *request to turn back* was understandable, even logical; yet it wasn't of God. They recognized as much when they here attributed Paul's insistence to go to Jerusalem despite the danger as **the will of the Lord**.

ii. It is easy to do - and a source of trouble - when we add our interpretation or application to what is thought to be a word from God, often thinking that it is also from the Lord. We *often* find it too easy to judge God's will for someone else.

7. (15-16) Departing Caesarea and going up to Jerusalem.

And after those days we packed and went up to Jerusalem. Also some of the disciples from Caesarea went with us and brought with them a certain Mnason of Cyprus, an early disciple, with whom we were to lodge.

a. **We packed and went up to Jerusalem**: Paul and his companions finally were on the way to Jerusalem. Paul's deep love for his Jewish brothers and sisters made every trip to Jerusalem important (Romans 9:1-3).

b. **Mnason of Cyprus, an early disciple**: Based on the dating of Paul's Corinthian ministry at about A.D. 51 (Bruce) and other considerations, it is reasonable to think Paul arriving in Jerusalem in A.D. 57. Even though this was only some 25 years after the beginning of the Book of Acts, some Christians were already recognized as "**an early disciple**," one who had been associated with the followers of Jesus from the earliest years.

B. Paul comes to Jerusalem.

1. (17-20a) Paul reports the good work of God among the Gentiles.

And when we had come to Jerusalem, the brethren received us gladly. On the following *day* Paul went in with us to James, and all the elders were present. When he had greeted them, he told in detail those things

which God had done among the Gentiles through his ministry. And when they heard *it*, they glorified the Lord.

a. **He told in detail those things which God had done among the Gentiles through his ministry**: Upon arriving in Jerusalem, Paul met with the leaders of the church there (**James** and **all the elders**), and gave them a full report of his work in preaching and planting churches.

i. Williams on **told in detail**: "The Greek has the sense of recounting every single thing." Paul told these Christians from a Jewish background everything God had done in his missionary efforts.

b. **And when they heard it, they glorified the Lord**: The elders in Jerusalem were thankful for what God was doing among the Gentiles. They saw some of the Gentile converts with Paul and could tell of their genuine love for and commitment to Jesus.

2. (20b- 22) Paul learns of his bad reputation among some of the Christians of Jerusalem.

And they said to him, "You see, brother, how many myriads of Jews there are who have believed, and they are all zealous for the law; but they have been informed about you that you teach all the Jews who are among the Gentiles to forsake Moses, saying that they ought not to circumcise *their* children nor to walk according to the customs. What then? The assembly must certainly meet, for they will hear that you have come."

a. **You see, brother, how many myriads of Jews there are who have believed, and they are all zealous for the law**: The elders of Jerusalem were happy for what God was doing among the Gentiles. Yet in Jerusalem the Christian community was almost entirely from a Jewish background, and these Christians still valued many of the Jewish laws and customs. They were still **zealous for the law**.

b. **They have been informed about you that you teach all the Jews who are among the Gentiles to forsake Moses**: The Christian community of Jerusalem heard bad, false rumors about Paul. They heard that he had become essentially anti-Jewish, and told Jewish Christians that it was wrong for them to continue in Jewish laws and customs.

i. Based on Romans 14:4-6, it seems that Paul didn't have a problem with Jewish Christians who wanted to continue to observe old customs and laws. It seems that he himself did so sometimes, such as when he took and fulfilled a vow of consecration in Acts 18:18-21 (probably a Nazirite vow). Paul seemed fine with this, *as long as they didn't think it made them more right before God.*

c. **What then? The assembly must certainly meet, for they will hear that you have come**: This has the sense of, "Paul, this is controversial and people will hear about it. Let's do something about this."

3. (23-25) The leaders of the Jerusalem Church make a recommendation.

"Therefore do what we tell you: We have four men who have taken a vow. Take them and be purified with them, and pay their expenses so that they may shave *their* heads, and that all may know that those things of which they were informed concerning you are nothing, but *that* you yourself also walk orderly and keep the law. But concerning the Gentiles who believe, we have written *and* decided that they should observe no such thing, except that they should keep themselves from *things* offered to idols, from blood, from things strangled, and from sexual immorality."

a. **We have four men who have taken a vow. Take them and be purified with them, and pay their expenses**: They advised Paul to both *join* and *sponsor* these four Christians from a Jewish background.

i. **Four men who have taken a vow**: The particular vow of consecration was probably similar to Paul's Nazirite vow mentioned in Acts 18:18-21.

b. **That all may know**: The Jerusalem elders believed this would convince everyone that Paul did not preach against Jewish laws and customs for those Christians who wanted to observe them.

i. Paul agreed to do this, to demonstrate that he never taught Christian Jews *to forsake Moses* and *not to circumcise their children* and that they were required to ignore Jewish customs, as he had been false accused by some among the Jerusalem Christians.

c. **But concerning the Gentiles who believe**: The Jerusalem elders understood that this had *nothing* to do with **Gentiles who believe** in Jesus. It didn't mean that *they* had to perform any Jewish rituals to be right with God. Paul would rightly refuse to compromise on this important point.

4. (26) Agreeing with the recommendation, Paul sponsors and joins some Christians in a Jewish purification rite.

Then Paul took the men, and the next day, having been purified with them, entered the temple to announce the expiration of the days of purification, at which time an offering should be made for each one of them.

a. **Then Paul took the men**: Paul could agree to this and sponsor the four men taking the vow of consecration because there was never a hint that such things would be required of Gentiles as a test of righteousness.

i. "He had shown them that their ceremonies were *useless* but not *destructive*; that they were only dangerous when they depended on them for salvation." (Clarke)

ii. Many commentators believe this was a terrible compromise on Paul's part; that he was a hypocrite. Yet the motive behind Paul's sponsorship of these Christian Jews completing their Nazirite vow is explained in 1 Corinthians 9:20: *And to the Jews I became as a Jew, that I might win Jews; to those who are under the law, as under the law, that I might win those who are under the law.*

b. **At which time an offering should be made**: It's important to understand that this offering – an animal sacrifice – was not in any way for the purpose of atonement or forgiveness. Paul absolutely understood that *only the sacrifice of Jesus on the cross* atones for sin. Yet not every sacrifice in the Jewish system was for atonement; many were for thanksgiving or dedication, as this one was.

5. (27-30) Jews from Asia stir a mob against Paul.

Now when the seven days were almost ended, the Jews from Asia, seeing him in the temple, stirred up the whole crowd and laid hands on him, crying out, "Men of Israel, help! This is the man who teaches all *men* everywhere against the people, the law, and this place; and furthermore he also brought Greeks into the temple and has defiled this holy place." (For they had previously seen Trophimus the Ephesian with him in the city, whom they supposed that Paul had brought into the temple.) And all the city was disturbed; and the people ran together, seized Paul, and dragged him out of the temple; and immediately the doors were shut.

a. **Jews from Asia, seeing him in the temple, stirred up the whole crowd**: They claimed that Paul was **against the people** [Israel], **the law, and this place** [the temple], but these accusations were unfounded. Paul simply rejected trust in any of these as a basis for righteousness before God, which comes only through Jesus Christ.

i. The charges against Paul in Acts 21:28 were an echo of the charges Stephen was executed for (Acts 6:13). Paul helped preside over that execution; now he is accused in a similar way.

b. **All the city was disturbed; and the people ran together**: The crowd was *enlarged* because it was feast-time (Acts 20:16). It was *enraged* because they believed Paul not only preached against the people, the law, and the temple, but also profaned the temple by bringing Gentiles into its inner courts (they said, **"he also brought Greeks into the temple and has defiled this holy place"**).

c. **Trophimus the Ephesian... whom they supposed that Paul had brought into the temple**: It was absolutely prohibited for Gentiles to go beyond the designated "Court of the Gentiles" in the temple grounds. Signs were posted which read (in both Greek and Latin): "No foreigner may enter within the barricade which surrounds the temple and enclosure. Any one who is caught trespassing will bear personal responsibility for his ensuing death." The Romans were so sensitive to this that they authorized the Jews to execute anyone that offended in this way, even if the offender was a Roman citizen.

6. (31-36) Roman soldiers rescue Paul.

Now as they were seeking to kill him, news came to the commander of the garrison that all Jerusalem was in an uproar. He immediately took soldiers and centurions, and ran down to them. And when they saw the commander and the soldiers, they stopped beating Paul. Then the commander came near and took him, and commanded *him* to be bound with two chains; and he asked who he was and what he had done. And some among the multitude cried one thing and some another. So when he could not ascertain the truth because of the tumult, he commanded him to be taken into the barracks. When he reached the stairs, he had to be carried by the soldiers because of the violence of the mob. For the multitude of the people followed after, crying out, "Away with him!"

a. **Now as they were seeking to kill him**: Paul had been seized by an enraged mob, and the mob didn't just want to take him out of the temple courts. They wanted to kill him, right there in the outer courtyard area of the temple mount. Paul had been near death because of the attacks of murderous mobs before (Acts 14:5, 19), and he must have thought, "Here we go again!"

b. **News came to the commander of the garrison that all Jerusalem was in an uproar**: From the Tower of Antonia, at the northwest corner of the temple mount, more than 500 Roman soldiers were stationed only two flights of stairs from the Court of the Gentiles.

c. **When they saw the commander and the soldiers, they stopped beating Paul**: The Romans didn't sympathize with Paul, but they were interested in keeping public order, so they arrested Paul both for his own protection and to remove the cause of the uproar.

i. **Two chains** means Paul was handcuffed to a solider on either side. Paul must have immediately remembered the prophecy of Agabus (Acts 21:11).

d. **The multitude of the people followed after, crying out, "Away with him!"** When the mob cried out for his death, Paul must have remembered when he was part of such a mob, agreeing with the martyrdom of Stephen (Acts 7:54-8:1).

i. Or, perhaps, it even reminded him of the trial of Jesus: "The shout *Away with him!* which pursued him as he was carried up the steps was the shout with which Jesus' death had been demanded not far from that spot some twenty-seven years before (Luke 23:18; John 19:15)." (Bruce)

ii. Boice on **Away with him!** "They did not mean, 'Take him away from the temple area.' They meant, 'Remove him from the earth.' They wanted him dead."

7. (37-39) Paul speaks to the Roman commander.

Then as Paul was about to be led into the barracks, he said to the commander, "May I speak to you?" He replied, "Can you speak Greek? Are you not the Egyptian who some time ago stirred up a rebellion and led the four thousand assassins out into the wilderness?" But Paul said, "I am a Jew from Tarsus, in Cilicia, a citizen of no mean city; and I implore you, permit me to speak to the people."

a. **As Paul was about to be led into the barracks, he said to the commander**: At first, the Roman **commander** thought that Paul was a terrorist, and was surprised that Paul was an educated man and could **speak Greek**.

i. *The language was a surprise*, because both the language and phrasing showed that Paul was a man educated in the Greek world, not a rabble-rouser. *The phrase itself was a surprise*; it seems far too polite and reserved. We would expect Paul to be screaming, "Help, help!" and not, "Pardon me sir, may I have a moment with you?"

ii. **The Egyptian** mentioned (also mentioned by the Jewish historian Josephus) led a ragged army of four thousand men to the Mount of Olives where they declared they would take over the temple mount. Roman soldiers had quickly scattered them, but the leader got away.

b. **I am a Jew from Tarsus, in Cilicia, a citizen of no mean city**: When Paul identified himself to the Roman commander, it put him in an entirely different standing. He was a citizen of **Tarsus**, not a suspected terrorist.

c. **I implore you, permit me to speak to the people**. At this moment, when his life was in danger from an angry mob and he was suspected of being a dangerous criminal, Paul had one thing on his mind: "Let me preach the gospel!"

> i. It's amazing that Paul could think and speak so clearly, considering that he had just been beaten. Some critics – such as the German theologian Ernst Haenchen – think that this proves that this whole account is a fabrication. What they don't take into account is the power of the Holy Spirit and Paul's great passion.

8. (40) Paul is permitted to address the mob that wanted to kill him.

So when he had given him permission, Paul stood on the stairs and motioned with his hand to the people. And when there was a great silence, he spoke to *them* in the Hebrew language, saying,

a. **So when he had given him permission**: The Roman commander bound Paul with two chains (Acts 21:33) because he suspected Paul was a troublemaker. Yet, he gave Paul **permission** to speak to the crowd, probably because he hoped that Paul's speech might quiet the mob. At first, it did quiet the people down.

b. **Paul stood on the stairs and motioned with his hand to the people. And when there was a great silence, he spoke to them in the Hebrew language**: What a dramatic moment! Paul, standing on stairs overlooking the massive open courtyard of the temple mount, made a dramatic sweep of his hand – and the angry, rioting mob fell silent. Then, Paul **spoke to them in the Hebrew language**, identifying himself with his Jewish audience, not with his Roman protectors.

> i. This was an opportunity Paul had waited a lifetime for. He had an incredible passion for the salvation of his fellow Jews (Romans 9:1-5), and had probably thought of himself as uniquely qualified to effectively communicate the gospel to them - if he only had the right opportunity.

> ii. Similarities between Jesus and Paul as shown in Acts 20 and 21:

> > • Like Jesus, Paul traveled to Jerusalem with a group of disciples.

> > • Like Jesus, Paul had opposition from hostile Jews who plotted against his life.

> > • Like Jesus, Paul made or received three successive predictions of his coming sufferings in Jerusalem, including being handed over to the Gentiles.

- Like Jesus, Paul had followers who tried to discourage him from going to Jerusalem and the fate that awaited him there.

- Like Jesus, Paul declared his readiness to lay down his life.

- Like Jesus, Paul was determined to complete his ministry and not be deflected from it.

- Like Jesus, Paul expressed his abandonment to the will of God.

- Like Jesus, Paul came to Jerusalem to *give* something.

- Like Jesus, Paul was unjustly arrested on the basis of a false accusation.

- Like Jesus, Paul alone was arrested, but none of his companions.

- Like Jesus, Paul heard the mob crying out, *Away with him!*

- Like Jesus, the Roman officer handling Paul's case did not know his true identity.

- Like Jesus, Paul was associated with terrorists by a Roman official.

iii. In a way unique to most of us, Paul really did know *the fellowship of His sufferings, being conformed to His death* (Philippians 3:10).

iv. Paul's particular call and ministry make these similarities especially striking, but we are called to follow after Jesus also. We shouldn't be surprised when events in our lives are like events in Jesus' life. There may be a time of temptation in the wilderness, a time when people come to us with needs only God can meet, a time when we seem at the mercy of a storm, a time when we must cry out to God as in the Garden of Gethsemane, a time when we must simply lay down our lives and trust God will gloriously raise us up. We, like Paul, are *predestined to be conformed to the image of His Son* (Romans 8:29).

v. However, Paul's experience was obviously different in many ways, not the least of which was the manner in which he will make his defense in the next chapter, while Jesus refused to defend Himself before His accusers.

Acts 22 - Paul's Jerusalem Sermon

A. The sermon to the crowd in Jerusalem.

1. (1-2) Paul begins his message to the mob.

"Brethren and fathers, hear my defense before you now." And when they heard that he spoke to them in the Hebrew language, they kept all the more silent. Then he said:

a. **Brethren and fathers, hear**: Paul began his great defense before the Jews the same way Stephen did: *Men and brethren and fathers, listen.* (Acts 7:2)

i. "Paul gave a magnificent defense. He actually used the word 'defense' (Acts 22:1). In Greek it is the word *apologia*, from which we get our word 'apology.' It refers to a formal defense of one's past life or actions." (Boice)

b. **They kept all the more silent**: Once the wild crowd heard Paul address them in Hebrew (Aramaic), they became quiet and ready to listen.

i. At the end of the previous chapter, Paul's audience for this sermon had just tried to kill him, thinking that he had profaned the temple by sneaking a Gentile in past the Court of the Gentiles.

2. (3) Paul tells of his Jewish upbringing and background.

"I am indeed a Jew, born in Tarsus of Cilicia, but brought up in this city at the feet of Gamaliel, taught according to the strictness of our fathers' law, and was zealous toward God as you all are today.

a. **I am indeed a Jew**: Paul spoke as a Jew unto Jews. He was careful to lay the common ground between them. With this, Paul began telling the story of his life before Jesus Christ and then his conversion.

i. Luke told the story of Paul's conversion in Acts 9. After that, Paul told the story in some way at least four more times in the New Testament, each with its own intention.

- Acts 22: Telling the story to persuade the Jews.
- Acts 26: Telling the story to persuade the Gentiles.
- Philippians 3: Telling the story for theological understanding.
- 1 Timothy 1: Telling the story to give encouragement.

b. **Born in Tarsus of Cilicia, but brought up in this city at the feet of Gamaliel**: Paul noted that though he was **born** outside of the Promised Land, he was **brought up** in Jerusalem, and **at the feet of Gamaliel**, one of the most prestigious rabbis of the day (Acts 5:34).

c. **Taught according to the strictness of our father's law, and was zealous toward God**: As Paul stated in another place, he was *a Hebrew of the Hebrews; concerning the law, a Pharisee* (Philippians 3:5). To the smallest detail, Paul kept the law as understood by the spiritual elite of his day.

d. **Zealous toward God as you all are today**: It's as if Paul searched for the nicest thing he could say about a mob that had just tried to murder him. "Well, I can say that you are **zealous toward God**."

3. (4-5) Paul tells how he persecuted Christians.

I persecuted this Way to the death, binding and delivering into prisons both men and women, as also the high priest bears me witness, and all the council of the elders, from whom I also received letters to the brethren, and went to Damascus to bring in chains even those who were there to Jerusalem to be punished.

a. **I persecuted this Way to the death**: This was evidence of the zeal mentioned in the previous line. Paul was so energetic as a persecutor that he, in some cases, was responsible for the death of some followers of Jesus. Paul communicated to the crowd, "You tried to kill me, but I succeeding in killing many." This had to be surprising news to many in the crowd.

b. **Binding and delivering into prisons both men and women**: Paul didn't kill every Christian he met; some were simply bound and imprisoned. But he was unsparing, persecuting **women** as well as **men**.

c. **The high priest bears me witness, and all the council of the elders, from whom I received letters**: Paul did his work of persecution with the official approval of the religious leaders.

d. **Went to Damascus to bring in chains even those who were there**: Paul was energetic enough to carry on his campaign of persecution beyond Judea, into Syria and the city of Damascus.

i. The message is clear: "I understand why you have attacked me. I was once an attacker also. I understand where you are coming from." Paul had been a Christian for more than twenty years, but could still relate to those who were not Christians.

4. (6-11) Paul describes his supernatural experience on the way to Damascus.

Now it happened, as I journeyed and came near Damascus at about noon, suddenly a great light from heaven shone around me. And I fell to the ground and heard a voice saying to me, 'Saul, Saul, why are you persecuting Me?' So I answered, 'Who are You, Lord?' And He said to me, 'I am Jesus of Nazareth, whom you are persecuting.' And those who were with me indeed saw the light and were afraid, but they did not hear the voice of Him who spoke to me. So I said, 'What shall I do, Lord?' And the Lord said to me, 'Arise and go into Damascus, and there you will be told all things which are appointed for you to do.' And since I could not see for the glory of that light, being led by the hand of those who were with me, I came into Damascus.

a. **Suddenly a great light from heaven shone around me**: Paul was a determined persecutor of Christians and Jesus until this heavenly light shone on him. It is as if Paul said: "I was just like you all, until I had an encounter with Jesus. Jesus met me and my life was dramatically changed."

b. **I am Jesus of Nazareth, whom you are persecuting**: Paul also came to understand he was persecuting Jesus Himself, the shining Lord of glory, brighter than the noonday sun. He didn't really know who he was persecuting until this.

c. **And since I could not see for the glory of that light**: The brightness of that light made Paul blind. In persecuting Jesus he was spiritually blind, and then he was also physically blind – and had to be humbly be **led by the hand** into the city of Damascus.

5. (12-16) Paul describes his response to the supernatural experience in Damascus.

"Then a certain Ananias, a devout man according to the law, having a good testimony with all the Jews who dwelt *there*, came to me; and he stood and said to me, 'Brother Saul, receive your sight.' And at that same hour I looked up at him. Then he said, 'The God of our fathers has chosen you that you should know His will, and see the Just One, and hear the voice of His mouth. For you will be His witness to all men of what you have seen and heard. And now why are you waiting? Arise and be baptized, and wash away your sins, calling on the name of the Lord.'

a. **Ananias, a devout man according to the law, having a good testimony with all the Jews**: Paul noted that it was **Ananias**, a man with credentials as a good Jew who received him into the Christian family.

b. **The God of our fathers has chosen you that you should know His will**: In Paul's speech, we see that both he and Ananias both simply acted like good Jews. They did not resist God nor deny their heritage.

i. Paul wanted them to know that he *still* served the God of his fathers. He had not rejected Judaism. Instead, many in Judaism had rejected God as revealed in Jesus Christ.

c. **The God of our fathers has chosen you that you should know His will, and see the Just One, and hear the voice of His mouth**: Acts 22:14 is a wonderful capsule of the duty of every one before God: To **know His will**, to **see the Just One** (Jesus), and to **hear the voice of His mouth** (His word).

6. (17-18) Jesus speaks to Paul in a trance at the temple in Jerusalem.

"Now it happened, when I returned to Jerusalem and was praying in the temple, that I was in a trance and saw Him saying to me, 'Make haste and get out of Jerusalem quickly, for they will not receive your testimony concerning Me.'

a. **When I returned to Jerusalem and was praying in the temple**: Paul told them about something that happened about 20 years before, when he had been a follower of Jesus for 2 or 3 years. Even though he had been a Christian for a few years, yet he still came to Jerusalem to pray in the **temple**. He wanted the crowd to know that even though he trusted in Jesus, he was not against all Jewish ceremonies and rituals.

b. **I was in a trance and saw Him saying to me**: Paul had an impressive vision of Jesus while in the temple; yet he never referred to this vision in his letters, and seems to only mention it now out of necessity. Paul's Christian life was founded on God's truth, not spiritual experiences, and he didn't even like to talk a lot about his spiritual experiences.

c. **Make haste and get out of Jerusalem quickly, for they will not receive your testimony concerning Me**: This word from Jesus probably was a surprise to Paul. With good reason, he probably thought of himself as the *perfect* one to bring the gospel to his fellow Jews. Nevertheless, Jesus gave him this warning, even telling him to **make haste**.

7. (19-20) Paul answers Jesus

So I said, 'Lord, they know that in every synagogue I imprisoned and beat those who believe on You. And when the blood of Your martyr

Stephen was shed, I also was standing by consenting to his death, and guarding the clothes of those who were killing him.'

a. **Lord, they know that in every synagogue I imprisoned and beat those who believe on You**: This was Paul's gentle objection to the warning Jesus just gave him in his vision. Paul's idea is, "Lord, they will listen to me. They know I used to persecute Christians, so my story will be powerful and persuasive to them."

b. **And when the blood of Your martyr Stephen was shed, I also was standing by consenting to his death**: Paul thought his early, energetic persecution of the church gave him *more* credibility with the Jewish people who were against Christianity. He tried to explain to Jesus why he should really stay in Jerusalem and work to tell the Jewish people about Jesus.

8. (21) Jesus replies to Paul's response.

Then He said to me, 'Depart, for I will send you far from here to the Gentiles.'"

a. **Then He said to me, "Depart"**: Jesus didn't agree with Paul's response. Jesus knew that it was not Paul's time and place to preach to the Jewish people the way Paul wanted to. Instead, for his own safety, 20 years before this, Jesus told Paul to simply **depart** from Jerusalem.

b. **For I will send you far from here to the Gentiles**: When Paul was touched by God in Damascus, he was told then of his call to preach to the Gentiles (Acts 9:15), so the words from Jesus to him in the temple at Jerusalem were not new. However, we can see that in his first visit to Jerusalem after his conversion, it would have been easy for Paul to care so much for the conversion of Israel that he would want to concentrate on that - that's why Jesus gave him the reminder in the temple.

i. Paul made it clear that it wasn't *his* idea to preach to the Gentiles; this was God's plan, not his. He hoped it also explained to the crowd why he seemed so friendly to the Gentiles: Paul was simply obeying Jesus and His word to him.

9. (22-23) The crowd riots in response to Paul's message.

And they listened to him until this word, and *then* they raised their voices and said, "Away with such a *fellow* from the earth, for he is not fit to live!" Then, as they cried out and tore off *their* clothes and threw dust into the air,

a. **And they listened to him until this word**: The crowd that had tried to kill Paul, and had then listened intently to his whole sermon, erupted into rage over the saying of **one word**. That **one word** was "*Gentiles*." (Acts

22:21) This Jewish mob was outraged at the thought that God's salvation could be given freely to believing Gentiles.

> i. The mob listened carefully up to this point. In their minds, they didn't mind this talk about Jesus, but they could not stand the idea that God might save Jews and Gentiles alike and in the same way.

> iii. The message of Jesus – that both Paul and the New Testament preached – is this: You may come to God just as you are – Jew, Gentile, foreigner, high, low, rich, or poor – but *you must come to Him through Jesus Christ.*

> iii. These Jews of that day did not have a problem with Gentiles becoming Jews. But they were incredibly offended at the thought of Gentiles becoming Christians *just as* Jews became Christians, because it implied that Jews and Gentiles were equal, having to come to God on the same terms.

b. Away with such a fellow from the earth, for he is not fit to live! This outraged, violent response was over one word: *Gentiles.*

> i. In Acts 22, the Jewish mob expressed their hatred of others through violent rage. Others express their hatred of the perishing through indifference. We may not riot like what the mob in this chapter did, but we may say much the same thing by our inaction.

B. Paul in Roman custody.

1. (24) The commander demands an explanation of the riot.

The commander ordered him to be brought into the barracks, and said that he should be examined under scourging, so that he might know why they shouted so against him.

> a. **The commander ordered him to be brought into the barracks**: It must have been a strange sight for the Roman **commander**. He saw Paul passionately address this huge crowd in a language he didn't know. He saw the crowd in rapt attention, until suddenly, they erupted into a riot.

> i. But when it was explained to him, he must have thought it absurd and offensive: All this rioting springing out of the hatred of Gentiles, people just like the commander himself.

> ii. From now until the end of the Book of Acts, Paul will be in Roman custody. As far as this book is concerned, this was the end of his time as a free man, though not the end of his witness or his usefulness to God and God's people.

> b. **Examined under scourging**: It is suggested that Paul be beaten with a **scourge**. This was quite different from being beaten with a rod or a normal

whip (which Paul had experienced, 2 Corinthians 11:24-25). Men often died or were crippled for life after a **scourging**.

> i. "This was not the normal Jewish flogging, which was bad enough, but the dreaded Roman flagellum. It was a beating so severe that in some cases it resulted in the death of the victim." (Boice)

c. **He should be examined under scourging**: This was brutal, yet customary in that time - but only upon people who were *not* Roman citizens.

2. (25-26) Paul reveals his Roman citizenship.

And as they bound him with thongs, Paul said to the centurion who stood by, "Is it lawful for you to scourge a man who is a Roman, and uncondemned?" When the centurion heard *that*, he went and told the commander, saying, "Take care what you do, for this man is a Roman."

a. **As they bound him with thongs**: Paul had his hands tied with leather straps so his hands joined around a wooden pole and his back was totally exposed. He was ready for a brutal beating, one that would not stop until he confessed to the crimes he was suspected of.

b. **Is it lawful for you to scourge a man who is a Roman, and uncondemned?** At that moment Paul announced his Roman citizenship.

c. **Take care what you do, for this man is a Roman**: When this became known, the reaction was immediate. It was a serious violation of Roman rights wrong to even *bind* a Roman citizen without due process, and they had *already* violated Paul's rights by binding him in Acts 21:33.

3. (27-29) The commander questions Paul about his citizenship.

Then the commander came and said to him, "Tell me, are you a Roman?" He said, "Yes." The commander answered, "With a large sum I obtained this citizenship." And Paul said, "But I was born *a citizen.*" Then immediately those who were about to examine him withdrew from him; and the commander was also afraid after he found out that he was a Roman, and because he had bound him.

a. **Tell me, are you a Roman?** The penalty for lying about one's Roman citizenship was significant. It wasn't the kind of thing people commonly lied about, so the commander could simply ask Paul directly.

> i. "The verbal claim to Roman citizenship was accepted at face value; penalties for falsifying documents and making false claims of citizenship were exceedingly stiff - Epictetus speaks of death for such acts." (Longenecker)

b. **With a large sum I obtained this citizenship**: Because of all the commotion and the beating Paul had received, he probably looked terrible.

The commander wondered how someone who looked like this could purchase his citizenship.

> i. "Something of this sort may have been in the tribune's mind as he said, *It cost me a very large sum of money to obtain Roman citizenship* - the implication being that the privilege must have become cheap of late if such a sorry-looking figure as Paul could claim it." (Bruce)

> ii. According to Stott, Roman citizenship could not be bought for a fee, only for a bribe. Normally, only right or reward only granted it. "The point was not that the tribune doubted Paul's claim, but rather he was implying that anybody could become a citizen these days!" (Marshall)

c. **But I was born a citizen**: Paul's parents (or grandparents) must have been awarded the rights of citizenship for some good done on behalf of Rome.

> i. "How the citizenship was acquired by Paul's father or grandfather we have no means of knowing, but analogy would suggest that it was for valuable services rendered to a Roman general or administrator in the southeastern area of Asia Minor." (Bruce)

> ii. Paul was an extremely rare individual. It was uncommon to find such an educated, intelligent, devout Jew who was also a Roman citizen. God would use this unique background to use Paul in a special way, even as he wants to use *your* unique background to use you in a special way.

d. **The commander was also afraid after he found out that he was a Roman, and because he had bound him**: Knowing what he now knew about Paul, the commander was very concerned for his own sake.

4. (30) The Roman commander arranges a hearing of the charges against Paul before the Jewish council (the Sanhedrin).

The next day, because he wanted to know for certain why he was accused by the Jews, he released him from *his* bonds, and commanded the chief priests and all their council to appear, and brought Paul down and set him before them.

a. **He wanted to know for certain why he was accused**: Luke presents the Roman commander as a fair and upstanding man. Though he did not know the details of the dispute between Paul and the religious leaders, he seemed to work hard towards a fair resolution.

> i. The Roman commander "must have thought that once he had a concrete accusation he would be able to decide what to do." (Boice)

b. **And commanded the chief priests and all their council to appear, and brought Paul down and set him before them**: Paul received what he probably thought of as a dramatic second chance. The opportunity to preach to the mob on the temple mount ended in another riot, but he would speak before the Sanhedrin (**their council**) the next day.

i. The Sanhedrin was the Jewish congress or parliament. Paul would be given the opportunity to speak before the group that he was once a member of. Acts 26:10 clearly says that Paul had a *vote* - usually, that would be used as a member of the Sanhedrin.

ii. Paul would logically think this was the opportunity of a lifetime, to preach to those he loved so much and knew so well.

iii. God had revealed a plan to Paul right at his conversion. Paul was *a chosen vessel of Mine to bear My name before Gentiles, kings, and the children of Israel. For I will show him how many things he must suffer for My name's sake* (Acts 9:15-16). Paul knew the general plan; but just like us, he didn't know how it would all work out. He had to trust God, just like every believer.

Acts 23 - Paul in Protective Custody, From Jerusalem to Caesarea

A. Paul's defense before the Sanhedrin.

1. (1-2) Paul begins his speech before the council.

Then Paul, looking earnestly at the council, said, "Men *and* brethren, I have lived in all good conscience before God until this day." And the high priest Ananias commanded those who stood by him to strike him on the mouth.

> a. **Paul, looking earnestly at the council**: The previous day Paul saw a great opportunity go unfulfilled when the crowd at the temple mount did not allow him to finish his message to them, but started rioting again. Now Paul had another opportunity to win Israel to Jesus, and perhaps a *better* opportunity. Here he spoke to **the council**, with the opportunity to preach Jesus to these influential men.

> b. **Men and brethren**: According to William Barclay, this address meant that Paul was bold in speaking to the council, setting himself on an equal footing with them. The normal style of address was to say, "Rulers of the people and elders of Israel."

> c. **I have lived in all good conscience before God until this day**: Paul probably thought this was an innocent enough way to begin his preaching. He didn't mean that he was sinlessly perfect and that his conscience had never told him he was wrong. Rather, he meant that he had responded to **conscience** when he had done wrong and had set things right.

> > i. Nor would Paul ever consider a clear conscience a way to be justified before God. "Paul might well appeal to the testimony of conscience as he stood before the supreme court of Israel; it was on no righteousness of his own, however, that he relied for justification in the heavenly

court. The purest conscience was an insecure basis of confidence under the scrutiny of God." (Bruce)

ii. Paul's statement in 1 Corinthians 4:4 is relevant: *For I know nothing against myself, yet I am not justified by this; but He who judges me is the Lord.*

d. **And the high priest Ananias commanded those who stood by him to strike him on the mouth**: Paul's claim of a **good conscience** offended the high priest. He thought that someone accused of such serious crimes should never claim a clear conscience.

i. Or, perhaps, he was convicted in his heart by the inherent *integrity* of Paul's claim. He *was* a man with a **good conscience**, and it was evident in his speech and countenance.

ii. No matter what his motive was, "This order was illegal, for the Jewish law said, 'He who strikes the cheek of one Israelite, strikes as it were the glory of God,' and 'He that strikes a man strikes the Holy One.'" (Hughes)

iii. The **Ananias** who was high priest at this time did no honor to the office. He was well known for his greed; the ancient Jewish historian Josephus tells of how Ananias stole for himself the tithes that belonged to the common priests.

iv. "He did not scruple to use violence and assassination to further his interests" (Bruce). Later, because of his pro-Roman politics, Ananias was brutally killed by Jewish nationalists.

2. (3-5) Paul's response to the punch in the face.

Then Paul said to him, "God will strike you, *you* whitewashed wall! For you sit to judge me according to the law, and do you command me to be struck contrary to the law?" And those who stood by said, "Do you revile God's high priest?" Then Paul said, "I did not know, brethren, that he was the high priest; for it is written, 'You shall not speak evil of a ruler of your people.'"

a. **God will strike you, you whitewashed wall!** We wish we knew *how* Paul said these words. It would have helped to hear Paul's tone of voice; was it an outburst of anger, or was it a calm, collected rebuke with that much more weight to it?

i. Whatever the tone, the rebuke was entirely accurate and justified. The man who commanded that a defenseless man be punched in the face indeed was a **whitewashed wall**; a white veneer of purity covering over obvious corruption.

b. **For you sit to judge me according to the law, and do you command me to be struck contrary to the law?** Paul exposed the hypocrisy of the man who made the command.

> i. The men of the council were supposed to be *example* of the Law of Moses. The command to have Paul struck was in fact contrary to both the spirit and the letter of the law. Deuteronomy 25:1-2 says only a man found guilty can be beaten, and Paul had not yet been found guilty of anything.

> ii. **God will strike you**: "Paul's words, however, were more prophetic than he realized. Ananias' final days - despite all his scheming and bribes - were lived as a hunted animal and ended at the hands of his own people." (Longenecker)

c. **Those who stood by said, "Do you revile God's high priest?"** Paul instantly knew that he was wrong in his outburst, no matter how he said it. He agreed that it was wrong to **speak evil of the ruler of your people** (Exodus 22:28). Yet Paul excused himself, claiming that he **did not know** that the man who commanded the punch was Ananias, the high priest.

> i. This isn't unreasonable, since Paul had been away from the council and the high circles of Jewish authority in Jerusalem for more than 20 years. Probably, he simply didn't recognize the man who gave the command to strike him as the high priest. However, some think he **did not know** because Paul's eyesight was bad. This is an inference from Galatians 4:14-15 and 6:11, as well as from early written church traditions.

> ii. Others think that Paul was sarcastic, with the idea "I didn't think that anyone who acted in such a manner *could* be the high priest."

3. (6) Paul's clever ploy.

But when Paul perceived that one part were Sadducees and the other Pharisees, he cried out in the council, "Men *and* brethren, I am a Pharisee, the son of a Pharisee; concerning the hope and resurrection of the dead I am being judged!"

a. **Paul perceived**: Paul seems to have read his audience and saw they were not conducive to the gospel - the actions of the high priest and the attitudes of those present made this plain. So, Paul gave up on preaching the gospel, and did what he could to preserve his liberty before a council that wanted to kill him.

b. **One part were Sadducees and the other Pharisees**: Paul's course was to divide the Sanhedrin among their party lines - to get make side (the **Pharisees**) sympathetic to him, instead of having them united against him.

c. **I am a Pharisee, the son of a Pharisee**: Knowing his audience, Paul referred to his heritage as a Pharisee, and declared, **"concerning the hope and resurrection of the dead I am being judged."** He knew this was a matter of great controversy between the two parties.

i. Of course, this was an essentially true claim. The center of Paul's gospel was a resurrected Jesus. He was **being judged** over the matter of the **resurrection of the dead**.

4. (7-9) The council is divided.

And when he had said this, a dissension arose between the Pharisees and the Sadducees; and the assembly was divided. For Sadducees say that there is no resurrection–and no angel or spirit; but the Pharisees confess both. Then there arose a loud outcry. And the scribes of the Pharisees' party arose and protested, saying, "We find no evil in this man; but if a spirit or an angel has spoken to him, let us not fight against God."

a. **When he had said this, a dissension arose between the Pharisees and the Sadducees; and the assembly was divided**: Paul picked the right issue. Framed in these terms, he immediately gained the Pharisees as an ally, and he let *them* argue it out with the Sadducees.

i. **Sadducees** were the theological liberals of their day, and denied the reality of life after death and the concept of resurrection. Luke rightly wrote of them, **Sadducees say that there is no resurrection; and no angel or spirit**.

ii. The **Pharisees** were more likely to find some ground of agreement with Paul, being the more the Bible believers in the Jewish world of that time. They took the Bible seriously, even if they did err greatly by *adding* the traditions of men to what they received in the Bible.

iii. Usually the **Saducees** and the **Pharisees** were bitter enemies, but they were able to unite in opposition against Jesus (Matthew 16:1, John 11:47-53) and Paul. It's strange how people with nothing in common will come together as friends to oppose God or His work.

b. **Let us not fight against God**: In saying this, the Pharisees recommended a return to advice of their great leader Gamaliel as recorded in Acts 5:38-39.

5. (10) Paul is rescued by the Roman commander.

Now when there arose a great dissension, the commander, fearing lest Paul might be pulled to pieces by them, commanded the soldiers to go

down and take him by force from among them, and bring *him* into the barracks.

a. **Now when there arose a great dissension**: The commander had to be certain that these Jews were crazy in their endless and violent disputes. Previously, they rioted over the one word "*Gentiles*," now the distinguished men of the council fought over the one word "*resurrection*."

b. **The commander, fearing lest Paul might be pulled to pieces by them, commanded the soldiers to go down and take him by force from among them**: The commander removed Paul for his own safety, and left him in custody in the barracks.

i. Paul's clever ploy rescued him from the council, but he could not have been happy with the result. He had the opportunity to preach to a huge crowd of attentive Jews on the temple mount and it ended in failure. Then he had the opportunity to preach to the influential Jewish council, and it also ended in a fistfight.

ii. Later. Paul seemed to suggest that this tactic of bringing up the resurrection controversy in the way that he did *was not* good. He suggests that it was "wrongdoing" on his part (Acts 24:20-21).

6. (11) Jesus comforts Paul in the night.

But the following night the Lord stood by him and said, "Be of good cheer, Paul; for as you have testified for Me in Jerusalem, so you must also bear witness at Rome."

a. **But the following night**: This must have been a difficult night for Paul. His heart longed for the salvation of his fellow Jews (Romans 9:1-4), and two great opportunities came to nothing. It would be no surprise if Paul blamed himself for the missed opportunity before the Sanhedrin. It could be said that his reaction to the punch commanded by the High Priest spoiled everything.

i. Perhaps with tears, Paul mourned these lost opportunities for God and how he might have spoiled them. At moments like these, one is often tormented with a deep sense of unworthiness and un-useableness before God. Perhaps this was his end of ministry.

ii. "Bold, courageous, fearless during the day, the night of loneliness finds the strength spent, and the enemy is never slow to take advantage of that fact." (Morgan)

iii. It was in the darkness of that night when the fears came upon Paul; when his trust in God seemed to falter; when he worried about what

God was going to do and if he was going to make it. It was in the darkness of that night that Jesus came to Paul and **stood by him**.

b. **But… the Lord stood by him**: Jesus' physical presence (as it seems was the case) with Paul was a unique manifestation. But Jesus promised every believer to always be with them (Matthew 28:20).

i. Jesus knew where Paul was; He had not lost sight of Paul because he was in jail. When John Bunyan, author of *Pilgrim's Progress*, was in jail, a man visited him and said, "Friend, the Lord sent me to you, and I have been looking in half the prisons in England for you." John Bunyan replied, "I don't think the Lord sent you to me, because if He had, you would have come here first. God knows I have been here for years." God knows where you are today; even if you are hiding it from everyone else, God knows where you are.

ii. Paul was alone, but he wasn't alone; if everyone else forsook him, Jesus was enough. Better to be in jail with the Lord than to be in heaven without him.

iii. Paul had been miraculously delivered from jail cells before; but this time, the Lord met him right in the jail cell. We often demand that Jesus deliver us *out* of our circumstances, when He wants to meet us right *in* them. We sometimes think we are surrendering to Jesus when we are really only demanding an escape. God wants to meet us *in* whatever we face at the moment.

c. **Be of good cheer, Paul**: Jesus was not only with Paul; He gave him words of comfort. The words **be of good cheer** tell us that the night brought with it an emotional and perhaps spiritual darkness upon Paul. Jesus was there to **cheer** His faithful servant after he had spent himself for Jesus' sake.

i. Jesus would not have said **be of good cheer** unless Paul *needed* to hear those words. Paul knew his situation was bad, but he didn't know the half of it! The next day, forty Jewish assassins would gather together and vow to go on a hunger strike until they murdered Paul. Paul didn't know this would happen, but Jesus did. Yet He still could say to Paul, **be of good cheer**.

ii. You might think that things are bad right now, but you may not even know the half of it. But Jesus knows, and he still says to you, **be of good cheer**. Why? Not because everything is fine; but because God is still on His throne, and He still holds to His promise that *all things work together for good to those who love God, to those who are the called according to His purpose* (Romans 8:28).

iii. Anyone can **be of good cheer** when everything is great; but the Christian can **be of good cheer** when everything is rotten, knowing that God is mighty and wonderful no matter what the crisis of the moment.

iv. **Be of good cheer** is only one word in the ancient Greek, and is used five times in the New Testament – each time by Jesus.

- Jesus told the bedridden paralytic, *Son, be of good cheer; your sins are forgiven you* (Matthew 9:2).

- Jesus told the woman with the 12-year bleeding problem, *Be of good cheer, daughter; your faith has made you well* (Matthew 9:22).

- Jesus told His frightened disciples on the Sea of Galilee, *Be of good cheer! It is I; do not be afraid* (Matthew 14:27).

- Jesus told His disciples the night before His crucifixion, *In the world you will have tribulation; but be of good cheer, I have overcome the world* (John 16:33).

- And here, in Acts 23:11 – Jesus told Paul, **be of good cheer**.

d. **For as you have testified for Me in Jerusalem, so you must also bear witness at Rome**: Jesus remembered what Paul *had* done in Jerusalem, and told Paul that there *remained more* work for him to do in Rome.

i. Paul could have been discouraged about the lack of results from the sermon in Jerusalem. But the results were not his responsibility. His responsibility was to bring the Word of God and to testify of Jesus; the results were God's responsibility. **You have testified for Me in Jerusalem** means that Jesus complimented Paul on a job well done.

ii. Yet, though Paul had done a good job, there was more to do. **So you must also bear witness at Rome** was Paul's next assignment. The greatest words a faithful child of God can hear are "There is more for you to do." Those words grieve the lazy servant, but bring joy to a faithful servant.

iii. It can be said to every child of God: *There is more for you to do.* More people to bring to Christ, more ways for you to glorify Him, more people to pray with, more humble ways to serve His people, more hungry to feed, more naked to clothe, more weary saints for you to encourage.

iv. "A divine decree ordains for you greater and more trying service than as yet you have seen. A future awaits you, and no power on the earth or under the earth can rob you of it; therefore be of good cheer." (Spurgeon)

e. **So you must also bear witness at Rome**: The promise of more work to do was also a promise of continued protection. Paul had to live until he had finished the course God had appointed for him.

i. Paul really *wanted* to go on to Rome (Acts 19:21 and Romans 1:9-12). Sometimes we think that just because we *want* something a lot, it couldn't be God's will for us. But God often gives us the desires of our hearts (Psalm 37:4).

ii. The *timing* of this promise was especially precious. It didn't look like Paul would get out of Jerusalem alive; much less make it to Rome. God not only knows what we need to hear; He knows *when* we need to hear it.

iii. Paul faced his enemies the next day with a smile, knowing that they were powerless against him, *because God had more for him to do!*

iv. "This assurance meant much to Paul during the delays and anxieties of the next two years, and goes far to account for the calm and dignified bearing which from now on marks him out as a master of events rather than their victim." (Bruce)

B. Paul is delivered from the plot of assassins.

1. (12-15) Forty men vow to set an ambush and kill Paul.

And when it was day, some of the Jews banded together and bound themselves under an oath, saying that they would neither eat nor drink till they had killed Paul. Now there were more than forty who had formed this conspiracy. They came to the chief priests and elders, and said, "We have bound ourselves under a great oath that we will eat nothing until we have killed Paul. Now you, therefore, together with the council, suggest to the commander that he be brought down to you tomorrow, as though you were going to make further inquiries concerning him; but we are ready to kill him before he comes near."

a. **Saying that they would neither eat nor drink till they had killed Paul**: In the days of Paul and Jesus, there was a secretive group of Jewish assassins who targeted the Romans and their supporters. They were dagger-men, because they often concealed daggers and stabbed Roman soldiers as they walked by. It seems that these same kind of assassins now targeted Paul.

i. They were so zealous that they made a vow to not eat or even drink until Paul was dead. This was a high level of commitment.

ii. These men lacked nothing in *commitment* or *zeal*. But their zeal was *not according to knowledge* (Romans 10:2). Zeal and devotion by themselves never prove that someone is right with God.

b. **Suggest to the commander that he be brought down to you tomorrow, as though you were going to make further inquiries concerning him**: The assassins wanted **the chief priests and elders** to lie to Roman commander, pretended they wanted another meeting with Paul.

i. Their lie was a sin; and men who should have been committed to the law of God were instead happy to sin against Him. They were zealous, but still willing to lie and sin to accomplish their supposedly godly goals.

2. (16-22) Paul's nephew learns of the plot and warns the Roman commander.

So when Paul's sister's son heard of their ambush, he went and entered the barracks and told Paul. Then Paul called one of the centurions to *him* and said, "Take this young man to the commander, for he has something to tell him." So he took him and brought *him* to the commander and said, "Paul the prisoner called me to *him* and asked *me* to bring this young man to you. He has something to say to you." Then the commander took him by the hand, went aside and asked privately, "What is it that you have to tell me?" And he said, "The Jews have agreed to ask that you bring Paul down to the council tomorrow, as though they were going to inquire more fully about him. But do not yield to them, for more than forty of them lie in wait for him, men who have bound themselves by an oath that they will neither eat nor drink till they have killed him; and now they are ready, waiting for the promise from you." So the commander let the young man depart, and commanded *him*, "Tell no one that you have revealed these things to me."

a. **When Paul's sister's son heard of their ambush**: It was no accident that this happened. God had to protect Paul because Jesus promised that he would go to Rome to testify of Him (Acts 23:11).

b. **Paul the prisoner**: Paul had committed no crime; yet he was a prisoner. Because the Roman commander suspected he might be a revolutionary of some kind, Paul had to be kept in custody until the facts of the case could be discovered.

3. (23-24) Paul escapes to Caesarea, with a full military escort and a letter referring his case to the provincial governor.

And he called for two centurions, saying, "Prepare two hundred soldiers, seventy horsemen, and two hundred spearmen to go to Caesarea at the third hour of the night; and provide mounts to set Paul on, and bring *him* safely to Felix the governor."

a. **Prepare two hundred soldiers, seventy horsemen, and two hundred spearmen**: 470 trained Roman soldiers would escort Paul out of Jerusalem.

It was as if God wanted to exaggerate His faithfulness to Paul, and show him beyond any doubt that the promise of Jesus was true.

b. **Provide mounts to set Paul on, and bring him safely to Felix the governor**: Not did Paul escape Jerusalem alive, he did so riding a horse – actually, *several* **mounts** were made available to Paul.

4. (25-30) The letter from Lysias to Felix.

He wrote a letter in the following manner:

Claudius Lysias,
To the most excellent governor Felix:
Greetings.
This man was seized by the Jews and was about to be killed by them.
Coming with the troops I rescued him, having learned that he was
a Roman. And when I wanted to know the reason they accused him,
I brought him before their council. I found out that he was accused
concerning questions of their law, but had nothing charged against
him deserving of death or chains. And when it was told me that the
Jews lay in wait for the man, I sent him immediately to you, and also
commanded his accusers to state before you the charges against him.
Farewell.

a. **I rescued him, having learned that he was a Roman**: In his letter, Lysias implied that he learned of Paul's Roman citizenship right away, and he said nothing of the way Paul was bound twice and almost scourged for the sake of interrogation.

b. **Had nothing charged against him deserving of death or chains**: For Luke, this was the important line in the letter. It was likely that Roman officials reviewed the Book of Acts before Paul's trial before Caesar. Here, Luke showed that other Roman officials had judged Paul "not guilty."

i. "One of Luke's prime motives in writing his twofold history is to demonstrate that there is no substance in this charge of subversion brought not only against Paul but against Christians in general - that competent and impartial judges had repeatedly confirmed the innocence of the Christian movement and the Christian missionaries in respect of Roman law." (Bruce)

5. (31-33) Paul arrives in Caesarea.

Then the soldiers, as they were commanded, took Paul and brought *him* by night to Antipatris. The next day they left the horsemen to go on with him, and returned to the barracks. When they came to Caesarea and had delivered the letter to the governor, they also presented Paul to him.

a. **Took Paul and brought him by night to Antipatris**: The 200 soldiers only went as far as Antipatris because the most dangerous part of the road was only up to this point.

i. "Up to Antipatris [about 25 miles] the country was dangerous and inhabited by Jews; after that the country was open and flat, quite unsuited for any ambush and largely inhabited by Gentiles." (Barclay)

b. **They also presented Paul to him**: Paul made it out of Jerusalem and to Caesarea on the coast. The plot of the 40 assassins failed.

i. Some wonder if the men who made the vow of fasting died because they failed in their mission to kill Paul. This was probably not the case. Ancient rabbis allowed for four types of vows to be broken: "Vows of incitement, vows of exaggeration, vows made in error, and vows that cannot be fulfilled by reason of constraint" - exclusions allowing for almost any contingency. (Longenecker)

6. (34-35) Paul awaits trial in Caesarea.

And when the governor had read *it*, he asked what province he was from. And when he understood that *he was* from Cilicia, he said, "I will hear you when your accusers also have come." And he commanded him to be kept in Herod's Praetorium.

a. **When he understood that he was from Cilicia**: Perhaps Felix hoped that Paul came from someplace that required that someone else hear his case. Apparently, learning that **he was from Cilicia** meant that Felix would indeed be responsible to hear and rule on his case.

b. **I will hear you when your accusers also have come**: This would be Paul's first opportunity to speak to someone at this level of authority (**the governor**). This was the beginning of the fulfillment of the promise made to Paul some 20 years earlier: that he would bear the name of Jesus to kings (Acts 9:15).

c. **And he commanded him to be kept in Herod's Praetorium**: This began a two-year period of confinement for Paul in Caesarea. After that he spent at least two years in Rome. Taken together with travel time, the next five years of Paul's life were lived in Roman custody. This was a striking contrast to his previous years of wide and spontaneous travel.

i. Paul lived many years with great freedom, and had to trust the promises of God through those years. Yet he also had to trust the promises of Jesus in his years of little freedom – and to know that God could work just as powerfully through those more difficult circumstances.

ii. Paul needed to receive the promise of Jesus – both promises from 20 years before, and promises recently made – to receive them with confident faith, allowing those promises to make a difference in how he thought and even felt. Every believer must do the same.

Acts 24 - Paul's Trial Before Felix

A. The accusations against Paul.

1. (1) The Jews assemble their case against Paul.

Now after five days Ananias the high priest came down with the elders and a certain orator *named* Tertullus. These gave evidence to the governor against Paul.

a. **Now after five days**: The Jewish leadership (**Ananias the high priest** and the **elders**) brought a man named **Tertullus** - a skilled lawyer – to present their case.

b. **These gave evidence to the governor against Paul**: The presence of all three (**Ananias**, the **elders**, and a skilled lawyer) at the court of Felix reminds us of how serious the Jewish leadership was about obtaining a conviction against Paul.

2. (2-4) Tertullus introduces his accusation against Paul with flattery towards Felix.

And when he was called upon, Tertullus began his accusation, saying: "Seeing that through you we enjoy great peace, and prosperity is being brought to this nation by your foresight, we accept *it* always and in all places, most noble Felix, with all thankfulness. Nevertheless, not to be tedious to you any further, I beg you to hear, by your courtesy, a few words from us.

a. **Most noble Felix**: Antonius Felix began life as a slave. His brother Pallas was a friend of the emperor Claudius; through such influence, he rose in status – first as a child gaining freedom, and then through intrigue he became the first former slave to become a governor of a Roman province.

i. But his slave mentality stayed with him. Tacitus, the Roman historian, described Felix as "a master of cruelty and lust who exercised the powers of a king with the spirit of a slave" (*Historiae* 5.9, cited in Longnecker).

ii. "The picture drawn by Tacitus of Felix's public and private life is not a pretty one. Trading on the influences of his infamous brother [Pallas, a favorite of the emperor Claudius], he indulged in every license and excess, thinking 'that he could do any evil act with impunity' (Tacitus, *Annals* 12.54)." (Williams)

b. **Seeing that through you we enjoy great peace, and prosperity is being brought to this nation by your foresight**: These were lies presented as flattery. Felix did not bring **peace** or **prosperity** to those he governed.

i. "In reality he [Felix] had put down several insurrections with such barbarous brutality that he earned for himself the horror, not the thanks, of the Jewish population." (Stott) In particular, he ordered a massacre of thousands of Jews in Caesarea, with many more Jewish homes looted by the Roman soldiers.

ii. Flattery is an often-neglected sin, one that the Bible speaks about more often than one might think. Romans 16:18 speaks to us of those who *do not serve our Lord Jesus Christ, but their own belly, and by smooth words and flattering speech deceive the hearts of the simple.* Jude 1:16 speaks of those who *mouth great swelling words, flattering people to gain advantage.*

iii. Four different times the Book of Proverbs connects flattery with the sin of sexual immorality. Many people have been seduced into immorality through simple flattery.

iv. Proverbs 20:19 says, *He who goes about as a talebearer reveals secrets; there for do not associate with one who flatters with his lips.* This means that we aren't to make flatterers our close friends.

v. Psalm 78:36 says we can even flatter God: *Nevertheless they flattered Him with their mouth, and they lied to Him with their tongue.* When you give God insincere praise, it is flattery, and God doesn't want it.

vi. "I suppose that even Felix was shrewd enough to have listened with tongue in cheek. What is it that these Jewish leaders are after that they should come all the way from Caesarea and flatter me in this fashion? he must have wondered." (Boice)

3. (5-6) Paul's accusers state their specific charges.

For we have found this man a plague, a creator of dissension among all the Jews throughout the world, and a ringleader of the sect of the

Nazarenes. He even tried to profane the temple, and we seized him, and wanted to judge him according to our law.

a. **For we have found this man a plague**: The charges against Paul were essentially that he was politically dangerous (**a plague...a ringleader of the sect of the Nazarenes**) and that he had profaned the temple.

i. Ancient Judea was filled with would-be messiahs and revolutionaries against Rome. Tertullus wanted to put Paul in the same group with these kinds of terrorists.

b. **A ringleader of the sect of the Nazarenes**: The reference to Paul being a **Nazarene** was intended to connect him to a generally despised and lowly place. It was term of slight scorn used for the followers of Jesus. Nazareth had a poor reputation as a city (John 1:46).

c. **Among all Jews throughout the world**: Here, Tertullus gave an unintended compliment as he described the extent of Paul's work in the Roman Empire.

d. **He even tried to profane the temple**: This was the only really specific charge against Paul; but Tertullus gave no *evidence* for this charge because there *was* no evidence. This was a fabricated charge based on rumor only (Acts 21:26-29).

i. Paul had nothing to fear from the truth; but he knew that the truth does not always win out in a court of law.

ii. Significantly, the same man who found it so easy to flatter also found it easy to accuse with no evidence. The two almost always go together; the person who flatters today will likely tomorrow accuse without evidence.

4. (7-9) Tertullus concludes his accusation against Paul.

But the commander Lysias came by and with great violence took *him* out of our hands, commanding his accusers to come to you. By examining him yourself you may ascertain all these things of which we accuse him." And the Jews also assented, maintaining that these things were so.

a. **The commander Lysias came by and with great violence took him out of our hands**: The Roman commander **Lysias**, who rescued Paul, was here put into a bad light. Clearly Paul's accusers regretted that the case had come this far, having preferred to settle it with mob justice.

b. **By examining him yourself you may ascertain all these things of which we accuse him**: Tertullus did not even pretend to offer outside evidence of the charges. His only hope was that Paul would incriminate himself under examination by Felix.

> i. "His oration has been blamed as *weak, lame,* and *imperfect*; and yet, perhaps, few, with so *bad a cause*, could have made *better* of it." (Clarke)

c. **The Jews also assented, maintaining that these things were so**: The other Jewish accusers present (the high priest and the elders) agreed with the charges, but they also offered no supporting *evidence*.

B. Paul's defense.

1. (10-13) Paul exposes the weakness of the case against him.

Then Paul, after the governor had nodded to him to speak, answered: "Inasmuch as I know that you have been for many years a judge of this nation, I do the more cheerfully answer for myself, because you may ascertain that it is no more than twelve days since I went up to Jerusalem to worship. And they neither found me in the temple disputing with anyone nor inciting the crowd, either in the synagogues or in the city. Nor can they prove the things of which they now accuse me.

> a. **I do the more cheerfully answer for myself**: Paul was happy to answer for himself, knowing that the facts of the case were in his favor - and notably, Paul used no flattery in his address to Felix.

> b. **Nor can they prove the things of which they now accuse me**: Even though it had been **no more than twelve days**, and many witnesses could be easily found, Paul's accusers gave no witnesses to **prove** that he was in fact **in the temple disputing** or **inciting the crowd**. There was simply no proof for their accusations.

2. (14-21) Paul explains his ministry, and why he was arrested.

But this I confess to you, that according to the Way which they call a sect, so I worship the God of my fathers, believing all things which are written in the Law and in the Prophets. I have hope in God, which they themselves also accept, that there will be a resurrection of *the* dead, both of *the* just and *the* unjust. This *being* so, I myself always strive to have a conscience without offense toward God and men. Now after many years I came to bring alms and offerings to my nation, in the midst of which some Jews from Asia found me purified in the temple, neither with a mob nor with tumult. They ought to have been here before you to object if they had anything against me. Or else let those who are *here* themselves say if they found any wrongdoing in me while I stood before the council, unless *it is* for this one statement which I cried out, standing among them, 'Concerning the resurrection of the dead I am being judged by you this day.'"

a. **According to the Way which they call a sect, so I worship the God of my fathers**: Paul made it clear that he had not abandoned the **God of my fathers** or the **Law and the Prophets**. Instead, he acted in fulfillment of them both.

i. Tertullus called Christianity *the sect of the Nazarenes* (Acts 24:5; Paul called it **the Way**.

b. **That there will be a resurrection of the dead**: This was believed by many or most devout Jews of Paul's day, though not by the Sadducees (Acts 23:8). Paul's belief that there **will be a resurrection** was connected to his specific trust in the resurrection of Jesus (1 Corinthians 15).

c. **Both of the just and the unjust**: Paul clearly believed in a resurrection for both the righteous and the unrighteous. The idea of soul-sleep or annihilation for the unrighteous is not accurate according to New Testament teaching.

d. **I came to bring alms and offerings**: This refers to the collection Paul made for Judean Christians among the Gentile churches of the West (Galatians 2:10, Romans 15:26, and 2 Corinthians 8-9).

e. **They ought to have been here before you to object**: In this, Paul reminded Felix that there was no eyewitness *testimony* to prove the charges of his accusers.

i. "This was a strong point in his defense: the people who had raised the hue and cry in the first instance, claiming to be eyewitnesses of his alleged sacrilege, had not troubled to be present." (Bruce) Because Paul was in the right, he consistently called the case back to the *evidence*, the very thing his accusers avoided.

ii. Christians should never be timid about or ashamed of the truth or of the evidence. If we are truly following God, the truth and evidence are our friends, not our accusers.

C. Felix's decision in the case.

1. (22-23) Felix avoids making a legal decision.

But when Felix heard these things, having more accurate knowledge of *the* Way, he adjourned the proceedings and said, "When Lysias the commander comes down, I will make a decision on your case." So he commanded the centurion to keep Paul and to let *him* have liberty, and told him not to forbid any of his friends to provide for or visit him.

a. **When Lysias the commander comes down, I will make a decision on your case**: Felix avoided a decision under the pretense of waiting for more evidence through the Roman commander Lysias. But Felix clearly *had* enough evidence to make a decision in Paul's favor (**having more accurate knowledge of the Way**).

b. **Let him have liberty**: Yet, knowing Paul's innocence, he granted Paul generous liberty even while he was held in custody.

i. Felix tried to walk a middle ground. He knew Paul was innocent, yet he did not want to identify himself with Paul's gospel and the Christians. So he made no decision and kept Paul in custody.

2. (24-25) Felix avoids making a spiritual decision.

And after some days, when Felix came with his wife Drusilla, who was Jewish, he sent for Paul and heard him concerning the faith in Christ. Now as he reasoned about righteousness, self-control, and the judgment to come, Felix was afraid and answered, "Go away for now; when I have a convenient time I will call for you."

a. **Felix came with his wife Drusilla, who was Jewish, he sent for Paul and heard him concerning the faith in Christ**: Felix wanted his wife to hear Paul's testimony, either as a curiosity or so that she could advise him. After all, he claimed to have insufficient evidence for a decision.

b. **With his wife Drusilla**: This woman was the sister of Herod Agrippa II and Bernice mentioned in Acts 25. Drusilla was beautiful, ambitious, and about 20 years old at this point. Felix seduced her away from her husband and made her his third wife.

i. "The lax morals of Felix and Drusilla help to explain the topics on which Paul spoke to them." (Stott)

c. **He reasoned about righteousness, self-control, and the judgment to come**: These were the three points Paul used when he spoke to Felix and Drusilla. These are three points many modern preachers would avoid speaking about, especially in speaking to a high figure like Felix.

i. We don't know exactly how Paul developed these three points, but we can speculate on something like this:

• The **righteousness** that is ours in Jesus Christ.

• The need for Christian ethics (**self-control**) that was evidently lacking in the life of both Felix and Drusilla.

• Eternal accountability before God (**the judgment to come**).

ii. We admire Paul's bold preaching, directed right to the issues of Felix's life: "Are there not some to be found, who think the highest object of the minister is to attract the multitude and then to please them? O my God! how solemnly ought each of us to bewail our sin, if we feel we have been guilty in this matter. What is it to have pleased men? Is there aught in it that can make our head lie easy on the pillow of our death? Is there aught in it that can give us boldness in the day of judgment when we face thy tribunal, O Judge of quick and dead? No, my brethren, we must always take our texts so that we may bear upon our hearers with all our might." (Spurgeon)

iii. "But some men will say, 'Sir, ministers ought not to be personal.' Ministers ought to be personal, and they will never be true to their Master till they are...But now we poor craven sons of nobodies have to stand and talk about generalities; but we are afraid to point you out and tell you of your sins personally. But, blessed be God, from that fear I have been delivered long ago. There walketh not a man on the surface of this earth whom I dare not reprove." (Spurgeon)

d. **Felix was afraid**: Hearing this message made Felix **afraid**. Knowing something about his life, at least we can say that he probably understood it. The gospel should make those who are intent on rejecting Jesus **afraid**.

e. **Go away for now; when I have a convenient time I will call for you**: However, Felix was unwilling to *declare* his decision *against* Jesus. Instead, he rejected Jesus under the pretense of *delaying* his decision.

i. Many respond to the gospel in this way; they express their rejection through delay, by delaying their decision to commit to Jesus Christ - but it is rejection none the less. The Bible tells us to come to Jesus in repentance and faith today: *Behold, now is the accepted time; behold, now is the day of salvation* (2 Corinthians 6:2).

ii. It is foolish to trust in **a convenient time** to repent and believe. "Thou sayest, 'Another time.' How knowest thou that thou wilt ever feel again as thou feelest now? This morning, perhaps a voice is saying in thy heart, 'Prepare to meet thy God.' Tomorrow that voice will be hushed. The gaieties of the ball-room and the theatre will put out that voice that warns thee now, and perhaps thou wilt never hear it again. Men all have their warnings, and all men who perish have had a *last warning*. Perhaps this is your last warning." (Spurgeon)

iii. "God to-day is pulling the reigns tight to check you from your lust; perhaps, if to-day you spurn the bit, and rush madly on, he will throw the reigns upon your back, saying, 'Let him alone;' and then it is a dark steeple-chase between hell and earth, and you will run it in mad confusion, never thinking of a hell till you find yourself past warning, past repentance, past faith, past hope." (Spurgeon)

iv. The claims of Jesus are never convenient for us. If we insist on waiting for **a convenient time**, we will wait for an eternity – an eternity spent in agonizing separation from God.

3. (26-27) The motive of Felix's heart is revealed: greed.

Meanwhile he also hoped that money would be given him by Paul, that he might release him. Therefore he sent for him more often and conversed with him. But after two years Porcius Festus succeeded Felix; and Felix, wanting to do the Jews a favor, left Paul bound.

a. **He also hoped that money would be given him by Paul, that he might release him**: Though Felix met often with Paul, it was not honest seeking. He hoped to be paid off with a bribe.

b. **After two years**: Under Roman law, the type of custody Paul was in could only last two years. Felix showed that he was willing to break Roman laws by keeping Paul for more than **two years**.

c. **Felix…left Paul bound**: Felix refused to release Paul, though he knew that he was innocent. He did this for the same reason Pilate condemned Jesus while knowing His innocence. They both acted out of pure political advantage (**wanting to do the Jews a favor**).

i. In a way, people like Felix and Pilate are the guiltiest of those who reject Jesus Christ. They *know* what is right but refuse to do right purely out of the *fear of man*. They have an eternally fatal lack of courage.

Acts 25 - Paul's Trial Before Festus

A. Paul appeals to Caesar to avoid a plot against his life.

1. (1-3) When Felix is replaced, Paul's Jewish accusers decide to re-try the case against Paul.

Now when Festus had come to the province, after three days he went up from Caesarea to Jerusalem. Then the high priest and the chief men of the Jews informed him against Paul; and they petitioned him, asking a favor against him, that he would summon him to Jerusalem—while *they* lay in ambush along the road to kill him.

    a. **Now when Festus had come to the province**: Acts 24 ended with the transition from the governorship of Antonius Felix to that of Porcius **Festus**. Felix was undoubtedly a bad man, but history tells us **Festus** was a basically good man. He governed well, despite all the problems left him by Felix.

        i. The statement, "**after three days he went up from Caesarea to Jerusalem**" hints at the good and energetic leadership of Festus. Upon arriving at **Caesarea**, the capital of the Judean province, he immediately made the trip to **Jerusalem**, probably the most important city of the province.

    b. **Then the high priest and the chief men of the Jews informed him against Paul**: Though it had been two years, the case of Paul was still important to the religious leaders. They hoped to make Paul appear before them again in Jerusalem.

        i. We can see that Paul's generous imprisonment in Caesarea was actually a providential provision of protective custody against the murderous intentions of the religious leaders. It was also a season of rest and replenishment after his years of hard missionary service, preparing him for the challenges in the years ahead.

c. That he would summon him to Jerusalem; while they lay in ambush along the road to kill him: The religious leaders knew that Paul would be acquitted in any fair trial. Therefore, they didn't really want Paul to be put on trial again; they wanted to **ambush** and murder him before the trial could take place.

> i. *These were religious men, religious leaders.* Their actions show the danger of religion that is not in true contact with God. If your religion makes you a liar and a murderer, there is something wrong with your religion.

> ii. "We see a growth of corruption. In Acts 23, where the plot to murder Paul was first launched, we find that it was the zealots who were responsible. Now, in Acts 25, we find that the leaders are initiating the very thing they were only tangentially involved in earlier." (Boice)

2. (4-6a) Festus refuses to put Paul on trial again in Jerusalem.

But Festus answered that Paul should be kept at Caesarea, and that he himself was going *there* shortly. "Therefore," he said, "let those who have authority among you go down with *me* and accuse this man, to see if there is any fault in him." And when he had remained among them more than ten days, he went down to Caesarea.

a. **Festus answered that Paul should be kept at Caesarea**: We don't know if Festus knew the intentions of the Jewish leaders or not. Either way, he refused to grant their request for a change of venue, and this was another way that God protected Paul.

b. **Let those who have authority among you go down with me and accuse this man, to see if there is any fault in him**: Festus was willing to put Paul on trial again, to resolve the matter. Yet he insisted that it would happen in Caesarea, not in Jerusalem.

3. (6b-8) Festus re-opens the trial in Caesarea.

And the next day, sitting on the judgment seat, he commanded Paul to be brought. When he had come, the Jews who had come down from Jerusalem stood about and laid many serious complaints against Paul, which they could not prove, while he answered for himself, "Neither against the law of the Jews, nor against the temple, nor against Caesar have I offended in anything at all."

a. **Sitting on the judgment seat, he commanded Paul to be brought**: Once again Paul was on trial before a Gentile ruler, accused by religious leaders. As before, Paul's life was in danger should he be found guilty.

b. **Laid many serious complaints against Paul, which they could not prove**: As before, the religious leaders made accusations without evidence against Paul. In response, Paul confidently rested on both the evidence and his apparent integrity.

i. Many in the Bible were the target of false accusations (such as Joseph and Daniel). Yet in another sense, *every* follower of Jesus is the target of false accusations by *the accuser of the brethren* (Revelation 12:10). Thankfully, Jesus is our defense against condemnation and false accusation (Romans 8:33-34).

4. (9-12) Paul appeals his case to Caesar.

But Festus, wanting to do the Jews a favor, answered Paul and said, "Are you willing to go up to Jerusalem and there be judged before me concerning these things?" So Paul said, "I stand at Caesar's judgment seat, where I ought to be judged. To the Jews I have done no wrong, as you very well know. For if I am an offender, or have committed anything deserving of death, I do not object to dying; but if there is nothing in these things of which these men accuse me, no one can deliver me to them. I appeal to Caesar." Then Festus, when he had conferred with the council, answered, "You have appealed to Caesar? To Caesar you shall go!"

a. **Festus, wanting to do the Jews a favor**: Though he was a good man, Festus also understood that it was important for him to have and keep good a good relationship with the Jewish people of his province.

b. **Are you willing to go up to Jerusalem and there be judged before me concerning these things?** Festus found it difficult to decide the case. Paul's standing as a Roman citizen apparently prevented Festus from *commanding* the trial to be moved to Jerusalem, so he asked Paul about this.

i. It's interesting to wonder if Festus *knew* of the plot to murder Paul or not. If he did know, then he knowingly asked Paul to walk into an ambush and be murdered. If he did not know, then he merely thought that this would please the religious leaders to have the trial in Jerusalem.

c. **So Paul said, "I stand at Caesar's judgment seat, where I ought to be judged…I appeal to Caesar."** Paul saw through the plot against his life. Perhaps it was through supernatural knowledge, or perhaps through God-given common sense and deduction. Therefore, he demanded to stand trial before Caesar.

i. Rightly and wisely, Paul wanted to avoid martyrdom if he could. He wasn't afraid to face the lions, but he didn't want to put his head in a lion's mouth if he could avoid it.

ii. Paul's appeal made sense. He was convinced that the evidence was on his side and that he could win in a fair trial. He also had reason to wonder if his current judge (Festus) was sympathetic to his accusers, the religious leaders among the Jews.

d. **I appeal to Caesar**: It was the right of every Roman citizen to have his case heard by Caesar himself, after initial trials and appeals failed to reach a satisfactory decision. This was in effect an appeal to the supreme court of the Roman Empire.

i. "God, who has appointed courts of law, also gives his people liberty to use them lawfully." (Calvin, cited in Hughes)

ii. Paul appealed specifically to Caesar Nero, who was later an notorious enemy of Christians. But the first five years of his reign, under the influence of good men around him, Nero was regarded as a wise and just ruler. Paul had no reason at this time to believe that Nero would be anti-Christian.

B. Paul's hearing before King Agrippa.

1. (13-14a) Herod Agrippa and Bernice visit Caesarea.

And after some days King Agrippa and Bernice came to Caesarea to greet Festus. When they had been there many days, Festus laid Paul's case before the king,

a. **King Agrippa and Bernice came to Caesarea**: Herod Agrippa II ruled a client kingdom of the Roman Empire to the northeast of Festus' province. **Agrippa** was known as an expert in Jewish customs and religious matters. Though he did not have jurisdiction over Paul in this case, his hearing of the matter would be helpful for Festus.

i. Of this **King Agrippa**, his great-grandfather had tried to kill Jesus as a baby; his grandfather had John the Baptist beheaded; his father had martyred the first apostle, James. Now Paul stood before the next in line of the Herods, Herod Agrippa.

ii. **Bernice** was Agrippa's sister. Secular history records rumors that their relationship was incestuous.

iii. Herod Agrippa II didn't rule over much territory, but he was of great influence because the emperor gave him the right to oversee the affairs of the temple in Jerusalem and the appointment of the high priest.

b. **Festus laid Paul's case before the king**: Festus, new to his post and perhaps unfamiliar with Jewish traditions and customs, seemed to be somewhat confused by Paul's case. Therefore, even though there was not enough evidence to convict Paul, his investigation continued.

i. The case was probably confusing to Festus because of the lack of concrete evidence. But, *of course* there wasn't enough evidence to convict Paul of the accusations against him, because he had *done no wrong*! This was reason enough for acquittal.

ii. This appearance before **King Agrippa** was really a *hearing*, and not a *trial*; Agrippa did not have jurisdiction in the matter. Yet he could have an important influence upon Festus.

2. (14b-22) Festus explains the case involving Paul to the visiting King Agrippa.

Saying: "There is a certain man left a prisoner by Felix, about whom the chief priests and the elders of the Jews informed *me*, when I was in Jerusalem, asking for a judgment against him. To them I answered, 'It is not the custom of the Romans to deliver any man to destruction before the accused meets the accusers face to face, and has opportunity to answer for himself concerning the charge against him.' Therefore when they had come together, without any delay, the next day I sat on the judgment seat and commanded the man to be brought in. When the accusers stood up, they brought no accusation against him of such things as I supposed, but had some questions against him about their own religion and about a certain Jesus, who had died, whom Paul affirmed to be alive. And because I was uncertain of such questions, I asked whether he was willing to go to Jerusalem and there be judged concerning these matters. But when Paul appealed to be reserved for the decision of Augustus, I commanded him to be kept till I could send him to Caesar." Then Agrippa said to Festus, "I also would like to hear the man myself." "Tomorrow," he said, "you shall hear him."

a. **Asking for a judgment against him**: The religious leaders hoped that Festus would decide against Paul without ever hearing Paul's defense.

b. **It is not the custom of the Romans**: Festus appealed to the strong tradition and system of law. He would not condemn Paul without a fair trial.

c. **They brought no accusation against him of such things as I supposed**: Festus was surprised, thinking that their accusations against Paul were unimportant. Their accusations focused on matters of their **religion** and **a certain Jesus, who had died, whom Paul affirmed to be alive**.

i. It is amusing to think of the religious leaders protesting to Festus that Paul won't stop talking about the risen **Jesus**, and hoping that the governor would *make* Paul stop.

ii. The words "**a certain Jesus**" show that Festus didn't know much about Jesus. It is good to remember that the great and important people of Paul's day didn't know much about Jesus, and they had to be told. "Brethren, this is why we must keep on preaching Jesus Christ, because he is still so little known. The masses of this city are as ignorant of Jesus as Festus was." (Spurgeon)

d. **A certain Jesus, who had died, whom Paul affirmed to be alive**: The limited knowledge Festus *did* have regarding Paul's preaching shows that in his preaching, Paul emphasized the death and resurrection of Jesus.

i. By implication, it also shows that Paul emphasized *the cross*. It's hard to believe that Festus knew that Paul preached that Jesus died, without also hearing about *how* Jesus died.

e. **I also would like to hear the man myself**: Agrippa's curiosity meant that Paul would have another opportunity to speak God's truth to a Gentile ruler. This would be the third such opportunity for Paul in Acts 24-26 (Agrippa, Festus, and now Agrippa).

3. (23) Paul the prisoner is brought before Agrippa, Bernice, and Festus.

So the next day, when Agrippa and Bernice had come with great pomp, and had entered the auditorium with the commanders and the prominent men of the city, at Festus' command Paul was brought in.

a. **When Agrippa and Bernice had come with great pomp**: This was more than a hearing of evidence; it was an *event*. It was held in an **auditorium**, and all the **commanders and the prominent men of the city** were there. This was another tremendous opportunity for Paul.

b. **At Festus' command Paul was brought in**: Surrounded by the important and powerful people of Caesarea and beyond, Paul came into the auditorium. All the **pomp** and pageantry was meant to communicate who was important, and who wasn't important.

i. Most everyone present – excepting, possibly, the Apostle Paul – was wrong in their estimation of who was important and who was not. Paul had an authority and a dignity greater than any of the important people at this hearing.

ii. "All these very important people would have been greatly surprised, and not a little scandalized, could they have foreseen the relative estimates that later generations would form of them and of the prisoner who now stood before them to state his case." (Bruce)

4. (24-27) Festus makes an opening statement at the hearing of Paul before Agrippa.

And Festus said: "King Agrippa and all the men who are here present with us, you see this man about whom the whole assembly of the Jews petitioned me, both at Jerusalem and here, crying out that he was not fit to live any longer. But when I found that he had committed nothing deserving of death, and that he himself had appealed to Augustus, I decided to send him. I have nothing certain to write to my lord concerning him. Therefore I have brought him out before you, and especially before you, King Agrippa, so that after the examination has taken place I may have something to write. For it seems to me unreasonable to send a prisoner and not to specify the charges against him."

a. **When I found that he had committed nothing deserving of death**: It was important for Luke to record these words of Festus. They clearly state that Festus understood that Paul was innocent.

b. **So that after the examination has taken place I may have something to write**: Festus wanted to use this trial to prepare an official brief for Paul's upcoming trial before Caesar.

i. Festus simply could not send Paul to Caesar with a letter that said, "I really don't know what this man is accused of and he is probably innocent of any wrongdoing, but I thought I should send him to you anyway." That was no way to be popular with Caesar.

c. **It seems to me unreasonable to send a prisoner and not to specify the charges against him**: Paul was so innocent that Festus could not actually describe or **specify** the charges against him.

Acts 26 - Paul's Defense Before King Agrippa

A. Paul speaks in his hearing before King Agrippa.

1. (1-3) Paul's introductory words.

Then Agrippa said to Paul, "You are permitted to speak for yourself." So Paul stretched out his hand and answered for himself: "I think myself happy, King Agrippa, because today I shall answer for myself before you concerning all the things of which I am accused by the Jews, especially because you are expert in all customs and questions which have to do with the Jews. Therefore I beg you to hear me patiently.

a. **Then Agrippa said to Paul**: Paul stood before the man whose great-grandfather had tried to kill Jesus as a baby; his grandfather had John the Baptist beheaded; his father had martyred the first apostle, James. Agrippa's family history made him unlikely to receive Paul warmly.

b. **I think myself happy, King Agrippa, because today I shall answer for myself before you**: Though he was a prisoner, Paul *was* **happy** to speak before Agrippa. First, because he was pleased to have the evidence of his case examined closely by the highest officials, but also because he was pleased to preach the gospel to kings and rulers.

i. In the auditorium in the city of Caesarea Paul spoke to Festus, Agrippa, Bernice, commanders of the Roman Legion, and all the prominent men of Caesarea (Acts 25:23). This was a tremendous opportunity, and Paul was certainly **happy** for that opportunity.

ii. This was a partial fulfillment of what the Lord promised Paul at his conversion: *Go, for he is a chosen vessel of Mine to bear My name before Gentiles, kings, and the children of Israel.* (Acts 9:15)

2. (4-5) Paul's early life as a faithful Jew and Pharisee.

"My manner of life from my youth, which was spent from the beginning among my own nation at Jerusalem, all the Jews know. They knew me from the first, if they were willing to testify, that according to the strictest sect of our religion I lived a Pharisee.

a. **My manner of life from my youth, which was spent from the beginning among my own nation at Jerusalem**: Paul was born in Tarsus, several hundred miles from Jerusalem. Yet at a relatively young age he came to live **at Jerusalem**.

b. **According to the strictest sect of our religion I lived a Pharisee**: Not only was Paul a faithful Jew, but was known as a faithful man among the Jews, living **according to the strictest sect of** the Pharisees.

3. (6-8) Paul as a faithful, believing Jew confronts Agrippa for his lack of faith.

And now I stand and am judged for the hope of the promise made by God to our fathers. To this *promise* our twelve tribes, earnestly serving *God* night and day, hope to attain. For this hope's sake, King Agrippa, I am accused by the Jews. Why should it be thought incredible by you that God raises the dead?

a. **Now I stand and am judged for the hope of the promise made by God to our fathers**: Paul made it clear that in both his heart and mind, he remained a faithful Jew. His trust in Jesus was an outgrowth of his trust in **the hope of the promise made by God** and he argued that **for this hope's sake… I am accused by the Jews**.

b. **Why should it be thought incredible by you that God raises the dead?** Since Agrippa was an *expert in all customs and questions which have to do with the Jews* (Acts 26:3), he should have understood the belief that God could, or would, raise the dead.

i. **Why should it be thought incredible** that God can do *anything?* As Jesus said, *with God all things are possible* (Matthew 19:26). Yet it should be especially easy for Agrippa to believe **that God raises the dead**, given some clear statements in the Old Testament (such as Job 19:25-27), the nature of God, and the intuitive grasp of the eternal among mankind.

4. (9-11) Paul explains that at one time he persecuted the followers of Jesus.

"Indeed, I myself thought I must do many things contrary to the name of Jesus of Nazareth. This I also did in Jerusalem, and many of the saints I shut up in prison, having received authority from the chief priests; and when they were put to death, I cast my vote against *them.* And I punished them often in every synagogue and compelled *them* to blaspheme; and being exceedingly enraged against them, I persecuted *them* even to foreign cities.

a. **I myself thought I must do many things contrary to the name of Jesus of Nazareth**: Before his conversion, Paul believed he **must** persecute the followers of Jesus. Some he imprisoned (**shut up in prison**), some he killed (**they were put to death**), and some he forced to renounce Jesus (**compelled them to blaspheme**).

i. Paul later speaks of the great regret he had over his prior life as a persecutor (1 Corinthians 15:9, 1 Timothy 1:15). Perhaps the fact that he **compelled them to blaspheme** weighed especially on his conscience.

b. **I cast my vote against them**: This clearly implies that Paul was a member of the Sanhedrin, having a **vote** against Christians who were tried before the Sanhedrin (as Stephen was in Acts 7).

i. If Paul was a member of the Sanhedrin, it also means that at that time he was married, because it was required for all members of the Sanhedrin. Since as a Christian, he was single (1 Corinthians 7:7-9), it may mean that Paul's wife either died or deserted him when he became a Christian.

c. **Being exceedingly enraged against them**: Before his conversion, Paul was an angry man. His great rage showed that his relationship with God was not right, despite his diligent religious observance.

5. (12-15) Jesus reveals Himself to Paul on the road to Damascus.

"While thus occupied, as I journeyed to Damascus with authority and commission from the chief priests, at midday, O king, along the road I saw a light from heaven, brighter than the sun, shining around me and those who journeyed with me. And when we all had fallen to the ground, I heard a voice speaking to me and saying in the Hebrew language, 'Saul, Saul, why are you persecuting Me? *It is* hard for you to kick against the goads.' So I said, 'Who are You, Lord?' And He said, 'I am Jesus, whom you are persecuting.

a. **As I journeyed to Damascus**: This is Paul's fullest account yet of his experience on the Damascus Road. He first noted that he went on his mission of hate and persecution with the **authority and commission** of the same religious leaders who now accused him.

b. **I saw a light from heaven, brighter than the sun**: Paul *literally* saw the light before he *figuratively* saw the light. Paul went to Damascus supremely confident that he was right; it took a light brighter than the **midday** sun to show him he was wrong.

c. **Saul, Saul, why are you persecuting Me? It is hard for you to kick against the goads**: Paul repeats the words from Acts 9:3-6. These words emphasize:

- The personal appeal of Jesus (**Saul, Saul**).
- The misdirected nature of his persecution (**Me**).
- The folly of persecuting Jesus (**Why**).

d. **I am Jesus, whom you are persecuting**: These words changed Paul's world. He immediately understood that Jesus was alive, not dead. He understood that Jesus reigned in glory instead of being damned in shame. He realized that in persecuting the followers of Jesus he persecuted Jesus, and in persecuting Jesus he fought against the God of his fathers.

> i. Paul had to *repent* – make a transformation of mind leading to transformed action – instantly. Paul lived a moral life, so he didn't have to repent of immorality – but of misguided religious zeal and wrong ideas about God.

6. (16-18) Jesus commissions Paul on the road to Damascus.

But rise and stand on your feet; for I have appeared to you for this purpose, to make you a minister and a witness both of the things which you have seen and of the things which I will yet reveal to you. I will deliver you from the *Jewish* people, as well as *from* the Gentiles, to whom I now send you, to open their eyes, *in order* to turn *them* from darkness to light, and *from* the power of Satan to God, that they may receive forgiveness of sins and an inheritance among those who are sanctified by faith in Me.'

a. **But rise and stand on your feet**: Jesus called Paul up to his feet. This was not because his humility wasn't proper, but because he was sent to go somewhere, and he had to **rise and stand on** his **feet** if he was going to go anywhere. This was a way to say, "Come now, let's be going."

b. **For I have appeared to you for this purpose**: The religious leaders sent Paul to Damascus for a purpose, with authority and commission. Now he must choose *another* **purpose**, the **purpose** of Jesus.

c. **For I have appeared to you for this purpose, to make you a minister and a witness**. Paul was commissioned to be a **minister**, which means he was to be a *servant* of **the things which** he had **seen, and of the things which** Jesus would **yet reveal** to him. The commission of the Christian is not to make the message or his testimony serve him; he is called to *serve* the message.

d. **To make you a minister and a witness**: Paul was also called to be **a witness** of those **things**. The commission of the Christian is not to create experience or create the message, but to **witness** it and experience it.

e. **To whom I now send you, to open their eyes**: Jesus described the work Paul would do. At that moment on the road to Damascus Paul was blinded by the great light from heaven. *His* eyes were not yet opened physically, but Jesus sent him to **open** the **eyes** of others (both Jews and Gentiles).

> i. Jesus then told Paul of four results that would come from the opening of the eyes:
>
> - Being turned **from darkness to light**.
> - Being turned **from the power of Satan to God**.
> - To **receive forgiveness of sins**.
> - To receive **an inheritance among** God's people.

f. **Among those who are sanctified by faith in Me**: This was how Jesus described His followers, His people, His family. They **are sanctified** (set apart from sin and self), and they **are sanctified by faith in** Jesus (not by works or spiritual achievement, but by their connection of love and trust to Jesus).

> i. The auditorium where Paul spoke was filled with important people and dignitaries (Acts 25:23), but we may fairly imagine Paul speaking these words with special attention on and focus towards Agrippa. This was an invitation to Agrippa to become one of **those who are sanctified by faith in** Jesus. His eyes could be opened just as Paul's were on the road to Damascus.

7. (19-20) Paul's obedience to Jesus.

"Therefore, King Agrippa, I was not disobedient to the heavenly vision, but declared first to those in Damascus and in Jerusalem, and throughout all the region of Judea, and *then* to the Gentiles, that they should repent, turn to God, and do works befitting repentance.

a. **I was not disobedient to the heavenly vision**: Given the experience Paul just described, this was logical. No one should disobey the God who revealed Himself so powerfully. Paul made a strong case before Agrippa and all there as to *why* he preached and lived the way he did.

b. **That they should repent, turn to God, and do works befitting repentance**: This is a neat summary of Paul's message. Paul sets **repent** and **turn to God** close, understanding them as two aspects of the same action. One can't **turn to God** unless they do **repent** – and actions will confirm true repentance (**do works befitting repentance**).

8. (21-23) Paul summarizes his defense.

For these reasons the Jews seized me in the temple and tried to kill **me. Therefore, having obtained help from God, to this day I stand, witnessing both to small and great, saying no other things than those which the prophets and Moses said would come–that the Christ would suffer, that He would be the first to rise from the dead, and would proclaim light to the *Jewish* people and to the Gentiles."**

a. **For these reasons the Jews seized me in the temple and tried to kill me**: Paul plainly states the truth of the case. It was only because he sought to bring the gospel of Jesus Christ to the Gentiles that the Jews **seized** him and **tried to kill** him. It wasn't because he was a political revolutionary or because he offended the sanctity of the temple.

b. **Having obtained help from God, to this day I stand, witnessing both to small and great**: During his more than two years of confinement, Paul *did* receive **help from God**. Yet to that point it wasn't help that released him; it was help that gave him opportunity and ability to speak to **small and great** about who Jesus is and what Jesus had done.

i. This seems to have been fine with Paul. He was more interested in telling people about Jesus than in his personal freedom.

c. **Saying no other things than those which the prophets and Moses said would come**: Paul also stated his unswerving commitment to the same gospel, because that gospel was based solidly on the Word of God (**the prophets and Moses**) not on the traditions or spiritual experiences of man.

d. **That the Christ would suffer, that He would be the first to rise from the dead, and would proclaim light to the Jewish people and to the Gentiles**. These were the three main points to Paul's preaching: Jesus' death, His resurrection, and the preaching of this good news to the whole world, without respect to either Jew or Gentile.

B. The response from Festus and Agrippa.

1. (24-26) Festus asserts Paul is mad, and Paul responds.

Now as he thus made his defense, Festus said with a loud voice, "Paul, you are beside yourself! Much learning is driving you mad!" But he said, "I am not mad, most noble Festus, but speak the words of truth and reason. For the king, before whom I also speak freely, knows these things; for I am convinced that none of these things escapes his attention, since this thing was not done in a corner."

a. **Paul, you are beside yourself! Much learning is driving you mad!** Paul was obviously an intelligent man, a man of **much learning**. Still, at this moment Festus thought he was crazy, saying this **with a loud voice** among all present. Given Paul's conduct at this hearing, there are some reasons someone like Festus might think Paul was **mad**.

- Though a prisoner in chains, he said he was happy (Acts 26:2).
- He insisted that God could raise the dead (Acts 26:8, 23).
- He experienced a heavenly vision and changed his life because of it (Acts 26:14-19).
- He was more concerned about proclaiming Jesus than his personal freedom (Acts 26:22).
- He believed in a message of hope and redemption for all humanity, not only Jews or only Gentiles (Acts 26:23).

    i. The gospel, when properly proclaimed and lived, will make some people think we are crazy. Paul put it this way: *the message of the cross is foolishness to those who are perishing* (1 Corinthians 1:18).

b. **I am not mad, most noble Festus, but speak the words of truth and reason**: Yet, Paul knew that not only his gospel was *true*, it was also *reasonable*. God may sometimes act *above* reason, but never *contrary* to reason.

c. **For the king...knows these things...none of these things escapes his attention**: Festus recently came from Rome, and perhaps didn't know much of what had happened with Jesus and the early Christian movement. Yet King Agrippa *did* know, and Paul appealed to *his* knowledge of the open, historical events that were the foundation for Christian faith – things that were **not done in a corner**.

    i. Paul's message was characterized by **truth** and **reason**, because it was based on *historical events* (such as the crucifixion and resurrection of Jesus), things which were **not done in a corner**, but open to examination.

    ii. The historical foundation of Paul's message made it **true**. As for **reason**, it simply isn't reasonable to ignore or deny things that actually happen. Who Jesus is and what He did *must* be accounted for.

2. (27-29) Agrippa is *almost* persuaded to become a Christian.

"King Agrippa, do you believe the prophets? I know that you do believe."
Then Agrippa said to Paul, "You almost persuade me to become a
Christian." And Paul said, "I would to God that not only you, but also

all who hear me today, might become both almost and altogether such as I am, except for these chains."

a. **King Agrippa, do you believe the prophets? I know that you do believe**: Paul used Festus' outburst to appeal to what King Agrippa knew (Acts 26:26). Then Paul brought the challenge directly to Agrippa, asking him: "**do you believe?**"

i. Paul didn't first ask Agrippa if he believed on Jesus; he asked, "**Do you believe the prophets?**" Paul did this because he knew that if Agrippa did believe the prophets, truth and reason would lead him to believe upon Jesus. He wanted to connect what Agrippa already believed to what he should believe.

ii. With this, Paul brought the challenge and a point of decision directly to Agrippa. This is a good and often necessary part of the presentation of the message of who Jesus is and what He did for us – calling the listener to *decision*.

b. **You almost persuade me to become a Christian**: When Paul called Agrippa to faith in the prophets and in Jesus, Agrippa *refused* to believe and to say he believed. Paul **almost** persuaded him.

i. The literal idea behind **almost** is "in a little, you seek to persuade me to act a Christian." The meaning of *little* could be "in a short time" or it could mean "there is little distance between me and Christianity." However close Agrippa was to becoming a believer, it wasn't close enough.

ii. If the sense is "almost," Agrippa's reply is especially sorry. Of course, **almost** being a Christian means that you **almost** have eternal life and will **almost** be delivered from the judgment of hell; but **almost** isn't enough.

iii. Far from being admired for how far he did come, Agrippa condemned himself even more by admitting how close he has come to the gospel and how clearly he has understood it, while still rejecting it.

c. **To become a Christian**: We may say that Paul recounted the words of Jesus on the road to Damascus, saying what a Christian is (Acts 26:18). Agrippa didn't want it.

- He didn't want to turn from darkness to light.
- He didn't want to turn from the power of Satan to the power of God.
- He didn't want to receive forgiveness of sins.
- He didn't want a place among God's people.

• He didn't want to become one of those set apart by faith in Jesus.

d. **You almost persuade me to become a Christian**: What stopped Agrippa short? Why did he only **almost** become a Christian?

i. Why was Agrippa only **almost** persuaded? One answer was the person sitting next to him - Bernice. She was a sinful, immoral companion, and he may have rightly realized that becoming a Christian would mean losing her and his other immoral friends. He was unwilling to make that sacrifice.

ii. On the other side of Agrippa sat Festus - a man's man, a no-nonsense man, a man who thought Paul was crazy. Perhaps Agrippa thought, "I can't become a Christian. Festus will think I'm also crazy." Because he wanted the praise of men, he rejected Jesus. "Alas, how many are influenced by fear of men! Oh, you cowards, will you be damned out of fear? Will you sooner let your souls perish than show your manhood by telling a poor mortal that you defy his scorn? Dare you not follow the right though all men in the world should call you to do the wrong? Oh, you cowards! You cowards! How you deserve to perish who have not enough soul to call your souls your own, but cower down before the sneers of fools!" (Spurgeon)

iii. In front of Agrippa was Paul - a strong man, a noble man, and man of wisdom and character – but a man in chains. Did Agrippa say, "Well, if I became a Christian, I might end up in chains like Paul; or at the least, I would have to associate with him. We can't have that - I'm an important person." "O that men were wise enough to see that suffering for Christ is honour, that loss for truth is gain, that the truest dignity rests in wearing the chain upon the arm rather than endure the chain upon the soul." (Spurgeon)

e. **I would to God that not only you, but also all who hear me today, might become both almost and altogether such as I am, except for these chains**: Paul declared his continued trust in the gospel of Jesus Christ. He did not retreat from his stand one inch, despite his long imprisonment for the sake of the gospel.

f. **Except for these chains**: With a dramatic gesture, Paul showed that even though he was in chains, he had more freedom in Jesus than any of the royalty listening had.

i. "O that men were wise enough to see that suffering for Christ is honour, that loss for truth is gain, that the truest dignity rests in wearing the chain upon the arm rather than endure the chain upon the soul." (Spurgeon)

3. (30-32) Agrippa admits Paul's innocence, yet forwards him to Caesar.

When he had said these things, the king stood up, as well as the governor and Bernice and those who sat with them; and when they had gone aside, they talked among themselves, saying, "This man is doing nothing deserving of death or chains." Then Agrippa said to Festus, "This man might have been set free if he had not appealed to Caesar."

a. **When he had said these things, the king stood up**: Paul's direct challenge was too much for Agrippa, Festus, and the others on the platform. It was getting too close, to personal, and they felt they had to end it quickly by standing up and ending the proceedings.

b. **This man is doing nothing deserving of death or chains**: Agrippa also saw there was no *evidence* offered to support the accusations against Paul, and he respected Paul's great integrity even while rejecting Paul's gospel. So, Agrippa and the others pronounced a "not guilty" verdict.

c. **This man might have been set free if he had not appealed to Caesar**: Yet, Paul could not be **set free**, because he had **appealed to Caesar**. It seems that once an appeal was made, it could not be retracted.

d. **Appealed to Caesar**: It seems that Paul might have been set free here if he had not appealed to Caesar. So, was Paul's appeal to Caesar a good thing or a bad thing?

i. Some people believe it was a bad thing, and that Paul was trusting in the power of the Roman legal system instead of in the power of God. They say that Paul might have been set free by Agrippa if he had not appealed to Caesar.

ii. However, we should see the fulfillment of God's plan through all these events. By his appeal to Caesar, Paul will have the opportunity to preach to the Roman Emperor the way he had to Felix, Festus, and Agrippa, thus fulfilling the promise that Paul would *bear My name before...kings* (Acts 9:15).

iii. The appeal to Caesar, and his subsequent journey to Rome at the Empire's expense, were also the fulfillment of the Holy Spirit's purpose that Paul should go to Rome (Acts 19:21, 23:11). This also answered a long-standing desire in the heart of Paul to visit the already present Christian community there (Romans 1:9-13).

Acts 27 - Shipwreck on the Way to Rome

A. From Caesarea to Fair Havens.

1. (1-2) Paul and his companions leave Caesarea.

And when it was decided that we should sail to Italy, they delivered Paul and some other prisoners to *one* **named Julius, a centurion of the Augustan Regiment. So, entering a ship of Adramyttium, we put to sea, meaning to sail along the coasts of Asia. Aristarchus, a Macedonian of Thessalonica, was with us.**

> a. **Julius, a centurion of the Augustan Regiment**: We don't know much about this specific **Augustan Regiment** (several held that title), but it was common for Roman soldiers to accompany the transport of criminals, those awaiting trial, and merchant ships filled with grain going from Egypt to Rome.

> b. **Aristarchus, a Macedonian of Thessalonica, was with us**: Aristarchus and Luke (notice the **us** of verse 2 and beyond) accompanied Paul on this voyage. The favor Paul enjoyed from Julius (as in Acts 27:3) meant he was allowed to take these companions with him.

2. (3-8) From Caesarea to Fair Havens.

And the next *day* **we landed at Sidon. And Julius treated Paul kindly and gave** *him* **liberty to go to his friends and receive care. When we had put to sea from there, we sailed under** *the shelter of* **Cyprus, because the winds were contrary. And when we had sailed over the sea which is off Cilicia and Pamphylia, we came to Myra,** *a city* **of Lycia. There the centurion found an Alexandrian ship sailing to Italy, and he put us on board. When we had sailed slowly many days, and arrived with difficulty off Cnidus, the wind not permitting us to proceed, we sailed under** *the shelter of* **Crete off Salmone. Passing it with difficulty, we came to a place called Fair Havens, near the city** *of* **Lasea.**

a. **Julius treated Paul kindly and gave him liberty to go to his friends and receive care**: The ship first sailed to **Sidon**, where Paul met with Christians and could **receive care** from them. The Roman commander gave Paul a lot of liberty because he wasn't a condemned man (yet), but waiting for trial before Caesar. Paul's godly character and display of Christian love were also helpful in gaining favor.

> i. Paul was different from the other prisoners on board. The other prisoners were probably all condemned criminals being sent to Rome to die in the arena.

b. **An Alexandrian ship sailing to Italy**: This was a grain freighter, taking grain grown in Egypt to Italy. According to Hughes, the typical grain freighter of that period was 140 feet long and 36 feet wide. It had one mast with a big square sail, and instead of what we think of as a rudder, it steered with two paddles on the back part of the ship. They were sturdy, but because of its design, it couldn't sail into the wind.

c. **Along the coast of Cilicia and Pamphylia, we came to Myra...off Cnidus...off Salmone...Fair Havens**: The ship began to make its way west, eventually coming to the port called **Fair Havens** on the south side of the island of Crete.

3. (9-10) Paul's advice to the captain and crew of the ship.

Now when much time had been spent, and sailing was now dangerous because the Fast was already over, Paul advised them, saying, "Men, I perceive that this voyage will end with disaster and much loss, not only of the cargo and ship, but also our lives."

a. **Sailing was now dangerous because the Fast was already over**: The **Fast** date in question here was probably October 5, which was the date of the Day of Atonement in A.D. 59. The idea is that as winter approached, the weather became more dangerous for sailing.

> i. "The dangerous season for sailing began about September 14 and lasted until November 11; after the latter date all navigation on the open sea came to an end until winter was over." (Bruce)

b. **Paul advised them, saying, "Men, I perceive that this voyage will end with disaster and much loss, not only of the cargo and ship, but also our lives"**: Paul did not necessarily speak here as a prophet of God, but perhaps as an experienced traveler on the Mediterranean, having already traveled some 3,500 miles by sea. Knowing the seasons and conditions – and perhaps with supernatural wisdom – Paul advised that they not go on.

i. 2 Corinthians 11:25 tells us that by this time, Paul had already shipwrecked three times. He, like most everyone, knew that sailing in this season was dangerous.

4. (11-12) The decision is made to sail on.

Nevertheless the centurion was more persuaded by the helmsman and the owner of the ship than by the things spoken by Paul. And because the harbor was not suitable to winter in, the majority advised to set sail from there also, if by any means they could reach Phoenix, a harbor of Crete opening toward the southwest and northwest, *and* winter *there*.

a. **Nevertheless the centurion was more persuaded by the helmsman and the owner of the ship than by the things spoken by Paul**: It isn't a surprise that the **centurion** had more respect for the opinion of the chief sailor and the owner of the ship than for Paul's opinion. They both had much to lose if the ship didn't make it to Rome.

b. **Because the harbor was not suitable to winter in**: The name *Fair Havens* (Acts 27:8) was not entirely accurate - at least not accurate in the winter. The position of the bay made it vulnerable to winter winds and storms. It was not an ideal place to wait out the coming season.

i. It was also not a *fun* place to spend all winter, and the crew of the ship didn't look forward to months in a small town. One commentator suggests that the local Chamber of Commerce named the place "Fair Havens."

c. **The majority advised to set sail from there also**: Taking a vote of the crew, they decided to sail on to the harbor of **Phoenix**. The port at Phoenix was on the same island of Crete and only about 40 miles away. It didn't seem crazy to them to make it to Phoenix and be spared a miserable winter at Fair Havens.

i. Yet they failed to properly regard the wise word from the Apostle Paul, which turned out to be prophetic: *This voyage will end with disaster and much loss.* They should have listened to Paul, and later told them so (Acts 27:21).

B. The stormy journey from Fair Havens to Malta.

1. (13-16) A good start is made from Crete, but the ship quickly encounters great difficulty in a storm.

When the south wind blew softly, supposing that they had obtained *their* desire, putting out to sea, they sailed close by Crete. But not long after, a tempestuous head wind arose, called Euroclydon. So when the ship was caught, and could not head into the wind, we let *her* drive. And

running under *the shelter of* an island called Clauda, we secured the skiff with difficulty.

a. **When the south wind blew softly**: The winds looked favorable, so they set out from Fair Havens. Just beyond Crete, the wind turned dangerous.

b. **A tempestuous head wind arose, called Euroclydon**: This wind was feared among ancient sailors for its destructive power. Helpless to navigate with this wind in their face, all they could do is **let her drive**.

c. **We secured the skiff with difficulty**: The skiff was normally towed behind the boat, but taken aboard at bad weather – so they brought it in.

i. *We* **secured the skiff with difficulty** may be quite literal from Luke's perspective. The doctor was probably pressed into service pulling ropes.

2. (17-19) Measures taken to save the ship.

When they had taken it on board, they used cables to undergird the ship; and fearing lest they should run aground on the Syrtis *Sands,* they struck sail and so were driven. And because we were exceedingly tempest-tossed, the next *day* they lightened the ship. On the third *day* we threw the ship's tackle overboard with our own hands.

a. **They used cables to undergird the ship**: This was a normal emergency measure, helping to prevent the ship from breaking apart in a storm.

b. **They struck sail and so were driven**: The fear of crashing **on the Sytris Sands** (an infamous wrecking area of ships off the coast of North Africa) made them go with the wind and give up hope of navigating the ship in the storm.

c. **They lightened the ship... threw the ship's tackle overboard**: These were the final two things done to help save the ship – first throwing over the cargo and then the ship's equipment. Even with this, the ship continued to drive in the wind *for many days.*

3. (20) The hopelessness of crew and passengers.

Now when neither sun nor stars appeared for many days, and no small tempest beat on *us,* all hope that we would be saved was finally given up.

a. **When neither sun nor stars appeared for many days**: On the open sea they could only navigate with either the **sun** or the **stars**. Many days in this storm drove the crew to desperation. The great **tempest** drove them blind westward across the Mediterranean.

b. **All hope that we would be saved was finally given up**: Acts 27:37 tells us there were 276 people on board, both passengers and crew. It seems that they had all **finally given up**, and had no hope of survival.

4. (21-22) Paul tells the crew to take heart.

But after long abstinence from food, then Paul stood in the midst of them and said, "Men, you should have listened to me, and not have sailed from Crete and incurred this disaster and loss. And now I urge you to take heart, for there will be no loss of life among you, but only of the ship."

a. **After long abstinence from food**: We shouldn't think that the sailors fasted and sought God. Instead, their **abstinence from food** probably was due to the poor condition of the food and seasickness.

b. **Men, you should have listened to me**: Paul could not resist (rightly so) an "I told you so" moment. Had they listened to his wisdom at Acts 27:10, they would not be in this seemingly hopeless situation.

c. **I urge you to take heart**: As a messenger of God, Paul hoped to bring hope to these passengers and crew who had given up all hope. His point wasn't simply to tell them he was right, but to bring them good news.

d. **There will be no loss of life among you, but only of the ship**: This was a mixed message. The promise that no **life** would be lost was hard to believe if the **ship** were to be lost. It was also bad news to hear that the voyage would be a complete financial loss, with the cargo already overboard (Acts 27:18) and the ship to be lost.

5. (23-26) Paul tells the crew of the angelic visit.

"For there stood by me this night an angel of the God to whom I belong and whom I serve, saying, 'Do not be afraid, Paul; you must be brought before Caesar; and indeed God has granted you all those who sail with you.' Therefore take heart, men, for I believe God that it will be just as it was told me. However, we must run aground on a certain island."

a. **There stood by me this night an angel**: God sent an angelic messenger to Paul to bring good, encouraging news when all else seemed hopeless. This wasn't a direct appearance of Jesus (as in Jerusalem, Acts 23:11), but of **an angel**. God's word came to Paul different ways at different times.

b. **An angel of the God to whom I belong and whom I serve**: The angelic presence was an encouragement; this was also. Paul remembered that he *belonged* to God and that he *served* God. God never forgets those who belong to Him and serve Him.

i. That doesn't mean everything goes easy for those who **belong** to God and **serve** Him. Paul's present calamity proved that. It does mean that God's watchful eye and active care is present even in that kind of calamity.

c. **Do not be afraid**: There was a *reason* Paul needed to hear this. He was also afraid in the storm (at least some of the time). In his strong moments, Paul *knew* he would make it to Rome because God promised it. Yet in the storm (here, a literal storm) it was easy to doubt and Paul needed the assurance.

d. **Indeed God has granted you all those who sail with you**: This implies that Paul *sought* God for the safety of everyone on the ship. He already had a promise for his own safety, but that wasn't enough for Paul. He labored in prayer for the safety and blessing of those with him, believers and not-yet-believers. Paul cared for them and loved them, and he labored for them in prayer until God **granted** the apostle their safety.

e. **Therefore take heart, men**: Paul encouraged them to take heart just a moment before (Acts 27:22). He repeats the encouragement again, this time in light of the revelation from God. "You have reason to take heart – God has given me assurance of your safety, and **I believe God**."

i. Paul *couldn't keep his hope to himself*. He had to pass it on to both the believers on board the ship and to those who had not yet believed.

f. **I believe God that it will be just as it was told me**: Paul's confident word to the troubled sailors on a storm-tossed ship express the essence of what it means to put our faith in God and His Word. God said it to Paul (through an angel) and Paul said, "**I believe God**."

i. Take note of what Paul said: "**I believe God**." He didn't say, "I believe *in* God." Every demon in hell agrees with the existence of God. Paul declared his total confidence in God's knowledge of his situation and His promise in his situation.

ii. Paul believed God when there was nothing else to believe. He couldn't believe the sailors, the ship, the sails, the wind, the centurion, human ingenuity or anything else - only God. This was not a fair-weather faith; he believed God in the midst of the storm, when circumstances were at their worst. Paul would say along with Job: *Though He slay me, yet will I trust Him* (Job 13:15). The storm and the danger were real, but God was more real to Paul than the dreadful circumstances.

iii. Paul was not *ashamed* to say that he believed God. "I would to God that all Christians were prepared to throw down the gauntlet and to come out straight; for if God be not true let us not pretend to trust him, and if the gospel be a lie let us be honest enough to confess it." (Spurgeon)

iv. Paul's unshakable confidence in God made him a leader among men, even though he was a prisoner of Rome.

g. **However, we must run aground on a certain island**: This was mixed news, and in these circumstances to **run aground** might be fairly called *to shipwreck*. Paul essentially said, "We're all going to shipwreck on an unknown island, but everyone will be alright."

i. **A certain island** means that God did not tell Paul *everything* about what was going to happen. Paul had to trust that *God* knew which island they would **run aground** on, even if Paul didn't know.

6. (27-29) Drawing near land.

Now when the fourteenth night had come, as we were driven up and down in the Adriatic *Sea*, about midnight the sailors sensed that they were drawing near some land. And they took soundings and found *it* to be twenty fathoms; and when they had gone a little farther, they took soundings again and found *it* to be fifteen fathoms. Then, fearing lest we should run aground on the rocks, they dropped four anchors from the stern, and prayed for day to come.

a. **When the fourteenth night had come**: They spent two entire weeks in the misery and terror of the storm.

b. **The sailors sensed that they were drawing near some land**: Sensing land was near (probably by hearing the breakers in the distance) the sailors took proper precautions against being crashed against some unknown rocks (**they dropped four anchors from the stern, and prayed for day to come**).

c. **And prayed for day to come**: The threat of shipwreck and death made them men of prayer.

7. (30-32) Some sailors seek to escape from the ship.

And as the sailors were seeking to escape from the ship, when they had let down the skiff into the sea, under pretense of putting out anchors from the prow, Paul said to the centurion and the soldiers, "Unless these men stay in the ship, you cannot be saved." Then the soldiers cut away the ropes of the skiff and let it fall off.

a. **As the sailors were seeing to escape from the ship**: These **sailors** didn't care for the passengers. Seeing a chance to save their own lives in the darkness, the hoped to abandon the ship leaving the passengers.

b. **Paul said to the centurion and the soldiers, "Unless these men stay in the ship, you cannot be saved."** Paul knew two reasons why they had to stay together. First, the ship's passengers desperately needed the crew's expertise, and it would be fatal if the crew abandoned the passengers. Second, Paul probably sensed that God's promise to give him the lives of the whole ship's company assumed that they would stay together.

c. **The soldiers cut away the ropes of the skiff and let it fall off**: At this point, it seems the soldiers had great trust in Paul.

8. (33-38) Paul encourages the passengers and crew at dawn.

And as day was about to dawn, Paul implored *them* all to take food, saying, "Today is the fourteenth day you have waited and continued without food, and eaten nothing. Therefore I urge you to take nourishment, for this is for your survival, since not a hair will fall from the head of any of you." And when he had said these things, he took bread and gave thanks to God in the presence of them all; and when he had broken *it* he began to eat. Then they were all encouraged, and also took food themselves. And in all we were two hundred and seventy-six persons on the ship. So when they had eaten enough, they lightened the ship and threw out the wheat into the sea.

a. **Since not a hair will fall from the head of any of you**: Paul had a word of faith and confidence from the Lord for the frightened crew and passengers. But this word only benefited those who *believed* it.

i. God has scores of promises of His comfort and care for us in desperate times, but they only benefit us if we *believe* them.

b. **And when he had said these things, he took bread and gave thanks to God in the presence of them all; and when he had broken it he began to eat. Then they were all encouraged**: There are hints that Paul regarded this meal as communion at the Lord's Table for the Christians present.

c. **They lightened the ship**: Throwing **out the wheat into the sea** reflected their great desperation. This was the last of the essential cargo of the ship, after they had already lightened the ship (Acts 27:18). This was a struggle for survival.

9. (39-41) The ship runs aground and breaks apart.

When it was day, they did not recognize the land; but they observed a bay with a beach, onto which they planned to run the ship if possible. And they let go the anchors and left *them* in the sea, meanwhile loosing the rudder ropes; and they hoisted the mainsail to the wind and made for shore. But striking a place where two seas met, they ran the ship

aground; and the prow stuck fast and remained immovable, but the stern was being broken up by the violence of the waves.

a. **They did not recognize the land**: They did not know it at first, but they came to an island called Malta. The place where the ship came aground is now called St. Paul's Bay.

i. "Only the rarest conjunction of favorable circumstances could have brought about such a fortunate ending to their apparently hopeless situation…all these circumstances are united in St. Paul's Bay." (Ramsay, cited by Bruce)

ii. "If they missed Malta, there would have been nothing for it but to hold on for 200 miles until they struck the Tunisian coast, and no one could have expected the ship to survive that long." (Bruce)

b. **The prow stuck fast and remained immovable, but the stern was being broken up by the violence of the waves**: As the ship was **stuck fast** on shore, the still-stormy sea pounded the weakened vessel and started breaking it apart. All on board had to jump ship or be **broken up** with it.

10. (42-44) Leaving the ship and coming safely to shore.

And the soldiers' plan was to kill the prisoners, lest any of them should swim away and escape. But the centurion, wanting to save Paul, kept them from *their* purpose, and commanded that those who could swim should jump *overboard* first and get to land, and the rest, some on boards and some on *parts* of the ship. And so it was that they all escaped safely to land.

a. **And the soldiers' plan was to kill the prisoners, lest any of them should swim away and escape**: To the soldiers, it made sense to kill the prisoners, because according to Roman military law a guard who allowed his prisoner to escape was subject to the same penalty the escaped prisoner would have suffered - in the case of most of these prisoners, *death*.

b. **But the centurion, wanting to save Paul, kept them from their purpose**: God gave Paul favor in the eyes of this Roman **centurion**, and that favor kept Paul and all the prisoners alive – in fulfillment of the word spoken to Paul, *God has granted you all those who sail with you* (Acts 27:24). God's word never fails.

Acts 28 - Paul Arrives in Rome

A. Paul's ministry on the island of Malta.

1. (1-2) The islanders of Malta are impressed when Paul is miraculously unharmed by a snake-bite.

Now when they had escaped, they then found out that the island was called Malta. And the natives showed us unusual kindness; for they kindled a fire and made us all welcome, because of the rain that was falling and because of the cold.

> a. **They then found out that the island was called Malta**: These experienced sailors would certainly have known the island of Malta, but not this side of the island. Almost all the traffic to Malta came to the main port, on the other side; they didn't recognize this side of the island.

> b. **Made us all welcome, because of the rain that was falling and because of the cold**: Luke wrote as someone who experienced this, both the kindness of the Malta natives and the cold and wet of the storm. **Malta** means *refuge*, a fitting name.

2. (3-6) Paul and the snakebite.

But when Paul had gathered a bundle of sticks and laid *them* on the fire, a viper came out because of the heat, and fastened on his hand. So when the natives saw the creature hanging from his hand, they said to one another, "No doubt this man is a murderer, whom, though he has escaped the sea, yet justice does not allow to live." But he shook off the creature into the fire and suffered no harm. However, they were expecting that he would swell up or suddenly fall down dead. But after they had looked for a long time and saw no harm come to him, they changed their minds and said that he was a god.

> a. **When Paul had gathered a bundle of sticks**: The great apostle gathered wood for the fire, even though there were probably scores of people among

the 276 passengers and crew far more suited for the job. Paul's servant heart was always evident.

b. **A viper came out because of the heat, and fastened on his hand**: Paul was faithful to God and living as a true servant. But this did not keep him from this trial. His humble service brought out a **viper**, and the **viper** didn't just nibble on Paul – it **fastened on his hand**.

i. Paul didn't let it bother him. He didn't scream, "Why God? I can't take any more of this!" or "Can't You see I'm serving You?" Paul didn't look at those sitting by the fire and say, "You lazy people! If you gathered wood instead of me, this wouldn't have happened to me!"

ii. Paul's reaction seemed calm and unconcerned: **He shook off the creature into the fire**.

c. **No doubt this man is a murderer…yet justice does not allow to live**: The natives were convinced that **justice** had finally caught up with this prisoner. **Justice** is actually a reference to the Greek goddess of justice, *Dikee*. The natives, knowing Paul was a prisoner, assumed he committed a great crime, and the goddess of justice would not permit Paul to escape unpunished.

d. **And suffered no harm**: God didn't preserve Paul from the storm just to let him perish by a snake. Paul was protected. It was promised he would go to Rome (*you must also bear witness at Rome*, Acts 23:11), and Paul wasn't to Rome yet. It wasn't so much that nothing would stop Paul as it was that nothing would stop God's promise from being fulfilled.

i. Paul could take God's *past* faithfulness as a *promise* of future blessing and protection.

ii. By extension, we also see that "Divine Justice" had no more claim against Paul - it had all been satisfied by Jesus' work on the cross. God's justice could never harm Paul, nor anyone who has had all his or her sins paid for by the work of Jesus on the cross.

e. **Said that he was a god**: This is a typically human reaction. For these natives, Paul had to be seen in extremes. Either he was terribly evil or considered **a god**. In truth, Paul was neither a criminal deserving punishment *nor* **a god**. This is all the more reason we must be cautious about what others think of us, either for good or bad.

2. (7-10) Paul heals the father of Publius, and many others.

In that region there was an estate of the leading citizen of the island, whose name was Publius, who received us and entertained us courteously for three days. And it happened that the father of Publius lay sick of a

fever and dysentery. Paul went in to him and prayed, and he laid his hands on him and healed him. So when this was done, the rest of those on the island who had diseases also came and were healed. They also honored us in many ways; and when we departed, they provided such things as were necessary.

a. **The leading citizen of the island…who received us and entertained us courteously for three days**: This was a great blessing and a strong contrast to the misery of the previous two weeks at sea. God gave Paul, Luke, and Aristarchus a season of relief and replenishment.

i. **Leading citizen of the island**: This "is the exact technical term for the person who represented Rome in that place; it is another example of Luke's extraordinary accuracy." (Boice)

b. **The father of Publius lay sick of fever and dysentery**: Some think this was a malady known as *Malta fever*, which comes from a microorganism found in the milk of Maltese goats. Its symptoms usually last about four months.

c. **Paul went in to him and prayed, and he laid his hands on him and healed him**: God healed this man; yet it happened through the willingness and activity of Paul. God did the work, but Paul made himself ready and available for the work.

d. **The rest of those on the island who had diseases also came and were healed**: Soon, the work Paul did went to many others. This word for **healed** is not the customary word for a miraculous healing. The word more literally means, "*to receive medical attention.*" It may be that Luke (who was a physician according to Colossians 4:14) served as a medical missionary on Malta.

B. Paul at Rome.

1. (11-15) The final part of Paul's journey towards Rome.

After three months we sailed in an Alexandrian ship whose figurehead was the Twin Brothers, which had wintered at the island. And landing at Syracuse, we stayed three days. From there we circled round and reached Rhegium. And after one day the south wind blew; and the next day we came to Puteoli, where we found brethren, and were invited to stay with them seven days. And so we went toward Rome. And from there, when the brethren heard about us, they came to meet us as far as Appii Forum and Three Inns. When Paul saw them, he thanked God and took courage.

a. **After three months**: They spent **three months** on Malta, gathering strength and waiting for the winter to end.

b. **Landing at Syracuse**: This was the first stop from Malta. **Syracuse** was a famous city in the ancient world, being the capital city of the island of Sicily.

> i. Archimedes, the famous mathematician, had lived at **Syracuse**. When the Romans conquered the island, a solider put a dagger to his throat as he worked on a math problem, drawing in the dirt. Archimedes said, "Stop, you're disturbing up my equation!" and the solider killed him.

c. **Rhegium… Puteoli… and so we went toward Rome**: As Paul and the others made their way northward up the Italian peninsula, they spent time with fellow followers of Jesus they met along the way (**we found brethren, and were invited to stay with them seven days**).

d. **When the brethren heard about us, they came to meet us as far as the Appii Forum and Three Inns**: Eventually they were greeted outside Rome by Christians from city who came to meet them. They honored Paul by greeting him as the emperors were greeted when they arrived at Rome: they went out to meet him as he came into the city, traveling a full day's journey to the **Appii Forum** to do it (about 43 miles or 69 kilometers).

> i. They had received Paul's famous letter to the Romans a few years before, so they probably felt like they knew him already – and they certainly wanted to honor him. In light of the love and honor behind this greeting, no wonder that Paul **thanked God and took courage**.

> ii. "Luke is far from giving the impression that Paul was the first person to bring the gospel to Rome…the presence of those Christians - *the brothers*, as Luke calls them - provides evidence enough that the gospel had reached Rome already." (Bruce) There were Jewish people from Rome present at Peter's preaching on Pentecost many years before (Acts 2:10), so there had probably been Christians from and in Rome from the beginning.

> iii. One could say that they treated Paul as if he were a king. "It was a custom when an emperor visited a city for the people to go out and meet him and escort him back into the city." (Horton)

> iv. Yet, during his second Roman imprisonment, Paul was left alone and forgotten (2 Timothy 4:9-16), meaning that in some sense, the Christians at Rome didn't (or perhaps couldn't) maintain their love and honor of Paul.

2. (16) Paul's status as a prisoner in Rome.

Now when we came to Rome, the centurion delivered the prisoners to the captain of the guard; but Paul was permitted to dwell by himself with the soldier who guarded him.

a. **When we came to Rome**: Finally, the promise of Jesus was fulfilled. Paul determined that he would go to Rome as early as his third missionary journey (Acts 19:21, Romans 1:15). At Jerusalem, Jesus promised Paul he would make it to Rome (Acts 23:11) and repeated the promise during the two weeks of storm at sea (Acts 27:23-25).

i. "Now, at the very end of the book, the apostle comes to Rome. Thus Jesus' prophecy that his disciples would be his witnesses 'to the ends of the earth' is fulfilled." (Boice)

ii. When Paul came to Rome, the city had existed for almost 800 years. The famous Coliseum was not yet built; but the prominent buildings were the temple of Jupiter, the palaces of Caesar, and a temple to Mars (the god of war). At the time, Rome had a population of about two million - a million slaves, and a million free. Society was divided into roughly three classes: A small upper class, a large class of the poor, and slaves.

b. **The centurion delivered the prisoners to the captain of the guard**: This was a happy moment for Julius the **centurion**, who fulfilled his duty and successfully brought all the prisoners from Caesarea (Acts 27:1) to Rome – with much help from Paul.

c. **The soldier who guarded him**: Paul wasn't in a normal prison. He was allowed to **dwell by himself** and provide his own living space (a *rented house* according to Acts 28:30). Yet he was constantly under the supervision of a Roman guard, and often chained. The rotation of the guards gave him a constant supply of people to talk to.

i. "To this soldier he would be lightly chained by the wrist…the soldier would be relieved every four hours or so, but for Paul there was no comparable relief." (Bruce)

ii. In Philippians 1:13, written from this Roman custody, Paul told of how his message reached the palace guards of Rome. Though he was the prisoner, he had a genuinely captive audience.

3. (17-20) Paul appeals to the Jewish community of Rome.

And it came to pass after three days that Paul called the leaders of the Jews together. So when they had come together, he said to them: "Men *and* brethren, though I have done nothing against our people or the customs of our fathers, yet I was delivered as a prisoner from Jerusalem into the hands of the Romans, who, when they had examined

me, wanted to let *me* go, because there was no cause for putting me to death. But when the Jews spoke against *it,* I was compelled to appeal to Caesar, not that I had anything of which to accuse my nation. For this reason therefore I have called for you, to see *you* and speak with *you,* because for the hope of Israel I am bound with this chain."

a. **Paul called the leaders of the Jews together**: Paul followed his consistent practice of going to the Jews first in every city he came to as an evangelist. It took him only **three days** to have a meeting with the **leaders of the Jews** in Rome.

b. **Men and brethren**: Paul wanted them to know that he had not forsaken Israel and that they were still **brethren** to him. As Paul explained to the crowd on the temple mount at the beginning of this ordeal, *I am a indeed a Jew* (Acts 22:3).

c. **I have done nothing against our people or the customs of our fathers**: Paul wanted them to know that he was innocent of any crime against the law or the Jewish people.

d. **When they had examined me, wanted to let me go**: Paul wanted them to know that the Romans were ready and willing to release him.

e. **Not that I had anything of which to accuse my nation**: Paul wanted them to know that he did not make a counter-suit or accusation against the Jewish leadership that had accused him.

f. **Because for the hope of Israel I am bound with this chain**: Paul wanted them to know that he was a prisoner because of his belief in Israel's Messiah, the **hope of Israel**.

i. As the year A.D. 70 approached, time was running out before an unparalleled national calamity struck a Jesus-rejecting Israel. In 10 years or so it would be clear that Jesus was **the hope of Israel**, yet a hope that many of them rejected.

4. (21-22) The Jewish leaders respond to Paul.

Then they said to him, "We neither received letters from Judea concerning you, nor have any of the brethren who came reported or spoken any evil of you. But we desire to hear from you what you think; for concerning this sect, we know that it is spoken against everywhere."

a. **We neither received letters from Judea concerning you**: This demonstrates that the religious leaders who accused Paul in Jerusalem and Caesarea knew their case was hopeless. They made no effort to send ahead documents confirming their case against him.

b. **Nor have any of the brethren who came reported or spoken any evil of you**: Paul wanted to know what they heard from Jerusalem about him. The Jewish people of Rome had not yet heard anything about Paul.

c. **We desire to hear from you what you think, for concerning this sect, we know that it is spoken against everywhere**: Though they did not know anything about Paul, they had heard that Christianity was unpopular among some, being **spoken against everywhere**. They should be complimented on wanting to hear the story from Paul himself.

5. (23-24) The Jewish community of Rome hears the gospel from Paul.

So when they had appointed him a day, many came to him at *his* lodging, to whom he explained and solemnly testified of the kingdom of God, persuading them concerning Jesus from both the Law of Moses and the Prophets, from morning till evening. And some were persuaded by the things which were spoken, and some disbelieved.

a. **He explained and solemnly testified of the kingdom of God, persuading them concerning Jesus from both the Law of Moses and the Prophets, from morning till evening**: In what must have been a wonderful time of teaching, Paul spoke of the **kingdom of God**, and gave an exhaustive study of how the Old Testament spoke of Jesus - **from morning till evening**.

b. **Testified of the kingdom of God**: In speaking of **the kingdom of God**, Paul undoubtedly taught what Jesus taught: That in Jesus God brought a spiritual kingdom that would take root in men's hearts before it took over the governments of this world. Most of the Jewish people of Jesus' day and of Paul's day looked for a political kingdom, not a spiritual kingdom.

c. **Some were persuaded by the things which were spoken, and some disbelieved**: In response to this remarkable, day-long teaching from Paul, some believed and trusted Jesus. Others did not, and **disbelieved**. Even the best teaching from the best apostle in the best circumstances could not persuade them.

6. (25-27) Paul explains the rejection of the gospel from Isaiah 6:9-10.

So when they did not agree among themselves, they departed after Paul had said one word: "The Holy Spirit spoke rightly through Isaiah the prophet to our fathers, saying,

'Go to this people and say:
"Hearing you will hear, and shall not understand;
And seeing you will see, and not perceive;
For the hearts of this people have grown dull.
Their ears are hard of hearing,

And their eyes they have closed,
Lest they should see with *their* eyes and hear with *their* ears,
Lest they should understand with *their* hearts and turn,
So that I should heal them.'"

a. **When they did not agree among themselves**: This suggests that those who were persuaded and those who disbelieved started arguing among themselves.

b. **They departed after Paul had said one word: "The Holy Spirit spoke rightly through Isaiah the prophet to our fathers."** Paul understood that Isaiah prophesied of their hardness of heart. Certainly, Paul was happy that *some* received the gospel, but he was undoubtedly distressed if even *one* of them rejected Jesus.

c. **Hearing you will hear, and shall not understand**: Essentially, Isaiah said this in this passage from Isaiah 6:9-10: "If you reject Jesus, you can hear, but never understand; you can see but never perceive. You heart is, and will be, hard, your ears closed, and your eyes shut - because you really don't want to turn to God and be healed of your sin."

i. This is a message just as true *today* as it was when Isaiah first said it - or when Paul quoted it. Many hear and reject simply because they don't want to turn to God and be healed of their sin.

7. (28-29) Paul tells them he will take the message of salvation to the Gentiles.

"Therefore let it be known to you that the salvation of God has been sent to the Gentiles, and they will hear it!" And when he had said these words, the Jews departed and had a great dispute among themselves.

a. **Therefore let it be known to you**: If some of them rejected **the salvation of God**, it did not make that salvation of no effect. It just meant that God would find those who would **hear it** – in this case, the Gentiles.

i. Paul plead for men to receive Jesus, but not as a beggar might plead. Paul ached not for himself, but for those who rejected - and solemnly warned those who rejected of the consequences.

ii. The preacher of the gospel really preaches two messages. To those who respond to the gospel with faith, he is a messenger of life. But to those who reject Jesus, the preacher *adds* to their condemnation. *To the one we are the aroma of death to death, and to the other the aroma of life to life.* (2 Corinthians 2:16)

b. **When he had said these words, the Jews departed**: This mixed group – some who believed, some who did not – left Paul arguing with each other (**a great dispute among themselves**).

i. In just a few years after Paul's rebuke of those Jews who rejected Jesus, the Jewish people of Judea were slaughtered wholesale and Jerusalem was destroyed. God's judgment was coming, and part of Paul's frustration was that he sensed this.

8. (30-31) Paul spends two years in Rome before his trial in Caesar's court.

Then Paul dwelt two whole years in his own rented house, and received all who came to him, preaching the kingdom of God and teaching the things which concern the Lord Jesus Christ with all confidence, no one forbidding him.

a. **Then Paul dwelt two years**: Paul spent more than two years at Caesarea waiting for his case to be resolved (Acts 24:27). Now he spent another **two years** waiting for his case to be heard before Caesar.

i. "The two years' prolongation of Paul's stay in Rome could be accounted for adequately by congestion of court business. It took that time for his case to come up for hearing." (Bruce)

b. **His own rented house**: Probably, Paul continued his work as a tentmaker (leatherworker) to supply the rent for his house (as in Acts 18:1-2 and 20:33-35). Paul was always a hard-working man.

c. **Received all who came to him**: One example of someone who he **received** in Rome was a convert of Paul's, a runaway slave named Onesimus (Philemon 10), who Paul told to go back to his master Philemon.

d. **Preaching the kingdom of God and teaching the things which concern the Lord Jesus Christ with all confidence**: Though Paul could not travel, he could teach and preach to all who came to him – and this he did. He also wrote letters; we have these two years of Roman custody to thank for the letters to the *Ephesians*, the *Philippians*, and the *Colossians*.

i. These two years were not wasted, and God didn't waste Paul's time in Rome. God never wastes our time, though we may waste it by not sensing God's purpose for our lives at the moment.

ii. Paul eventually had his appearance before Caesar Nero. It's entirely reasonable to believe that he boldly and powerfully proclaimed the gospel to him - as God had promised he would (Acts 9:15 and 23:11).

iii. It seems likely that Paul was acquitted of these charges, and by most estimates was free for another four or five years until he was arrested again, imprisoned, condemned, and executed in Rome at the command of Nero in A.D. 66 or 67 – as the historical traditions of the early church state.

iv. Probably, Luke did not record Paul's appearance before Caesar because the Gospel of Luke and the Book of Acts were written to give the Roman court the background and facts of Paul's case in his trial before Caesar.

e. **No one forbidding him**: This has the idea of *completely unhindered*. Paul's chains and custody mattered nothing. The word of God was unhindered.

i. As Paul came to Rome, the sea, the soldiers, and the snake all threatened his life. But God delivered him from them all. Through Paul, God shows that God's man, fulfilling God's will, *cannot* be stopped - though all kinds of difficulty may come in the way.

ii. Finally, even the disbelief of some of the Jews - or anyone else's rejection of Jesus - will not hinder the gospel. The gospel will go forth and find those who will believe.

iii. Matthew 22:1-14 is a parabolic illustration of the Book of Acts. God prepared a feast for Israel, and invited them to come (in the days of Jesus' ministry), but they would not come. Then, He sent out a second invitation, after *all things* were *ready*. But they did not come then either; instead, they killed God's servants who brought the message of the feast. Finally, God invited all that would come, including Gentiles - but they could only come if they were clothed in the garments of Jesus.

f. **With all confidence, no one forbidding him**: There is no end to the story, because the history of the church continues this story on and on through the centuries. Trusting in Jesus, relying on the power of the Holy Spirit and the guidance of the Father, the word of God will continue to spread without hindrance and continue to change lives for the glory of God. The Book of Acts really is a never-ending story.

i. "Now unto him, who is able to work so as none can hinder, be all honour and glory, dominion and power, for ever and ever. Amen." (Poole)

Acts - Bibliography

Barclay, William *The Acts of the Apostles* (Philadelphia, Pennsylvania: Westminster Press, 1976)

Bruce, F.F. *The Book of the Acts* (Grand Rapids, Michigan: William B. Eerdmans Publishing, 1988)

Calvin, John *Calvin's Commentaries Volumes XVIII and XIX, Commentary on the Acts of the Apostles* (Grand Rapids, Michigan: Baker Book House, 1979)

Clarke, Adam *The Holy Bible, Containing the Old and New Testaments, with A Commentary and Critical Notes* (New York: Eaton and Mains, ?)

Gaebelein, Arno C. *The Acts of the Apostles* (Neptune, New Jersey: Loizeaux Brothers, 1983)

Horton, Stanley M. *The Book of Acts* (Springfield, Missouri: Gospel Publishing House, 1981)

Knowling, R.J. "The Acts of the Apostles," *The Expositor's Greek Testament, Volume II* (London: Hodder and Stoughton, ?)

LaSor, William Sanford *Church Alive* (Glendale, California: Regal Books, 1972)

Lenski, R.C.H. *The Interpretation of the Acts of the Apostles* (Minneapolis, Minnesota: Augsburg Publishing, 1961)

Longenecker, Richard N. "The Acts of the Apostles," T*he Expositor's Bible Commentary, Volume 9* (Grand Rapids, Michigan: Zondervan, 1981)

Lovett, C.S. *Lovett's Lights on Acts* (Baldwin Park, California: Personal Christian- ity, 1972)

Marshall, I. Howard *The Acts of the Apostles* (Grand Rapids, Michigan: William B. Eerdmans Publishing, 1980)

Morgan, G. Campbell *The Acts of the Apostles* (Old Tappan, New Jersey: Fleming H. Revell, 1924)

Ogilvie, Lloyd-John *Drumbeat of Love: The Unlimited Power of the Spirit as Revealed in the Book of Acts* (Waco, Texas: Word, 1976)

Poole, Matthew *A Commentary on the Holy Bible, Volume 3* (London, Banner of Truth Trust, 1968)

Ramsay, Sir William M. *Pictures of the Apostolic Church, Studies in the Book of Acts* (Grand Rapids, Michigan: Baker Book House, 1959)

Smith, Chuck *New Testament Study Guide* (Costa Mesa, California: The Word for Today, 1982)

Spurgeon, Charles Haddon *The New Park Street Pulpit, Volumes 1-6* and *The Metropolitan Tabernacle Pulpit, Volumes 7-63* (Pasadena, Texas: Pilgrim Publications, 1990)

Stott, John *The Spirit, the Church, and the World: The Message of Acts* (Downers Grove, Illinois: InterVarsity Press, 1990)

Wiersbe, Warren W. *The Bible Exposition Commentary, Volume 1* (Wheaton, Illinois: Victor Books, 1989)

Personal Remarks from the Author

Much thanks to the many who have helped me prepare this commentary. My wife Inga-Lill and our children have given me so much support in this and all the ministry. Special thanks to Debbie Pollaccia for her proofreading, though remaining errors are all my fault! Thanks to Craig Brewer, to Kara Valeri, and to Gayle and Ricky for their kind words. I'm very grateful to Stretch and all the others who give the gift of encouragement. Much thanks to all those who have supported and helped through the years, and to the whole church family at Calvary Chapel of Simi Valley. Through you all, God has been better to me than I have ever deserved.

David Guzik's Bible commentary is regularly used and trusted by many thousands who want to know the Bible better. Pastors, teachers, class leaders, and everyday Christians find his commentary helpful for their own understanding and explanation of the Bible. David and his wife Inga-Lill live in Santa Barbara, California.

You can email David at
david@enduringword.com

For more resources by David Guzik,
go to www.enduringword.com

LASCIVIOUS

Isaiah 17:7
Isaiah 19:23

In Science we have been Reading only the
notes to a poem, in christanity we find
the poem itself.

C. S. Lewis (miracles)

Ezek 36, 25-26 Jeremiah 33:8

CPSIA information can be obtained
at www.ICGtesting.com
Printed in the USA
BVHW081235300919
559784BV00001B/47/P